PERSONAL AND FAMILY

NAMES

A Popular Monograph on the Origin and History of the Nomenclature of the Present and Former Times

BY

HARRY ALFRED LONG

Glasgow School Board

"Names?" Could I unfold the influence of names, which are the most important of all clothings, I were a second Trismegistus!"—CARLYLE.

LONDON: HAMILTON, ADAMS & CO.
GLASGOW: THOMAS D. MORISON
EDINBURGH: JOHN MENZIES & CO.

1883

REPUBLISHED BY GALE RESEARCH COMPANY, BOOK TOWER, DETROIT, 1968

Library of Congress Catalog Card
Number 68-26584

PREFACE.

ABOUT the year 1856 my attention was specially directed to the study of personal names, and circumstances at that time led me to concentrate attention upon this field of literature. Having laboured therein for the period of about fourteen years, the result was produced in a work entitled "The Names We Bear." So little did I expect my book to take the market that it was brought out privately. Howbeit, the edition of two thousand copies was not long in the hands of readers when a succession of complimentary critiques and encouraging notices began to flow in from both sides of the Atlantic. Frequent applications for the work from far and near induced me to put forth extra exertions to produce a work yet more worthy of the subject and of our times. After thirteen years additional labour thereat, I venture to come before the public again as an author and to ask the patronage of the general community. This may be regarded as an entirely new work, being rewritten throughout, and in extent exceeding the previous volume by about one-half.

Much study is but an effort to make the past present. What else does the Historian, whether in ordinary prose or in epic poem? the Geologist, when unfolding the stony pages of primary deposits? the Dramatist, if presenting the lives and actions of the heroic dead, than revivify past ages, or rather, re-present the illustrious departed, whose memory man treasures? Educated men cannot rest while the past remains unveiled. My book is a tiny effort to reproduce the great actors of past generations in greater numbers than history can take cognisance of. Much of this work refers to periods when as yet the history of nations, passed under review, was unwritten. Even when national life and action found a recorder, that historian only chronicled in broad outlines the facts brought out in the growth of an empire or the clash of battle. History makes known what patriarchal clansman founded a kingdom, but not who marched to the tented field, not those who shared with him the perils involved in rearing an infant nationality. In this book will be found the names of hundreds of the rank and file who fought in the battle of Hastings.

Nor should the bearing of this study upon a more thorough understanding of the nomenclature of geography be lost sight of. Thereby will be seen evidences in physical and political geography that the designations of countries, mountains, rivers, districts, towns, villages, hamlets, are associated with the names of persons whom we daily meet, suggesting to the thoughtful mind most interesting topics regarding the histories of families and places.

And further, like all other products of the earth, language is variable, transitory, and subject to loss. In this study of words, readers will recover archaic forms of speech, obsolete expressions, and colloquially lost words will reproduce themselves in unlooked for and refreshing forms.

One of the many difficulties in composing a work of this type is overcoming dryness, which, if unconquered, however meritorious the book may otherwise be, its utmost attainment is to be shelved for reference. In view of this fact the author has constantly had before his mind the desirableness of presenting a work, on the one hand readable by reason of explanations being presented in a popular form, and yet, on the other, scholarly.

The writer hopes that the verdict passed upon his second effort will be as encouraging as that kindly accorded to his previous work.

GLASGOW, *July, 1883.*

CONTENTS.

——:o:——

PERSONAL AND FAMILY

NAMES

PERSONAL AND FAMILY

NAMES.

CHAPTER I.

THE PHILOSOPHY OF PERSONAL NAMES.

THE subject of the following work is a branch of nomenclature known as the study of personal names. An objection to attention thereto in this utilitarian age is the *vis inertiæ* which this preface is written to overcome. " *Cui bono ?*" cries the objector, " what end is answered thereby other than the satisfaction of barren curiosity ?" Such objection must be fairly met, which is readily done in the following words.

By this study we obtain a more accurate view of the construction and power of our language. A new field of thought is entered upon. Besides by it many words are prevented from being lost which are links necessary to unite the vernacular of to-day with obsolete forms of speech. For, through ignorance of this branch of education, we, though having the same words, yet, being unaware of their meaning and force, would virtually be without them, inasmuch as we should be in the position of one looking upon cuneiform writings not having the cipher whereby to interpret them. Belshazzar saw the mysterious words on the plaster, but they were inanimate signs until Belteshazzar inspired them with a life of meaning. This study throws much light upon British history. If the literature of Britain were to perish, and only our names remained, very many of the mighty deeds which have made this country what it is might be fairly elaborated therefrom. It lifts the historic veil higher than the ordinary historian can. He records the births and deaths of kings, sieges fought and battles won ; but it minutely details the precious things of home, love, worship, and the social condition of the toiling million, of which matters history takes little heed. The pen of the historian is a jet of flame, dazzling at day-dawn ; the science of names is many sparklets at the noon of night. But

2

apart from such considerations, we cannot allow that the desire
to know why I am named as I am is vain curiosity, any more
than it is vain to ask whence I came. The extreme utilitarian
might as justly say, "What boots it whence you came? The
true questions are: What you *are*, and what you *will be*." This
is only two-thirds true, inasmuch as the *I am* of to-day is
built equally with the *will be* of to-morrow upon the *was* of
yesterday. Can it be a matter of indifference what a human
being is called, seeing that Infinite Wisdom named, before
birth, Ishmael, Isaac, Josiah, Cyrus, John, and Jesus,—not to
mention those changed by God after birth? If, then, the
name, involving its meaning and surroundings, was, if it be
lawful so to say, a subject of Divine consideration, on what
defensible principle should the meaning of my name be to me
a matter of indifference? The Providence which counts hairs
has more to do with names than the unthinking multitude
suspect. Many acts of highest heroism and historic interest
found as lowly an origin as that of the suggestion afforded by
a name. Of such cases several illustrations are given in the
body of this work. No word appeals so powerfully to the
spirit within us as our proper name. The Rabbi of Galilee
stood at the grave of His friend whom He called from Hades
by *name*, though had He said, "Man, come forth," the *power*
would have been the same, but the *love* manifested would not.
In like manner, when a sorrowing disciple yearned for a glance
at the body which had so lately passed through its bitter baptism, she was called to recognition of Him as related to her,
not by saying, "Woman," but "Mary." As illustrating the
affection involved in *knowing by name*, nothing can be more
appropriate than the negative evidence of the four biographers
of Jesus. They represent Him as not addressing Judas once
by name. So, in like manner, God makes no mention of the
name of either Laban or Balaam, when revealing their respec-
tive messages to them. The passage where it says, "Judas,
betrayest thou the Son of Man with a kiss," upon the authority of that king of critics, Tischendorf, should be given,
"Friend, betrayest," &c.; agreeing with the mode in which the
king addressed the man not having on a wedding garment—
"Friend, how camest thou," &c. Nor was it by chance, but
on the principle under consideration, that, in the three lists of
the Apostles, Judas is the last mentioned. There is no more
certain proof of the favour of God than the reduplication of
the name of the person addressed, whether by Jehovah in the
Old Testament, or Immanuel in the New. It begins at Gen.
xxii. 11, "Abraham, Abraham," and concludes at Acts ix. 4,
"Saul, Saul." Only one woman had this high distinction conferred upon her, "Martha, Martha." This view of names allies

them more closely to persons, giving all pertaining to their use an air of grandeur and solemnity. Some think the name of a man is to be viewed in the same light as street names or the numbers of houses, simply as a distinction given on business principles. Not so. However common-place or even comic the appellation of a human being may now be, from the very fact of union with one who is the offspring of God it is dear to the bearer and those who love him; yea, even sacred, by reason of relationship to a deathless being. There are fallen names as well as fallen persons, but not the less is each of high, nay, Divine origin. I was deeply affected in reading the experience of an educated convict as to the pang suffered when, instead of being called Charles, a name endeared by associations of home, religion, and love, he was roughly called No. 44. It is the *Christian name*, not the *surname*, which appeals to profounder emotions. The private soldier on the battle-field and the common sailor on the perilous flood are commanded by surnames, but it is the dear one in the arm chair by the fireside that is addressed by his Christian name.

> " Peace to these pangs! Mother! put forth
> Thine elder, holier claim ;
> And the first word I hear in heaven
> May be—my Christian name."

He who knew nature thoroughly—what was in man—did not say, Peter, lovest thou Me ? but, " Simon, son of Jonas, lovest thou Me ?" Take the compound appellation Simon Peter, and Simon would be what we term the Christian name. Being imposed by parents in circumcision, it would be familiar and sacred. Jesus brought out the family relationship more strongly by saying, " Son of Jonas." The surname tells of ancestry, business, struggle, dignity, heroism, office, it is our world name—but the Christian name speaks of father, mother, home, love, familiarity, heaven, God. And yet in this work they are not distinguished, forasmuch as the surname of one is the Christian name of another ; but this in no way weakens the charm of it to its possessor. Whatever it may be, it is the most personal and precious part of the entire appellation. Should he have many Christian names—a sentimental mistake —that one by which he is most generally addressed will contain the talismanic power. Pride will, at the baptismal font, select many names. Nature, at home, elects one, and that is the *Christian name*. This phrase originally meant that name which was given to the recipient when he became a Christian. Our missionary records teem with illustrations of my meaning. Surname is a form of Supernomen, above the name—as John Williams—where Williams, being given to the person over and

above John, is termed his surname. Some authors are of
opinion that sur, above, is to be taken in its most literal sense,
inasmuch as the surname was formerly written $\dfrac{\text{Williams}}{\text{John.}}$

Observe.—The arithmetical sign for equality (=) will be
used to indicate that two or more names are synonymous or
nearly so, as Herschell = Kouli Khan, *i.e.*, that the former
name was originally used in a similar sense to that which was
primarily given to the latter. *Con.* stands for connected with,
Ab. for abbreviated, *Pats.* for patronymics, *Dim.* for diminutive. Names under explanation will be given in large type as
DUPANLOUP. A colon (:) will be placed to signify "means," as
Balloon: (means) great ball. When a name is followed by a
word or words within a parenthesis, the word or words are
added to suggest some well known instance of its use as Landseer (painter). It is not professed that meanings herein given
are infallibly correct. The basis of this book being etymolo-
gical analysis and comparative nomenclature, the value of any
statement of the meaning of a name is to be measured by inter-
nal and external evidence in respect thereto, as well as by
authority. Britain being placed between northern ice floes
and southern fruit fields, birds and fishes make for our island
in their migration to and fro as to a half way house. Hence
we possess a more varied fauna than any other spot on the
globe of equal dimensions. Just so with regard to nations—
Gaels, Romans, Saxons, Danes, Norsemen, Normans and Jews
led by ambition, driven by necessity, or urged by hope, have
made for our island. The consequence is our nomenclature is
the fullest and most mixed of any known. This in the order
of Providence is needful for this land was destined to supply
the United States and our fifty colonies with names. Yet for
this reason the analysis of a directory is very difficult, and in
giving the meanings of so great a number, it is hardly possible
there should be no mistake.

CHAPTER II.

THE ORIGIN AND FORMATION OF WORDS.

UR.

BEFORE the study of names can profit, it is necessary to be acquainted with the way in which words are formed. This preliminary chapter will, therefore, be devoted to elucidating that subject. But lest our reader should think he is being invited to seat himself in standard four, the motto of this chapter shall be a fragment of Plato in Cratylo, by Taylor, upon the assumption that to study a subject which engaged the close attention of that immortal founder of the Academy cannot be unworthy of a scholar, "Do you know on what account *Pur* was so called? Consider whether this is not of barbaric origin—for it is by no means easy to adapt this to the Greek tongue ; and it is manifest that the Phrygians thus denominate *fire*, with a certain trifling deviation." We read in the earliest recorded history extant, that Abram migrated from Ur of the Chaldees. The Chaldees, among whom he dwelt, worshipped fire, the symbol of the Invisible God, who is Light. These ancient pyrolatrians correspond to the Guebers of the current time. A change of religion is of rare occurrence in the history of nations. Forms of government have been held as very convertible : dynasties have been changed like garments ; even languages yield to the action of time, but religion is nearly as inelastic as rock. The Reformation was a moral miracle, without parallel in all the ages of the past. Yet in some unrecorded manner, and for reasons wholly unknown, the Chaldees passed from being fire-worshippers to the grosser form of made image-worship, while, on the other hand, the aboriginal Persians became pyrolatrians. Hence, in the time of Daniel, they are found worshipping gigantic idols, and punishing recusants by casting them into fire, and that in no less than five cases, viz., Zedekiah, Ahab, Shadrach, Meschech, and Abednego. Now, no fire-worshipper would pollute, according to his notions, fire with flesh. So, then, when Daniel was to suffer as a criminal, it was in a den of lions. In those ages, when the sun received special honours in any locality, such centre of heliolatria was named from the fact, as Bethshemesh : house of the sun ; Bethshan : house of the shiner ; Heliopolis (On) : city of the sun=Luxembourg, and, nearer home, Greenock : sun hill ; Tinto : fire hill, which coincides as nearly

as possible with Dunedin : hill (of) fire.   These all formerly
being sun-worship centres.

Ur (of the Chaldees) : light, brightness, burning, primarily
spelled Aiur, gives

Ur (Gaelic) : fresh, new as though just out of the fire, as we
say "bran new" for burn new.   From the Chaldee Ur we
have

URIJAH : (whose) light (is) Jehovah, *ab.* to URIAH (Hittite).
URIEL : (whose) light (is) God.

> " The Archangel *Uriel,* one of the seven
> Who in God's presence, nearest the throne."

JAIR : he (will) enlighten.   Probably given to a child in the
hope he would be the light of the house = ECOLAMPADIUS.

JAIR gives JAIRUS.   In some cases Jair : a river = BROOKS,
as in Jordan : river of (flowing from) Dan.   Of course,
these Jairs, though spelled alike, are different words like our
corn : fruit of earth (*con.* kernel), and corn : horn like.

HORUS (Egyptian Apollo) : the light, whence OROSIUS : son
of Horus, protected by that god.

AARON : great light (of household) = HAUSSCHEIN, takes
form Haroun, as in HAROUN AL RASCHID : Aaron the just.

ARELI (m) : lights of God, born at appearance of stars.

From Aiur comes the old Persian adjective Arta : great,
applicable to the sun, then to altar flame.   As ARTABANUS :
having charge of altar flame, temple servant = ABDUL MEDJID.

ARTAPHERNES : great shepherd, *con.* HOLOFERNES : head
shepherd, chief commander.

ARTAXERXES : great king = MAHARAJAH.   From Arta in its
connection with light we have

ARTEMIS : Diana, Selene ; the shiner, the moon giving
ARTEMESIA (Carian) : daughter of Diana.

ARTEMIS is usually given as perfect, but this is preferable.

ARIDATHA : great by birth, of noble descent = BURNS,
CHILDERS.   Also from Arta, the Punic favourite we have

HAMILCAR : great melech, king.   It is also the root of the
Latin, Arduus : lofty, through the Celtic Ard ; Airt : quarter,
whence wind ; AIRD.   From the same we obtain

Ardeo : to shine, to burn, to glitter.   Allied is the Celtic

Aodh : fire, ardour, whence Edui : men burning for the
fight, also—

AIDAN (St.) : fiery one, ready for battle = BROWN, whence,
nominally, another saint, viz.—

HAYES, and HAY, the latter being identical with High and
Arta.   Originally—

High : the towering of the altar flame.   This Aodh gives—

HUGH, the most prolific and ancient of British names,

being a pet with Gaels, Irish, and Cymri. It is thoroughly
aboriginal, being common in the Highlands, Ireland, and
Wales long before the dawn of authentic history. It simply
means heat for fight, battle ardour.

HUGH is followed through its ramifications in chapter on
Patronymics.

Ard, AIRD, Ardeo, Arduus, Dunedin, and the ancient name
ARTHUR are forms of Arta, which primitive word gives the
endings—

Art, Ard in such words as WISHART: of a wise nature.

BALLARD: of a bold nature ; MAYNARD : of a manly nature.
In such cases a flavour of highness, greatness, superiority is
generally supposed. This ending, for the two are truly one,
gathered diverse meanings as it passed into different nations,
places, and languages, but they all fairly find their germ in
arta. This is corroborated by observation upon—

HAMILCAR (Carthiginian general), which in the Punic is a
form of

HA-MELK-ART (Sidonian Hercules): the great king, in
which melk for melech. It looks unreasonable to say that
the affix in WISHART and HAMILCAR are identical, but
philology shows such to be the case. Without violence to
accuracy, we may say that *arta* is equivalent to the better
known

AUGUSTUS : sublime, *con.* altar service from Auruspex (from
avis specio), who told events by condition of bird-victims.

GUZMAN is formed on Augustus, as though august man.

ARTHUR is identical with those ancient Milesian names—

(M')ARTNEY, (M')ARTHY, M'CARTHY, and (O)HART. This
origin is corroborated by comparing these from Arta : great,
with the old Amalekite name from Ag, a primeval Semetic
word for fire, and root of Ignis, whence

IGNATIUS (martyr) : son of fire, fiery, choleric (= BANNA-
TYNE), *con.*—

AGNI, the Hindoo god of fire. Now, this Ag doubled gives

AGAG : fire ! fire ! ! alluding to the pyramidal altar flame
destroying the victim and soaring aloft. Thus it was Balaam
was made to say : " His King shall be higher than AGAG."
Self-sacrifice shall overtop the slaughter of others, as resurrection triumphs over death.

AGAG is the only Amalekite name known, but, nominally,
he had cousins, as—

OG (Bashan) : high, tall. Had his royal highness lived now
he might have been called

Lum : tall as a chimney, for Low : a flame, gives

Lum : a chimney, up which the low goes. We might probably claim

OGYGES (aboriginal Greek king): tall, or using it figuratively, exaltado, a magnate. The chief gate of Thebes was—

OGY-GIA : lofty, which was also the name of an island, and so = our Hoy : high, out of the water. Plutarch calls Ireland by this name Ogygia. The Hibernian

HOGAN, HAGAN are probably of *og*, *ag* origin in the sense of exalted, the son = EGAN, which consult.

GUZZI (Father) is an Italian diminutive formed on Hugo from Hugh.

Huguenot: little Hugh, a commonplace fellow daring to teach religion, and—

HOCHE (general) = ALT, ALTER, ULLMAN, all men of high standing comes very near to the Arta idea.

The Chaldee Aiur also gives the beautiful word Mar-garites : a pearl, whence—

MARGARET, similar to PENINNAH : pearl or coral, and ACHATES (fidus) : the agate. ISPAH : jasper, fair as. The original form is —

MERVARID : child of light. By a charming fiction the oyster was supposed to come up from the dark sea bottom to worship the moon, and when doing so it received a drop of congealed dew, which formed the pearl. Some derive the word from Mergret : grit of the sea. From it—

MARGAREDON (" bastard "), in the sense of pearl of knights. Many other derivatives from MARGARET will be presented in their order. From Aiur we have—

Urim (and Thummim : perfections) : lights, shining from the precious stones on the pectoral of the consulted priest. Also, from Aiur—

Seraph : to burn, whence Saraphim : burning ones (snakes), Seraphim : burning ones (with love), ardors.

Ardor : a seraph, *con.* Aiur, Arta—

> " From among
> Thousand celestial *ardors*, where he stood
> Veil'd with his gorgeous wings, up springing light
> Flew through the midst of heaven."

From Aiur is also derived the name of an inferior order of angels.

Orphanim, much spoken of among Jews, almost unmentioned by us, " Seraphim, cherubim, *orphanim*, hallelujah ! "

NER : a lamp, a lightgiver, from Aiur, whence the well-known

ABNER : father of Ner, probably like him. " They buried Abner in Hebron." Aiur tends to form Or, as Orfah, the Turkish name of the town and district of which Abram was a native. Also gives

ORION : son of fire = ZOROASTER, PYROSPORUS : seed of the

fire. One of the Persian titles of the sun is Arsa : burner,
from Aiur, whence

ARSES (Persian king) : burner, destroyer = AGAG, APOLLYON.
ORION was Nimrod's title after deification, as was

ALORUS : god of fire = AGNI. From Aiur, also the beautiful
name—

HOURI : flashing-eyes = LAPIDOTH : lamps, eyes like. The
Greeks transferred Ur into their languages in the form of

Pur : fire. Note Aiur, Ur has a tendency to take on the
consonants *p, b, f, v.* These are cognates (born together), produced by the same organs, the lips, and hence termed labials.
Pur gives

PYRRHUS (Epiriote king) : red headed, or ruddy = ROY,
REDMOND and FLAN.

PYRAMUS : inflamed (with love of Thisbe). " First *Pyramus*
must draw his sword to kill himself ; which the ladies cannot
abide." By change of a vowel we have

PERSEUS : lightning, burner = BARCA (also from Ur) and
ARSES.

BARCA, the Carthaginian gave name to Barcelona. The
name is cognate with

BARAK (Deborah) : whose spear glittered like lightning =
LLEWELLYN, and dagger from day.

ALBORAK (Koranic angel) : who went like lightning.

PYROIS (one of mares of the sun) : daughter of fire, quick
mover.

Pyre : the funeral pile,—

" For nine long nights, through all the dusky air,
The *pyres*, thick flaming, shot a dismal fire."

Pyrites : fire stones ; Lithos : a stone, to *lites,* then *ites.*

Empyrean : the ethereal heaven = Ouranos : burning like
the lambent flame of the Aurora Borealis, heaven, whence

URANIA : heavenly (muse), in which the root Ur becomes
prominent. Ouranos, Air, Aur are formations upon Aiur, as
is Ether for Aither, from the old verb Aithoı I burn. In
Porphyros, purple is reduplicated as though written pur, pur,
os : son of a very fiery colour, at least that is its literal meaning.
Hence the anti-christian philosopher—

PORPHYRY : dressed in purple = PEPLOE : clad in peplum.
The word is also applied to red granite. " Within the which
(labyrinth) a number of columns and statues there be, all of
porpyrit, or red marble." Hence the title of Byzantine
Emperors—

PORPHYROGENETUS : born in imperial purple, or in the
porphyry palace, the Alhambra of the Greeks.

ZOPYRUS : fire of Zeus, destroying like lightning = BARAK,

PERSEUS. The Greeks had yet another word for redness, probably traceable to the patriarchal Aiur, Ur, viz., Erythros, whence—

ERYTHRAS (son of Perseus): flaming = ASTRAFIAMMANTA: flaming star.

Erytheia (also from it): ruddyish, from which Hercules took the oxen of Geryoneus.

Erythean Sea was the name the sons of Javan gave to the Red Sea. From same source—

Erythematous: inflamed, reddened by disease. Aiur, Ur varied to Er gives

Thermos: heat, whence Thermopylæ: hotgate, pass at which were warm springs. Warm is identical with Therm-os, so that—

Thermopylæ = Warmbrunn, in Silesia. A Persian district is known as

Gurmsir: warm region. Therm, Warm, Gurm are essentially one. Again Aiur, Ur to Er gives

ERINNYS (eris nous): *fury* of the mind, *ire* of the soul.

ERIS = Fury, from Furo, from Pur, from Aiur, Ur. The Latin for anger is

Ira, whence Ire, is undoubtedly from Ur. Ira = Hatred, from Hate, from Heat. In like manner the Cornish Forkhan means both fire and hatred, being as to first syllable a form of Pur. In corroboration, it may be observed that a title of Odin is

BROWN: burning (for the fight) = ERINNYS (of course literally). Also from Pur—

PYROSPORUS: seed of the fire = ZOROASTER (archimagus). The former alludes to the birth of Bacchus, the latter to fire worship, and each is literally = ORION: fire son.

ZOROASTER, *con.* Zero: semen; Zemindar (dominus): seed lord, a Hindoo farmer. " May not the name of the Nereid MARA (Od. xi. 326) express the phosphoric flashing of the surface of the sea, as MAIRA expresses the sparkling of the dogstar Sirius ?" If so, MARA and MAIRA are claimable as of the seed of Ur. Again Pur gives

Parsee : a pyrolatrian. These Parsees are called Guebers, Giours, by the Mahometans. Some claim as of this source

Fars, giving Faristan : land of the Parsees.

Aurum: gold, the shining metal is from Aiur; whence also—

AURORA (rosy fingered): golden hours, *con.* Horologe : hour discoverer = Clock : that which clicks. It is highly probable that Fire is from Pur. It is called Vuur by the Danes. The Swedes call it Rod. In New Guinea it is For. Of

That, Pur, Vuur, For and Fire are in essence one word ramified, there seems little doubt. Focus : the hearth, gives

Fuego : fire, (Spanish) Terra-del-Fuego : land of fires, volcanic.

Curfew : cover fire ; Fuel : (good for the) fire. After Feu : fire, of the French we have the Italian Fuoco : fire. Pur gives Purus : cleansed by fire ; our Pure : cleansed.

Puritan : a catharite, who keeps to the *pure* word without notes or comment.

Purgo : I cleanse ; when by adding *s* Spurge : a medicinal plant, whence

Spurge : an herbalist. Purus gives Puer : a boy. Varro says : " So called because free from vices acquired by imitation." Puer takes the *dim.* Puella : a girl ; and Pupilus : a little boy, one under tuition, as boys ought to be.

Orbius Pupillus (Grammatist of Beneventum) : little orphan boy. Pupil when applied to eye is so called because one seems to see a little boy therein. Pupil exactly answers to

Lad : one led, giving La (dde) ss = Pais Paidos : one led.

Pedagogue : a child leader. That Pure is identical with Puer by no chance coincidence is made probable by analogy, as seen in the language of nature. " In the Delaware language, a youth is called Pilape, a word compounded from the first part of Pilsit : innocent ; and the latter of Lenape : a man, which, therefore, means innocent man."

Purgatory : place of purgation, and many other derivatives from Purgo.

Uro : I burn, almost traces itself to Aiur, Ur, whence Urn : receptacle of human ashes.

Inure : to burn into, to make used to. The smith's hand is inured to labour by handling hot iron.

Adure : to burn up. " A degree of heat which doth neither melt, nor scorch, doth mellow and not *adure*."

Urtica : a nettle (needle), so called from its inflammatory quality.

Combustible : that which may be burned, from Ustus, from Uro, from Ur. The Com is a form of Cum : with, while *b* is formative. Ustus gives

Locust (locus ustus) : burnt place. Locusts leave the country in a condition like to that of its being burnt. " A fire devoureth before them ; and behind them a flame burneth."

Locusta (poisoner) : woman living in marshes, bare places. Allied to Ustus we have the Italian names—

Foscaro, Foscani : dark coloured, swarthy = Swartz. Hence too—

Obfuscous: a dun brown (an old Oxonian colour). Ur also gives

Areo : to be dry, on which is formed Torreo : to be parched, torrid (zone).

Torrent : a water course subject to drouth = Ghau ; though some give it from Terra : earth, a land flood.

TORRANCE (when not from Turra : a tower) ; TORRENTIUS = WATERS, BORROMEO (bore) : persons living near such.

Areo : to be dry, gives Arena : sand, where gladiators fought, sand being thrown to absorb blood, and prevent slipping.

Area : a court-yard, an open space where corn was dried. Aiur gives Ardeo : to burn, whence Ardent : inflamed, and "Arson ab ardendo," is the malicious and wilful burning of the house or outhouse of another man. From Areo, also

Arunda : a reed, a dry plant, whence Arun : reedy, sedgy stream, whence

ARUNDEL (ian Marbles) : a settler thereon. This is sometimes given from

Hirondelle : a swallow, but similitude has inveigled the guesser.

Ferveo : to boil, to seethe, to make hot, is also from Pur.

Fervent : zealous ; Ferment : to effervesce. Fever is clearly from Ferveo, meaning in a fervid state of body.

Febrifuge : herb to make fever flee. Fever is a zymotic disease, a fermentation of the system.

> " A feuer it (jealousie) is cotidian
> Which every daie wol come aboute
> Where so a man be in or oute."

Pruriency : itching heat through feverish state of blood is from Pur by transposition. Burke, in an oration against Pitt, told that statesman, "He had a *pruriency* of taxation that seemed to infect his blood." Changing *p* into its cognate *f* and reduplicating Pur, we have—

Furfur : bran, brown, so called from colour. To it, too, we trace

Fornax : a furnace, an archway like a furnace roof.

FORNARIUS (Italian) : furnaceman, a baker ; and giving

Fornication : the act of frequenting the habitations of harlots, which, in Rome, were under archways. Milton, in his "Reason of Church Government," says : "She gives up her body to mercenary whoredom under the *fornicated* archways which she calls God's house."

Forceps : a fire-rake, a fire-comb, now shears. Capio : I take, to Ceps and Pecten : a comb, to fex. Ur transposed gives

Ruber : red ; Rubus : a bramble, producing red berries.

Ruby : red (coloured gem) ; Rubric : red (letter service).

RUTILIUS (consul) : carroty-pated = PYRRHUS. Rutilent : of a red colour. "Parchments coloured with this rutilant mixture."

RUFUS, RUFFINUS, BURRHUS (Pretorian guardsman) = REDHEAD = REDMOND, FLAN.

Biretta, is *con.* herewith, being so called in respect to colour, as Alb: white. Purus gives Puto: I judge, prune, dress vines, think. Hence—

Amputation: the act of cutting round about, ambiputo. Here it is pertinent to trace the rise of ideas, as well as the formation of words. Pur: fire, is observed to cleanse; hence Purus leads to consider a quality of fire, cleansing. Puro gives Puto, *con.* the purgation of vines. Now, to purge trees involves thought, whence by another abstraction we have Puto: I think, giving Compute to reckon, which contracts to Count: to expect through reckoning. What a gulf between *fire* and *expectation*—yea, between Aiur and Count, yet both are bridged by these processes. Pur turns up again in the German—

Purpuroth: red as purple, in which there is a triplication from the root Ur.

Feursbrunt: empyrosis, conflagration it is duplicated. The words *con.*

Roth: red, are many in English, as Penrith: red hill, gravel hill =

RADCLIFFE, RAWCLIFFE. Rotherhithe: red hyde, harbour. RUTLAND: red land, sandy soil = Damascus.

Ridley: red field = ROWLEY, RILEY, ROTHACKER. With the French Ur beccmes

Rouge: red; LEROUX: the red (headed) = BURRHUS. Through the French and Italian we get the following names applied to florid complexion or redness of hair :—

ROUSE (bravo!), ROUS, ROUSSEAU (Jean Jacques), ROSSI, ROSSINI (composer), ROSSETTI, RUST (bishop of Dromore). Doubt attaches to

ROSSI, ROSSINI, ROSSETTI, as they are derivable from Ross, which consult.

RUSSELL is from a Norman town, yet that town may be named from some notable red headed person.

Rust (*ru*bigo): brown or red coloured oxide of iron, is clearly of Ur descent.

> " Whole provinces
> Appear to our sight then, even leek
> A *russet*-mole upon a lady's cheek."

To return to German offshoots of Ur, we have

ROTHSCHILD: red shield, a wounded crusader. In the Spanish we have

Rosso: red, as Cape Rosso: red cape. Also Braza: a burning coal, charcoal.

Brazier: pan containing burning coals. From this Braza we have the name

Brazils, producing red coloured wood. The English

BRAZIER: *brass* worker, has nothing to do with brazier, except form.

Burra, Borrico, names given to mules from their being a reddish brown colour. "The *Burra* plied her feet most nimbly, and shortly after nightfall brought me to a village about two leagues from the river's bank." "I had the appearance of a person between sixty and seventy years of age, and drove before me a *Borrico* with a sack of Testaments lying across its back." Burra, Borrico = French

Saure: yellowish brown colour, whence Sorrel, Sord, SAURIN (Miss): auburn tressed =

FLAVIUS and the Milesian SORLEY (M^c) = XANTHUS and JACINTA.

> "For a *roan*-gelding, twelve hands high,
> All spurr'd and switch'd, a lock on's hoof,
> A *sorrel* mare."

XANTIPPE (wife of Socrates): a sorrel mare. Sorrel found in meadows, and eaten by boys, means sour plant. Burrel Roan, Sorrel =

Hamor: a ruddy ass from Hamar: to be red, inflamed, from which

Alhambra: the red, Arabic palace literally = Porphyry (built). The man

HAMOR was probably so called from the ass, that being, in the East, a symbol of wisdom because of its strength and patience. The judges of Israel rode on white asses to signify wise judgment. So Jesus entered Jerusalem on an ass "whereon never man sat." What He has He must have *wholly* or it cannot be *holy*. "The sepulchre that Abraham bought for a sum of money of the sons of

EMMOR, the father of Sychem." Hence Amorites: descendants of HAMOR, EMMOR. In the Erse we have Aiur, Ur in Lough Dearg: red lake = Erythean (sea).

In Irish names Ur assumes the form Roo, as in

O'CONNOR ROO: the red headed eldest son of Connor, for none but first-born sons were allowed the O. Similarly we meet with

ROURKE (Teddy O'): the red = RUFUS. Roo and ROURKE form, in England—

ROOK, ROE, ROWE, when not from Rue: a street. We have many words in English directly, indirectly, or by combination from Ur, as—

Roan: reddish brown = Burra. Rose, which simply means red though it be white.

> "Four yoked stedes full different of hewe,
> The first was *sord*, with mane as reed as *rose*."

Rose: a cultivator, a nobleman's gardener.   Out Parch and Burn are variations of Pur.   Burn gives Brimstone: stone that burns.

Burnish: to make bright as though burning.   Burnish is identical with Furbish: to polish, whence the worthy—

Frobisher: a whitesmith, polisher of metal.   "Furbish the spears, put on the brigandines."   The French Brun, and the Brown, are forms of Burn.   The Parisian—

Le Brun is only Brown of English borough ubiquity.   So the engineer

Brunell is but = Brownell, each being = Brunette: of a brownish complexion.   From the same prolific source we have Borell, whence

Burwell: maker of borrell cloth; also means wearing it, humble conditioned.   Chaucer says :—

> " Had they themselves but light to see the ropes
> And snares of Hell, which for their fate are dresst,
> Because they pill and poll, because they wrest,
> Because they covet more than *borrel* men."

Bruin, the Alpine bear, is a form of brown.   Bronze is to make metal brown.

Auburn hair is yellowish brown, being to ladies what Sorrel, Sord, Roan, Brindle, are to horses and dogs.

Brindle : of a burned colour.   Brand : a partly charred stick. " A brand plucked from the burning" and grafted into the true vine.   Brindle, Burned = Ustus.

Bran-new, originally said of iron fresh from the fire.

> " Armado is a most illustrious wight,
> A man of *fire new* words, fashion's own knight."

Brent: the brand goose, neck having a black and white mark round it as though it had been branded, burned.   Gives name to hunter of it.

Brent.   Brand : to mark with charcoal.   Brunt : where fight rages hottest, as in " Brunt of the battle."   Brandy : burned wine, *y* for Vin.   From Ur the Welsh get Rhudd : red, whence Ruddle : red ochre.

Rudd = Rourke.   Ruthlan: red bricked temple = Alhambra, *con.* Scanlan : old temple, church.

Ruddock : little red (bird) = Robin, also from Ur and *uncon.* Robert.   Hence, too—

Red : fire colour; Ruddy, for rudly, for redly, for red like. Hertford is a form of

Herudford : red ford = Sandyford · and Radford.   Raw, Rear ; red, uncooked.

Roast : to redden.   Some derive this from Rotir : to turn ; but twisting the jack is accidental, reddening essential.   Scorch

smells too strongly of fire for us to allow it any origin but an
igneous one.

Ordeal: purgation, trial by fire. "A custom not differing
much from these (in use among the Greeks) that was practised
in this island by our Saxon ancestors upon the same account,
and was therefore called the fire-ordeal, for ordeal in Saxon
means purgation. The manner of undergoing this test was
thus: the person accused passed blindfold, with bare feet, over
certain ploughshares made red hot, and placed at equal dis-
tances." A king of Norway, named Magnus, came to Scotland
in his boyhood, and stayed here until he attained maturity.
Returning, his nobles denied his identity, which he proved by
ordeal, and was therefrom called BAREFOOT. Any so called
here do not trace their pedigree to MAGNUS: great, (Mc)
MANUS, but their ancestors, being tried by ordeal. There is a
firm at Boston known as

DISCALZEADO, an Italian word meaning bare-foot, a discalceated monk. The philosophy of monastic bare feet is this:
Barefooted signifies poor =

LACKLAND, LANDLESS, PAIR. "Now, this was the manner
in former times in Israel concerning redeeming (land) and
concerning changing (estates) for, to confirm all things; a man
plucked off his shoe, and gave it to his neighbour," thereby
intimating right to walk over it, else he would trespass. A
bye-law of the Temple forbade any to enter sandalled. All
must go barefooted to the All Possessor. "Put off thy shoes."
Where God is manifest there is the Temple. "Put shoes on
his feet" = restore his landed property. Bare feet meant, in
the symbolism of religion,—

> "No foot of land do I possess,
> No cottages in this wilderness,
> A poor wayfaring man."

Koh-i-noor: hill of light, shows our old friend Ur in Noor
in far off India. Compare it with NER: light; and Kohistan:
the hill country.

NUREDDIN (favourite Arab name): the light of religion,
suggesting: "Let your (religious) light so shine." The Mogul
Emperor,

GEHANGUIRE: conqueror of the world, took to himself a
bride called

MHER-UL-NICA, a name indicating superiority. The former
part is *con.* Major: greater, and is seen to advantage in

MAHARAJAH: great king. Of his uxorious gallantry he
changed her name to

NOURJEHAN: the light of the world. The former part of
his name is the latter part of hers, so that they were nominally

as well as personally married. When she died he erected that famous mausoleum to her memory known as Taj Mahal : the crown of the harem,—

" With the Light of the Harem his young Nourmahal."

NOURMAHAL : great light, beauty = OLYMPIA. Taj *con.* Dagh : a mountain ; as Daghistan : hill country, so— STEPHEN from Stephanos : a crown, allied to steep. As we have already seen, the Gaelic received tribute from Ur, to which we add as follows— Ruadh : red, as Ruadh-abhuinn (avon), contracts to the better known RUTHVEN : red river = Rio Colorado. Hence to ROY : red (headed).

We now summarise whereby it is seen that from the Chaldaic Aiur or Ur of the Hebrew, we obtain directly, indirectly, or by combination with other roots, the following words—

Hebrew : NER, Areli, ABNER, ALORUS, BARAK, HAMOR, BEOR, EMMOR, URIJAH, URIAH, URIEL, JAIR, JAIRUS, AARON, Urim, Seraph, Saraphim, Orphanim.

Arabic : NUREDDIN, NOURMAHAL, NOURJEHAN, Koh-i-noor, ALBORAK.

Egyptian : HORUS.

Persian (ancient) : ARTAPHERNES, ARTAXERXES, ARTA-BANUS, ARIDATHA, ARSES, arta, mervaid, arsa.

Persian (modern) : Gurmsir, Parsee, Fars, Faristan, houri.

Punic : BARCA, HAMILCAR, HA-MELK-ART.

Turkish : Orfah.

Papuan : For.

Greek : ORION, OROSIUS, ARTEMIS, ARTEMISIA, PYRRHUS, PYROIS, PYRAMUS, PERSEUS, URANIA, PORPHYRY, ZOPYRUS, PORPHYROGENETUS, ERYTHRA, ERINNYS, PYROSPORUS, MARA, MAIRA, ERIS, Thermopylæ, Erytheia, pyrites, ouranos, porphyros, erythros, thermos, pur, pyrolatria.

Latin : AURORA, PUPILLUS, RUTILIUS, RUFUS, RUFFINUS, BURRHUS, Edui, ardeo, arduus, furo, ira, aurum, fuscus, focus, purus, purgo, puer, puella, pupilus, fornax, uro, urtica, ustus, areo, torreo, arena, arson, russus, arunda, ferveo, febrifuge, furfur, forceps, purpura, forfex, ruber, rubus, puto, rubigo.

Italian : LOCUSTA, FOSCARI, FOSCANI, FORNARIUS, ROSETTI.

Spanish : Brazils, rosso, braza, borra, borrico.

French : LEROUX, ROUS, RUFUS, ROUSSEAU, SAURIN, Huguenot, rouge, saure.

German : ROTHACKER, ROTHSCHILD, purpuroth, feursbrunt.

Irish : (Mᶜ) ARTNEY, (Mᶜ) ARTHY, HART, SORLEY, HUGH, ROURKE, ROE, dearg, roo.

3

British : ARTHUR, RUDD, RUTHLAN, rhudd.

Cornish : Forkhan.

Danish : Vuur.

Gaelic : AIDAN, HAYES, HAY, RUTHVEN, ROY, HUGH, Dunedin, ard, aird, ruadh.

English : MARGARET, MARGAREDON, SPURGE, BALLARD, WISHART, BROWN, BRUNELLE, BURWELL, ROSE, FROBISHER, ARUNDEL, RADCLIFFE, RAWCLIFFE, ROOK, ROWE, TORRANCE (Latinised) TORRENTIUS, RIDLEY, RILEY, RUDD, Arundel, Penrith, Radcliffe, Rawcliffe, Rotherhithe, Hertford, Radford, borell, bruin, auburn, brindle, biretta, brand, rose, parch, burn, burnish, brimstone, sulphur, fervent, ferment, pruriency, compute, count, rust, russet, sorrel, sord, roan, brent, brunt, ruddle, ruddock, robin, raw, rear, scorch, ordeal, pyre, air, warm, empyrean, erythematous, puritan, pupil, purge, spurge, purgatory, urn, adure, inure, arson, ire, combustible, locust, area, obfuscous, ardent, torrid, torrent, fever, fuel, fornication, ruby, febrifuge, parch, rubric, rutilent, furbish, bran, brandy, bran-new, purple, red, ruddy, curfew.

Truly, Ur is a patriarchal word, nor is here all his progeny. There are few scholars who could not treble the presentation. Howbeit, our object is to illustrate the formation of words and genesis of ideas, to do which these may suffice. How such words passed from language to language is not here to be considered farther than to say that probably in the early ages it was entirely by word of mouth, in later times by oral intercourse and by manuscript, but in the last days by word of mouth, writing, printing, and wiring. Socrates and Plato discussed the origin of Pur in Athens when its ancestor Aiur, Ur had been exercising an influence upon language for twenty centuries ; we are considering it twenty centuries later. Our stand point is our superiority. They were giants standing on a plain, we, men pedestalled on the accumulated experience of four thousands of years. They knew not Abraham, and were unacquainted with the science of language as now understood.

CHAPTER III.

PERSONAL NAMES

PRECEDE all others with respect to time. Adam was a personal name. Not only does this kind claim priority as to order, but it could as to number up to the Christian era. Since then local, trade, and war names have left personal appellations far in the minority. Names of this type are, in the nature of things, non-transferable. Thousands of persons might get their name from the same locality (as SCOTT from Scotland), but not even two could be called Jacob, Moses, Virgil, except through a second-hand use of one of those names by adoption or popular application. Of course this is the outcome of so many personal names being obtained at birth and the nativity of no two children being born in identical circumstances, not even twins, as is seen by the remarkable case of Jacob and Esau. This is a period when more knowledge is extant on nearly every subject than in former ages ; yet in this we differ from the ancients. Then, as a rule, every man knew the meaning of his name ; now, as a rule, not a man in a thousand knows whether his name is local, personal, ancient, or modern. Of course, personal names are fairly divisible into three classes —physical, mental, and moral : the latter having respect to habits and manners. Howbeit, seeing that my reader can distinguish at once under what head to place any explained name, and yet more because it is convenient for philological purposes to link the three together, I have so done. Of those deemed most important as to meaning or historic association, the following is a typical selection.

ADAM is the same word as EDOM, and con. Dam : blood, as in Aceldama : acre of blood. Rabbinical tradition assures us that he was named from being made out of a sandy soil, like that on which Damascus = Sandy (Beds.) and PASCOVITCH, was built. It more probably means *ruddy*, like the Welsh GRIFFITH and the Irish name CORCORAN : rosy, like RUDDIMAN and the gallant SCARLETT, but answers most accurately to RHODOPIS : rosy-cheeked, like FLANN : ruddy, giving FLANIGAN : young Flann, FLINN, CLANCY, GLANCY, MACKLIN = FLANIGAN, and LINN. ADAM means generically man = anthropos, homo, *on*, as male or female. ONDEDIEU : man of God, a religeuse = GOTHER (bishop) : a good man. EVE, EVA is the English form of CHAVAH : living, life giving. ABEL : vanity, vapour, breath. " *Hebel, hebelim,* all is *hebel !*" CAIN : possession, " I have

cained the man," the Lord " promised should bruise that cruel
serpent." " Jehovah *cained* me in the beginning." ABIEL :
father of strength, strong = AMOZ. " Ner, the father of Abner,
was the son of Abiel." ABIALBON : the same with augmentative *on* " *Abialbon* the Arbathite," man of Hebron. GABRIEL :
strength of God, very strong, man of God, *cor.** to GEBBIE, as
MICHAEL to MICKIE.   MICHAEL : who like God ; CARMICHAEL :
dear to Michael, *con.* CARUS : cherished one, whence CHERRY,
DARLING, Mavourneen.

ALGEBAR : the strong (a title of the great hunter) "Nimrod
began to be great in the earth," varies to EL GEBER, Algebra,
and Gibberish : science to the ignorant. "Near the student
stood an antique bronze lamp, with strange figures carved
upon it.   It was a magic lamp, which once belonged to
the Arabian astrologer El Geber."   Tel-el-kebir : strong hill,
earthworks, *con.* Tellus : earth.   GIBBAR : manly = ANDREW,
WIGHT.   The Biblical names for a man are Ish (sexual),
ADAM (generic), ENOSH (sickly), GEBAR (strong).   " The
children of *Gibbar* (were) ninety and five."   AKBAR (Mogul
Sultan) = NERVUS :   strong, from   Neuron :   a   bow   string,
whence our *nerve.*   NERO :   strong ;   NERVANDER : a nervous,
strong man.   Hence also NERVA (emperor), MINERVA (goddess) :
strong ones = BIAS (one of seven wise) : full of vital energy,
con. Bios : life, whence Vis : force = BREE.   KRAFT (George
Wolfang) : strong, powerful, *con.* Kratos : power.   IPHIS :
strong, much used by Greek women, means strong as a python.
IPHIGENIA : strong born, or of pythonic descent, or daughter
of IPHIS   from   Ophis :   a   serpent.   ALCIMUS : strong.
"*Alcimus* commanded that the wall be pulled down."   This
is *con.* Elk : strong (deer), Auk : strong (bird).   But, observe,
some of these strong may be political.   ALCMAN (lyric poet) :
strong minded.   CRATERUS   (general) :   powerful = KRAFT.
ADRASTUS (king) : powerful, *con. drastic* and *draw.*   OUTRAM :
very strong, gives Tram, from one of that name invent-
ing tramways.   AGASTHENES (king of Elis) : very strong.
LASTHENES : stone strong, passive strength = PETER, *con. lithos,
lapis.*   LEOSTHENES : strong as a lion, active, strength.   HAR-
POCRATES (Egyptian) :   strong   as   a   harpy.   HIPPOCRATES
(hippocras) : horse strong.   VALENS : strong through health.
VALENTINIAN :   healthy,   strong,   *con.* Convalescent :   growing strong.   HALES (judge) :   a   *hale*   man,   whole = the
Milesian name FALLON and the English MERRY : not jocund,
but joyous through exuberant health.   VALENTINE is given by
some good writers as a form of GALENTINE, *con.* GALLIARDI
and GAY, all meaning happy through good health.   The latter

---

* *Cor.* for corrupted to, as Alexander *cor.* Sandy.

becomes JAY (Bath). WALDO (Waldenses): powerful, *con.*
Wield = ZUINGLE, ZUINGLIUS: he who *sways*, rules, each is
a sceptre wielder, swerver, swayer.
KEREN-HAPPUCH: horn of stibium, beautiful eyed = ORPAH.
Keren gives Keras: a horn, whence Corona: a crown; Cervus:
a stag, whence CERVANTES: swift as a deer = DEERFOOT. COR-
NELIUS: son of a crowned man, powerful, of a dynasty. Horns
were symbols of royalty. " I will make the horn of David to
bud." The Cornelian gens was the most powerful in Rome,
hence names thereupon are widely spread. Thus CORNEILLE
(dramatist), CORNARO (Italian noble), KORNILOFF (killed at
Sebastopol): son of Cornelius. COSTA: ribbed, strong;
COSTIGAN: son of. Compare IRONSIDES (Edmund with Costa),
Costa Rica: rich coast, the coast is a rib. SFORZA (duke of
Milan): man of force, *con.* Fortis: strong, whence LE FORT: the
strong. From Fear: vir, gebar, a strong man in the Celtic.
FERGUS: man of strength, FORGIE = FORBES (*con. vis.*), FORBIE,
FORDYCE: man of wisdom, though some gives this, man of
the south. FARQUHAR: a champion, a strong man. FORSYTH:
man of peace = SWEENY *con.* SYTH: peaceful. Kilsyth: his
cell. FERRAR, FERRIE: tall, strong man. FEARGHAL: a
strong man, gives (O) FERROL. TREMFEAR: strong man, gives
the better known TRAYNER, and Trimble, which also means a
strong man, and probably is the source of TURNBULL, TRUMBEL.
FORLONG: man of the sea. FIRGIL: a man of family = GENTIL:
a gentleman, a man of gens. FERGUS = ANGUS: one who is
strong. Carrickfergus: his rock. Fermanagh: the men of
Monagh. Fermoy: men of the lowlands. STARK: strong, brave,
con. Stirk, Starch, and = BALD: bold. Each mean *stark*-naked,
bald of clothing, ready for fight. BREE (Dr.): strong, so also
BREEN, when not formed on BRIAN. ANDREW: virtuous, manly,
a gymnast = MANLY, gives DANDIE (Dinmont) = ANDERSON,
whence *dandy*. TETRANDER: a four square man, well-built
= ARBA: four. PERIANDER (one of seven): very manly =
WIGHT: strong, wight like, manly. DOUGHTY: able to *do*,
formidable. Do gives deed, dead (do-ed), death (do-eth),
doughty,—

" Lordynges, lysten, and you shall here,
You shall well heare of a knight
That was in warre full *wyght*,
And *doughtye* of his dede."

Wight is *con.* weight and sway. Tom Doughty was Sir
Francis Drake's pet sailor, his Tom Bowling. SWITHIN (rain),
SUENO, SWAINE: strong man, able to sway things or persons,
con. ZWINGLE, swither, swivel, and SWIRES (smith). VARRO
(the learned): a manly man, from Vir and = WIGHT.
ALBINUS (Governor of Britain): of a pallid countenance =

BLAKE: bleached, when that is not Welch. CONSTANTINUS CHLORUS: Constantine the pale, as DONALD BANE. SULLIVAN (from Bain : white): fair eyes. The Ban and Boyne were so called from their bleaching properties, if not *con*. BOYD, which consult. The Elbe and Albula, from their whiteness. ARGELANDER : white man = LE BLOND : the fair, BLOUNT, BLUNT, BLONDIN (rope), BLONDELL (harp), also therefrom. GUIN : white, Gowan : a daisy. NELL GWYNNE (the Welch Venus): Ellen White. Gown : white garment. But GUINNESS (porter) is formed on M'Gee Inness : M'Gee's island, about = SKERRATT (scar): a rock : dweller on a rocky islet; Sherries : rocky isles. INCE, INNIS : an islander. Flathinnis : island of the brave. Innis gives Insula (Lat) Isola (It): an island, whence Isolated : lonely. WINNE, GUIN, BIANCO, BANCO, SNOW, BIANCHI, BLANC (Louis), BLANCHE, BLANCHARD : all fair as a banshee. Mont Blanc = Snowdon = Mount Niphates, *con*. NIPHEUS : very fair = CHIONE : snow white, *con*. Hiems, Chiems : snow time = Winter : wind time. GAM (David) GAME, CHAM (caricaturist) from Cam : crooked. CAMERON : crooked nose ; CAMBELL : wry mouthed, tortured into CAMPO BELLO : field of fight. Cam also gives Akimbo : arms at an angle. Cam : river. Cam also Camera : a chamber, arched, covered roof.

ANCUS (Martins): crooked arm, *con*. anchor, Ancona : built on an angle of the coast. BOYLE (philosopher) is often rendered, *affected by boils*, but is purely Milesian, meaning peril, probably born in a time of danger. BALLOCH, BROCHIE (captain): spotted = PIGOT : speckled = PYM, PIM (Hampden): pimpled. SYLLA : " As to his figure, we have the whole of it in his statues, except his eyes. They were of a lively hue : fierce and menacing ; and the ferocity of his aspect was heightened by his complexion, which was *strong red interspersed with spots of white.*" An Athenian droll drew the following jest upon his complexion,—

> " Sylla's a mulberry strew'd o'er with meal."

SULPICIUS : red-spotted face, gives SULPICE (St.) VARIUS, VARIOLUS (brain): troubled with small-pox, marked with variola. NEVIUS : birth-marked, or pustuled, from Novus : new,—

> " Was there no milder way but the small-pox,
> The very filthiness of Pandora's box ?
> So many spots like *naeves* on Venus' soil."

NEVE : a nephew = NEPOS, *con*. Neece : its fem. NEVINS : bighanded. RONQUILLO : rough voice, from Raucus, whence ROOK = BELCHER : bawlcher, *con*. BULL : that boos, makes much noise = GROGAN, FOGARTY = CREEK, CRAICK : war whoopers, *con.* Cricket: noisy insect; Crack: to make a sharp noise; Corncrake: noisy bird in corn. GAVAZZI (padre): loud laugher. Sometimes GELASIUS (pope), GELEE is given as its correspondent, but it means *servant of Jesus*, being identical with the Scotch GILLIS.

NOBAH: loud voiced: "*Nobah* went out and took Kenath, and called it Nobah, after his own name." PURCELL: little mouth = BOCCACIO. BLŒSUS, gives BLOIS (house of), BLASIUS, BLASE (wool comber's St), BLAS (Gil): babblers, blabberers, stammerers all = BALBUS, BALBOA (first European who descried the Pacific). These = the Milesian LALOR: stammerer. Such do not necessarily point to impediment in speech, but were also applied to sorcerers using strange words in a muttering way, and so answer to HALLOSHETH: enchanter, whisperer. "Next unto them repaired Shallum, the son of *Halohesh*, the ruler of the half part of Jerusalem, he and his daughters." HALOHESH (identical with former): a charmer, harmer, for harm is to hurt by a charm. AHENOBARBUS: brass or copper-coloured beard = BARBAROSSA: red-beard, Thor-like. BAREBONES: bonny beard. POGONATUS: bearded — SKEGG: shaggy beard. These answer to the Irish names VESEY, VOSE, VOSEY. BELLUS: beautiful, gives BALIOL, belle, BELLOTT (lieutenant) = Formosus (Pope), well made = FRAME. In some cases, FRAME: a stranger. TREBELLI: very beautiful = BRAVURA. KALI (goddess): black, beautiful, *con.* Kalos: beautiful, and Coal: beautiful (mineral). Calcutta: Kalis temple. CALLISTO (Lycaon's daughter): most beautiful. COSMO (de Mœdici): beautiful, adorned, *con.* Cosmos: beautiful order of the universe. Cosmetic: beauty aider. Comb: hair beautifier. EUTAXIA: she who decently arranged her garments, *con.* Syntax: arrangement of sentences. Tactics: good arrangements. PULCHERIA: fine skinned, *con.* Pellis: skin = VASHTI (Persian Venus). CŒCUS: blind, CECIL, CECILIA: dim sighted = CECCHI of the Italian and the Hibernian KEO, but not KEOGH: a horseman, *con.* COCHRANE. SCIPIO: a staff, to his blind father, *con.* Sceptre: staff, for a patriarch to lean on. ZISCA (Bohemian patriot): one eyed = TUERTO, *con.* Torso: twisted. GUERCINO: one who squints = STRABO, whence *strabism*; but SCHILLER (poet), often given as equivalent, is merely a cottager, one dwelling in a shiel, hut, and so = SHIELDS. EUROPA: big-eyed beauty = BOPIS, GLAUCUS, GLAUKOPIS: grey-eyed = GRAY, GLASS. PEKAH: open-eyed. "*Pekah* went up to Jerusalem to war against it, but could not prevail." CINCINNATUS (dictator): hairy at birth, CRISPUS (orator), CRISPIN (St.) = CROLY, CURLEY (Dan.): for curly, all having curly polls = KROLLMAN. NOTMAN (when not a neat herd): having the hair neatly cut, a round head. SHERLOCK: sheared locks = POLLARD: polled for

tonsure = KORAH. WHITLOCK: white headed = CANUTIUS,
CHANZY, in some cases = VANE (Sir Harry), FAINE, BAIN.
PETIFER: iron footed, a hard kicker, assumes odd form of
POTIPHAR. EDIPUS (of Colonna): swelled foot, PODIO: little
footed, *op.* of Patagon, FUSS. VIERFUSS: four-footed, running
as swiftly as a four-footed animal. PLANCUS (consul): splay-
footed. Splay for display. PANSA (and Hirtius): foot-spreader.
PANSA expanded his feet, PLANCUS displayed them. DASIPO-
DIUS = BROADFOOT. SCAURUS: weak-ankled, or club-footed.
NECHO (Pharaoh), CLAUDIUS (Cæsar): lame, *shut* in, *enclosed,*
Claudo: I shut, varies to CLODIUS, CLAUDE (Lorraine), GLAD-
USE. TAMERLANE (Tartar): Timour the lame. TIMOUR: iron,
constitution = HARAN (& Co.) ZILLAI: iron of Jehovah, His truth
and invariability. This metal (*lit.* the ringer, singer, sounder)
was used by Hebrews to symbolise truth and firmness, reli-
ability; we say "True as steel." BARZILLAI: son of Zillai.
"Now Barzillai was a very aged man, even four score years
old." TALHIRAN (king of Picts); iron forehead. TALIESIN
(Pictish king): brow shining like iron. These show *hiran,*
our iron, came in before historic times, and a good forehead
was regarded as an element in manly beauty. But we return
to our cripples. CRUICKSHANKS (Bacchus): bow-legged. LONG-
SHANKS: much daylight under the crutch. KORTMAN: a short
man = STUNT, PAUL, PETTIT, NINIAN, and MINGHETTI. CURT-
HOSE: short legs, *con.* CORTI (count) = SHORT. KRUPP (guns):
a cripple. VARUS: straddle, preva*ri*cator, as though trying to
walk both sides of the way at once. GRACCHUS: *gracile,*
slender, hence GROUCHY (marshal), GRUCCHIO = MACROS: long,
withered, *emaciated,* gives ALMAGRO (and Pizarro): the thin.
CAUNT (champion): gaunt, ge want, thin by hunger = the
French LARIDAN. GOURKO (general): a cucumber, which,
being a long fruit, was applied to a long person. Perhaps *con.*
Ghirkin (gourdkin): little gourd.

AWLEY: tall as a willow; hence (Mc) AULAY, (Mc) AULIFFE,
suggesting ORNAN. HAZZARD, HAGGER: *haggared,* hacked,
hagged, cut thin = CAUNT. LABEO (lawyer): thick-lipped, *con.*
Label: instructions attached to bottle-lip, gives LABIENUS: son
of LABEO. SILAS (when not contracted from Sylvanus), SIL-
ENUS, SIMON (when not Hebrew): simiœ-like, hemi, semi, half-
nosed = HARIM: snub-nosed, bent upwards. "The children of
Harim a thousand and seventeen." HARUMAPH: flat-nosed.
"Next unto him repaired Jedaiah, the son of *Harumaph.*"
COURTNEY (curt nez): short-nose = CAMOYS: nez retroussé,
nasus retro = SIMON.

> " This wenche thikke and well i-growen was,
> With *camoys* nose and eyghen gray as glas."

CAPPON, GROSSTESTE(Lincoln bishop): MAZZINI(young Italy), CHUBB (lock), FRONTO, *con.* Frond: that part of tree that pushes to the front, and the Sclavonic GOLAWTSCHEFF, each answer to BROADHEAD, GREATHEAD, the German KOPF (scoffee), and our TAIT (archbishop). KEAN: head, CANMORE, (Mc) CANN, Cantankerous: head full of fight. DOLGORUKY (Russian noble), MACROCHIER = LONGIMANUS (Artaxerxes): long-handed. MALE-BRANCHE: bad arm, failing in battle, the *op.* of ARMSTRONG. PLATO: broad-backed = SCUDMORE, SKIDMORE. CLEGG: big built. CLEGHORN = Benmore: great hill. DAFT (cricketer): deaf man = Absurd: answer *from* a *deaf* man. DEE, DOO, DOW (Neal), DOVE, DIBDEN (sea songs), DUNN, (Mc) DOUGALL: dark Gael, DOWALL, DUGALD, DOUL, DWYER (giving DIVER): wearing a black skirt, are variations played upon DHU: dark, whence DARN: dark. DARNLEY (Mary): a dark avised man. TARN: dark water, deep pool. RODERICK DHU: Roderick the dark, DUFF, DUFFY, (Mc) HAFFY, which becomes GUFFIE: all swarthy.

> "These are Clan Alpine's warriors true,
> And, Saxon—I am Roderick Dhu."

Hence, too, Dour: one who scowls, looks black, *con.* Adour = Blackwater, and ATREUS: blackavised, whence ATRIDES: sons of ATREUS, *con.* Atramentum: ink.

NIGER: black, gives Nigger, Nigritia = Caramania: country of the blacks = Mauritania: the Morian's land, the *op.* of Kordofan: the white man's land. NOIR (shot), NERI (Philip): dark visaged. VALLESNERI: dark valley. From a botanist so named the plant Vallesneria is so called. FOSCOLI, FUSELI, FUESLI, PELEUS (father of Achilles) = our BLACK when that is not a form of BLAKE. APPELES (painter): *con.* PELEUS, very dark, PELOPS: black face, giving Peloponnesus: island of Pelops, now Morea, for Romea: south Roman, from it, too, Roumelia, Roumania, Erzeroum: land of the Rouman, from Aretz: earth, *con.* Aro: to plough. ROUSTAN (politician French): Roum stan, or Rouman. ÆSOP: burnt face, an Æthiop = PELOPS, CUSH, African = TERENTIUS AFER: Terence the African = AFRICANER of mission fame. Cape colonists, born of European parents, are termed Africanders. SCHWARTZ (Indian missions): swarthy, gipsy like — CRONE, CRON (Mc) CRONE. OCYROE: quick runner = LIGHT, LIGHTBODY, GAL-LETLY = SWIFT: strong runner. OCYROE, *con.* Ocean: swift flowing. But TRUEBODY: a faithful messenger.

HIPPOTHOE, HIPPOTHOUN, HIPPOTHOUS: swift as a horse, *con.* NASITHOUS: swift as a ship. "My days are passed away as the swift ships." ALTHEA (huntress): the swift (in the chase). TACHUS (Egyptian king): quick (runner), tachydromus = SNELL. ASNAPPER: the swift, Assyrian title of the sun. "The nations

whom the great and noble *Asnapper* brought over." But the
Milesian NAPPER (Tandy) : baby taken by an *ape* to top of
Tralee church steeple, TANDY is DANDY, DE ANDY : son of
Andrew = ANDERSON. PARNACH : nimble, leaper, runner =
LAPPER, when not a trade name. " Elizahom, the son of *Par-
nach*," clearly is *con.* PHARNACES (Pontic king) : quick, active
= WIX, WICKS, SPRYE, THRALE, GRADY, NYM. Cæsar's famous
dispatch, " Veni vidi, vici : I came, I saw, I conquered," was
saying, I was too nimble for the quick man. Pharper is Phar
phar : swift, swift. " Are not Abana and *Pharpar* rivers of
Damascus?" Abana: stony from Eben: a stone. Such names
differ little from our modern ALLAN, SNAREY: the swift.

AURELIAN (gave name to Orleans) : golden-haired = FLAVIUS,
which was to Roman knights what CHLOE was to Greek
dames. FLAVIUS gives FLAVEL, FAVEL, and is = BOYD, which,
conjoined with Hugh, gives (Mac)EVOY : yellow - haired
Hugh = SORLEY and SAURIN: sorrel headed. FLACCUS: flap-
eared, whose ears are *flaccid.* But FLACK : son of LAKE.
GRANT : great, grandee, magnate. GRANDIUS (mathematician) :
full grown, bigman, the *op.* of PAULUS. MITCHELL : mickle,
from much, identical with MEIKLE = GROOT, GROTE (historian),
GROTIUS (Hugo), forms of great, as is Groat : great (piece of
money), Great, from Grow, whence Grass—Cress, from Cresco :
I grow. Big : that which is bigged out,—built. MEIKLEHAM,
MEIKLEM : great house = GRESHAM, CHEESE, HOUSE, BRIAN,
con. CHATEAUBRIANT : Bryant's Castle.

GRANT, MITCHELL, MEIKLE, GROTE, GROTIUS, MOIR, MORE,
STORY, (M')MANUS, MAGNUS, MUIR : the sea ; MOOR : un-
cultivated land, all mean great. The puzzling name ACE =
HOUSE, while AUDUS : living in the old house.

JUVENAL (satirist), JUNIUS (critic), JUNOT (marshal), JONG,
JUNCKER, YONGE (Miss) = our YOUNG. VAUGHAN, PETIT
(Petticoat : little coat), PAULUS, PAUL, MINUTIUS (killed at
Cannœ): minute person ; SMEE : small ; SMICKROS, KENYON :
a dwarf = KORT ; BASSET, BISSET : all = LITTLE, SHORT ; how-
beit, MEE : man of Meath. Names of this class are often
adjectives inverted and used as nouns, as in the case of
LONG. " A young gentleman of the family of Preux, an
attendant on Lord Hungerford, being of remarkably tall
stature, acquired among his companions the sobriquet of
Long Harry, and became the founder of a family who bore
Long as a surname." The Romans had LONGUS, as is plain
from LONGINUS (on the sublime): descended of LONGUS, and
LONGIUS (whom tradition says lanced the side of Jesus) : son
of LONGUS. It assumes the form of LAING, LANG in Scotland, and in Germany LANGE, but this in France is L'ANGE :
the angel (passion play), yet LONG is used in the French, as

is seen in name of one of the unfortunate Jeannette crew, DELONG = LONGIUS of the Latin, from which they received it. In the Chinese LONG : fortunate. In the Celtic LONG : a sailor. FORLONG : man of the sea. Lochlong : ship lake. So with Dun : a hill; Dunum : a fortress ; we have Longdunum, Londinum, London : ship fortress, the fort up to which ships come. As with Henry Long, so fared it with John Little. Will Stukely *loquitur,*—

" This infant was called John Little (quoth he),
Which name shall be changed anon ;
These words we'll transpose ; so wherever he goes
His name shall be called Little John."

LITTLEJOHN = PETTITJEAN : very common across the Channel. HAKKETAN : little. " Johanan, the son of *Hakketan,* and with him a hundred and ten males." JOKTAN is varied as to form, but similar as to meaning : little born. " Unto Eber were born two sons : the name of one was *Peleg :* for in his days was the earth divided ; and his brother's name was *Joktan.*" PELEG : division, whence Pelagos, Pelagus : the sea, the land divider. Archipelago : chief sea, containing most Greek islands. PHALEC is the Greek form of this name, as given in Luke's genealogy. JOKTAN = PICCOLI (giving PICCOLINIMI), CADE, NINA (Cardinal), NINION (brother of Jas. 2nd.) : a daisy, a little dear = Ninion, *con.* Mignonette : little, little plant; all these come under head of what the Negroes call piccaninnies, wee folk = MINGHETTI and NINIAN (St.)

MURPHY, MORPHEY (chess) are sometimes given as meaning scrofulous = GAREB : scabby, scautty, leprous. " *Gareb,* an Ithrite, Uriah the Hittite : thirty and seven in all,"—

" Whose band-less bonnet vailes his o'ergrown chin,
And sullen rags bewray his morphew'd skin."

Whereas MURPHY and MORPHEY are healthy Milesians, *con.* MORIARTY ; an admiral, from Muir : the sea, from Mor : great. MORRISEY : message from the sea ; MARMADUKE : a sea leader, captain. LEIPER, in like manner, has been sacrificed to cant (explaining names by sound) and made to mean *a leper,* but means carrying Scottish banner, with leopard thereon, being the exact correspondent of the Italian LEOPARDI (pessimist), similar to BERESFORD : bear, bearer.

SIDELAS (Ptolemy) : silent, little speaker = TACITUS : taciturn = MOODY, MUDIE : mute = OFFA (Mercian king). " He was dumb until twelve years old." EL MUDO (Spanish painter). " He was mute as a mackerel." STILL (bishop) = the foregoing. But SIDETES (Ptolemy) : a huntsman, *con.* SAID : fortunate in the chase ; Bethsaida : house of hunters, fishers. The following express shining, brightness, glory, or fame. Glory is an abstraction, but it was primarily a visible property—glare, glory, shining. It manifests something admirable in the physical nature (strength, speed in man, beauty in woman), mental (intricate calculations, high poetic powers, or the inventive faculty), or moral (always some form of self-sacrifice). In religion, glory promised to believers is nothing foreign put upon them, but moral character revealed. Glory is from *Clar*-us: glare. The Greek idea of glory was being spoken of in remote ages, fame (from Phemi : to speak), renown (*i.e.*, being re-named). The sons of Abraham meant by glory, the revelation of God. The difference between true and false glory is elegantly illustrated by Milton in his description of Satan, who, falling, was defigured from a star of high magnitude into a faxed star, whose meteoric flash soon fades,—

> " At last, as from a cloud, his *fulgent* head
> And shape *star bright* appeared, or brighter clad
> With what permissive *glory* since his fall
> Was left him, or false *glitter*."

LUCIFER (his well-known title) : light bringer, originates in the analogy between angels and stars ; as the morning star. PHOSPHORUS: light bringer, exceeds other stars, so he the other angels. Venus leads stars through the arch of heaven, so he misled angels. LUKE : shining, glorious, gives LICINIUS, LYCIDAS, LUCIUS, LUCRETIUS, LYCIAS (when not a man of Lycia), LUCAN, LUCANUS (if not men of Lucania), LUCIPOR : Luke's boy, slave. The Romans called slaves after their masters, by adding Puer : a boy, in the form of Por. In the late Slave States slaves were called boys until aged, and then were termed uncles. Lucania : grove country : *con.* Lyceum : the grove (where philosophers met).

LUCY, when masculine as (Shepstone) signifies good at pike catching. Helios : the sun, *lit.* shiner, entered the Cambro British as Houl, whence HOWELL, HOWLETT, as exceeding in glory, answering to SAMSON = PHARAOH : the sun, *con.* Pur : fire, Phos: light. Also from Helios: shiner, we have charming HELEN: skin shining with health, radiant with beauty, giving HELENA, ELEANOR, when not formed on ELLEN, the *fem.* of ALLEN. SLICK (Sam) : sleek skinned, skin soft and shining. HELEN is given by some from Hellas : Greece, and so meaning a Greek lady. NYMPHAS (Col. iv. 15) : a handsome fellow, shining with beauty, *fem.* NYMPHA, whence Nymphs : beauties, shiners, so pretty women were termed stars. ELECTRA (daughter of Atlas): drawing (by beauty). Electron : amber, from Elein: to draw. PHOSPHORUS, PHŒDRUS, PHOTINAS, NYMPHAS : all more or less brilliant. PASIPHÆ : all shining, the sun. PHŒBUS : light of life, the sun, *fem.* PHŒBE : the moon. The German Schon : beautiful, means shining, as

Sheen (Richmond): beautiful = WINTHROP: winsome thorp = Nain and SCHOMBURG (died at the Boyne) = GASTON: beautiful town. Cicero gives LUCINA as identical with Luna: the moon, both from Luceo: I shine, so SELINA (from Selene: the moon) = CLARA: shining, takes the Italian from CHIARA. Clarify: to make clear. CLARET: clear wine. CLARINDA: fancy names herefrom.

BERT, BERTIE, BERTHA are Germanic synonymes to foregoing, as seen in ADALBERT (Hungarian apostle), ETHELBERT (king), ALBERT, ALBRECHT: noble and bright. ALBERT gives BERT, from which BERTHOLET, BERTHOLON (chemist), BERTI, BERTOLI: Italians, and our English names BRIGHT and BURT. DAGFIN: fair as day = JEMIMAH gives DAFFIN, wrongly given from David.

HERCULES: glory of Hera, Juno, ERCOLE. From him forty cities were named Heraclea, whence HERACLITUS: native of Heraclea. Heraclidœ: descendants of Hercules. The same demi-god gives Herculaneum. CLEON (tanner) = famous, glorious = BRIGHT (John) = SHIMEI, from SHEM: a name, one whose name is often mentioned. CLEOMBROTOS (king): glory of mortals. AMBROSE (Milan): not mortal. Ambrosia: food of gods. PERICLES (the Olympian): very glorious. OLYMPUS: all shining, like the Olympian gods = CLEOPAS, CLEOPHAS, CLOPAS: all glory. EMPEDOCLES: whose glory remains,—

" He, who to be deem'd
A god, leap'd fondly into Ætna's flames."

Perhaps his name was his ruin through ambition to realise it. DAMOCLES (sword): glory of Damon. DAMON (tanner): conqueror. " A certain Persian, whose mother was a widow, was called by his neighbours, NAUARI: he who has nothing. The mother sees in her son germs of greatness, and to urge him to its development, transposed two letters of his unwelcome appellation, and called him ANUARI: the brilliant, the illustrious." He so signalised himself as to become worthy of his latter name. A Turk named NOURI = ANUAR, was imprisoned for helping to murder Abdul Aziz.

AHMED, MAHOMET, MARMOUD: glorious. " He shall give you another PARACLETE: comforter," from Kaleo: I call, as of Him who intercedeth. Mahometans give it from Kleos: glory, claiming PARACLETE: glorious one, as alluding to Mahomet when foretold by ISSU: Jesus. From this Arabian sham we have the old English for an idol, Maumet. " Little children, keep yourselves from *Maumets.*" STILPON (chief Stoic): shining, glorious = JAPHIA (king of Lachish): illustrious. CLYTUS (slain by Hector, CLITUS: sons of renown.

CLEOSTRATUS, HERBERT: glory of army, but HUBERT

(O'Grady) : glorious Hugh. SOPHOCLES : glory of Sophilus.
SOPHILUS = WISEMAN, SOPHIA : wise woman, *con.* Sophomore.
CUTHBERT (ken, couth as in uncouth) : bright, famous for
knowledge, *cor.* odd to say, to Cuddy : an ass. CUNARD (line) :
ken hard, very cunning. REDPATH (reed, rad, rath-bert bright,
pert) : famous adviser. DYCE (Sombre), DEAS (lord) : wise,
FORDYCE : man of wisdom = FROUDE : wise through age,
experienced. FRODOBERT, FLOBERT : famous for wisdom.
CLACK, CLOW also mean wise, and = CLEVER, common in the
south of England. KRISHNA (god), CARSHENA : illustrious,
shining. " The next unto the king was *Carshena.*"
NABAL : a fool, he who fails, falls, is deceived. Bal is
identical with Fal in Fallo : I deceive. Fool : one beguiled.
From Guile : deceit, we get Gull, Guilty. " The serpent
beguiled me." SOTTENVILLE (*con.* Sot : who *sits* long drinking) : fool in town = Verdant Green. Slav is the Russian and
Polish correspondent to Cleos. Greeks applied such names
generally, in infancy, Muscovites only in after life. DOBROSLAV
(Polish noble) : good glory = AGATHOCLES, if not glory of
AGATHOS : yet if not, still = EUCLEOS, whence EUCLID (of
Megara) : son of Eucleos. LADISLAUS, WLADISLAV : glorious
chief = CLEARCHUS (retreating myriad). JAROSLAV (Crimean
prince) : glorious George. BOLESLAUS, BOGOSLAV : the glory
of God = THEOCLES, THECLA. Suwarrow's famous dispatch to
Katharine clarifies the name,—

> " Slava Boga ! slava vam ! Krepost Vzala yia tam,
> Glory to God ! glory to you ! Ismael is our's."

RADOSLAV (Bosnian king) : glorious Conrad. PETROSLAV :
glorious Peter. PAULOSLAV : glorious Paul. Names given to
distinguished soldiers. Sclavons use *Mir* with a similar force,
though in a less exalted sense, as CAZIMIR (Polish king) :
good commander, *con.* Ukase : a command. PAULIMIR
(Radoslav's grandson) : Paul the prince, the good. VLADIMIR,
WALDEMAR : princely ruler. To come near home, we have
LEOFRIK : rich in love, fond, LEOFINGSTAN : most loved,
LIVINGSTONE (Africa) = FRITHESTAN. Former *con. love,* latter
friend.
    LIEBIG (chemist) : loved = MUNGO (St.), from which Strath-
bungo : valley of St. Mungo. LIEBROOD : lover of the cross,
con. Holyrood = SANTA CRUZ. DARWIN : dearly loved, a nurse
name = DARLING : little dear. In the 16th and 17th centuries
a mania came upon the learned to transmute names so as to
make an exodus from vulgarity by changing their appellations
from the vernacular into classical equivalents. Thus GERARD :
firm spearman, thinking his name meant amicable, exchanged
it for ERASMUS : amiable = ERATO. Not content with one

after the fashion of plebians, he went in for a triplet, adding
DESIDERIUS : desired, to be *desiderated,* takes *dim.* DIDEROT.
His name then stood Desiderius Gerard Erasmus. And he
rested. The fun and wonder is that the then best Greek
scholar in Europe could make such a *fiasco.* GERARD : a bold
spearman = GARNET (noth : bold) and GARIBALDI. But as "A
prophet hath," &c. The unknown is winsome. DESIDERIUS :
nearly = CUPID (Cupio : I desire), who causes *desire.*

SWARTZERD : swarthy earth, peat soil = ADRIAN (Atra :
black) = DARNLEY, became MELANCTHON : of same meaning,
and *con.* Autocthones: sprung from the earth itself, so ancient.
SOLANDER (however) : one who hunts the soland goose.
KONIGSBERG : shot up into REGIOMONTNUS = VILLEROY, our
KINGSTON. BROOKS (our WATERS, BECK, GOOLE) became
TORRENTIUS. WOODMAN disguised himself as XYLANDER =
FIDDAMAN. WHITMAN (our White) enlarged himself to ARGE-
LANDER (astronomer). REUCHLIN *(con.* auld Reekie : old
smoky = Rekiavick : vapour town) became CAPNIO. HAUS-
SCHEIN : house shiner, light of family (beautiful name), was
learned fool enough to augment into ECOLAMPADIUS : house
lamp = the pretty but little known HOUSGO : house joy.

BOECE from Bois : a wood (dweller) followed suit in Scotland by becoming BOETHIUS. A French writer of the 17th
century, remarkable for his pompous style, was GUEUSE : a
beggar : to assimilate his name to his gorgeous diction, he
assumed that of his estate, and is known to the world as
BALZAC. Some idea of the troubles befalling men through
name changing may be gathered from the following distress-
ing narrative. "Some gentlemen of our nation travelling in
Italy, and passing through Florence, there in the next church
beholding the monument and epitaph of the renowned English
knight and most famous warrior of his time, there named
JOANNE ACUTUS, have wondered what John Sharp this
might be, seeing in England they never heard of any such :
his name rightly written being indeed Sir John Hawkwood,
but omitting the H in Latin as frivolous, and the K and W
as unusual, he is here from Hawkwood turned into Acutus,
and from Acutus returned in English again unto Sharp."
HAWKWOOD : wood frequented by hawks, similar to HAPSBURG
and GLADSTONE. POWER, POE (Edgar) from LE POER : the
poor = LACKLAND : without estate = POOR, PUIR, LANDLESS,
living names originally used by monks going barefoot to intimate poverty. Had the Prodigal Son come home shod, that
would have signified that he had not forfeited his estate.

BELLAMY : fair friend (when not local), from Amicus : a
friend, from Amo : I love *con.* OM : mother, and AMEN : nour-
ishing faithfully. BELLAMY becomes LAMMIE, when that is

not for LAMBIE = DILK, nurse names. BELDAM : fair lady, ulti-
mates in meaning a hag. It is common in England, and seems
to be a case of bar sinister. PHILEMON : kisser, affectionate,
from Philema : a kiss, from PHILO : I love = PHILO (JUDÆUS :
the Jew). "Salute one another with a holy philema."
ONESIMUS : profitable, assisting. "I beseech thee for my
son *Onesimus*, which in time past was to thee *unprofitable*, but
now *profitable* to me and to thee." PHILETUS : beloved, *con.*
PHILTER : a love potion. PHILOLOGUS : lover of the word,
nearly identical with *Philologist.* PHILINNA = AMANDA : one
beloved. DIPHILUS (whence the proverb "Diphilo tardior") :
doubly loved. TRIPHILUS : most beloved = GOLD, GOUDIE, PRE-
CIOUS : nursery names given by affectionate mothers. Three,
in many languages, is used with the force of a superlative, so
TRITON : loud tone, high-sounding main, an allusion to his
buccinic conch and waves breaking on the shore.

"What are the wild waves saying?"

TREBELLI : very beautiful = TRYPHOSA : very shining, excell-
ing in beauty. TERPANDER : an out-and-out man. TETRANDER :
four man, square built, like Hercules Farnese. AGAPETUS
(pope) : esteemed, loved. "These are spots in your agapoi."
GRAINE : loved, connected with the sun, in the sense of beautiful, so = HELEN, OLYMPA, NYMPHA, and other shining ones.
CARO (Italian poet), CARUS, CAREY (missions), CHERRY, CHEERY,
CARADOC, all mean cherished, beloved, last, Romanised into
CARACTACUS, *cor.* CRADOCK. PREU, for PREUX : valiant. PLAY-
FAIR (speaker), a form of playfellow. ELIGIUS (St.) : eligible,
princely, gives ELOYSIUS, whence LOYSON (Pere) : son of ELOY-
SIUS, ALOYSIUS (patron St. of R. C. schoolmasters) : of the elect,
elite, from Lego : I choose, whence Legion : a thousand chosen
men, or thereby.

PENDERGAST, *cor.* PENDERGRASS : receiver of guest = LIEB-
GUEST, *con.* Prender : to take. MEAGHER, MEARA : hospitable =
POLYXENA, XENOPHILUS. FLATTERY : royal chief = VORTIGERN.
COGHLAN : man wearing a cowl-HOOD. BRADY, (Joe) : stupid,
it is not only = but identical with Brutii, from BRUTUS, *con.*
our Brute : stupid, in contrast with man. DRISCOLL : false
story, allusion unknown. LUCAS : wages, from Cas : money
= ISSACHER. If a birth name, the Milesian and Hebrew
strangely coincide. CASSIDY : treasurer, money holder =
ORDERS. MULVANEY, FEENY, from Fioun : *v*inum, *w*ine,
given to = BIBERIUS. VANS, VANCE (from Uain, Erse for a
lamb, in the accusative Oin *con.* Ovis) : a lamb-like man =
AGNEW (Andrew), but LAMB : carrier of flag emblazoned with
Lamb (of God) = CHRISTOPHER. From Uain, Oin : a lamb.
VANNAN : a little lamb = LAMMIE. FREDERICK : peace rich,

peaceful because no foe to kill, gives FRITZ, FERRY (Jules),
FRIZZLE. GRATIAN (emperor): gracious person. Grenoble (Polis):
city of Gratian. COMMODUS: obliging, *accommo*dating, courteous
= CURTIS (gunpowder). SEVERUS : harsh, severe = SUWARROW
(general). The Roman and the Russian justified their names.
TITUS : honourable, TATIAN, TATE, TITIAN (painter), TITIENS
(Madame), EL TATO : the honourable = HONORIUS. ETHEL :
noble. ATHELSTAN : most noble, HUDDLESTONE (locality from
man), the German form ADLER : an aristocrat, EDLIN and UDAL,
come of Ethel, as does (Edgar) ATHELING : of noble birth =
CHILDE (Harold): the well bred. These suggest ETHELRIDA :
noble councillor, *fem.* of ETHELRED, gives (St.) AUDREY, whence
Tawdry: vulgar fine. ARIDATHA (Esther ix. 8, *con.* Arta: great,
high): of high birth = TIRIDATES (king): nobly born, as BURNS
and BARING : bairns, born ones of superior origin = CHILDERS.
So, too, CHILDERIC : ruling son, noble governor, CHILDEBERT :
glorious son, great by descent. These about = BREWIN (Grant):
beloved ruler, re *con.* rex. And so INFANTA: royal daughter,
Spanish princess, *fem.* of INFANT : royal son, whence Infantry :
his soldiers. FAUNTLEROY (enfant le roy): king's son, RENE (roy
natus) = INFANTE and like to KNIGHT: a son (emphatic), (*con.*
Gnatus), an imp, a scion = CHITTY. These are to be arranged
with such names as UPP, HOPPS, ZOON, INGO, IMPEY, HEMP,
KIDD, ING, INGLE, MAGOT, HOGAN, MACCUS, all meaning son by
excellence, answering to O in Irish names, as O'Hara : eldest
son of Hara, his heir. Hence the Yankee puzzler, MULLHARE:
bald, HARE or HARA. Seed was anciently used with the force
son, supreme, most noble offspring. It is so used in the first
prophecy on record : " The seed of the woman," &c. And not
less so in
ZOROASTER: seed of the fire = PYRISPORUS: seed of the fire, but
yet more notably in (S) PORUS (fought Alexander): the seed,
con. "Spore: the productive substance of cryptogamic or flower-
less plants." ARSAMENES (satrap): strong minded = EUMENES :
remembering well, benevolent = CLEMENT, *con.* mens : the
mind. AGAMEMNON (king of men): remembering much—
(M) NESTOR: rememberer, *con.* Mnemonics: science of memory,
Amnesty: not remembering = MANASSAH. EUMENIDES: daughters of Eumenes, Furies, but used through superstitious fear
in sense of benevolent goddesses. (M) NEMESIS : avenging
remembrancer. ARSINOE (queen): strong minded, *con.* Arsenic:
strong poison, and Nous : the mind.
ALCMAN (lyric poet) and ALCINOUS (host of Ulysses): strong
minded. HUGIBERT (*con.* Hugo), HUBBARD (mother): mind
bright, clear thinker, gives HOBART (town), HUBERT (wrote
on bees), about = KENRICK: keen, rich, learned. But KENDRICK
(M') HENDRICK formed on HENDRY for Henry. KENNETH

4

(German savan): learned, kenneth, one of cognoscenti, a gnostic in literality. QUANT, KANT, KUNTH, CUNDLE (when not a war name): all ken, are cunning. OCHUS (Darius): wise = FROUDE. PINDAR (Theban poet): man of head, connoisseur. CONON (Athenian): man of nous, noun, mind as ARSINOE. MENTOR: rich in *mental* endowments, a guide. HACHMONI: very wise, a magus. WHITE (in some cases): witty man, a Saxon M.P., one attending Wittanagemot; meeting of the witty.

BUDDHA (becomes Fo): learned = Milesian LACEY (Sir Evans de). Botan: country of Buddha. This was not his name but title of Sackya Mouni, who originated the Buddhist religion, now stagnant. LEPIDUS (triumvir): witty. "Some elegant figures and tropes of rhetorick frequently used by the best speakers, and not seldom even by sacred writers, do lie very near upon the confines of jocularity, are not easily differenced from those sallies of wit, wherein the *lepid* way doth consist." DŒDALUS (invented sails): cunning. LEFROY: the cold, frigid, *con.* Refresh: to make cool. BENGEL (lexicographer): timid.

ASYNCRITUS: not to be judged with, incomparable, beyond criticism, nonpareil. ÆSCHYLUS (tragedian): shame faced, modest = ÆSCHINES (for the crown), though it is capable of an opposite meaning, viz., baseness. SOPHRONICUS (father of Socrates): of a wise mind, modest = PUDENS: shame faced, and SEMPRONIUS (consul): sound minded. ARISTOGITON: best neighbour = BEAUVOISIN, *con.* Vicinity, from Vicus: a village. Many names imply moral or social goodness, as AGATHO, PHELIM, GOODE = GOOD. GOTHER, the Scotch DUGUID = Greek EUERGETES, and the Latin BONIFACE. "The kings of the Gentiles exercise lordship over them; and they that exercise authority over them are called *benefactors.*" Was that an allusion to Ptolemy Euergetes? MAYNARD: of a man's nature, manly, humane.

AGATHOS: good, from Ago: I drive. With the Greeks he was good who drove away cattle from the enemy, as Caffres yet do. So our TURNBULL: turner of English cattle on to Scottish pastures, if it be not a formation on TREMBLE, which consult. BEST is beatest, he who beats all. Beat, beater (our better), beatest, contracted to best. EVANDER: good man = GUZMAN: a monk, as our English GOODMAN. EUPATOR (title of Mithridates): good father, whence Eupatoria. TREBONIUS (friend of Cæsar): very good. Bonus: good, gives BONIFACE = DUGUID, BOHN, BONING (son of Bohn), BONNET, BONNER (bon air): good manners = DEBONNAIRE (Louis): of good manners, polite = URBAN, TOWNLEY. LEBON: the good = MEDOC, whence MADOX. PROBUS: of probity, one approved. JUSTUS: who does right, JOSSELYN = DICE (Horce), DICEARCUS

(Messinia): just judge. FRY (Elizabeth): free, kindly, affable, gives FREW, *con.* FRAULEIN: free woman. These belonged to the order, called a thousand years since, Frelungi. CHARLES means whatever Carl, Churl formerly meant—strong with a flavour of roughness which time has rubbed out. We say Tom cat, Germans, Carl cat. Churlish does not necessarily mean sour, dour, but rough, boorish, colonial. CHARLESWORTH: the carls dwelling = BOORHAAVE.

" The miller was a stout carl for the nones,
For bigge he was of brawn and eke of bones."

KARL RITTER: Charles Knight. CARLOMAN = CHARLIER (vir), KAROLYI (count) CAROLUS, CAROLL, Carolina: country of Charles. CARLOS (don) HARLEY, M'ARL = CARLOVING and CARLOWITZ: son of Charles, CAROLINE, CHARLOTTE, its *fems.* CHARLEMAGNE, Charles the magnificent. CLEMENT (pope): man of clemency, gives MENZIES, MENSCHIKOFF: Clement's son = MENDELSOHN.

FOLLETT is no *dim.* of fool, but of FOLLEY (sculptor): a rock = FOLI. FELL: rock dwellers, hillsmen. PACKE: a deceiver = COSBI (slain by Phineas): one who cozens = DOLON (slain by Diomedes) gives PAXTON. SPOONER: enticer, allurer. Spooney: easily gulled. GULLIVER (De Foe): one who beguiles, gulls his audience = ALAZON. VARLEY (electrician): cautious, wary. HILARIUS (bishop of Poictiers): given to *hilarity.* "Hilary term begins." HILARY = L'Allegro: the cheerful, man of alacrity. Glarus is formed from Ecclesia and Hilarius: church of Hilary, and gives GLARES. GIOCONDO (built bridge of Notre Dame): jocund, jocose, jovial from Jove. At first sight looks = MERRYMAN, but that = CARLOMAN, for the merry is an outcome of rejoicing in strength. Merriment comes of exuberant health manifesting itself in laughter, singing, leaping. GAY (poet), JAY (Bath), GALLIARDI = HALES: healthy, hearty. LETITIA: frolicsome, joyous, LETTICE. FAUSTUS (Doctor), FRAUSTULUS (exposed twins) FAUSTINA (Antony's wife), FESTUS, FAUST, FUST (printer): joyous through favourable circumstances = the following well known names FELIX, FELICIA: felicitous persons = EUMERUS (Cyrenian): well fated. JAMIN (son of Simeon): adroit, dexterous, lucky, *con.* BENJAMIN, this about = SAID, SADI, *fem.* HAIDEE: happy, lucky in hunting, root of SIDETES: huntsman, is seen to advantage in (Port) Said, Bethsaida: house of hunting. EUTYCHUS, TYCHIUS, SYNTYCHE (last = FELICIA): lucky Greeks. Again SAID = HAVARD, HARVARD (they have, hap), GLUCK, HABO, EDDY, LUCKIE (and sometimes) RAE: all favoured by Fortune, and so = SECURIUS: cheerful, happy, who puts care (cura) aside (se). Secure abbreviates to Sure: free from anxiety. CURIUS (Dentatus): a man full of cares, who meets troubles half way. SADD : heavy hearted, set countenance. Sadness is settled grief. PENTHEUS (Theban): who grieves, whence PENTHESILEA : taking away sorrow by her charms, *con.* Nepenthe: (herb): no grief. TRISTAM : of a *tristful,* gloomy face = MORNY (duc): mournful, melancholic. Some authors give TRISTAM : a herald, *con.* tryst.

SHANDY (gaff): wild, uncontrollable, always in a shindy = WILDERSPIN : self-willed. MALATESTE : an Italian name corresponding with foregoing and HEADDY. PERTINAX : a man of *pertinacity,* and such are usually impertinent. The early Christians said " Vere Severus, vere Pertinax:" truly severe, truly obstinate. IGNATIUS (St.): fiery, whose wrath soon *kindles,* gives IGNAZIO, INIGO (Jones). BALLANTYNE, BANNATYNE : fiery child. Tyne for Tan : fire, Beltane : May : fire of Baal.

GRIG : fierce, GRIGGS, (M^c)GREGOR (*uncon.* Gregory), Anglicises to GRIERSON, where the Highlander doffs the garb of old Gaul. SAAD (Arabian favourite): joy, through luck in hunting, is seen in this *con.* MOHAMMED BEN HASSAN SAAD EDDIN : Mahommed, the son of Hassan, the joy of religion. So the great warrior, SALADIN : goodness of religion. ALADDIN (lamp): the religious. FUTHER EDDEEN : glory of religion. FADLADEEN (Lalla Rookh): the whiteness, purity of religion. Names combining with Deen : religion, are in daily use among Arabs.

GATLING (gun) for gadling : a gossip, who *gads,* goes from house to house. Go gives gadfly, goat, GADSBY, guest, gate, *con.* Ghaut : a pass. EUSTACE (Flemish count): standing well, firm, constant, gives EUSTACHIUS : (eustachian tube) = STITT, STOUT, STEADY, CONSTANT : standing by one in war or peace, *fem.* CONSTANCE. These = ECKHARDT : *oak hart,* figuratively, true = AMON, AMEN, AMEENA (Bou). CONSTANTINE : son of Constance, Constantinople : city of Constantine, and CONSEDINE is a common name in England corrupted therefrom.

RAYMOND, RAYMENT (rince mouth): pure mouth, truce keeper = VERUS: man of veracity. DROUIN (de Lhuys): truth win, winning honourably. AL SEDDEK : the just. " He was also termed Al Seddek, or the Testifier to the Truth, from having maintained the verity of Mahomet's nocturnal journey." ZADOK (high priest), SADOC (Sadducees): just, are identical with foregoing Arabic name. ZEDEKIAH : justice of Jehovah. " The king of Babylon made Mathaniah, his father's brother, king in his stead, and changed his name to Zedekiah." Expressing his opinion of the act by the name. MATHANIAH : the gift of Jehovah. MATTAN, MATTHEW, MATTY (meddlesome) : a gift, child given in answer to prayer. LYSIMACHUS (general) : loose strife = Puritan name, MAKEPEACE, and German FRIEDMAN. LYSANDER=FREEMAN and FREW. SYMMACHUS, looks like fighting with, querulous, but signifies commilitis : a fellow soldier. HUTIN (Louis) : the quarrelsome. IRENE (empress), IRENEUS (bishop): peaceable = SOLOMON. " In the Greek empire a certain officer had the title of Irenarch, nearly corresponding to our Chief Justice of the Peace." WINIFRED (well): winning by peace. FERDINAND : venturesome, takes form HERNAND as in HERNANDEZ or FERNANDEZ (Juan), son of Ferdinand.

CARPO : fruitful as to offering=ESCHOL : grape cluster, big family man. POLYCARP (martyr): much fruit. "Herein is my Father glorified that ye bear *karpon polun.*" Christian fathers should have spiritual sons. PIUS : one who has made an atonement, gives PIO (Nono), BIOT, BIOTTI, BIAGOTTI (Italian *dims.*) Pious : fond of parents. " The pious Eneas." PASITELES, PRAXITILES : all finished, accomplished, good all round, PRAXEDES : active, business like, practical. Zao : I live, gives ZOILUS (critic), ZOSIMUS (emperor), ZENO (philosopher), ZENAS (lawyer), ZEUS (Jupiter) : full of life = WICKS, SHARP, SMART, GRADY.

SMART : brisk, active, who can *smite* quickly, out of army sunk into meaning gay. Smart : sore, the result of being smitten. SMART = NYM and SPRY, sprightly. ZENOBIA (queen): life sustained by Zeus, *con.* Biology : science of life. ENEAS : praise = JUDAH = LAUDIUS : who receives applause, gives LO (St.) VASA (Gustavus) : keen, bold, originally Wass, whence WASSING : son of Wass, giving WASHINGTON (Sussex) : town of the descendants of WASS : bold, *con.* VASA. TRYPHO (the Jew) : TROPHIMUS : one nourished, a foster child = FOSTER. When from Phos : light, means very glorious, trebly bright. SHELAH : prolific = CARPO, NON, ESCHOL, ABRAHAM : father of a great multitude. KIRWAN : dark avised=DOW, DEE, from Dhu : dark, whence DONALD : dark haired, DUNDONALD : Donald's Castle, (Mac)DONALD varies to (Mc)WHANNELL.

PEABODY : handsome as a peacock, fine fellow, and consequential. HENNESY (Pope) · impetuous, heady, irritable. PURDIE : proudie, little. FEELY, FILSHILL : men of great teeth = TOOTH (ritualist) and MORDAUNT. OATES (Titus), OATTS, are from eat, in the sense of gigantic, gluttonous = JUTE, TURNUS, JOTUN : giants with an absorbing appetite. Oats (corn) means edible. Our *eat* and the Latin *edo* are from Eo : to go. Eat is the going of the jaws, and jaw : that which goes = Gueule. It is strange but true that jaw philologically = JANUS : he on whom the year (gir, gyre, time circle) goes, turns. Let us present the matter thus : eo, eat, oats,

edo, jaw, JANUS, OATES, OATTS. In keeping with above gluttons
we have SWAGEMAN : he who *assauges* at meals and begins
again. TANKEY : pugnacious, quarrelsome. Bowditch in his
"Suffolk Names," Boston, 1860, says that it is probably
connected with using the *tankard.* I knew a family of this
name. It is good English, and is preserved in combination
with the Celtic for the head, viz., Can, in Cantankerous:
thraw, cussed, head full of quarrelling. Can varies to KEAN :
head = KOPF (M') CANN : an Irish warrior given to cutting off
heads. Kanturk : the boar's head. KINTOR : HILLHEAD.
CANMORE :' great head = CHUBB : chubby headed. LENTO
(lenis : soft) : man of lenity, tender hearted, LENTULUS :
descended from. MANSI (mansuetus, manus suesco, sequor) :
suave as to manners, kind, obliging = BONNER. WORDIE : a
boaster, one of many words = ALAZON.

SOBRIQUETS, NICKNAMES, AND INSEPARABLE SURNAMES.

Sobriquet from super : above, is applied to grotesque appellations given to persons in addition to their proper name. Nicknames are names given with a contemptuous nick of the head,
because of some peculiarity real or supposed in the appearance
or character of those to whom they are applied. Often such
are biographies crowded into a word. When attributed to
the members of a dynasty they play the part of an ordinal.
We say George the First, Second, Third, Fourth. No Greek
would tolerate this. He added the patronymical or descriptive
appellation to each wearer of the purple. Thus, SELEUCUS :
shining, brilliant, *con.* Selene : the moon, gives SELEUCIDÆ :
descendants of Seleucus, from him also Selucia (on the Orontes):
city of Seleucus. The following are some of the cognomens
fixed on members of that race of kings :—EPIPHANES : the
illustrious, *con.* Epiphany : glorious appearing. The Jews
called him EPIMANES : the maniac. CALLINICUS : splendid
conqueror, by irony, his reign being feeble. CERAUNUS :
thunderbolt, by a sarcasm on his weakness. POGON : bearded
= BAREBONES : beard bonny, and the Milesian VESEY. GRY-
PHUS : the griffin, griper, rapacious = HARPALYCE : harpy wolf
= CYBIOSACTES : scullion, mean, avaricious. Of course Seleucus
is understood before each.

So with the Grœco-Egyptian dynasty of the Ptolemies.
LAGUS : the hare, the timid = ZIPPOR : a bird, gave name to
race called LAGIDE : sons of Lagus. SOTER : saviour, preserver
= HAFIZ, HAFID : given by Rhodians whom he helped.
EUERGETES (eu) : doer of good = DUGUID, *con.* evangelist and
energy. He was so called by the Egyptians for rescuing their
Gods from Cambyses. PHILOPATER : lover of father. He was
a parricide. Another of the dynasty was PHILOMETER : lover of

mother. He hated her. PHYSCON : big bellied (*con.* Physics : study of nature) = WAMBA, WOMBA = MICKLEWAIM. "The bairns hae nae meal to put in their wame." Also answers to PANZA (Sancho) : paunchy = HOGARTH (caricaturist) : hog girth, as big round as a grass fed pig. But Pansy (flower) : thought, Pensee from Pendeo : I hang. We naturally hang our head when thinking, meditating, but hold it up when recollecting. Pansy : pensive (flower). To the HOGARTH class belong CARNOT and CARNO (of the French) : fleshy, *con.* Carnis : flesh = CRASSUS and GRASSELLI. LATHYRUS : pea nosed, wart upon it = CICERO, from Cicer : a vetch. LAMYRAS : the buffoon, who puffs out his cheeks, so making them big. SIDELAS : the silent = MUDIE, MOODIE, STILL, TACITUS, DUMAH. SIDETES : the huntsman, *con.* SAID, Bethsaida and JAGARD. POLIORCETES (Demetrius) : destroyer of cities, *con.* Police, Politics, Policy. Nor were the Romans in the rear of the Greeks as to nicknames. One of their witty hits was changing two letters in Tiberius Nero and so making it BIBERIUS MERO : drinker of wine = BIBULUS (consul) and FEENY, MULVANY. There is a flourishing name in Italy, BEVILACQUA = our DRINK-WATER, which some claim as a form of DERWENTWATER, howbeit the name is teetotal not local = the German LOBWASSER : love water, and accurately answering to the great French BOILEAU from Bibo : I drink, whence Bevor : drunk out of in battle.

Witty France produced a heavy crop of sobriquets. Each Louis had his, as BEGUE : stammerer = MUTTER : LALOR (Shiels), though LALOR of the Greeks is a title of Apollo : *eloquent.* DEBONNAIRE : of good airs, manners = BLAND, CURTIS. Such names are found scattered through all history, as Cato CENSORIUS : the critic, judge, censor, census taker : Mutius (Scaevola) : the left-handed. Scaevus : unlucky, signs observed to left hand of augurs, but afterwards applied to unlucky words, as Mors : death, and then to improper language, whence Obscene. Diodorus SICULUS : the Sicilian. Sicily was called Trinacria : three - cornered. Dionysius EXIGUUS (brought reckoning from birth of our Lord, A.D., into use) : the thin, spare = CAUNT, ALMAGRO, MACROS, LONG, LARIDAN. Eric BLU-TAXT(Swedish king) : of the bloody axe, *con.* BLOTT, HACO. HAR-DICANUTE : Canute the bold, similar to HARDY (captain) : bold.

GAFFER (Gray) : grandfather = NANA (Sahib) = AVES, ANAX, LAVEAU. AVES : aged, *con.* Ævum : an age, Co-eval : same age, Ave ! age to you = Hail ! health to you, *con.* HALES : healthy = VALENS, giving VALENTINE, VALENTINIAN, *con.* Vale : farewell, *i.e.* may you be strong. From Avus, Avunculus : less by age, giving uncle, aunt. So NEPOS : a nephew, neipce, niece, and NEFF (Felix).

" Ho ! why dost thou shiver and shake, Gaffer Gray ? "

Hugh CAPET (founded Capetian dynasty) : the cap, kepi wearer, the monk's cap used for covering tonsure. Heraclitus PHYSICUS : the naturalist, physician, watcher of growth, *con.* Phuo : I grow, giving PHYLLIS : verdant, flourishing, and APPHIUS, APPIUS (Claudius), APPHIA : fruitful = BLASTUS : a sprout = CHITTY = FLORUS (Gessius), FLORA, FLORENCE : all flourishing like verdure, suggesting RAMOLINI (Napoleon's mother) : little branches, like RAIMES, RAMAGE : branches, one living where birds are heard singing in trees = FOULIS : where the foulis do singe. Suggestive of CRAIB, CRABBE (poet) : a branch, applied to a clan returning from battle with branches in their helmets as a token of victory. Nomos : law, gives NUMITOR : legislator, and NUMA Pompilius : Pompilius the law-giver = the Greek THESEUS. POMPILIUS : son of POMPEY : fifth born, *con.* Penta. TULLIUS HOSTILIUS : Tully the warlike. The Irish TULLY = TORRANCE and FLOOD, when not meaning tower dweller. Ancus MARTIUS : the warlike, Marslike, *con.* MARTIN = PTOLEMY. ANCUS : crooked-armed, suggests BOSSUE : boss-shouldered. Ancus yet lives in the word Ancona : city on sea bend = REACH in England, (Mc) SKIMMING in Lowlands, and COUDEREAU in France, ours applies to bend of stream. The word is also in Anchor : bent iron, angular grappler. Genoa is *con.* Gonia : an angle, Gonu : a knee, being at a bend of coast. Tarquinius PRISCUS : of the old stock = BEITH, COLL. Tarquinius SUPERBUS : the proud, who held himself *above* others.

TARQUIN : the archon, ancient, ruler = ANAX. Constantine PALEOLOGUS : old stock speaker, having a brogue. Constantine COPRONYMUS : dung name, because when being baptized he defiled his clothes, *con.* Copros : dung, Coprolite : dung stone. LALLA ROOKH : tulip-cheeked (Moore). LORENZO DE MEDICI : Lawrence of the Medicean family, at Florence. MEDICI : physician, medical man. Medeor : to cure by Median herbs. MICHAEL DE LA POLE (chancellor) : MICHAEL of the pool = POOL, POLLOCK, GLASSPOLE. LA BELLE SAUVAGE : forest beauty, lady of the park, a form of Isabella Savage. ROB ROY : red-headed Robert, similar to REDMOND : red Edmond. CALLUM O'GLEN : Callum of the glen, as 9 o'clock, 9 of the clock. MACCALLUM MORE : the great M'Callum, Argyll. MARCO POLO (Venetian) : Mark Paul. TAM O' SHANTER : Thom of the Shantie farm, broken down barns, old buildings. CLYM OF THE CLOUGH : Clement of the cliff (outlaw). From cliff, CLOW, CLIVE (India) = FOLLY, FELL = DU HALDE : of the hold, usually a rock = STERNHOLD : living in a stone hold, castle that could not be burned.

CHAPTER IV.

OUR Scriptures supply names to nearly half of civilisation. As well kick at Fate as at the Book. Eclectic, sceptic, agnostic are alike indebted with believers thereto for names of themselves or friends. In many cases these were indirectly derived from that sacred source when the recipient was unconscious of such origin and continues to be so life through. As in ordinary affairs, it consists with wisdom that all actions should be interpenetrated with religion rather than that certain acts should be viewed as secular and others as sacred, so it seemed good to blend biblical names with common through this book, consequently no exhaustive chapter will be devoted thereto. Yet, on the other part, seeing it is of Divine appointment, founded on human nature, that one day should be more. especially devoted to things sacred, so there seems a propriety in setting apart one chapter entirely to this subject.

No people, of any age, combined God's name and attributes with their name so much as did the Hebrews, Israelites, Jews. Take Old Testament names and compare them with those now used among Jews and two notable facts forthwith force themselves upon the observer. They alone, as distinguished from "the seventy nation," entwined the Divine name with their own in combinations so varied that a Jerusalem directory of B.C. 700 would only be less valuable than the Bible. The Jews no longer so act, presumably wholly or partially because some organic change in respect to them and the Divine name has taken place. That civilised nations could not now tolerate names varied from the parental stock, that Cohen's sons and daughters must be Cohens, does not cover the position, because, as in the Church of Rome, there is the recognition of the religious as well as the civil name : in like manner were the Jews anxious to act as they once did, no government in the world could prevent them. Not only do they not now so use the word Jehovah in conjunction with biographical changes, but there is one name they avoid—Joshua, or, as we British term it, Jesus. It is hard for the sceptic to account for this name being disused after the first century of our era other than the way Christianity accounts for it, viz., Jews looking upon it as accursed, and consequently to be avoided, while most Christians view it as too sacred for application to even the best of the sinful sons of Eve. Thus, between hatred and awe, the name Jesus became the heritage of Him to whom, in the highest sense, it can alone apply. We have shown that Jesus is a formation upon the word Jehovah, which former has been corrupted until it means hypocritical, as is seen in the too well known words, Jesuitical and Jesuitique of our neighbours the French. Yet, though the name Jehovah has been in use thousands of years, it, like Him of whom it is the sacred sign, has suffered no change. At one time Jove was thought to be a formation therefrom, but scholars agree that as Dies : a day, becomes Jour, so Dios : divine, becomes Jove, and Dios-pater : father Jove, becomes JUPITER. And yet THEOS : God, has been arrogated by the basest of men, as ANTIOCHUS THEOS : Antiochus the divine. So, too, Theos is applied to gods whose feigned stories are best untold. Now, as no man ever took to himself the title Jehovah, He who said : " Thou shalt not take the name of Jehovah, thy God, in vain," must surely have watched over it with jealous care through His love to man, for if nothing unpolluted were left to us, whereof shall Jacob's ladder be made ? how we travel the upward towards Him ? Considering the vile uses to which the words Lord, God, Christ, Jesus, have been applied, who can doubt that the peculiar name has been preserved like the uncorrupted manna in the golden pot in the ark of God. JEHOVAH : I am, *i.e.,* unvaried by time or conditions ; He to whom there is neither accession nor diminution of knowledge, happiness, power, or love ; He who is " without parallax or tropical shadow;" " He in whom is light and no darkness at all." The sun has spots, diamonds have flaws, creatures their foibles, Jehovah none. Whether this be ideal or real no sceptic can conceive of a being comparable thereto. One grander is not only impossible but unthinkable. Nay, there is only One. The man who thinks sublimely lands ultimately in the thought—God. The Hellenistic Jews called this name *Tetra-Grammaton,* because consisting of four letters. It was unused by pious Jews in conversation, they substituting EL or ADONAI therefor. Nor was this mere superstition, but a high form of wisdom. Similarly through awe of the Divine, inspired writers use the personal pronouns where we should reckon them inelegant, but their defence is they feared to mention His great name too often less familiarity should breed undeserved contempt. I turn by the merest chance to Job xxiii. where the weeper uses pronouns instead of the Divine name twenty-seven times, but the word God only once, and Almighty once. Much the same is seen in the book of Psalms, as also in the New Testament. Illustrations of this awe abound in all parts of it. Turn to 1 John ii. 25 to end. "And this is the promise that *he* hath promised us, eternal life. These things have I written unto you concerning them that seduce you. But the anointing which ye have received of *him*, abideth in you, and ye need not that any man teach you : but as the same anointing teacheth you of all things, and is truth, and is no lie, and even as it hath taught you, ye shall abide in *him*. And now, little children, abide in *him* : that when *he* shall appear we may have confidence, and not be ashamed before *him* at *his* coming. If ye know that *he* is righteous, ye know that everyone that doeth righteousness is born of *him*."

Theos was not corrupted so much because men are wicked or given to change, as because changing it at all the meaning must degrade. Thus DIABOLIS : accuser, slanderer, whence DIABLE, DEVIL, starts existence with a low meaning, whereby it may be raised. Thus we have *devil, devilled, devilish,* used in anything but a bad sense, as " He (a horse) is a devil to go." " He (a man) is a devilish (very) good fellow." The fact is as Jehovah is the holy name any change must needs be downwards. SATAN : adversary (of God and man) is much grander in conception and use than DEVIL. One of the most blessed titles applied to God is DESPOT : foot binder, he who governs without consultation. Despots are divisible into good and bad. Every father of a family, every captain of a ship, teacher of a school, is a despot, as is the Empress of India over Hindoos. Souls under the apocalyptic altar, cry, " How long, O Despot, holy and true dost Thou not avenge our blood ? " But so ill used has *despot* become, and in such ill savour is it that few of us find pleasure in applying it to God, although that aged saint Simeon did, " O Despot, now thou lettest thy servant depart in peace." Now I can go home and die.

The Hindoo for God is RAM, whence RAM-BUKAH : the gift of God = BOGDAN from BOG : God in the Sclavonic. When the word Jehovah enters into composition with personal names it assumes the forms of *jah, ah, a,* and is used either as a prefix or a postfix. The highest compliment ever paid to a woman (if it be lawful to term things so sacred compliments) was when the Almighty said, " As for Sarai thy wife, thou shalt not call her name SARAI (princess, aristocratic woman), but SARAH (" princess of Jehovah, greatest princess "). There the Lord takes part of his name and adds it to that of His nominee. Consult Israel. We find it again in combination with the name of a woman, Ex. vi. 20. JOCHABED (*con.* ICHABOD : where is the glory ?) : Jehovah's glory, perhaps an inspired promise of the Lord's power being manifested out of weakness. After the manifestation of the Almighty in the bush (God delights in paradoxes of speech and action) the cases in which the Divine name combines with the names of men become numerous, as ABIJAH, ABI : (whose) father (is)

Jehovah = JOAB. To me these are wonderful names. Nowhere is it revealed in the Old Testament as lawful to call the Eternal by so familiar an expression as Father. What prophet, which psalmist so addresses Him? Jesus was the first man who taught men so to address God. Howbeit, He did not, as our authorised version and revision lead us to suppose, teach us to say " Our Father," which puts the second table of the decalogue before the first, placed brotherhood before fatherhood. The Lord's prayer in Hebrew, Greek, and Latin places Father before our, and should do so in English. However, Father of us would now sound strange. Theology and reason have been sacrificed on the altar of idiom. The Greek and Latin churches have *Pater emoon* and *Pater noster* which is true teaching. By such names as ABIAH we know what the Scriptures do not explicitly teach that pious Israelites approached God with holy boldness, so that it is clear the spirit of adoption whereby we cry Abba : Father, wrought, though faintly, from Exodus to Pentecost.

SHINAB (Admite king): shining of the father, glory of = CLEOPATRA, which may mean glory of the country = LAMBERT. Shin is essential with schon, shine, sheen, skin, sun, all meaning that which shines, is beautiful. ABIEL, ELIAB : God (my) father. ABIBAL (Hiram's father) : my father (is) Bael. ABIATHAR : (whose) father (is) left. Father dying during infancy of son. NADAB : liberal, benevolent = GIFFARD : of a giving nature. But AMMINADAB (chariots of) : a willing people, may be noble people = ARISTODEMUS : best of the people, and PROTESILAUS: first of the people. NABAL : rough, boorish, churlish, dour, *con.* falls and fool. " The *nabal* shall no more be called *nadib*."—Isa. xxxii. 8.

ABINADAB : father of liberality, free with heart to feel and purse to help. ABIGAIL : (whose) father rejoiceth (at her birth), *con.* HAGGITH. ABIHU : (my) father (is) He = ELIHU : (my) God (is) He. ABIMELECH : (whose) father (is) king, of royal descent = FAUNTLEROY (banker): for Enfant le roy = FITZROY. But FAUNT : a fount. ABRAM, ABIRAM : high father, a patriarch. ABRAHAM : father of a multitude, gives IBRAHIM (pacha), BRAHAM (singer), ABBEMA (French), BRAM-WELL : Abraham's spring. MABERLY (poor man's friend) : Abraham's field. TABRAHAM, TABRAM (de Abraham) : son of Abraham. From Ab : father. BABOO (Hindoo title) = SIRE, SIR, and the Arabic ALI BABA (forty thieves) : the father. BABOO applies to Hindoo gentleman in his civil capacity, SAHIB to distinguished natives of India and foreigners, if military men.

ABISHALOM, ABSALOM : father of peace, born in quiet times = BISHLAM. JEHOSHAPHAT, SHAPHATIAH ⟩ : Jehovah's judge =

ADONIJAH, in the sense of God bringing out of trouble, *con.*
SUFFETES : Carthaginian judges. Adon becomes DAN : a judge,
whence DANIEL : judge of God = ELIPHAL, THEOCRITUS, used
passively with the force judged of God, helped by. Hence
DANIELS, s formative. AMARIAH : (whom) Jehovah spoke (of),
promised, from Amar : to speak, whence Amiral (some tall) :
commander, becomes ADMIRAL. From it the Arabic title
EMIR-AL-OMRAH : commander of commanders, generalissimo =
PHICOL (Philistine) : mouth (of) all, whom all obey, *con.* Pi-
hahiroth : mouth of Hiroth, pass so called. OMAR PASHA is a
double title. We have OMAR : a commander, word giver, Gen.
xxxvi. 11-15, the Mosque of Omar now in Jerusalem, and
lately had Omar Pasha, general of Abdul Medjid. OMRIAH,
OMRI : commander of Jehovah, greatest general. PUAH :
mouthy, wordy.

Uz, AMOZ : strong = HALES : hale, strong by reason of
health. UZZIAH, AMAZIAH ⅄ : strength (of) Jehovah, very
strong, *con.* UZZIEL : strength of God. AMITTAI (Jonah's
father) : amen (of) Jehovah, God keeping faith. A common
name in Arabia still is AMOUN (Ben) : amen (man) = FIDELIUS :
faith keeper. AMEEN-EDDEN : faithful in religion. ATHALIAH
(queen), ATHLAI (Bebai's son) ⅄ : whom Jehovah afflicted.
EZER : help, gives EZRA, ESDRAS = ALEXIS when ALEXIUS :
son of Alexis. EBENEZER : stone (of) help, *con.* Ben : a son,
Ebony : stone wood. AZARIAH, JOEZER ⅄ : helped of Jehovah.
that happening to the father about the time of son's birth,
ELAZARUS : helped of God = AZAREEL, AZIEL, AZRAEL (death
angel of the Koran). ELIEZER (Damascus) = the Arabic
ASRALLAH. LAZARUS (form of ELAZARUS) gives Lazaroni :
beggars like Lazarus. Lazaretto : lazar house, instituted for
lepers and contagiously diseased. LIZARS : medical attendant
on Lazaretto. Lazy : lying about like Lazarus. So *ill* and
idle are the same word.

ELISHEBA (Aaron's wife), *con.* Sabbath and meaning oath of
God, *i.e.*, God remembering his oath to Abraham, hence
ELIZABETH, ELIZA, ELSIE, BET, BETTY, BABINGTON : town of
St. Elizabeth's church. BARUCH : blessed = BEATUS, *fem.*
BEATRICE for BEATRIX. BARACHEL (Elihu's father) : blessed
(of) God, by increase of family. BERACHIAH : blessed (of)
Jehovah. Ben : a stone, gives Banah : to build, whence
BENAHIAH : built (of) Jehovah, increased in family. "When
I prophesied Peltahiah, the son of *Benahiah* died." BATH :
daughter, eldest girl. BATHONI : daughter of my sorrow.
BATHIAH : daughter (of) Jehovah, His worshipper. BATH-
SHEBA : seventh daughter. PEKAH : open eyed − BOPIS : ox
eyed, the opposite of MYOTIS : lady shutting her eyes peep-
ingly, winsomely. PEKAHIAH : (whose) eyes Jehovah opened

(to see divine visions). " *Pekahiah*, the son of Menahem, but *Pekah*, the son of *Remaliah*, a captain of his, conspired against him." REMALIAH : exalted (of) Jehovah, from Rama : high. ELIJAH : God (is the) Lord, ELIAS, ELLIS, ELLIOTT, ELLESTON : town of St. Elias. JOEL : Jehovah (is) God. Elijah is a creed in a name, and should be read by the light that lit on the altar on Carmel. " How long hop ye between two opinions ? if Jehovah be Elohim, follow Him." ELISHA : God (is) saviour, is like thereto, forming ELISEUS. HOD : praise, glory, *con.* Laudo and Plaudo, whence Explode : to make a loud noise like may persons clapping hands. EHUD (judge) : one praised = ÆNEAS. EPÆNETUS : praiseworthy. ISHOD : man, praised for his beauty. ABIHUD : father (of) praise, worshipper = *Theosebes*.

HODAVIAH ⎫
HODIJAH ⎬ praise (of) Jehovah.
HODEVAH ⎭

The Hebrew idea of glory is nearness to God, the Greek fame, the Roman applause. " Augustus, when dying, canvassed for the applause of those who were round his bed."

JEDAHIAH ⎫
JEHOIDA ⎬ known, loved, approved of by Jehovah.

" Depart from me, I never *knew* you."

JEDIDIAH : beloved (of) Jehovah, *con.* DIDO, DAVID, and = DEOCARUS : cherished by God. JEHOIKIM : Jehovah appointed. ELIAKIM : God appointed, *con.* JACHIM : firm. No stranger to Israel could know the difference between these two unless under Hebrew teaching. A beautiful illustration of " I will give him a new name," showing power over and interest in. JEHOIDAH : knowledge (of) Jehovah, loved of God, *cor.* JADDUA (high priest). ARAM : high, becomes Ramah : brae top, becomes Aramathea, and RAM : man of dignity. " Then was kindled the wrath of Elihu of the kindred of *Ram*."

JEHORAM JORAM : Jehovah exalted = JEREMIAH : raised (of) Jehovah, *cor.* JERRY. ADONIRAM (666) : the Lord (is) exalted. AHAZ (dial of) : seen (by God). " I have seen, I have seen the affliction of my people." JEHOAHAZ : beheld (of) Jehovah, *con.* GHAZI (ghau) : valley of vision, beautiful dale. MICAIAH : who (as) Jehovah ? MICHAEL : who (as) God ? " Who is like unto Thee, O Jehovah among the elohim ?" From latter MIGUEL (Don), Macclesfield : Michael's field. CARMICHAEL : dear to Michael, MIKE, MICKY, and Moke : a donkey. This is a pet name with the Irish, who view it thus :—As Michael conquered Satan, the first Protestant, and drove the rebel angels from heaven, so the Pope conquered Luther and excommunicated Protestants. Thus it means *conqueror of heretics*.

NAHUM : a comforter. NOAH : consolation (to parents) = MENAHEM. NEHEMIAH : comforted (of) Jehovah. From same root MANES: consolator, MANICHŒUS: son of Mani, whence Manicheism. ELIMELECH: God (is) king, the Lord reigneth. ELIZUR (conversely), ZURIEL: God is a rock, unchangeable. PEDAHAZUR: rock of redemption, *con.* PADON: redeemed. "Gamaliel, the son of a *Pedahazur*." ZURSHADDAI: rock Almighty. From Zur: a rock, we get Soor, whence Syria: country round Tyre, Sirocco: Syrian wind = Libecchio: Libyan wind, Suristan: Syrian land. AMMISHADDAI: people (of the) Almighty, covenant ones, those under the *shedder*, disposer. AMMIHUD: (one of the) people who are praised, "*Ammihud*, king of Geshur." SHEMER: guarded, kept, gives Samaria: hill of *Shemer*. ISHMERAI: guarded (of) Jehovah = THEOPHYLACT: God guarded, *con.* Phylactery: protection, sign of God's keeping.

TEBAH: confidence of parents = Greek ELPIS: hope, and Irish DIGNUM. " His concubine whose name was Reumah, she bare *Tebah*." REUMAH: lady, superior woman, exaltado, from Ram: high. JEHOVAH-ROPHI: (the) Lord, (the) healer. RAPHAEL: healer (of) God, sent to heal, whence RAFFLES (Sir Stamford) from whom the largest flower in the world is called Rafflesia. JEHOVAH-NISSI: (the) Lord (my) banner. JEHOVAH-TZKINU: (the) Lord (our) righteousness, *con.* SADOC: just, gives Sadducees: disciples of Sadoc, identical with Tunisian Bey, SIDIK = JASHER (book of), *con.* the *dim.* JESHURUN: little just one, darling because of goodness. ZACCAR: mindful. ZECHARIAH: remembered (by the) Lord, hence ZACHARY. ZERUIAH (ye sons of): balsam (from) Jehovah, pleasure giving birth = MORDECAI. When *Ah* for *Ach*: brother, begins a name, it is generally used figuratively, as AHITUB: good brother, worthy person, *con.* TABEEL: goodness (of) God. " Let us set a king in the midst of Jerusalem, the son of *Tabeal*." We, too, have GOODBROTHER.

AHINOAM: brother of pleasantness, good company = BUONAPARTE, LEDRU. AHIMELECH: king's brother = NOBLE, for notable, from Noto: I mark. AHIAM: mother's brother, maternal uncle. When born like him. AHAB: father's brother, paternal uncle = BRODERSEN: son of brother.

AHIMOTH: brother of death, sickly born, *con.* Mors, Mars, Mavors. AHITOPHEL: brother of foolishness = BRUTUS: dull, stupid. HAZELELOPONI: give *shade*, O thou who regardest me, *con.* ZILL ALLAH: shadow of the Almighty, Persian title. " The name of their sister was Hazelelponi." Blessed name. BEZALEEL: (under) (the) shadow (of) God. " He that dwelleth in the secret place of the Most High shall abide *under the shadow* of the Almighty," *con.* ZILLAH, ZALMON. ZALMUNNA: shelter forbidden, he who shows no quarter. SHALOM, SALMON, SELIM: peace, Salaam: to bow, wishing peace. SHALMANESER:

peaceful prince, *con.* Sar, Israel. SHEMULIEL : peace (of) God, friend (of) God, as Abraham. SHELOMI : peaceful man. SHELOMITH : peaceful woman, nearly = SHULAMITE : peaceful, filled with love, the bride, the Catholic Church. " Return, return, O Shulamite ; return. return, that we may look upon thee." Some derive SHILOH from this root and give it = PACIFICO = SHILONI : peacemaker. The Samaritans give the famous prophecy of Jacob, " The sceptre shall not be taken from Judah, nor a leader from his banners, until the PACIFIC shall come." But SHILOH : sent (of God), identical with Shiloah, Siloam : (water) sent (through strong arches). Apostle : sent from (the Lord Jesus). Missionary : sent (by the Church) = Envoy : sent (by Government).

SOLOMON : very peaceful, forms SULEYMAN (Pacha) in Turkey, SLOMAN, SOMAN in England. From Salem also we have Islam, Moslem, Mussulman. Istamboul : city of peace (boul polis), the Arabic for Constantinople, and = Islambad : city of the faith, Hindostan. SOLOMON = PACIFICUS : the pacifier, and the Irish SWEENEY : peaceful, but not FREDERICK : peace rich, one who makes peace by putting enemy so that they cannot fight. EL : God, the strong one, ELOHIM : strong ones, first met with in composition in MEHUJAEL (Lamech's grandfather) : struck of God, greatly afflicted. " We did esteem Him stricken of God and afflicted." MAHALEEL : praise (to) God, *con.* Hallelujah : praise Jah. HILLIL : singer, he who lilts. Lilt : to sing jerkingly and spontaneously. The two great rabbis of Hebraism were *Hillil* and Shammai. SHAMMAI : named, famous = INCLYTUS, *con.* SHEM ; a name. Ad : one, solus. BEDAD : solitaire, lonely. HADAD : one, one, the sun god, Sol : the sun, *con.* Solus : alone. " *Hadad*, the son of *Bedad*, who smote Midian in the field of Moab." BEOR : a torch = FLAMBARD : flaming sword, glittering like flame. " Balaam, the son of *Beor*, hath said." AMMIEL, conversely ELIAM : people of God. BALAAM : a foreigner, not of the people = OUTREMER : a stranger, one from beyond the sea. CALCOL : sustenance (of parents) = SCIPIO : sceptre, staff of his blind father. But CALCOT, for CALDECOT (English) : cold house, open to winds = BALFOUR.

DARDA : pearl (of) wisdom, wisest = HACHMONI : very wise. DEBIR : an oracle. " *Debir*, king of Eglon." He would be good at advising, and so = EUBULUS and ALFRED. DEBORAH (a bee, *i.e.*, patient, industrious, others give) : eloquent woman = CHRYSOSTOM : golden mouth, CHRYSOLOGUS (St.) : golden discourser = BILSHAN : son (of the) tongue = PHUVAH : mouth, *con.* PHICOL.

PHINEHAS (Cozbi) or PHINEAS : serpent-mouthed, persuading to evil, as the worm did Eve, from Pi or Phi : mouth, and

Nahash : a hisser, serpent. " Thy two sons, Hophni and *Phineas,* are dead." TIDAL : who is feared = ALDRED : whom *all dread,* whence Mrs. Stowe's DRED. " Tidal king of nations," *i.e.,* a mixed people, as Abyssinia : a mixture. Pamphylia: all tribes intermixed. ZIZA : full-breasted, abundance (of milk), whence JAZIZ : he will bring abundance. " Over the flocks was Jaziz, the Hagerite," Hagarene. What name could be better for a shepherd ? ARDON : a fugitive, who flees to high place, *con.* Arduus = PHYGELLUS and FLEMING. " Caleb had a son named *Ardon.*" AGEE : a fugitive, *con.* Hagar. " Shammah, the son of AGEE." Arvad (*con.* ARDON): place of fugitives = Flanders : fleers = Servia : country of runaway serfs, slaves. " The inhabitants of Zidon and *Arvad* were thy mariners." BALAK : licking up, destroying. " Now shall this company *lick up* all that are round about us, as the ox licketh up the grass." ISHMAEL : heard of God, had three sons, viz., MISHMA : hearing, *con. Ishmael,* Simeon, DUMAH : silence, *con.* Dumb : silent, MASSA: patience. The rabbis weld these into a proverb—" Hear much, say little, bear much." GAMALIEL (at feet of) : reward from God. Birth name. " The fruit of the womb is His reward." GOLIATH : an exile, an emigrant = GALES : of the Gaels, strangers. NEAL : new Gall. METANASTE (*n*euphonic) : city changer, *con.* ASTYANAX : city king. HINNOM : lamentation (of parents), born in bad times = BERIAH, *con.* Hinnio : I neigh, Hinny : bred of a horse, Whine : to lament. " The border went up by the valley of the son of *Hinnom.*" Ghau : a valley, and *Hinnom* gives Gehenna : hell, *con.* Gehazi. IZHAR : anointed = MESSIAH, CHRIST, UXOR : a wife. The Romans anointed the door lintel under which the newly arrived bride passed, whence from Unguo ; I anoint, we have Unguent, Unction, Uxor, Uxorious : inordinately fond of wife.

JAMIN : dexterous, adroit, right-handed, strong = Stark, STARKEY (stark naked) : stripped for battle, made strong as David was by throwing off armour. When men so did they were called by the Saxons, Bold : bald. *con.* Yemen : the south, to the right is BENJAMIN : son of my right hand, honour, strength ; if not, BENJAMIM : son of my days. LOT : a veil, a secret worker, artful, gives LOTAN (duke). Lot *con.* lid, clot, clod, cloud, lotto, lottery : all covers. " Behold, I have given thy brother a thousand pieces of silver, he is to thee a *lot* to thine eyes." NIMSHI : drawn out, elected, one of the elite = ELIGIUS, ALOYSIUS, and *con.* Moses. REUBEN : see ! a son, from Reu : to see, whence RUTH : fascinating. REHUM : he who looks pitifully, also from Reu, where it slides into the English RUTH : she who rues, pities through seeing. JERAHIMEEL : (he will obtain) mercy (of) God, *i.e.,* God will look at him. IKKESH

5

(son of Ira) : crooked = CROOKS, GAM, BOSSUE. Probably used
figuratively for *a deceiver* = SPOONER and Hindoo Thug: a deceiver. PACKE (whence PAXTON : Packe's town): a deceiver,
cheat, subtle scamp.

SHEBA : an oath, sacred, rest-giving. "A man of Belial,
whose name was *Sheba*" ASHBEA : I swear, adjure. "The
families of them that wrought fine linen of the house of
Ashbea." AMOS : a burden, gives AMASA : burdensome one.
"Absalom made *Amasa* captain of the host instead of Joab."
AMASIAH : burden (of) Jehovah, sustained by God. "Roll thy
burden on Jehovah, He will sustain *thee.*" THADDEUS : who
praises = PYAT : a pious man, atoned for, *expiated.* The French
have THADE, but THADY (Irish) : a poet. The Italians TADE-
ONI : great Thade. HABAKKUK : a wrestler, embracer, he who
wrestles with God and embraces His promise. ZACCHIAH :
(the) Lord (is) pure, ZACCHEUS, *con.* Saddoc. "Zaccheus, make
haste and come down." The Romans rarely had the natives
of conquered countries to be chief publicans, hence some
scholars attempt to derive *Zaccheus* from a Latin root, but in
vain, seeing he is "a son of Abraham." CHUZA (Herod's
grieve) for CHUZIAH : (the) Lord seeth, *con.* GEHAZI, also given
as meaning Seer : he who sees what is commonly hidden.

SOSIPATER, SOPATER (Berea): father saver, who protected
him. ONESIMUS : beneficial, profitable — a runaway slave.
ONESIPHORUS : profit bringer—his master.

ASYNCRITUS : not to be criticised with another, incomparable,
none such. LYSIAS (Claudius): liberator, *con.* Analysis : loosen-
ing, separating. LIBERIUS : one freed = FREEMAN, from Libero :
I loosen, gives Liberty. LYSIMACHUS : looser of strife = the
Puritan name MAKEPEACE. PENTHESILEA (Amazonian queen):
who by her charms *takes away grief.* AQUILA (Paul's fellow
weaver): an eagle = HERNE, twisted into ONKELOS. ZOHAR,
ZERAH, ZORAH : dawn brightness, birth bringing hope. "If it
be your mind that I should bury my dead out of my sight;
hear me, and entreat for me to Ephron, the son of *Zohar.*"
Zorah, the Danite, had a descendant named Manoah, who had
a son whom he named from Shemesh : the sun. SAMSON (with
the augmentative *on*): splendid sun, glorious man.

ZERAHIAH ⎱ Jehovah arises, the Lord is my Light. "The
IZRAHIAH ⎰   glory
of the Lord is risen upon thee." EUTYCHUS : lucky, fortunate,
gives through the French TOY = GLUCK, LUCKIE, *con.* SYNTYCHE
= FELICIA, EDITH : fortunate ladies. "There sat in the window
a certain young man named EUTYCHUS." SACAR : hire = the
Irish name LUCAN : one hired, whence ISSACHER. PEULTHAI :
wages or reward of Jehovah. "Moreover, the sons of Obed—
Edom .... *Sacar* the fourth .... *Issacher* the seventh, *Peulthai*

the eighth, for God blessed him (with many sons)." That was
a paying family. PARMENAS: who remains with you in trouble
= CONSTANCE. PARMENION (Alexander's friend): son of
Parmenas.

AMAL: labourer = BAUER, and root of ÆMILUS: a worker.
"The sons of his brother Helem (were) Zophah, and Imna, and
Shelesh, and Amal." ZOPHAH: an early riser = our EARLY,
con. ZEPHON: great watcher. ANER: an exile, expatriated =
GOLIATH. "The men which went with me, Aner, Eschol, and
Mamre." ESCHOL: a cluster (of grapes), he who has many
children. "Thy wife shall be as a fruitful vine." MAMRE:
rising, lifting up, who causes the rise of his clan. LEMUEL
(king of Massa): consecrated (to) God = ALLGOOD. BETHUEL:
virgin (of) God, pure man, *con.* Bethulia = Parthenope: maiden.
ENOCH, HANOCH: dedicated, a devotee. "The sons of Midian
city (were) Ephah, and Epher and *Hanoch.*" HELEM: hammerer = SCHMIDT. "The sons of his brother Helem."

IDDO: long lived = POLYBIUS, MACROBIUS. "Iddo the chief
at the place Casiphia." IDDO: timely, born when expected,
"Zechariah, the son of Berechiah, the son of Iddo." IDDO:
loving, *con.* DIDO and DAVID, of the class ERASTUS: amiable,
PHILETUS: worthy of friendship, PHILEMON: beloved. "Of
the half tribe of Manasseh in Gilead, *Iddo,* the son of Zechariah."
Three different persons whose names are diverse in the original.
JACHIN: He (will) establish (the covenant with us). "Of the
priests Jedaiah, and Jehoiarib and Jachin." UZZAH: strong,
like a goat butting, powerful in attack. AZAZ: strong, strong
= BOAZ. "He set up the right pillar, and called the name
thereof *Jachin ;* and he set up the left pillar and called the
name thereof *Boaz.*"

JEHISHAI: grey headed = CHANZY, CANUTIUS, HOARE: who
is hoary. Hoar: white, as hoar frost. JOKTAN: small (born)
= CADE. "Who hath despised the day of *joktan* things."
JUBAL: joyful sound, giving Jubilo: I rejoice, Jubilee: time
of joy. "*Jubal* was the father of all such as handle the harp
and organ." KALLAI: a runner = CURTIUS (Quintus), SNELL,
SWIFT, SHARP, PODARGUS. KEDAR: dark skinned = TARTAN,
ÆSOP: an Ethiop. "Arise ye, go up to *Kedar,* and spoil the
men of the east," *i.e.,* the descendants of Kedar. KEDEMAH
(son of Ishmael): swarthy, man from the east = CADMUS
(alphabet). LO-AMMI: not my people, *con.* AMMON: my people.
LO-RUHAMA: not looked on, without mercy. Names of mystical
children of Hosea.

MATRI: a gaoler, watcher = GAYLOR, WARD. "The family
of *Matri* was taken." A name of interest, as gaolers were few
among orientals, their punishments being awfully summary,
as cutting off the hand for theft, etc. MADAI: middle (land),

gives Media, Medes, probably *Medius:* the Middle, and Medeor: to cure by Median herbs, whence Medicine: the healing art. Isaiah (*con.* Hosea. His name was a sign to Israel): salvation of Jehovah, shamefully *cor.* to Easy (midshipman). Maphish (son of Ishmael): soul, active = Quick, Grady. Chavah : life, living, our Eve, giving Eva.
Oren, Ornan : (tall like) an ash = Pinus : pine tall = Rowan, Tann : a pine, Longfellow. Peleth : swiftness, a runner = Galletly, Trotter, Light, gives Pelathite. " Benahiah was over the Cherathites and *Pelathites*," *i.e.*, the slashers and runners, light infantry. Pethuel : vision of God, he whose eyes are opened so that he sees God. Penuel, in the N. T. Phanuel : face of God, to whom He manifests Himself much. " Balaam, the son of Beor, hath said, and the man who had his eyes shut, but now opened." Poratha : lot given, born on a lucky day, *con.* Purim : lots, Pur = Fortuna as though Sortuna : born according to Sors : lot. Fortunatus from Sors : a lot, and Natus : born. " The Jews slew 500 men . . . and *Poratha*." And the odd thing was he should be slain on a day chosen by Pur : lot. Ribai : adversary, antagonist = Satan. " Ittai, the son of Ribai." Seth : appointed, ordained to be progenitor of men, which Abel seems not to have been. " God hath *appointed* to me another *seed* instead of Abel." Sippai, Saph : doorkeeper, who stands on the threshold = Durward, Salmon, Usher, Lusher. " At which time Sibbechai slew *Sippai* that was of the children of the giants." Sibbechai : thicket man = Broglie, Forrest, Woods, Savage. Tebaliah : immersed (of the) Lord, baptized of God, consecrated for an office. " Tebaliah (was) the third."

Zichri, Zithri : remembered, illustrious = Euphemius : well spoken of, *con.* Zechariah : remembered of Jehovah. " The Lord remembered Noah." Melech : a king, a fighter who drives pell *mell,* who *mauls.* Melchiah (Pashur's father) : (my) king (is the) Lord, varies to *Melechias.* Malchus : royal = Abimelech : of kingly fatherhood, noble descent = Aridatha (*con.* Arta : great), Tiridates (king) = our Atheling.

Mithredath (treasurer) : gift of Mithras, in Greek, Mithridates. Mithras : mother, like Cybele and Diana, applied to the sun as producer. Adramelech (Syrian Apollo) : brilliant king, the sun = Horus. Anamelech (Syrian Hercules) : powerful king. The former worshipped under the form of a peacock. The sun sees much, has many eyes. Anamelech was worshipped as a horse. Compare with story of Argus (*con.* Ergon : work) : sharp, acting quickly with his eyes, as Podargus : swift-footed (Hector's charioteer), Podarce = Golightly. Moloch (dreadful king) : king (god of Moab).

MELCHIZEDEK : righteous king, *con.* SADOC : just = JUSTUS : who does right. MANASSEH : amnesty, causing to forget. "God hath made me forget all my toil." NEITH : wisdom, skill in weaving, the Egyptian Minerva, whence ASENATH : belonging to Neith, a wise person = APOLLONIUS : son of Apollo, wise. ZAPHENATH : who receives Neith, wisdom, is inspired. NITOCRIS (Chaldee Queen): Neith's victory, one overcoming by wisdom. PAANEAH : who flies pollution, an allusion to flight from Potiphar's wife. Joseph was not the only man so called. It was applied to an Egyptian nobleman 150 years before. POTIPHAH : priest of the bull. POTIPHERAH : priest of the sun = HOPHRAH (Pharaoh). When Zaphenath married Asenath it was like to like, wise to wise. SHADDAI (El): the almighty shedder, disposer of life, judge of men, dividing unto them severally, even as He will. The farther we go back in language the nearer we approach a use of words common to those who are now many nations. Who would think when speaking of a water shed, or shedding of the hair (crease), that he was using a word so near akin to a name of God ? "Man, who made me a judge or a divider over you ?" SHADDAI : the shedder = PARCE : apportioner, *con.* Upharsin : divided.

OF THE ENDINGS IM, OTH, ONI.

Little comes of telling *what* names mean unless *how* they come so to signify be made clear. This sub-Chapter on "Scripture Names" is an effort to present the *how* in a pleasant form. It will not be a formidable array of dry words culled from the book of Chronicles, like ammonites from limestone, but a lively presentation of the laws and ways by which words in general and names in particular are formed.

The Hebrews used three numbers :—Singular, indicating one thing ; Dual, for two of same kind ; Plural, to represent more than two. The Greeks also had a dual, but its form was fading when the Christian era began. Hence it is not met with in New Testament proper names. Though the dual was then obsolescent in Hebrew and Greek (for it was waning in the former), it was active in others, as in the Sanscrit, the sacred language of India. It is now wanting in all Indian languages derived from the Sanscrit, as French, Spanish, Italian, Portuguese are from Latin. The dual was common in the Syriac of the first century, whereas now only two words of that number are colloquial in Syria. William Von Hum-

boldt shows its use among the aboriginal Indians, extending
from Patagonia to the verge of the Arctic, where Esquimaux
converse by its aid. One European nation retains it, Lithuania.
Russia is discouraging its use; hence it follows the dual will
soon cease to be used in Europe, where it only existed as an
exotic, never flourished as a native. Plural forms are less
likely to become obsolete. The dual is a grammatical conven-
tionalism, the plural an essential part of language. Howbeit,
time does not make it fade in all places. The Arabs have it
in vigour. The Arabic enjoys as wide a geographical range
as any on the earth, English only excepted. It is spoken with
variable purity over the vast regions of central and northern
Africa, Persia, Syria, Hindostan, the Indian Archipelago, and
that peninsula which has, for forty centuries, sheltered the
unconquered sons of Ishmael. Through the Moors, Arabic
tinged the Spanish and Portuguese. Even English is enriched
thereby, for thereto we owe the words Alcohol, Alcove, Algebra,
Chemistry, Crimson.

IM.

The Hebrew Im (Dual) was formed by adding *im* or *aim*
to the singular, as Pharah: to be fruitful, EPHRAIM: doubly
fruitful. Elegantly applied by Joseph to his son. Bethlehem
Ephratah: Bethlehem the fruitful, another being in Zebulun.
Euphrates: fructifier, whose water makes fruitful. ADAH:
ornament, crown, Adithaim: twofold ornament. "Lamech
said unto his wives, *Adah* and Zillah, Hear my voice." Doth:
a well, Dothan for Dothaim: two wells. DATHAN: well-owner
= WELLS. EGLON: a fat calf = GALBA, MEDCALF. Eglaim:
two heifers. "Eglon was a very fat man," a John Bull.
HUR: a cave (dweller) = CAVOUR, WEMYS, HUME: troglodytes. Horonaim: double cavern. "Aaron and *Hur* stayed
up his hands." "From Zoar (they shall go) unto Horonaim,
as an heifer of three years old." Kir: dyke, wall, enclosed
dwellings. "Kir made bare the shield." Kirtan: double
city = Dupple (German) and Medina (Arabic). From Kir,
Carthage: walled, Castra: a camp, Caer, Cahir, KERR, ISCARIOT.
Mar: bitter, Marath: to rebel. NIMROD: he who is very
bitter, a rebel. Merathaim: double rebellion. "Go up against
the land of Merathaim," Babylon. NAHAR: a river = RIVERS.
Naharaim: two rivers, Euphrates and Tigris, as Doab: between Ganges and Jumna, so Senegambia, Senegal and Gambia
rivers. Aram-naharaim: highlands between the two rivers.
"Eliezer took ten camels of his master, and departed; and he
arose and went to Aram-naharaim." Septuagint calls it
Mesopotamia: midst of rivers, now called by Arabs Aljezireh:
the island, identical with Algiers. Mitzr: Egypt. MIZRAIM:

double Egypt, upper and lower. " The sons of Ham, Cush and Mizraim."

Aph: the nose. APPAIM: nostrils (nose thrills), two breathers. NAHOR: snorting, breathing hard, easily made angry, suggests STERTINUS (eighth wise man): snorter, snorer = NARES and NASONIUS (Ovid): nosy, big nose. An irritable person is called by orientals " a man of nose." " The sons of Nadab, Seled and *Appaim*." Shair: to separate, whence our sheer, share, shire, shore. Shaaraim: double gates, to a town. " The wounded of the Philistines fell down by the way to Shaaraim." Shahar: to dawn, the separation of gloom, its dispersion. SHAHARAIM: double dawn, joyous birth. "*Shaharaim* begat children in the country of Moab." Mahanaim: two camps, hosts.

> " Not that more glorious, when the angels met
> Jacob in *Mahanaim*, where he saw
> The field pavilion'd with his guardians bright."

Shunem: two resting places, good repose. " Elisha passed to *Shunem*, where was a great woman."

Hebrew differs from English not only in having a dual, but two kinds of plural—one masculine, the other feminine, distinguished by their endings. The masculine ending was *im*. It was exceedingly common, having a wide range as to time and space. Hence the Saxon en, as house, housen—hose, hosen —eye, een—shoe, shoon. " These men were bound in their mantles, their *hosen*, and their caftans." HOZIER (admiral): maker of leather buskins and leggings, same word as CHAUCER. So Chicken: fowls, plural of chick: a fowl, the modern *s* is added, Chickens being now orthodox. New words are pluralised by *s* or *es*, unless they are from classic languages, as Chasm: a gaping, an opening, Chasmata: openings (between stars). In two instances in the Bible, *im* is grafted upon Greek words, as Allophim: gauyim, those of other tribes, *con*. Pamphylia: all tribes. Sanhedrim: those sitting together, *con*. Cathedral: seat (of a bishop). In Arabic, *im* varies to *in*, as Bedowee: a desert dweller, llanero, karooman. Bedouin: dwellers in the desert. " The only noise heard from time to time in the city is the galloping of the steed of the desert: it is the janissary who brings the head of the *Bedouin*, or who returns from plundering the unhappy Fellah." Here Bedouin should be Bedowee. Fellah: a boor, labourer, takes the plural Fellaheen. Here *in*, *een*, identical with our *ine* in swine, for sowen, and *en* as shoon for shoe-en. " Put on your Sunday shoon." Sometimes plurals are used intensively, as Naib: a noble, NABOB: nobles, very noble, as possessing the good qualities of many nobles. The following are a few instructive cases of its Biblical use:—

Ail: strong. Elim: strong ones. " They removed from *Elim*, and encamped by the Red Sea." ELOALI: great adorable One. ELOHIM: the Triune Almighty. EL: God, forms ALLAH. " Hear, O Israel, Jehovah thy Elohim is one Jehovah." ANAK: long necked, tall. Anakim: descendants of ANAK, where *im* is patronymical as *ide* in LAGIDE: sons of LAGUS: the hare. AVAH: to overturn, ruin = ABADDON. Avim: desert dwellers, resident where they had destroyed all. "The *Avim* which dwelt in Hazerim, even unto Azzah, the *Caphtorim*, which came forth out of *Caphtor*, destroying them, and dwelling in their stead." Caphtor: a watch tower. " Have I not brought the Philistines from Caphtor?" The Avim were destructive tribes wanting in skill; so, then, they were bounded by Azzah: a strong place. Boch: to weep. Bochim: tears, weepers. " The people lifted up their voice and wept. And they called the name of that place *Bochim*." Charash: to cut. Cherathites: slashers. Charashim: cutters, engravers. " Seraiah begat Joab, the father of the valley of *Charashim;* for they were craftsmen." Chamar: to be black, *con.* HAM: hot, black = NIGER, prophetic of his dwelling, Africa. Chemarim: black men, men clothed in black, neri ; the priests of God were dressed in linen, pure and white. " Josiah put down the *Chemarim* whom the kings of Judah had ordained to burn incense. CUSH, CUSHAN: an Æthiop = ÆSOP: a negro, who has a burnt face. Cushistan: Ethiopia. CUSHI: dark skinned = DUFF. "Zephaniah the son of Cushi." Cushim: Æthiopians. " He shall lead *Cushim* captives, young and old, naked and barefoot."

DEDAN: leading forward (to increase of family). Dodanim: Dedanites, gives Rhodes: island of the Dodanim. "The sons Javan, *Elishah* and Kittim, Tarshish, and *Dodanim*." From Elishah comes Elis, a city of Greece, which country was called Kittim by the Hebrews. Balaam said, " Ships shall come from the coast of Kittim." EBER, HEBER: beyond, hyper, super. IBRI: from the other side = Hebrew : Euphrates-passer, an emigrant. Ebronah: passage (of the Red Sea). Abarim: passages, ghauts: passes, identical with gates. " Get thee up to this mount *Abarim* and see the land." HILLEL: who lilts to God's praise. Hallelim: praises. "Abdon, the son of Hillel, died and was buried in Pirathon." " Sing ye *Hallelim*." MELEK: a fighting king. MALLUCH: kingly descent = CREE and RENE. Melakim: kings.

MOPH: anxiety, a weakling at birth. MUPPIM: anxieties, weaker than the other. NATHAN: given (by God), a prayed for son. Nethinim: devotees, giving themselves without reserve to God's service. " We certify you, that touching any of the priests and Levites, singers, porters, Nethinim, or ministers of the house of God, it shall not be lawful to impose toll, tribute, or custom upon them." NEPHES : to stretch out, to increase. NEPHUSIM : expansions, spreadings, big family. " The children of *Nephusim* returned from Babylon." Nimrah : pure water. Nothing to do with Nimr : a leopard. Nimrim : flowing waters. " The waters of *Nimrim* shall become desolate."

OREB : a raven, a dark one. Orbim : dark ones, Arabs. " The *ereb* and the morning were the first day." Creation begins with the evening, that redemption may end with the resurrection morning." EREBUS (from ereb), who married KNOX : night. " As dark as *Erebus*." " Orbim brought him bread and flesh in the morning." Elijah fed by the Bedouin.

RAPHA : a giant, transposes to HARAPHA (Samson Agonistes). Rephaim : giants or descendants of Rapha. " Moza begat Binea : *Rapha* was his son." " Chedorlaomer smote the *Raphaim* in Ashtaro*th* Karna*im*, and the Zuz*im* in Ham, and the Em*im* in Shaveh Kiritha*im*." Five plurals and a dual.

Keren : cornu, a horn. Karnaim : two horns. Ashtaroth Karnaim : two-horned moon, where Astarte was worshipped as a moon in crescent. CHEDORLAOMER : Chedor, the servant of Lahmi, the god of the Susanim. SATAN : adversary, enemy. Satanim : accusers. " Now, the Lord my God hath given me sabbath on every side, so that there is neither *satan* nor evil occurrent." SEIR : rough, applied to rocky, scrubby districts = Thrace, Trachonitis, GARRIOCH, BADENOCH. Seorim : roughs, barley, because of spicular form, said of satyrs, goats, demons, and comets, the latter called by the Saxons faxed (hairy) stars. " Thus dwelt Esau in mount *Seir ;* Esau is Edom." When the Shepherd sends the goats to the Devil, it is rough to rough. " Owls shall dwell there and *seorim* dance there," goats shall caper over fallen Babylon.

SEPHAR : a book, learned therein, gives SAPHIR (Adolphe) = BOOKER, takes *fem.* SAPPHIRA (not from the sapphire). Sephar exactly corresponds to Surat (E. I.) : a book, place of pundits Sepharvaim : books, scribes, place of learned men, a college. SHAPHAT : a judge, skilful in counting = RICHTER : reckoner. Shophetim : judges, sanhedrim = Suffetes : Carthaginian senators. " Where are the gods of Sepharvaim ?" " Thou shalt not revile the Shophetim." Seraph : burning (with love). Seraphim : angels, ardors, burning ones. " Cherubim know most, *Seraphim* love most." Saraph : burning (with thirst), the dipsas. Saraphim : burning ones, serpents, inflamers. " Moses made a *saraph* of copper, and put it on a pole." " Who led thee through that great and terrible wilderness, wherein were *saraphim* and *akrabbim*," scorpions. " The coast of the Amorites, from the going up to Akrabbim, from Selah," the rock. Cherub: celestial, gives CHERUBINI (friar). Cherubim: heavenly ones. " John was a burning and a shining light," burned with love and shone with instruction, a combination of seraph and cherub. SHEBER : a breach, so named because born when the men of Ai made a breach in the ranks of Israel. Shebarim : breaches. " Maachah, Caleb's concubine, bare *Sheber.*" " For they (the men of Ai) chased them from before the (city) gate even unto *Shebarim,*" for there they made breaches.

Shilhah : a missive weapon, *con.* SHILOH : sent, gives. SALAH : a dart. " Arphaxad begat *Salah.*" METHUSELAH : man of dart = DOWD, DOWDS. Shilim : armed men, place of. But SALA (Augustine) identical with HALL and SALMON, saloon, hallkeeper. " Lebaoth (lions) and Shilhim," cities of Judah, and fighting ones too. Shittah : a thorn, the acacia. Shittim : thorns. " I will plant in the wilderness, the cedar, the *Shittah.*" " They pitched by Jordan from Beth Jesimoth, even unto the plains of *Shittim,*" place of acacias. Sokh : a shelter, a booth. Sukkim or Suckathites : tent dwellers. " The people were innumerable that came with Shishak out of Egypt : Lubim (Libyans), *Sukkim* and Cushim (Negroes)." The families of the scribes which dwelt at Jabez : Tirathites, Shimeathites, and Suchathites." ZEEB : a wolf, a terrifier = GUELPH : yelper. Zeboim : place of wolves, or hyænas. " Make them as Oreb and Zeeb." " How shall I make thee as Admah ? how shall I set thee as Zeboim ?"

SHUPHAM : an adder, glider, coluber (*con.* labor) = Elops and Gleed. SHUPPIM : serpents. " *Shuppim* also and Huppim, the children of Ir." Zephath : a watch tower = Migdol, whence Magdala, giving MAGDALENE. " They slew the Canaanites that inhabited Zephath." Zophim : watch towers, *con.* ZEPHON = VIGILANTIUS. " Balak brought Balaam into the field of Zophim."

The following are found in our authorised version only in the plural :—Emim : terrors, very terrible. " The *Emim* dwelt therein in times past, a people great and many, as tall as the Anakim." Gammadim : pygmies, dwarfs, wee folk like Ghoorkas. " Gammadim were in thy towers " defending Tyre. Gerizim : cutters, allusions to fruitfulness and what follows it, reaping and pruning. " Thou shalt put the blessing upon Mount *Gerizim,* and the curse upon Mount Ebal." Eb: a stone, gives ben, ebony, EBENEZER, Abana : stony river, Ebal : stony hill. " And some fell on stony ground." Blessing and fruitfulness, curse and barrenness always conjoin. Gebim : pits, caves, troglodytes = Horites. " The inhabitants of Gebim gather themselves to flee."

NAPHTALIM : wrestlings of God, severe pangs in childbirth.

"Of the tribe of *Naphtalim* were selected twelve thousand."
Telaim : young lambs. " Saul gathered the people and
numbered them in *Telaim.*" " He shall gather *Telaim* with
his arms." Zamzumim : ze, zu, zummers, noisy ones, like
Bos : an ox, booer, Moo-cow, Zebub : a fly, Tungri : old name
for German.ans because they gave *tongue* when going into battle.
Compare such names as BELCHER : bawlcher, BELI : bellower,
CREEK : who *cries* as he goes at the foe. CROKE, CROKER,
giving CROCKETT, also means swashbucklerism. GROGAN :
roarer, shouter. " Giants dwelt therein in old time, and the
Ammonites call them Zamzumim. So the Zulus get their
name from their war-cry : Usutu, howled in a style which
none but a Kaffir can. Their great organiser was CHAKA
(murdered 1828) : the fire brand = FLAMBARD, BEOR. He was
uncle to CETEWAYO : doomed one. Zamzumim answers to Zulu
in a most remarkable manner, clearly illustrating how names
originate and tribes obtain their designations.

OTH.

The feminine ending *oth* had a more contracted range than
IM. Had is said, has might be, for we yet have it in many
Anglo-Saxon words as Moon, *mas.*, Monath, *fem.*, our Month.
The following examples illustrate its use in Biblical proper
names :—
Alam : hidden, a virgin, secluded in the harem, veiled, is
applied to unknown period, hidden time : "From *olam* to
olam thou art God." "The Earth with her bars was about me
for *olam.*" Applied to eldest as ELAM. Alamoth : virgins,
pure men, free from idol service. " Behold *alam* shall conceive
and bear a son and shall call His name Immanuel." Olam, he
whose years are hidden, was to come of alam. " For the sons
of Korah: a song upon Alamoth." Alam = PARTHENOS: virgin,
goddess, Minerva, Parthenon : her temple. PARTHENIA = VIR-
GINIA, BETHULIA (female names). PARTHENOS (Sciote monk)
= VIRGINIUS, BETHUEL ; virgin of God = ENOCH. IMMANUEL,
EMANUEL : God with us, disguised to MANUELL. Arabah :
desert plain, gives Arabia, Arboth : desert plains. " The
border went up to Beth-hoglah, and passed along by the north
of Beth-arabah."
ATARAH : a crown—ADAH : head ornament, a tiara,
ATAROTH : crowns. " Jerhameel had also another wife whose
name was *Atarah.*" Ail : strong, ALLON : an oak, robust
man, ELON : a terebinth. "*Elon* the Zebulonite judged Israel."
ELON = ECK. Elath : oak trees. " At that time Rezin, king
of Syria, recovered Elath." CHISLON : firm confidence (of
parents). Chisloth : confidences, bulwarks in which people
trust. " Elidad, the son of *Chislon.*" " Unto the border of

Chisloth-Tabor." Fortified city at foot of Tabor. Gath : a
wine press. Gittite : native of Gath. Gethsemane : wine press
valley. Gittith : harps used by wine pressers when making
merry. "To the chief musician on *Gittith.*"
Hazor (*con.* Az: strong): an enclosed village, Hazeroth :
villages. "The people journeyed from Kibroth-hataavah unto
Hazeroth." Kab: the grave, a cave, sepulchre, Kibroth :
graves (Hataavah : lusters). Aram : high, Jaram : to be high
= Augustus. Jerimoth : high places = Bamoth. Former
figurative for one in whom we trust, latter local. "Rehoboam
took him Mahalath, the daughter of *Jerimoth*, the son of
David, to be his wife."
Jerah : to tremble, to shake like a tent curtain, very shy.
Jerioth : tremblings. "Caleb begat children of Azubah, his
wife, and of *Jerioth.*" Kedemah : eastward, beginning, where
the light dawns, Kedemoth : beginnings, *con.* Cadmus : an
eastern, as Sterling : son of eastern man. "Jetur, Naphish,
and *Kedemah.* These are the sons of Ishmael." "I sent
messengers out of the wilderness of *Kedemoth* unto Sihon."
Jetur : nomadic village built by men seeking pasture, hence
Iturea, nearly = Numidia : pasture or grazing land. Kir : a
wall, Caer, Castra, Kerr, Pinkerton from pen : a hill, caer : a
fortified place, ton : a town, meaning a strong city set on a
hill. Kirioth : walls, bulwarks = Gederoth. Iscariotes : (Ish) :
a man of Kirioth, as Ishod : a man of glory, fine made, now
Izod.
Lib : a lion, from Leba : to roar, Lebaoth : lionesses =
Leontopolis : city haunted by lions. "*Lebaoth* and Shilhim
and Ain and Rimmon ; all these cities are twenty and nine."
Mar : bitter, Mare : the sea, bitter water, Marath : bitterness,
Meraioth, Maroth : bitternesses. "The son of Zadok, the
son of *Meraioth.*" "The inhabitants of *Maroth* waited carefully for good." Mahar : to behold. Mehazioth : visions,
con. Gehazi : ghau of vision, beautiful valley = Belcombe.
"*Mehazioth*, the son of Heman."
Nain : pleasant, the opposite of Mar : bitter, Naioth :
pleasantnesses, opposite of Maroth. "He went into a city
called Nain." "Samuel and David dwelt at *Naioth.*" Nain
= Winthrop : winsome thorp, dorf = Sheen. Nebo : budding,
fruitful. Naboth : fruitfulnesses = Ephraim. Nebaioth (mountains) : very fruitful. "I will give thee the vineyard of
Naboth." "The rams of *Nebaioth* shall minister unto thee."
Rabbah : great (city) = Mecklenburgh : Muckleborough. Rabbath : great cities. "Appoint a way that the sword may come
to *Rabbath* of the Ammonites." Rehob : open space, street
enlarged = Straduarius (violin), *con.* Rehabiah (grandson of
Moses) : enlarged of Jehovah, the Lord's freedman = Freeman.

RAHAB (harlot): free woman = JUNGFRAU : young free woman. REHOBOAM: who makes the people free = PUBLICOLA, LIBERATOR from Libero: I loosen, whence Liberal : bond breaker, or socially, who loosens his purse strings. " David smote also Hadadezer, the son of Rehob, king of Zobah." Rehoboth : places, spaces. " Isaac called the name of the place Rehoboth, and he said—' For now the Lord hath made room for us.' "

NAAMAH : a fascinating woman = BELVIDERA, *con.* Nain, NAOMI. Naamoth : localities of amenity. " The sister (first woman so termed) of Tubal-Cain was *Naamah.*" Saba : a host, *con.* Sabre : army weapon, Sepoy : swordsman, Sabaism : worship of the host of heaven, sun, moon, and stars, Sabaoth : armies, Jehovah Sabaoth : Lord of armies, infinite in reserves and resources. Sokh : a booth. Succoth : tabernacles. " The fifteenth day of this month shall be the feast of *succoth.*" The men of Babylon made Succoth - benoth : tabernacles of daughters. Ben : a son, Benoth : daughters. The harlots of Astarte, the Syrian Venus.

SHEM : a name, one heard of = CLEON (the tanner), INCLYTUS. ARAM : to be high, RAM : exaltado, from former Syrians called Aramæans. SHEMIRAMOTH : most exalted, SEMIRAMIS (female Napoleon). Tob : good, fertile soil = Aleppo. TABBAOTH : goodnesses. " The children of *Tabbaoth.*"

The following in the plural only :—Behemoth : beasts, great beasts, plural used as an augmentative. " Behold, now, *Behemoth,* which I made." Megilloth : canticles, little songs, liltings. Mazzaroth: zodiacal signs, twelve constellations. "Canst thou bring forth *Mazzaroth* in his season ?" Pi, Phi : mouth, as PHICOL : mouth all (obey). PUAH : mouth, an orator when *mas.,* chatterer when *fem.* These may be said to be from the Hebrew *P,* which was shaped like a mouth. PUAH : a loquacious person of the *fem.* gender. Hur: a cave, Horonite: cave dweller. Pihahiroth : mouth of caverns. Shigionoth : many-stringed instruments. " Habakkuk, the prophet, upon Shigionoth.'

ON, UN, ONI.

These endings do not refer to number but are suffixed to nouns, verbs, or adjectives, as augmentatives. Thus from Zabal : to dwell, ZEBULUN : a dwelling-place with an intensified force, *i.e.,* very fond of dwelling there. " Now will my husband *dwell* with me." Ayal : a stag. Ajalon : a great stag. Gibeah : a hill, curved ground, *con.* Gibbus : humped, like the moon in crescent. Gibeon : a high hill. " Sun, stand thou upon Gibeon ; and thou moon, in the valley of Ajalon." Ail : strong, ALLAH : strong God. HELON : very strong. " Eliab, the son of *Helon*." Alam (as a verb) : to hide. Almon : hidden (by trees).

Am : people, Amon (No) : great (many) people = Puebla : populous, but MILCHOM : king of the people. Some have it great king, for MILCHION, from *Melech:* a fighting king. AMMON : (of) my people. AMMISHADDAI (Dan's son) : the Almighty's people, one of. AMMON (David's first born) : very amen, faithful one. "Art thou better than No-Amon, that was situate among the rivers ?" Nile branches.

En : a well, *con.* Een : eyes, Ænon : much water, great many streams. "And John also was baptising in *Ænon*, near to Salim, because there was much water there." ROSS (when oriental) from Rosh : head, ROSCONI : great head, leader = CAPPON.

Azaz : to be strong, Azmon : very strong (fortifications). "The border shall fetch a compass from *Azmon* unto the river of Egypt." Bathar : to divide, BETHUEL : separated to God, a patriarchal Nazarite. Bithron : great division, hills and dales. "Abner and his men walked all that night through the plain, and passed through all *Bithron*." Kiydh : destruction. Chidon : great destruction. Nakhah : to smite, NACHON : smiting very much = THRESHER, SMITH. "When they came to *Nachon's* threshing floor of Chidon, Uzzah put forth his hand." He was called NACHON because he owned a Nachon : place of much smiting with the flail. That place was then called Chidon because there Uzzah was destroyed. There is a climax—touching, smiting, destruction. Kasal : to be firm, Chesalon : firm confidence (of dwellers in its strength) = Chisloth. "Mount Jearim, which is *Chesalon*." Oren : an ash, as tall as, ORNAN : an exalted personage, *lit.* a great ash = ROWAN. Kileah : to destroy, CHILION : consumption, destruction by disease. Maleah : to be diseased, *con.* Malis : bad, MAHLON : great infirmity. "The name of his two sons *Mahlon* and *Chilion*."

Dan : judgment. Madon : great contention, that which is greatly striven for before the judge. Shamar : to guard, Shimron : vigilantly guarded. "He sent to Jobab king of *Madon*, and to the king of *Shimron*." DAG : a fish = NUN, NON : a fish, symbol of productiveness. One of the letters of the Hebrew alphabet. "*Non* his son, Jehoshuah his son." From Dag we have Tagus : prolific in fish = the African stream, Great Fish river. Dagon : great fish = Grampus, Rabba-dag. "Now, Jehovah had prepared *rabba-dag* to swallow Jonah." Dum : to be silent, gives DUMAH = MOODY, MUDIE. Dumb gives Dumps : time of muteness. Dimon : place of undisturbed silence. "The waters of *Dimon* shall be full of blood." As though the prophet said, It shall be no more Dimon but Damon, from Dam : blood, *lit.* red, as

Aceldama : acre of blood, Edom, Idumea, Adam, Damascus :
sandy soil = Sandy (Beds) : red gravelly earth = PASCOVITCH.
Eghel : a calf. EGLON : great fat calf = GALBA, MEDCALF.
Epher : a young hart, EPHRON : great = CERVONI : great stag,
fine deer (" Cervoni lies"). " Abraham weighed to *Ephron*
the silver." EPHRON = our BUCK and the German BOCK.
Ezeb : to form, EZBON : well framed, fine fellow = ISHOD,
BRAVO, IZOD, and ARBA : four, a square built man, like the
Hercules Farnese. " Sarah died in Kirjath-arba (city built by
him) which is Hebron." To the order of the fine made belonged
ESAU : formed, made, finished. " The first came out red, all
over like an hairy garment ; and they called his name *Esau.*"
Hair is only expected on the well grown. The moral of
Esau's superior make as compared with Jacob is :—The wicked
are best at first, worst at last. One apparently begins well,
the other truly ends well. " The sons of God *Ziphion* and
Haggi, Shuni and *Hezbon.*" Zepha : to look out. ZIPHION :
sharp sighted, good spy = *Spiers.* ZEPHON : a watcher,
guardian angel,—

> " Ithuriel and *Zephon*, with wing'd speed
> Search through this garden ; leave unsearch'd no nook ;
> But chiefly where those two fair creatures lodge,
> Now laid perhaps asleep, secure of harm."

ZEEB : the golden wolf, terrifier, howler, ZIBEON : great
wolf, rapacious man = AUTOLYCUS. " Esau took Aholibamah,
the daughter of Anak, the daughter of *Zibeon*, the Hivite."
Of a bad breed she. Haleb or Heleb : fat, fertile, Helbon :
very fertile, Aleppo : fat soil, GALBA (emperor) : fat as a calf,
the Roman John Bull = LIPPO (Memmi) thought to be formed
on Philip, but means a plump man = TURNUS : a jotun, big eater.
" In the wine of *Helbon* and white wool." Geda : to cut down,
GIDEON : a powerful feller. " The time would fail me to tell
of *Gideon.*" Shemesh : the sun, SAMSON : splendid sun. " Of
Barak and of *Samson.*" Gen : a garden, Gennessaret (*con.*
Sarah) : princes garden, very fertile, GINNETHON : plant
protector = JARDINE : gardener. Pi : mouth, Pison : great
mouthed, wide spreading river. " The name of the first is
Pison." Gihon : great breaking forth of waters = Swale
(Yorks) : swelling with rains. " The name of the second is
in Gihon."

Kedar : dark, Cedar : dark foliaged. Kedron : very dark =
DOUGLAS, BLACKWATER. " Over the brook *Kedron.*" Quosh :
a bow ; Kishon : bending, winding much = Meander : river of
Meonia, CROMBIE, CARRON and ILISSUS : helix shaped, running
like a cork-screw = Serpentine. " That ancient river, the river
Kishon." Ranan : to make a tremulous sound, like water running amongst stones, Arnon : loud sounding = Rio Sonora.

Hhakam : to be wise, HACHMONI : very wise, a magician.
" David's uncle was a counsellor, a wise man, and a scribe ; and
Jehiel, the son of *Hachmoni*, was with the king's sons."
LABAN : white, a fair man = BLONDIN, FINIGAN, BAIN, Lebanon :
very white (with snow). " His fruit shall be like *Lebanon*,"
much. The idea is the same as in POLYCARP : much fruit, large
family = NON, NUN, ESCHOL. Pathah : to be open, like a
mouth, PITHON : great enlargement, of territory. " The sons
of Micah were *Pithon* and *Melech*." Padhah : to redeem,
PADON : great redemption. " He returned from captivity. Probably received his name through parental belief in return."
Pim : to be perplexed, PINON (duke) : distraction. Perhaps
born when parents were in sore distress, like MARY, BERIAH.

SHAMAR: to guard, SHEMER: a watchman = WARE and WARD,
SHIMRON : vigilant guardian = ZEPHON. " Job and *Shimron*,
the sons of Isaacher." Aman : to support, nourish, be faithful
to = FOSTER, TRUMAN (Hanbury, Buxton & Co.), the last *con.*
GOTTREU (*Tholuck*) : one who trusts God. AMNON : very true,
AMMITTAI : the amen, said of Jehovah. "These things saith the
AMEN," the faithful The underlying thought in PATER, FADER,
FATHER, AMEN AM (mother), EMMA : nurse, is one, viz., feeding,
sustaining, being as true as a good nurse to a baby. Cazab :
to deceive. COSBI (Phineas) : great deceiver, subtle, artful.
Gashan: to lay waste territory of enemy ; SHIMON: great desert,
despopolado. " The sons of *Shimon* were *Amnon* and Reumah." Shamah : to hear (ISHMAEL, SAMUEL), SIMEON, SIMON :
much heard, listened to with acceptance. " Because the Lord
heard she called his name *Simeon*." SIMON gives a *dim.* in
the French SIMONOD, whence MONOD. SIMON when Greek, as
SIMONIDES : son of Simon, is from Hemi : semi, half, meaning
half nosed, *con.* Simiœ : monkey kind, snub-nosed. NASA : to
lift up, Sion : very lofty = ALTAMONT. " Mount *Sion* which is
Hermon." Hor : hill, giving Oros : a mountain, whence Orontes : a mountain stream = Torrens (terra) : a land flood. Hermon : lofty peak. Some *con.* Shemesh : the sun, with Sion :
much shone on, a hill having a sunny aspect. Tsayah : to be
dry, Zion : very dry = DURLEY : dry field, DRYDEN : dry valley.
" We wept when we remembered *Zion*." Sharah : to shine,
Sirion : great shiner, a metal cuirass, " Which Hermon the
Sidonians call *Sirion*, and the Amorites call it Shenir :" the
shiner, *con.* Schon : beautiful, SHEEN (Richmond) : shining,
beautiful, Skin : the shining part. But SCHINNER (cardinal)
is none other than our SKINNER who takes off the pelt. Zill :
shadow (ZILLAH), ZALMON (captain) : great shadow, comfort.
ZALMUNNA. Salem : peace, Solomon : very peaceful = SALMONI.
Shar : to be smooth, Sharon : great plain, llano (loco plano),
savannah. " Who has not heard of the rose of Sharon ?"

JASHER (book of): righteous, JESHURUN : entirely righteous, then used as of affection to a good child in the sense of darling. From the Hebrew augmentative we have the Italian ONI, ONE, the French ON, ILLON, and the English ON, OON = Celtic *more*. " GIORGO (George) was called GIORGONE, or great George, from a certain grandeur conferred upon him by nature, no less of mind than form." CARRION : great Charles. " Carrion had a complete ovation in La Somnambula." FABRONI : great Fabius. Italians affect descent from Roman aristocrats. RICCOBONI : great Richard. TASSONI (Rape of Bucket): great Tasso. ALBERONI (cardinal): great Albert. LORENZO for LORENZONI : great Lawrence. SACCHONI (cardinal): great Isaac. VENERONI, for VIGNERON : great vine, family man = Eschol. Vignette (frontispiece : artistic piece in book *front* : a little vine. CASTIGLIONE : great castle, dwelling in, the *op*. CASTRIOTTO (George): little castle, his true name and title SCANDER BEG : Alexander the Bey. PECCI (cardinal): eater, paunchy = PANSA, PACCHIONI (of Reggio): great eater. TAMBRONI (Joseph) : big drummer. BORRONI : great torrent, *con*. "*Bore*, of the Ganges." BORROMEO (St.) : living on banks of a *bore*, torrent, that *bears* every thing before it = *Torrentius*.

ALBIS : fair, pale = BAIN, ALBON, ALBONI : very pale, *cor*. to the grotesque ALLBONES. The Italian queen of song being corpulent, the Parisians said, " Alboni is an elephant that has swallowed a nightingale." PORDENONE (painter): great gatekeeper = SALMON, PORTMAN : who had gate rights, a citizen. Caput: the head, CAPPON : great head = KEAN, TAIT, CANMORE. Pectus : the breast, as *in petto*, PETION (bastile breaker): big chested. TAGLIONI (danseuse) : great cutter, slasher, prehistoric war name, *con*. TAGLIAPIETRA : stone splitter, who smashes stone helmet. Belongs to neolithic age. SCLATER : stone slitter = LATTA : lath splitter. TAGLIABUE : buffalo killer (bos) = TUVEE (vacca): slayer of cow. These *con*. Entaglio : art of cutting precious stones. The Latin nations affect the *o*, as it makes words sonorous, hence *oni* is often used formatively, mere verbal padding. Thus Lazaroni : lazy ones, is formed on Lazarus. Macaroni : food for the happy, *con*. MAZARIN: a pastry cook. PELLON : great Peter = English PEROWNE, French PERILLON. PERILLON is thus analysed Per (for Peter) il (for filius) on : son of great Peter. CREBILLON (French Eschylus) great CRIB, which CRIB : basket maker. MASILLON (divine) : great Thomas. MABILLON (benedictine) : great Abraham. PHILIPON : great Philip, the French equivalent for PHILLIMORE, FILMER. ROUSILLION : great Russell. BIBRON : great *bibber*, drinker, *con*. BEVILACQUA (Italian) : water drinker = DRINKWATER. " According to the naturalist, *M.*

6

Bibron, the sand lizard," &c.   SANDON : great Alexander,
SANDY.   " A few years ago, *Dr. Tardieu* was blamed for the
facility with which he signed the certificate of insanity for
the unhappy advocate, *Sandon*."

SANDS (George) : sandelier, sandal maker = GRACY : brogue
maker.   TARDIEU : slow footed, tardigrade, the *op.* of
PODARGUS, SWIFT, FLETT,—

> " He to my *tardy* feet shall lend
> The swiftness of the roe."

DILLON (when French) : great David (when Irish) : great
flood, born at time of.   Our use of this augmentative may be
illustrated thus : Ballo : I throw, Balœna : a whale, the
thrower, Ball : a missile, with *dim.* becomes Bullet or Ballot :
little ball, but by assistance of our old friend *oni*, swells into
Balloon : great ball.   So from Bouche : the mouth to Buff, we
have Buffoon : great cheeks, puffing them out in fun.   Opera
Bouffe : buffonic acting and bucolic music.   Cartoon : great
card, chart = Magna Charta.   Caisson : great chest, *con.* Cash :
metal money that goes in a box.   CASH : caisson maker = ARK,
ARKWRIGHT : makes box for *archives.* = Lagoon : great lake,
con. Lagos : lake district of Africa = LACHLAN : lake land =
Fermanagh : lake country.   Gabion : great cave, hollow to be
filled, *con.* CAVOUR, CAVE : troglodytes.   Saloon, Salon : great
hall, *con.* INGERSOLL, *con.* Entresol.   Alp : a mountain, Alb :
Britain, ALBANACH : son of the mountain.   Albion : great
Britain, ALBANY : north Britain.   Patagon (Spanish) from
Planta : foot-sole, pad, means great footed, Patagonia, BROAD-
FOOT (Bertha), DASIPODIUS, ŒDIPUS (Colonna) : swelled foot,
the *op.* of PODIO : little foot, man with.   The name PEED
(for *pied de bœuf*): slow footed, walking like a cow.   The
French contrast it with PIEDLEU *(pied de loup)*: swift footed,
like a wolf.   PEED forms PAY, whence Payson and also gives
the *dim.* PEDDIE : little Peed, so that in literality PAYSON =
PEDDIE.   VIERFUSS : fourfooted, flat = PIEDLEU.   PROUDFOOT :
foot of the Pryd (hill).   Pryd-hill = BEAUMONT : pretty hill.
The augmentative *on* with variations entered the Greek.

Ergon : work, gives Urge : to move, to work, as goad to
an ox, GEORGE : earth worker, Argos : cultivated all round.
ARGUS : sharp, good worker, Energy : working actively, Ergo :
therefore, Organ : a work by excellence, Organon : great
work = Magnus Opus.   Peri (very) was used by Greeks to add
intensity of meaning, like *on, oni.*   PERIANDER : very manly,
con. ANDREW = FERGUS and AGENOR (Phenician King) : agan-
aner, very much a man.   MENANDER : a man indeed = BARRON,
MANNUS, WIGHT, BRAVO.   PERICLES : very glorious, much

spoken of = SEMIRAMIS. PERIGONUS: true son = ICILIUS, PATROBAS, SHINAB, each of whom was sides up with his father. The Greeks also used Bous: an ox, for big, as we do *bull.* BUCEPHALUS: great head, BOPIS: big eyed, Bulimy: ox hunger, hungry as a bull. The Celts, and from them the Saxons, used More: great, as CANMORE (Malcolm): great head = TATE (when from the Normans), CHUBB (locks), MAZZINI (Joseph), great mazzard. ORANMORE (lord): great fountain = LISMORE: great leas, meadows, garden. CONMIR: great dog, noble warrior. Consult DOIG. MORVEN (ben): great mountain, Ben More = Grammont. BRITHMOR: great Briton, as FRANCONI: great Frank, a` magistrate. CATHMOR: great in battle, *con.* KATH-LEEN: battle eyed, eye sparkling like a warrior going into combat. WHITMORE: great man, from WHITE: a man, WIGHT. WILLIMORE, WILMER: great William. But LONGWILL = LONGUE-VILLE, LANGTON. OBERON: great elf, comes thus, Albis: white, ALVA (duke): white man, ELF: a fairy = BANSHEE: white woman, from Bain: white. OBERON was a puck coming out of hill side by moonlight to play tricks. Hence PUXLEY: field haunted by fairies, and POOK: a fairy, very pretty, a common name.

> " This *Puck* seems but a dreaming dolt,
>   Still walking like a ragged colt,
>   And oft out of a bush doth bolt
>   Of purpose to deceive us.

> " And leaving us, makes us to stray,
>   Long winter nights out of the way;
>   And when we stick in mire and clay,
>   He doth with laughter leave us.

> " Do you amend it, then; it lies in you:
>   Why should Titania cross her *Oberon?*
>   I do but beg a little changling boy
>   To be my henchman."

PAPILLON (Norman knight): campaigning with a *great tent,* exactly = Pavilion. Certain sacred names we should never expect to find in directories, on door plates, and public house signs, are so found. In the New York Directory we have several persons called CHRIST: anointed = MESSIAH, UXOR and O. E. HŒLAND, and GOTT: GOD, identical with Goth: good in fighting. How comes this? From the mediæval passion plays. Successful personators of any character as VIRTUE, HOPE, FAITH, SCRIPTURE, or parties mentioned in the Bible often took the name of the character as a surname. Thus in Germany he who took the part of Satan was called TEUFEL, TUFFIL: devil, or MANTEUFEL: man devil, identical with MANDEVILLE, from which Maundrel: to tell absurd stories like

Sir John. Amongst the French Satan wore wings and was called LANGE : L'ange, the angel. Doubtless if Joseph Muller had played Christ as cleverly seven hundreds of years since as he did last year at Oberammergau, instead of being known as Muller he would be called Christ. GOTT, GOD, GOODE, GOTHER enter largely into British names, so GOTHRUM : famous Goth. King Alfred stood as godfather for him, having his name changed to GODMAN : goodman = EVANDER, whence Godmanchester : Goodman's camp. So Godalming (Surrey) : almshouse of GODA in the field. GODA is *fem.* of Goode : man of God, and GODA : godly woman. GODARD : of a godly nature, *con.* GODIVA : God given. Gossip (God sib) : akin through God, *con.* SIBBALD : bold kinsman. SEBLEY : field of a kinsman. Gossip is ecclesiastical as is NOVELLO : one passing his novitiate in a religious house = NEW, NEWCOMEN : new comers, NOVATIAN (heretic) : *lit.* son of a novice.

FLOWERS : Easter born when flowers were scattered through church = FLOURENS, LORELIAS, as LLORENTE omits initial *f.* These = EOSTER, though the last is heathen, having to do with the worship of the Saxon goddess corresponding to Astarte. It is still in use. "The master of the ship, Robert *Eoster*, was drowned." Ecclesiasticism also gives MARNOC (St.) : devoted to Mary, whence his *cell* Kilmarnock. MURROCH (Mc) is equal thereto. So (Mc)ILVRIDE for (Mac)GILLIBRIDE : servant of St. Bridget, to whom we owe Hebrides : islands of St. Bride, from chapel on coast. Scotch fondness for *gil* is seen in GILKISON for GILKINSON = WILKINSON, and M'GILL : son of Gill or Gil.

But we have unconsciously glided from names Biblical into names common through ecclesiasticism. Alas ! that this should so often happen in actual life. We have been true to nature, but she is faulty. We atone by concluding our chapter with an essay upon the word God. The Greeks called Him THEOS : placer, arranger, systematizer, who brings cosmos (order) out of chaos (confusion). Hence THETIS (mother of Achilles), THETA (Sun's mother) = MITHRAS : mother of light. Theos in combination with Doron : a gift, supplies THEODORUS, THEODORE, TUDOR, which get mixed with Gothic words from Theod : people, whence THEODERIC, DERRICK, DIRK, which suffer more confusion with the Celtic DARACH, DARRACH : son of an oak, strong = HELON, ECKIUS. DERRINGER : oaken spear, who being famous for pistols suggests PISTOL, which in the time of Shakespeare meant pistolier = carbineer. THEOS gave the Romans DEUS, whence the French DIEU, the Spanish DIOS, and the Italian DIO, and DEITY to us. Goodbye : God be with you = Adieu (Fr.) and Addio (It.) : I commend you to the keeping of God. Before Christianity was introduced among the Celts he was known as BAA-UL : life all, *baa* identical with Bios : life and *ul* with all. When the Celts were Christianised they called Him DIA, in the plural DY. Seventy millions in Europe know Him as Bog, whence BOGDAN : gift of God = THEODORUS and ELNATHAN. BOGOSLAV : glory of God = THEOCLES, THECLA, HODIJAH. BOGATSKY : city of God = Allahabad : the habitation of God. By the time Bog reached western Europe it sank into BOGEY : a nursery terror. The generic name amongst the Egyptians was THOTH : God. As a rule the name of God in all languages is expressed by four letters or less. It is so with JEHOVAH, ADONAI, ALLAH, THEOS, THOTH in the original, while ZEUS : living one, GOTT, GOD, BOG, DEUS, DIO, DIA, TIN, TI, TU, TUIS (last four supposed to be connected with Tuisco and the idea of earth born), AS, AZ (these two mean *strong*), AD (one) all divine names plainly come under the rule of the Tetragrammaton : four letters. TEWSON, TUSON are common names in England, meaning of divine descent = DIOSCURI : sons of Dios, Jupiter. Either so or they mean Tuesday born, sacred to Tuisco. TEW also is in daily use. Seeing the name of God might have been ten lettered as Omnipotent. But is four—Why ?

I (M).

Eastern nations have yet another augmentative, and, if brevity is the soul of wit, it is the wittiest used by man. We have seen that the Hebrews have two forms of the plural, as we have child*en* hors*es*, they have seraph*im* *(mas.)* ashtar*oth*, gitt*ith* *(fem.)*. From *im*, by omission of *m*, they formed a very complimentary intensitive ending, thus Rab : great, Rabb*an* : very great, RABBONI(m) : a teacher equal to several masters. Mary used it well when saluting her risen Lord as "Rabboni!" for His rising from the dead was an effective way of teaching "I am the life." So ISHI(m) : a noble man = many men = NABOB *plu.* of NAIB : a noble one giving the word of command. Sometimes ISHI : my man, *i.e.*, husband. ARABI (m) = many Arabs. The scamp justified his designation. When it is Turkish, ARABI : driver of an arabah cart, and then = WAGNER. This augmentative has become common all over civilisation, as is seen by such names as JOSEPHI(m) : the best of the Josephs, equal many of them. JACOBI(m) : superior to any named Jacob. SIMEONI(m) : a better man than any called Simeon. Every observer of men and manners can enlarge this list of examples.

Reu : a shepherd, who *looks* after sheep. REI(m) : who watches like many shepherds. SHEM : a name, famous SHIMEI (m): much spoken of = SEMIRAMIS. "Nathan the prophet, and *Shimei* and *Rei*." Ur: light, joy, URI(m): great light (of family) = HOUSEGO, ECOLAMPADIUS. "See, I have called by name Bezaleel, the son of *Uri*." As BEZALEEL: (under) the shadow of God, these two may be said to be the light and shade of Bible names. Ur: light. ARELI(m): the lights of God, born when the stars appeared. SHUNI(m): great sleeper, long in bed and loud at it = STERTINUS: great snorer. ZEPHON: (his brother): great watcher. Both sons of Gad. Ah: brother. AHI (m): a brother indeed, or my dear brother. He was grandson of Guni. Gen: a garden. GUNI (m) very fruitful, great family man = ESCHOL, POLYCARP. CARMI (m): vineyards, very prolific. A son of Reuben. He bred in Egypt like a fish (NUN). Carmel: the vineyard of God, a very fruitful hill. ZIMRI (m).: vine with many branches = ZETHAR: an olive. Family men. Az: strong. UZZI (m): very strong. "Bukkie begat *Uzzi*." BUKKI (m): dispersions, scatterings, he who scatters the enemy. EZER, EZRA, ESDRAS: strong helper. EZRI (m) = the help of many. Ben: a son. BANI (m): worth ten sons. "The children of Bani, 642." Dad: dear. DODAI (m): very dear, *con.* DIDO, DAVID, JEDIDIAH: dear to Jehovah. "Over the course of the second month was Dodai."

HUSH: quick. HUSHAI (m): very swift = PODARGUS, GALLETLY, LIGHTBODY. "*Hushai* the Archite came to meet David with his coat rent." HOD: praise, JUDAH: who is praised. HIDDAI (m): who praises very much, great psalm singer = HILLEL.

Meribah: strife. JERIBAI (m): contentious, cantankerous, querulous. JERUBBAEL: let Baal contend. RIBBAI (m): great fighter = POLEMON. ITTAI (m): fine strong man. "Ittai the son of *Rabbai*, out of Gibeah." NAOMI (m): fair as many daughters, *con.* NAAMAN, the handsome Syrian. Pi: mouth. PUAH: talkative. PAARAI (m): an awful jabbler. Ziph: a watch tower. ZIPHON: very vigilant. ZEPHI (m) = many on guard. SHEMER: a watchman. SHIMRI (m): a very faithful guardian. Salem: peace. SHALMAI (m): very peaceful = SOLOMON.

GEMALLI (m): many camels, possessor of = POLYMELES: many sheep. SHILHI (m): carrying many arrows in his quiver, or darts, *con.* SHILOH: sent, *con.* METHUSELAH: man of the dart. Not brave like swordsmen. NAPHTALI (m): wrestlings of God. "Of the tribe of Nephthalim 12,000." HACHMONI (m): very wise man indeed. Quosh: a bow. Kishon: very winding. KISHI (m-dual): the double bow, a bow in the clouds appearing when he was born = KUSHAHIAH. ELIOENI (m-dual) : my eyes (een) are to God (El). He had seven sons, and gave each a religious name. His last born was ANANI (m) : prophecyings, foretellings, given when His words were fulfilled. Ghor : a valley. GEHAZI (m) : valley of visions, where one sees many things to please. LABAN : white = BAIN. LIBNI (m) : very pale = ALBON, ALBONI, CHLORUS. Sin : a bush. Sinai (m) : much bushy undergrowth, the *op.* of PENROD. ZACHER, ZACCUR : having a good memory = MNASON ("an old disciple)." ZICHORI (m) : exceedingly attentive. ZECHARIH : remembered of Jehovah. ROSH : head, leader. RASHI (m) = many captains, suggests Rabboni (m).

CHAPTER V.

BIRTH NAMES

ARE of high antiquity. Their age often prevents discovery of the attendant circumstances in which such were given, so that even when the meaning of a birth name is known, its appropriateness being unknown, our information receives no great increase. Names of this class are generally souvenirs of faith, hope, prayer, or gratitude, developed into expression by the birth of an immortal whose destiny is veiled by a mystery which time only can uprear. In the nature of things national history could not take cognisance of all births, but if able, unless we knew the circumstances under which a child appeared, the mere name would be small gain. As it is impossible that biography can be co-extensive with history, the mass of mankind must pass away unrecorded. Clio cannot take office as Registrar-Generaless. She tells, in some cases, the gross amount, but never the digits which go to form it, informs us that Napoleon marched on Moscow heading half a million of men, but the historic Muse is silent as to who the rank and file were. The million cannot reach the van and be visible to all save by a combination of circumstances and possession of faculties that meet only in a few persons. In other words, the many cannot be known, must be anonymi. Hence, famous names are to those unknown as one blade of grass to a wide meadow. Yet those we have are samples of what we lack. By them we know the principles employed in nomenclature by all nations now civilised and in many yet savage. As it was customary with parents to name children at birth as recorded Gen. xxix., xxx., the probabilities are, that nearly all names were originally of this class. Nor may we lose sight of the pious Hebrew deferring that act until the eighth day, while the classic Greek and law-abiding Roman conferred the appellation on the ninth or tenth days. "Circumcised the eighth day," because seven days complete the weekly circle, so that the eighth day is the first portion of a new period of time. The child was then pictorially regenerated, entering into relationship with the covenant people, before which it was on a level with Gentiles. So Jesus rose from among the dead on the eighth day, for first and eighth are identical,—the former having respect to this week, the latter to last. He rose on the first or eighth to begin a new life on a new day. So, also, as to the number saved in the ark. Eight souls begin a new world. Eight = new, in biblical symbolism. Few birth names descend to our age, most being exchanged for names won. Our nomenclature may be enriched as to number by birth names, of whose meaning no man knoweth. If any such they fitted periods when names were simple and descriptive, and, as a rule, became obsolete at the death of their original possessor. In case these won a great name, that given at birth lived by adoption of admirers, but more a life of sound than of sense. That nature urges to name at birth is seen in the case of our great ancestress who, when she brought forth the first born of many brethren, called him—

CAIN : possession. "I *have gotten* the man from the Lord," him whom He promised." "Jehovah *cained* me in the beginning of His way." Many of her daughters since named their offspring with the same yearning hopefulness, like poor Eve, to be distressed by blighted hopes. Her bitterness of disappointment was indicated when she called her next born ABEL, HEBEL : vanity. "All is *hebel.*" Of the millions who followed her example, the following illustrations may suffice :—

ISHMAEL, ISMAEL : God shall hear. "As for Ishmael I *have heard* thee." SAMUEL, SHEMUEL, ELISHAMA : heard of God, gives SCHAMYL (Circassian) SMOLLETT (Tobias) : little Samuel, SIMNEL (Walter), SIMSON, SIMPSON, SAM, SAMSON (when English), but not SAMBO, from ZAMBO (Spanish) : bandylegged. ABENBROD (evening bread) : born at time of family taking supper. ABENDROTH (evening red) : born at ruddy sunset. ANASTASIUS : born at anastasis, resurrection, Easter, gives ANSTEY (Chisholm), STACEY = PASCAL (Blaise) : passover time born when pascal (suffering) lamb was eaten = PASCHASIUS (abbot of Corbie, 844, first to use the word Transubstantiation), PASCHINO (Roman cobbler ; had shop near statue of gladiator, to whom young fellows compared him : hence *pasquinade*), PARASKEVA (Russian lady) : born on Easter Sunday. Spaniards called Easter-day Pascua Florida, as they then scattered flowers on the church floors. Florida (U.S.) discovered on Pascua Florida, A.D. 1518. Fleury (cardinal), from Flos, floris : a flower. LLORENTE (inquisition), for Florente : flourishing = TANTALUS, FLOURENS (Gustave), all Easter-born save Tantalus. Pace eggs are Pascal eggs. As the chicken comes out of the egg, so Christ out of the sepulchre. EOSTER : born when the goddess Eoster (Astarte) received special honours. This name is in common use in this form and also as HESTER, and is the ancient heathen correspondent to the foregiven. THEOPHANIUS : time of *God's manifestation* to magi by the star, *cor.* TIFFANY = EPIPHANIUS : epiphany born, Jan. 6th. The Italians *cor.* it to BEFANA, whence BETTANA. These = BERTHA : bright born. The Eastern church calls that season theophany, which the Western church terms epiphany. Tradition makes the wise men, corresponding to Europe, Asia, and Africa, naming them GASPER : the jasper stone, BALTHAZAR : treasure master, MELCHIOR : kingly, royal. These are the three kings of Cologne. The first gives the well known GASPARDE. In the Middle Ages children were often called from saints days on which they were born.

VIGILANTIUS : born at vigils. SALVERTE : born when the "Salve Regina" was being chanted. TOLLIDAY : on St. Olave's day, gives TULLY, when English, Tooley Street named from St. Olave's church. CROUCH, CROSS : at crouch mass, December 18th, *con.* crutch. FRANCIA (dictator): born September 17th, feast of St. Francis Stigmata. LOVEDAY : on day appointed for making up quarrels and grievances. HAGGAI : feast of the Lord, born at, "Shimeah, his son HAGGIAH, his son." From Hagh : a feast, HADJI : feast keeper, pilgrim, a man who went from feast to feast, so HAGAR : a stranger (Egyptian), *con.* Hegira : era of Mahomet's flight, July 16th, A.D. 622. Hagarenes : strangers, gauyim. HAGGITH : parents rejoiced at his birth like those keeping *hagh.* "Then Adonijah, the son of *Haggith,* exalted himself, saying, I will be king."

JERAH, JAROAH : born at appearance of *wanderer,* the moon, so called because of its phases. LEBONAH (from laban: white): at moon's appearing. HODESH : a new moon = NUMENIUS. "He begat of *Hodesh,* his wife, Johab and Zibi." "For this cause we choose *Numenius,* son of Antiochus," *con.* Mene : numbered. "Mene, Tekel, Upharsin." Moon : numberer. Almanack (all moon ac): giving all moons. So KRONOS (Saturn), gives Chronos : time, as that star told time. Meniscus : little moon, lunette, glass. Menology : register of months. Mensis : a month (moon-eth). Menstruum : solvent caused by the moon. Mensuration : numeration of months. The Hebrew name for the moon proper, Jerah : the wanderer, is supposed to give Jericho : city where the moon received special religious honours, as Greenock : from Graine : the sun. MOON = the foregoing upon which is formed the baronial MOHUN : born at appearance of the queen of night. KUSHAHIAH : bow of the Lord (from Quosh : a bow, whence Kishon : winding river = Ilissus : helix river, and KISH : bird snarer = our SNAREY, for snarer): born when a rainbow was visible, which parents accepted as an omen that the little stranger was connected with the covenant. KISHI (m): double bow, born when a rainbow was seen.

VIRGIL (Publius Maro. Correctly Vergilius): at appearing of constellation Vergiliœ, from Ver: spring, *con.* Vergulta : a rod which buds in spring, giving Verger : who carries rod.

Hereby we are taken to the days of astrology. Maro's wife suffers the hour of nature's need. He, husband and augur, watches the starry host, eager for a prophetic index of the child's future. The wished for message, "A man child is born," comes, and at the same time the Vergiliœ rise above the horizon, indicating fruitfulness and inciting hope. Maro salutes his son with the omen Vergil ! Vergil !! This name = GAD : a troop, cutting through, an eventual success, fortune. The sun sets over the western wilderness, and the gloaming slowly veiled the tents of Jacob. Zilpah labours, Leah watches. A voice in the tent said, "I have gotten a son." The sky searcher cries Gad ! Gad !! ARELI (m) : born when the lights of God appeared, the stars rose. This tribial designation = SAID, FELIX, FORTUNATUS, BONHEUR (Rosa) : good hour. BONAVENTURA : well come, FESTUS, LUCKIE, GLUCK : lucky names, LONG, when Chinese. From GAD AZGAD : strong in fortune. "The children of *Azgad,* 1222." Such names more or less verge on astrology. METTERNICH (statesman) : at *middle* of the *night, con.* NACHMAN : night watchman, and = the well-known French MINUIT. We also find in common use MITNACHT : born at night's noon.

SHEMA, SHIMEON, SIMEON, and SIMON : heard (of God), gives *simony* (Simon Magus), SYMES, SYMINGTON (where church of St. Simon), SIMPSON, SIMS (Reeves), XIMENES (cardinal). " Because the Lord *heard* that I was hated." These answer to ARATUS (*con.* Oro : I pray) : prayed for = DESIDERIUS : much desired. SHAMMUAH : heard of the Lord = SAMUEL. ASHER : blessed, happy, assumes the modern form ASSER = BEATUS : blessed, whence BEATRICE. "Happy am I." But ASHET = ZOPPI : maker of pie dishes, and VARSARI (George). JUDAH : praise, one spoken well of = ÆNEAS, gives JUDAS, JUDE, JUDITH, JUDY, JUDD, JUDSON, JUDEUS (Philo): the Jew, JEWELL (bishop), JUKES, Judea, Jewry, Ghetto, but JULER : a jeweller, a trade name, and JULES : of the Julian gens, and JULIAN (apostate) : son of Julius.

BAPTISTA and BATTISTA : June 24th, John the Baptist's day, gives BATTI, BABTY, BATTINI, ZITA (all in Don Juan), BAPTIST, GAMBETTA for Gian Baptista. NOEL, NOLAN (captain), and NAULET : December 25th, natal day of Jesus. Natal (Port) discovered by Vasca de Gama, Christmas Day, 1497. CARNA-TION (Gypsy name) : at time of Incarnation. ANNUNCIATA (Spanish lady) : March 25th, feast of Annunciation gives SUNTER. I have met with it in Yorks. CONCETTA and CONCHA : December 8th, named in honour of Immaculate Conception. IMMACULATO : unspotted, also born December 8th. Since decree of December, 1854, thousands of children have been named IMMACULATO, the English of which is AFFLECK :

without flick. DOLORES: in honour of seven dolours of Mary, gives LOLA (Montes). LADYMAN: March 25th, Lady-day, *con.* TOPLADY and NOSTRODAMUS (astrologer): Notre Dame, Nuestra Senora, our lady = MARIO: devotee to Mary. Ladybird: insect having five spots upon wings, thought sacred to five wounds, stigmata, of our Lord.

> " Ladybird ! ladybird ! fly away home,
> The daisies have shut up their sleepy red eyes."

Marigold: her gold, sacred flower. Tobermory = MOTHERWELL and Ladywell: spring sacred to B. V. M. TEMPLEMORE: Mary-kirk. The oath Marry! means by Mary. MARY: bitter, born at a time of bondage, hence MIRIAM, MIRIAMNE (Herod's wife), MARIA, MARIANA (Sp. jesuit), MARAT (French red), MOLL, MOLLY (Bourne), MOLLISON, Malkin: a cat, Marionette: little Mary dancing. MARIAN (Maid), MARIOTT, MARRYATT (captain), MARO (monk, whence Maronites), MAR, when it does not mean illustrious, when it does, gives MERLING: son of the illustrious = PATROBAS. MURROCH (Mc): a Maryite = (Mc) MARRY, (Mc) MURCHIE, MURCHISON = MURTOGH: dedicated to Mary, though in some families it means an admiral, sea leader. To these add DAMIAN (John): son of the mother, devotee to B.V.M. Among the Latin race thousands of men are named Mary. We have all possible variations of her names and supposed titles applied to a man child. Some Bourbons have twenty such inanities instead of an honest healthy Christian name. Such is GLORIOSA: the glories of Mary. Pio Nono's name in English was John Mary Thomas Smith. We now have the Infanta MERCEDES: mercy of the mother of God. "I was accompanied by my aide-de-camp, Colonel Solis, and the Generals Cordova and Alaminos. Don Enrique de Bourbon was accompanied on the fatal morning by Don Frederico Rubio, Don Emigdio Santamaria, and Don Andrez Ortiz." SOLIS: a southerner, from Sol: south, as Solano: hot south wind. RUBIO = RUFUS, RUDD = EMIGDIO (amo Deus, Dio): lover of God = GODFREY. SANTAMARIA: holy Mary. ANDREZ: son of Andrew = ANDERSON, born on St. Andrew's Day, November 30th. Who would suppose that this religious company were on for a duel? To these we may yet add MARR (music) and MARIS, besides others too numerous to mention.

LOMAS, LAMAS: loaf mass, Lammas, born August 1st, time of offering first fruits. MIDDLEMASS is *cor.* from Michaelmass, and *cor.* into the less distinguishable name of MIDDLEMISS: September 29th. QUARTERMASS (local): living where four seas meet. MIDWINTER: December 25th, the secular correspondent to the ecclesiastical NOEL, but before the former there was in use YULE and YUILL: born when the yule log was burning in honour of Jul, at time of winter solstice. GENARO (Naples): January born. Rio Janeiro: river of St. Januarius, discovered by Cabral in 1499. WHITGIFT (archbishop): Whit Sunday born (whit·for white, dressing in) = PENTECOST: born on seventh Sunday after Easter. INNOCENT: at Childermas, December 28th, in commemoration of Herod's slaughter. SUNTION is the old English Assumption: born August 15th. CREAM (for Careme, from Carnis: flesh, as Carnival: farewell flesh): lent born. TOUSSAINT and OGNISANTI: on November 1st, All Saints Day = MILCENT (de mille sanctis). MORTIMER and MUTIMER: death of martyrs, day observed in memory of, wrongfully given as MORTIMER: dead sea, a pilgrim calling thereat, this being a cant fancy, guess by sound. FAITH: born October 8th, St. Faith's Day. HEGEL (Hegelian philosophy): born at time of hail-storm. SABBATHIAS (Zwi, Pretender to Messiahship, A.D. 1641): Sabbath born, *con.* Sabbation: river not running on Sabbath. SHABBATHAI: Sabbath born. "*Shabbethai*, the Levite, helped them." PAUSIUS and PAUSANIUS: born on day folks *paused* from labour, *con.* PAULUS, PAUL: little, who has *paused* in growth, allied to Parvus, Pauper, and our English LITTLE: at birth = PETTIT, KLEIN, MINNOCH, and MINION.

KURIAKOS (Iconium), CYRIACUS, CYRIL (Jerusalem), and CYR (St.): on Lord's day (kurios) = DOMINIC (dies dominicalis). Domingo discovered on Lord's day by Columbus, 6th December, 1492, *cor.* to the English DOWNIE. To these Spanish writers add MENDEZ, whence MENDOZA = SONTAG (Madam): Sunday born. In the West Indies negroes name piccaninnies from their birth day, thus,—QUASHEE: Sunday born, QUASHEBA, if a girl. One Quashee discovered the virtue of a medicinal plant, from him called Quassia. So common is Quashee and Sambo that they are generic for any unknown negro. MACREADY (tragedian): Wednesday born, Mercredi: Mercury's day, but M'CREADY is a formation upon that prolific name Reid. There is actually a MICKLEREID (much, muckle): greatest of the Reids, the Reid. LUNDY is often given Monday born, Luna dies, but is formed on London, and means a Cockney. LONDON (Robert) flourished in 1180. Proof that then London was small. FREYTAG (Nuremburg): Friday born = FRIDAY (my man) = JUBA, COUBA, negro names, giving to the yellow girls JUBINA, CUBINA. Friday is the next most sacred day after Sunday all over the world, save in Scotland, where it is set apart for courtship and marriage, which is in keeping with pre-Christian times, as the day was specially sacred to the Norse Venus, Freya, Frigga. In many families FREE means Friday born, given by Freya; but FREEMAN: freedman = FREW, one of the Freelungi. MITTAG: midday

born = MESEMBRIA, *con.* Mesembryanthemum : flower blooming at midday. The above = DOUBLEDAY : born at a mid-
summer's noon. NOON, NUN (when English) : born at nones.
LAUD (Archbishop) : at lauds, time of praise. Laudo from
Plaudo : to clap hands, whence explode : to make a noise like
hand clappers. PRIME : at primes, first service. But PRIM
(General) : first born. MATTENS : born at matins, matutinal
service, morning worship. MEZZANOTTE (Italian) : midnight
born = METTERNICH. COCKSHOT : born when the *cock shuts*
the day. Sometimes a form of Cocksholt : wood frequented
by cocks. Holt becomes shot as Aldershot : alderholt, wood.
PHOTIUS : son of light, born when day is dawning. MANIUS :
born at *mane:* morning = the better known TITUS MANLIUS :
son of the morning = LUCIUS : son of daylight (lux).
MORGANROTH : born when sky began to redden, good omen.
DOLLINGER (theologian) : day-linger, born at *tw*ilight, *between*
lights, *i.e.,* of son and moon = AHISHAHAR : dawn brother =
SHAHARAIM : two dawns, mid-dawn = ZERAH ˙ (Ethiopian),
Zarah : dispersion (of darkness). DOLLINGER is often met
with in the clearer form of DALLINGER. Novelists would be
hard put to it to fancy names more poetical, so much does
fact outstrip fiction. DAGO and TAGG (when German) :
born at daybreak, *con.* Dagger : flashing, glittering like the
day ; in some cases = ALBA, ALVA : born when day whitens.
DAGOBERT : glorious as the day. BERTHEIM : when born the
brightness of the home = HOUSEGO. MEZZOFANTI (cardinal) :
half an infant, very small at birth = PAULUS, MINNOCH, and
con. VENT, VENTRISS : little, infantile as to size. MOAB : of
the father. AMMON : my people. Their issue was absorbed
or perished, but the Jew remains to the fore. THOMAS : a
twin = DIDYMUS (*con.* dis bis) = ZWI : two. GEMMELL (*con.*
Gemini). TWINN : one of twain. THOMAS gives TAMASSIER
(Rose). MASSENA (Marshal), MASSON, great Thomas, MAS-
SEY, MACE (when not mace bearer), MASTAI (count), TAM
(O'Shanter : of the shanty farm, old buildings), combines
with AGNELLO, ANELLO : an angel, as in MASSANIELLO,
but GIOTTO (s O) is from ANGLIOTTO : little angel, a nurse
name. THOMASINA as a *fem.* is becoming common. In the
Gaelic we have OMISH, as in M'OMISH = THOMPSON, so
(M') COOMBE, (M') CUMBER = TOMSON. The conventional mean-
ing of Thomas in the Middle Ages would be born on his day.
The following are actual family names = foregoing, viz., TWA,
COUPLES, DOUBLES. VOPISCUS (Syracuse) : one who lives of
two = AHIMOTH : brother of death, twin brother died. HAM-
MEDATHA : a twin. "Haman, the son of *Hammedatha.*"
AVENTIN (St.) for Adventinus : happy event, advent, welcome.
BONAVENTURA (St.) bonny advent.

DENTATUS: born with teeth, *con.* Indentures: indented parchment. FAIRBAIRN, FAIRCHILDS, FAIERS: like Moses, beautiful from the womb = ESAU: perfect, well formed, hair upon his body showed his perfection to which others grow. When it is given ESAU: hairy, the name is confused with SEIR: rough, goat-like, Seorim: satyrs, demons. PROPERJOHN: John who was a fine baby. But LITTLEJOHN: small at birth = LITTLE of us, and ZUAR of the Hebrews. " Oh, let me escape thither (is it not a little one?). Therefore the name of the city was called Zoar." " The son of *Zuar* shall be captain." FLANN: ruddy at birth = EDOM. SCARLETT (heavy dragoon), ROSE, and the German ROTH.

JOLIFFE: jolly child, from LIFFE: son, one loved, life of parents, liffe, life, love. GOODLIFFE: child devoted at baptism = HOSIUS, ALLGOOD: hallowed, so CUNLIFFE, WICKLIFFE. KOSKIUSKO (Poland): weak boned = HOLBEIN (painter): hollowbones. TOLA (judge): a worm, weak, little. " I am a *tola,* and no man." GEBAR: strong (man) is its contrast, GABRIEL: the strength of God, very strong. TICKEL (friend of Addison): feeble, trembling, made into Kittle: shaky, delicate, critical in Scotland, as " It is a kittle point." So TIDDLER (Tom's ground): all of a totter. TOTTIE: a little girl.

" O weake life! That does leane
On things so *tickle* as th' unsteady ayre."

ARAM (Eugene): weakly born, feeble baby. But ARAM (Biblical): high. HAGAB: a grass hopper, locust, AGABUS (prophet): little at birth. AMOZ: strong, robust, from AZ: strength, probably applied to strong infant. SAUL: asked for: " Saul died and *Baal-hanan* reigned in his stead." Gen. xxxvi. 38. The first place his worship is implied. BAALHANAN: born of the grace of Baal, *con.* HANNAH: grace. ACHBOR, AKBAR: a mouse, small child = MUSCULUS (reformer): a little mouse, identical with *muscle.* Symbolic meanings were attached to mice, now lost, hence their mission to afflict Philistines. Rats and cats are unmentioned in Bible. DANCER (Daniel), DAUNCY, DANCY: who is dauncy, nigh to death, done, born more dead than alive. From do comes death (doeth), dead (doed), dauncy, done.

CADE (Jack): born little. Cad pig: least of litter, Cadet: younger brother = puny, puisne, post natus. Puny gives Pony: little (horse). Some give Cadet from Capdet from Caput: the head. Cade. " We John *Cade,* so termed of our supposed father, Dick. Or rather, of stealing a *cade* of herrings." Cask is formed on cade and casket on it. Of all English names it answers most closely to PAUL: one whose growth has been arrested, whence PAOLI (Corsica), PALAFOX (Saragossa),

Pablo (Fanque), Pawley, Paley : Paul's field, dedicated to,
Polk (president), (Mc)Phail, Paulus (Sergius), Paulicians :
followers of Pauline epistles, ancient puritans. Semple : born
January 25th, feast of St. Paul's conversion. Agrippa : sharp
pains, æger, ægrotat, acer. De las Penas: born of great pains,
is the Spanish equivalent. Jabez corresponds. " His mother
called his name *Jabez,* saying, ' Because I bare him with
sorrow.' " Tahrea : delaying cries, slowly born—" The sons
of Micah were Pithron, and Melech, and *Tarea.*" Varies to
Terah whence Teraph : an image, Teraphim : household gods.
Some have Teraph a form of Seraph, as Tekel : weighed, is
identical with Shekel : a weight. Cordus, Corder (Maria
Martin), Cordelia : born slowly. Leah : wearied, fatigued
mother to give her birth. " The name of the elder was *Leah.*"
= Cordelia. Bilhan (Ezer's son. Gen. 36) : terror, conster-
nation (of mother in labour). Bilhah is its fair *fem.* Ahab :
father's brother, when born had features of his uncle = our
Farebrother : father's brother, born like him. Ishni : like
his father, the born image of papa. Aharah (son of Benjamin):
after his brother, as Jacob after Esau. Another of the names
like Nun : a fish, breeding like one, telling how prolific the
Hebrews were in Egypt. Ulysses (named of Autolycus) :
anger with, odious to, annoyance at. Grandpa in ill skin.
Cadena (Sp. lady) : born August 1st, feast of Peter's chains,
from Catena : a chain, whence concatenation. Azmaveth :
strength of death, implies mother died = Todleben (Sebastopol):
dead alive, child lives, mother dies. "Over the king's treasures
was Azmaveth."

Ichabod : inglorious. "She named the child *Ichabod,* saying, The glory is departed." Ishod : glorious man, fine shaped
male child, *con.* last and Judah, becomes Izod, Izett = Bravo.
Hophni : little fist = Pygme : the fist (size when born), *con.*
Pugno : I fight, Pugil : a champion, pugilist, Pygmalion
(Tyrian king) : son of Pygme. Trepoff (shot by Nihilist) : a
foundling discovered on *treppe :* the steppe, moor, wilderness,
son of the steppe. Benoni : son of my sorrow. "It came to
pass as her soul was in departing (for she died), that he called
his name *Benoni.*" This being an evil omen Jacob made it
Benjamim : son of my days = Shanegan (Irish) : old man's son.
Benjamin : son of my right hand is *con.* Yemen : right hand,
south. To a man in Hebron looking due east Syria was
reckoned north (left hand) and Arabia south (right hand).
Gives Ben, Binney, Benson, howbeit Bendigo is a form of
Benedict.

Nephtalim, Naphtali : the wrestlings of God. " With the
wrestlings of God have I wrestled." Adding the Divine name
gives superlative force : River of God (Bog, Euphrates), Moun-

tain of God (Benledi, Sinai). Hush : to hasten gives HUSHAI (David's friend), HUSHAH (Hushathites) HUSHIM, (Dan's son), HUSHAM : all prematurely born. " When Jobab died, *Husham*, of the land of the Temanites, reigned in his stead." The Kaffirs name children on same principles. For example, a child is sometimes called by the name of the day on which it was born, as Robinson Crusoe called his servant FRIDAY. If a wild beast is heard to roar at the time the child is born, this circumstance would be accepted as an omen, and the child called by the name of the beast, or by a name representing its cry. If the animal heard were the hyena, which is called *impisi*, the name of the child might be either UMPISI, or U-HUHU, an imitative sound representing the laugh-like cry of the beast. A boy, whose father prided himself on the number of his stud, called his child USO-MAHASHE : father of horses, as their number would be increased by the time he inherited them. A girl, whose mother had been presented with a new hoe, was called UNO-NTSMBI : daughter of iron. PANDI (Zulu king) got his name from *impande*, an esculent root in use among the Kaffirs. Hyena : is from Hus : a sow, whence *S*us, whence *sow, sow-en, swine*. The daughter's name *con*. the hoe, compares well with BARZILLAI : son of iron. "*Barzillai*, of Regelim, brought beds to David." Many Biblical names are illuminated by being studied from the Kaffir point of view.

AIAH : howler, hooter, schirler : a vulture, hawk, or kite = U-HUHU. " But the king took the two sons of Rizpah, the daughter of *Aiah*, whom she bore to Saul." The wife suffers in her harem, her husband goes forth, and seeing a vulture hovering, calls his newly born daughter AIAH. THACKOMBAU (Fiji king) : evil to Bau (the island). The Wesleyans craned him up from a cannibal into a christian. PROCULUS (opposed Probus) : born while father was *procul*, afar. APICIUS (wrote on pleasures of eating) : born *out of the house, Apo* oikos. From Oikos : a house, Œcumenical Council : a council called from wheresoever a house is. ASTOR (Astoria) : Thursday born, dedicated to the Asir Thor = DONNER and TONNER : born on Thursday, and marked with his hammer. TEWSON (auctioneer) : son of Tuisco, Tuesday born. By a mythological fiction, which was grafted on to Christianity, when a child was born on a day connected with a god, if a male, he was called the son of that god, all to the glory of the family. CÆSAR (Julius) : from Cœdo : I cut, cœsus : cut, born by incision, whence that operation is called Cœsarian. NONNATUS : not born, before the death of his mother. " Raymond *Nonnatus* was born at Portel, in the diocese of Urigel in Catalonia." NEPUMUK (St. John) : born at Pomuk, in Bohemia.

7

NEVUS, NEVIUS, NEVINS (when not big fisted): born with a birth mark. Nœvus, from Novus : new.   Certain new arrivals were named in the prosaic form of numeral adjectives, as PROTOGENIA (Deucalion's daughter): first born girl = PRIMA (Romulus's daughter) = PRIM (Madrid) = PROTUS. These = LANE (le ane, antiqus : old. When not Irish): eldest = MAXIMUS, MASSIMO : chief by birth, maximus natu.   Frederick 7th being a great admirer of the Roman generals Fabius *Maximus* and Scipio *Emilianus* compounded them calling his son MAXIMILIAN : patient and valiant.   In Psalm xc. 2 we read, " From *olam* to *olam* thou art Elohim." Olam : hidden, veiled, gives ALAM : a virgin, one veiled. Jonah was in sheol for *olam* as he lost count of time, it was veiled from him. Applicable to hills whose duration is hidden, or to eternity. It is then applied to anything old.   Shem gave it to his eldest son ELAM : first born, ELYMAS : Persia, Elymais : capital of ULAM: as above. " His sons were *Ulam* and Rakem." JETHER and JETHRO : excellent, excelling in age. " He said unto *Jether*, his first born, up and slay them." REUBEN : Reu : see, whence RUTH : desire of eyes, Ben : a son.   " *Reuben*, thou art my first born, my might, and the beginning of my strength, the *excellency* of dignity, the *excellency* of power." Hence RUBENS (painter), RUBINI (physician).   SONNEBORN : a son born to parents who had previously, in despair, adopted a son.   SIR, SIRE : father, SIRET = EXCELLENCY : excelling by years, and presumably by knowledge.   ZELOPHEHAD : first rupture = BECHER : ripe early, giving BECHORATH, BICHRI : my first born.   " Becher is called *Bered* in Chronicles."   " *Zelophehad* had no daughters." SECUNDUS : second (born) from Sequor : to follow, gives SECUNDINUS : son of *Secundus* (St. Patrick's companion) called by the Irish St. SECHNALL, whence MAOLSEACHLAN : bald to, disciple of Sechnall, tortured to MALACHI (of the golden collar) being supposed = the Hebrew MALACHI : messenger of the Lord.

VASHNI (son of Samuel) : second born, probably a sister first. SHILSHA : third son.   " The sons of Zopah. Shammuah and *Shilshea*" = TIERS (French statesman) = TERTIUS, whence TERTULLUS, its *dim.* which is foolishly given, in some works, very earthy.   QUARTUS : fourth (son) = CODRUS (Athens) = REBA (Moabite king), but as Reba is a transposition of Arba : four, and that is applied to a square built, handsome man, REBA may mean fine made.   TETRICUS (almost emperor) : fourth son. QUINTUS: fifth (son), gives St. QUENTIN, QUINTILLIAN : son of *Quintus*, also QUINZE (when French): fifth birth.   POMPEY : fifth (son) though given from Pompeii, said to have been founded by Hercules with great *pomp, con.* Penta : five, Punjaub : five river country, Punch : made of five ingredients, Pampeluna

for Pompiopolis: city of Pompey. Cæsar's rival had a son,
viz., SEXTUS: sixth, XYSTUS (pope), hence Sistine (chapel)·
The Roman = Hebrew SHESHAI (son of Anak). SEPTIMUS:
seventh (son), *con.* September: seventh month = BARSABAS:
seventh son, BATHSHEBA: seventh daughter. OCTAVIUS: eighth
(son), OTTO when Italian, Otto (roses) eighth essence. From
Octo we get Ides: eight days after Nones. NONUS, ENNIUS
(Calabrian poet): ninth born, *con.* Noon: ninth (hour), from
which Luncheon for Nuncheon: noon-day repast. DECIUS
(patriotic devotee), DECIMUS: tenth child, *con.* Decade: ten
years. QUINCE (when Spanish): fifteenth by birth. IMOGEN:
last born—TELEGONUS and the Italian SEZZI = POSTHUMUS
(postremus): last. Our great Will took it to mean Posthu-
mous: born after father was in ground.

> " What's his name and birth ?
> I cannot delve him to the root: his father
> Was called Sicilius, who did join his honour
> Against the Romans, with Cassibelan ;
> But had his titles by Tenantius, whom
> He served with glory and admir'd success :
> So gain'd the sur-addition, Leonatus :
> And had, besides, this gentleman in question,
> Two other sons, who, in the wars o' the time,
> Died with their swords in hand, for which their father
> (Then old and fond of issue) took such sorrow
> That he quit being ; and his gentle lady,
> Big of this gentleman, our theme, deceas'd
> As he was born : The king, he takes the babe
> To his protection : calls him *Posthumius* Leonatus,
> Breeds him and makes him of his bed-chamber."

SICILIUS is a form of ICILIUS : equal son, as good as his father
(*con.* Isosceles: equal legs) = PATROBAS. SERVIUS: preserved,
foundling = GERYON and TREPOFF. In those ages infanticide
was not considered immoral. PIAZZA : a foundling discovered
in a portico. LEONATUS: lion born, of warrior parentage.
MOSES: drawn out = NIMSHI: chosen, elect, taken out of, suggesting HYDROGENES: water begotten, Hydrogen : water producer. Moses was his Egyptian name, his Hebrew appellation
is lost. The Rabbis say it is one of these :—Chabar, Jecothiel,
Jared, Ahizamach, Abisuco, Abigedur or Schemiaia. But
which ? In Arabic, and cognate languages, it varies to MUSSA
(Pasha Silistria) or MOUSSA.

> " The gleams miraculously shed
> O'er *Moussa's* cheek when down the Mount he trod
> All glowing from the presence of his God."

Hence MOYSE, MOSS, MOSELEY, MOWATT (when they do not
mean a little hill = KNOWLES), MOZART (king of composers) but
MOSS (local) = PETLEY : living on a peat field, whence MOSS-
MAN, MOSSCROP, MOSSCRIP = PETMAN : turf digger. In this

case MOSSMAN = CESPEDES (Spanish), but sometimes stands for a moss-trooper, moor robber. BISHLAM: born in time of peace, con. Salaam : to bow and wish peace. " In the days of Artaxerxes wrote *Bishlam.*" GALAL : rolled (reproach from parents, barrenness), con. Gallus : a cock, crows when darkness is rolled away, Globus : any round thing. BERIAH : calamity, born in. " He called his name *Beriah,* because it was evil with his house" = MARY from Mar : bitter = HARMS (pastor) : born at an *evil* time. ACHILLES (tendon) : without the lip, dry nursed = GALLIO (deputy), LACTANTIUS (Latin father) : brought up on milk. NORRISS, NURRISH : one nursed, fostered = FOSTER, but sometimes used actively for a nurse.

GIORDANO (Bruno), JOURDAN (marshal), JORDAN : baptised with Jordan water = SANTHAGUE : holy water. HALDANE : half Dane, of Saxon mother and Danish father. GOLLACHER, GALLACHER : born of a strange woman, con. Gael. GALLYON : son of an Englishman. Englishmen were called Gaels : strangers, 700 years ago in Ireland, where the three last were originally born. D'AUBIGNE (Reformation) : of an alien, becomes DABNEY. BRANCHUS : throat, con. Bronchitis : disease of throat. Varro says—" The mother of *Branchus* being in child, dreamed the sun entered into her mouth and passed through her belly ; whence the child was called *Branchus* from Bronchus : the throat." ARCHEMORUS : beginning with death. His death foretold by Amphiarus as soon as he was born. The Nemean games were solemnised in his memory.

CHARILAUS : people's joy = DEMOCHARES, so named of Lycurgus. DESIDERIUS (pope), DIDIER, DIDEROT : child greatly desired = BRAMMANTE (architect), SAMUEL, SAUL, and ARATUS. MACBETH : son of life, whose birth enlivens parents = HAGGITH. SAMBORN and WINTERBORN are not nativity names, but mean *sandy burn* = GRIESBACH and *winding burn* = CROMBIE. In some cases BURNS is not from Burn : a brook, and so = BROOKS, but con. bear, bairn, born, meaning emphatic bairn, of noble descent = TIRIDATES and GNATHO : the son, con. KNIGHT. DAVID : beloved, a pet, con. JEDIDIAH : beloved of Jehovah, gave to Carthage DIDO : beloved (woman) and to us the *fem.* VIDA, DAVIE (fought in war of independence), DAVY (Humphrey), DAVIES, DAWE (painter), DAFFY (elixir), DAVIS, DAVITT (land leaguer), TAFFY, applied to a Welshman from St. David, as SAWNEY, a Scotchman from St. Andrew, and PADDY, from St. Patrick, though some good authors insist on having it from St. Palladius. DAKIN, DAWSON = DAVIDOFF. DILLON (M.P.), DILKIE, DILK, DILLY : little David. The Arabs have SALMAH EBEN DAOUD : Solomon, the son of David, and SCHAH DAOUD : king David. " All Israel and Judah *loved* David."

HOBAB: beloved. "Yea, He *hobabed* the people; all his saints are in thy hand." WINE: beloved. "My *winsome* deary O!" = MUNGO (St.). WINNOC: little dear = DARLING and WINNIE (the waif). These are nurse names, as MEDAD: loved, ELDAD: loved of God, greatly beloved, and DAD. "There ran a young man, and told Moses, and said, *Eldad* and *Medad* do prophesy." Such are DEARLOVE, SWEET, ANGEL, ANGLIOTTO: little angel, LOVE, BABY, BURNS, ENFANT, INFANT, PETTS, PRECIOUS, PETTEE, GOLDING, ZERESH (Haman's wife): golden, GOLDIE, GOWDIE, GOOD, GOODE, GOODCHILD, SPES, HOPE, ELPIS: whence ELPIDIAS: son of hope, and the Milesian name DIGNUM, which signifies hope (of parents). ZEPHO: watched for (by parents), *con.* ZEPHON: watcher, guardian. JOHN (world known) is composed of Jehovah: I am, and HANNAH: grace. From latter HANAN: merciful, and HANNE-THON: free gift. HANANIAH, ANANIAS, ANANUS: Jehovah's grace (given by). HANNO: gracious, HANUN (shaved ambassador). HANNIBAL (Carthage): (born of the) grace of Baal. ANN, ANNE, ANNVILLE: Ann's town. DANVILLE: of it. Annapolis: her city. NANNUCI (Italian), and NINA: little Ann. Shush: the lily (white), gives Shushan: the city of lilies, planted round it; compounding with Hannah, gives SUSANNAH, SUSAN: beautiful as the lily and gracious, SUKE, SUE.

The awful word JEHOVAH: I am, unchanging, contracts to *jah* and *ah* in composition. Thus Jah and Hannah: Jehovah's grace, gives JOHANNA, JOHANNES, JOHN, JEAN, as St. JEAN d'Acre: St. John of Accho. PRUJEAN: prudent John. GROSSJEAN: great John = MEIKLEJOHN: John who thinks *much* of himself. (M') FADYAN: long John, *cor.* to FADDAN. JOCKIE, JOCKEY: little John = JACKET, JOCK, (M') GEOCH: Jock in kilts. FROISSART tells that,—"Henry, Duke of Lancaster, on his return to England, entered London in courte *jacques* of cloth of gold, a la fachion D'Allmayne." These jacques, when little, were called *jacquette* by the French and Jacket by us. JACKET: properly means a retainer wearing one. Jack suggests poverty, and servitude, or inferiority, as jackass, jackpudding: a buffoon, jackanapes, who travelled with bear and monkey. Jack: instrument for roasting, formerly a boy called a turn spit. In Italy (Don) GIOVANNI, GIANNONE: great John, GIOVANETTI, VANELLI: little John = JANTJE (Dutch). The name John applying to beloved disciple, or the Baptist, is in double favour, and was given to children born on either of their days on the calendar. So fond are Italians of it that they combine it with many names in the forms *gian, giam,* as GIAMBIANCHI: white or fair John, becomes ZAM-BIANCHI (defended Rome in 1849). GIAMBATISTA: born June 24th. GAMBETTA, TISTA, TITA. Sometimes patronymical,

GIAN-ANTONIO: John, son of Anthony, GIANFIGLIAZZI : John, son of Azzi. Giovanni, *cor.* to GIANNA, forms ZANONI : great John, which *cor.* to ZANY : a merry *andrew.* Zan for John gives ZAMPA (musician): John's father, Zanpere = Arabic ABRI YAHYA. ZANCHIUS (Jerome) : John's son (filius) = ZANCOFF. The Mexicans call him JONTLI. The Hungarians have GUY, whence GUYON (Kars): great John. Germany has HANS, whence HEYNE, HANKS, HANCOCK, HANDLEY : John's field, attached to his church, HANS-WURST: Jack sausage. The Dutch say JAN, JANSEN (spectacles) = JOHNSON. The Spaniard prefers JUAN, DON JUAN : lord John JUANITO : little John = VANELLI. BOBO JUAN : booby John. The Celts had AIN, OIN, OWEN, SHANE, SHAN, the two latter formed on Ain as though Shane : the John. Shane gives SHENKIN, SHONEEN : Jackie, Johnnie, a boy. STRICHEN, STRAHAN : John's strath, valley. Russia has IVAN, CZENTIVANNY : St. John's (Cathedral, Moscow). Wales rejoices in EVANS, JONES, the latter being, after Smith, the commonest name in Britain. The men of Portugal delight in JOAME, whence GOMEZ = JOHNSON. In Persia it is YOHANNAN. The Greeks have GIANNAKES. In India, through the Mahometans we find JEHAN, as Jehansi = our JOHNSTONE: John's town, where his church. The following all means son of John, HANNEFAN (enfant), UPJOHN, JANZOON, MᶜGEOCH, HANSOM (cab), IVANOVITCH, IVANOFF, FITZJOHN, BEVAN, BOWEN, ZANCOFF (Bulgarian), JANNŒUS (of John Hyrcanus), JUXON (bishop), JENNINGS, SHENKIN, JENYNS (Soame), JENKINS (aged), JANKOWITZ, JEHANPUTRA, ZANCHIUS. Who shall lay to the charge of John that he is Malthusian ? The following mean John's town, AINSWORTH (dictionary), GONVILLE (college), HAMBURG, VAN AMBURG : of Hamburg, Johannisburg (wine), SHENSTONE, Jambol (bol for Polis: a city). Shajehanpore : king John's town. In its *fem.* form we get JOHANNAH, JANE, JEAN, JINNIE, JANET, JEANETTE, JENNY, JOAN, "JEANETTE and Jeannot : little Jane and John." So that John interpenetrates more than twenty languages.

HAFIZ and HAFID : saviour = SOTER (Ptolemy) = SALVATOR (Rosa), *con.* Salvador (island). HOSEA : saviour, whence Hosanna : save thou, forms with Jehovah. JOSHUA : greatest saviour = HAFIZ - ALLAH : saviour of God, whence JESUS (Greek), ISSA (Arabic), JESUS (English) : saviour of Jehovah,—

> " Such the refined Intelligence that flow'd
> In Moussa's frame ;—and, thence descending, flow'd
> Through many a Prophet's breast ; in *Issa* shone,
> And in Mohammed burn'd."

The letters I.H.S. do not stand for Jesus Hominum Salvator : Jesus the saviour of mankind, but are an old Saxon abbreviation of Jesus, whence JESUIT : of the society of Jesus, giving Jesuitique : hypocritical.

"After that came his brother out, and his hand *a-kabhed* Esau, and his name was called JACOB:" heeler. From Kabh : heel, Kibes: chilblains, swellings caused by cold, blain, blown,—

> *Falstaff :*—" Well, sirs, I am almost out at heels."
> *Pistol :*—" Why, then, let *kibes* ensue."

" Esau said is he not rightly named Jacob ? for he hath *supplanted* me these two times." The figure is taken from wrestling : Sub : under, Planta : sole of the foot, Supplant : to place a foot under that of an antagonist, and so trip him, taking his place,—

> " He wonder'd but not long
> Had leisure, wondering at himself now more ;
> His visage drawn he felt to sharp and spare ;
> His arms clung to his ribs, his legs intwining
> Each other, till *supplanted* on his belly prone
> *Reluctant*, but in vain."

Planta gives Patagon : great foot = FUSS, *op.* of PODIO (Italian): little foot, whence Patagonia : country of great footed people. Lucto : I strive, struggle. Luctator (luttator) : a wrestler. Reluctant : wrestling back, antagonising. Satan suffered a greater grip than he could give.

Jacob is identical with AKKUB : insidious. " *Akkub* was a porter, keeping the wards of the thresholds of the gates." Same as AKABI (starved rabbi), JAAKOBAH (David's hero), DACOBI (1 Esdras v. 28). YAKOUB (Khan), JACOBUS gives JACOBIN : one meeting in St. James' Monastery. JACOBITE : follower of James II. Hence, too, COBB, COBBETT, COBBIN, COBELL, COBOS, COPP, COPPING : son of Cob for Jacob = COBEZ, which corresponds to the name of the Russian general SKOBE-LOFF. Here we seize upon the latter part of name, but by taking the former syllable we obtain the softer name JAMES, whence JAMIE, JEMMY, JAMIESON = GIMSON. The Spaniards have DIEGO, giving DIAZ = JAMIESON, also IAGO, as Santiago (city of St. James): our JAGG, JAGGARD when not = HUNTER. Santiago = JAGIELSKI (s Koumiss) : town of St. James. The Highlanders have it in the form of HAMISH. In Ireland it is SHAMUS (O'Brien). France has JACQUES, as JEAN JACQUES ROUSSEAU: John James Russell, JACQUELINE, JACQUARD (loom) : identical with JAGGARD. GIACOMO prevails in Italy, and this shared by Spain, as Compostella : Giacomo Apostolo : (city of) James the Apostle. COMO from Giacomo is common in Italy. St. James has charge of all Spain.

> " To thee fervent thanks Spain shall ever outpour ;
> In thy name though she glories, she glories yet more
> In thy thrice-hallowed corse, which the sanctuary claims
> Of high Compostella, O, blessed St. James."

English pilgrims were named COCKLE from visiting this shrine.

> " He shows St. James' COCKLE shell;
> Of fair Montserrat, too, can tell."

Also to this prolific James we trace JEX, JOCKELL (when not horse warrior = EMLY), LAPIDE (Cornelius A.) = JAMIESON, SIPPELL, wherein there is only one letter for a philologist to hold on by. As SAR : a prince, is root of SARAI : a princess, and also of ISRAEL ; prince with God, it follows that grandmother and grandson were allied by name as well as by blood. SAR, CZAR, HERR, DAR (Hindoo for lord), MAR (Syriac for lord) all have an originally similar meaning, one who marshals, puts men into line of battle, a military organiser. Now though Jesus named Peter who afore was Simon, and therefore it is not of nativity, yet it seems half a pity to dissever him from his con-freres James and John, so we will say PETER : a stone, a man firm yet moveable, one built *in*, but not built *on*, a lively stone quickened by The Living Stone. PETER *con.* to Pier : a jetty, a mole. Petrœa : rock (city)=Selah. Arabia Petrœa : Arabia the stony. Peter gives PETRULLA, PETRONIUS, PERKIN (Warbeck), PARKINS, PARKIN, PARKINSON, PURKISS, PARNELL (obstruction), PARR (old), PEREIRA (Dr.), PIERS (Gaveston) PIERCE, PERRON (cardinal), PERONI (last two) : great Peter. PIRRETT : little Peter, PERRY (when not a trade name, one making liquor from *pears*), PEDRO (don), PEREZ = PIERSON and PETRONIUS, PIETRO, PERUZZI, PERUGINO, from Perugia from Peter, and PETRARCH (poet). (St.) Petersburg : Peter's city, Petro-paulski : city of Peter and Paul, PETERLOO : Peter's meadow, *low* lying. Its French form is PIERRE, which is patronymical, showing how high Peter stood in Gallic favour. BASSOMPIERRE (general): Bassom, son of Peter, ROBESPIERRE (terror): Robert the son of Peter, DAMPIERRE, DAMPIER: Daniel, son of Peter. From last DAMPER: Australian bush meat. " At the sixth attack, DAMPIERRE, at the head of a picked detachment, charged a redoubt."

LEVI : joined, Levite : of Levi's tribe, Leviticus : law of Levites, Leviathan : joined scales, crocodile of Egyptians, being largest animal of the Nile applies to any big thing. " This time will my husband be *joined* to me." NATHAN : given (of God), Nethinim : given ones, devotees, NAT, NATHANIEL : given of God = JONATHAN : Lord given. THEODORUS, THEODOSIUS, THEODOTUS = GODIVA (Coventry): God given. MATTAN, MATTHEW : a gift, son. " From the wilderness they went to *Mattanah*. There the *Lord gave water.*" MATTANIAH : (son whom the) Lord gave. MATTHEW gives MADAI (Florentine confessors), MATYS (QUINTIN), MATHWIN, MADDISON, MACMATH = MATTHEWS for MATTHEWSON, MAITLAND : glebe

dedicated to St. Matthew, MADDOX, MATTOCK (some claim last
two as forms of Welsh MADOG: beneficent = BONIFACE). "Do
you know Matthew Mattocks?" MATTHIAS, MATTHIAH: gift
of Jehovah. ZABAD: a gift, as ELZABAD: God gave = ZABDIEL
answers to ZEBEDIAH, ZEBEDEE: gift of Jehovah = ZABDIAH,
ZABDI: the Lord's gift. Issue in answer to prayer. ISAAC:
laughter, gives HYKE, HICKS, (M')KISSOCK, NYE, NYKIN, SACY
(French). HICKS, when Hibernian, means doctor, surgeon,
HICKHOCKS: son of doctor = MACLAY.

These Oriental demonstrations of joy correspond to our
Occidental HAUSCHEIN: a baby whose birth makes the house
to shine. This German name was Greecised into ECOLAMPA-
DIUS: lamp of the house = UMBREIT (job): home brightness.
We English have one (London Directory) corresponding,
HOUSEGO: house joy; and the French have BERTHEIM:
brightness of home. These names, and such, supply the poetry
of onamatology, name giving or knowing.

THAMAH: laughing, joy of parents, welcome baby-girl. HUL-
DAH: a weasel, a little active girl. "So Hilkiah, the priest,
and Ahikam, and *Achbor*, and *Shaphan*, and Asahiah, went
to *Huldah* the prophetess: (now she dwelt in Jerusalem in
the college): and they communed with her." What a menagerie met in the Jewish Girton:—ACHBOR: a mouse, SHAPHAN:
rabbit, HULDAH: a weasel.

TIRAS: desire (of parents). Youngest son of Japhet, supposed to give name to Troas. This is the first record of a long
line of yearners for offspring. It answers to WUNSCH: much
wish for, and such names as SHEAL (son of Bani): prayer, and
SHEALTIEL (Ezra's father): asked of God = SAMUEL. BASS:
little (at birth), BASSETTI: very little = PETTY, PETTIT. IBRI
(son of Merari): (born) beyond the Red Sea). BYTHESEA
(commanded a man of war in 1869): found by the sea =
WITTON: son of the wood, foundling in some cases = GROVES.
PARRISH is also a foundling name, as is the Italian D'ONDES:
of the waves, found on shore, *con.* Unda: a wave, whence
UNDINE: a nereid, sea born, suggesting the widely known
APHRODITE: daughter of foam. Irish Protestants call their
sons WILLIAM when born July 12th, while Irish Catholics call
theirs PATRICK when born March 17th.

TAPHATH: a drop (of myrrh), applied to small infant girl,
then to short steps, then to a little girl making them, means
a regular little dear. "Which had *Taphath*, the daughter of
Solomon, to wife." Myrrh, from Mar: bitter, gives Myrtle,
Smyrna: (town amidst) myrrh plants. PERE-ET-MERE
(French): loved by *father and mother*, precious pet = DEAR-
LOVE: dearly beloved. "In the list of decorations in the
Moniteur de l'Armee appears the name *Pere-et-Mere*. The

gallant bi-sexual receives the Legion of Honour for good conduct during several campaigns." AMPERE is same as above in converse order, though it is given as identical with *empire*, and applied to a man belonging to the German empire. To him we trace the abbreviation, etc., called by English rustics Hampersand, *i.e.*, *Amper's and*, so used in his shorthand.

COPRONYMUS: dung name, *con.* Coprolite: dung stone, a nickname given to son of Greek Emperor, because while being baptised he defiled his baptismal robes. He was akin to PALŒOLOGUS: old style speaker, having a brogue. Not only have we children named from birth-day, but also from birthmonth, as LAVRILLIAT: April born. HERBEST, HARVEST (sermons): born at time of gathering in of herbs. DAVOUST (marshal): August born. MAY (in some cases): May born. The favourite month with the worshippers of Baal of old and Mary now. HALLIDAY (*con.* Halidom: holy dame, B.V.M.): born on a holy day. The notion that this was got by crying Halli (holy) day! when going on a raid is absurd as it implies the Hallidays came to fighting age without a name, or that this one took the place of their birth name. In the latter case what was that? GENTLES, GENTLEMAN: of a gens, clan, high birth = BURNS.

METRONYMICS.

SOME few masculine names may be traced to mothers. These though looked askance at by refined moderns took the place of patronymics with the Lycians. From the maternal side we have our DEVLIN, and the ancients had VESPASIAN: son of Aspasia, indicating filial affection. ASPASIA: an amazon from Asp: a horse. IBBOTSON (of course our's): son of Elizabeth. DYSON: son of Dy for Diana, but is capable of being placed with DYBALL: one of a bold people, in which case = DODDS. NELSON may be son of Nell, Ellen, or from Neil. Let him have the benefit of the doubt for the sake of the old sea lion. SUE (Eugene) looking so like Susan means *sweater*, *con.* Sudor from Hudor: sweat, water. UNA (an Irish name of soft sound): born at time of famine, gives UNITT: son of *Una.* MARRIOT, MARRYATT (novelist) are from Mary, but plead it is religiously, not socially. VYE is claimed as son of Sophia, but pleads for its being a formation on Devizes. M'JANET and M'JANNET: looking so like son of the girl. Janet is of the gens John, meaning literally son of little John, JANNET = LITTLEJOHN. TALMAGE (Brooklyn) is nothing but a name I met with in Toronto, TALLMADGE: son of tall Margaret, Madge, exactly = MARGERISON (soap manufacturer): son of Marjory. DE WITT is of Woods, son of a man so named, but is capable of being local, and meaning *of the wood.*

MOLLISON : son of Mary in the vulgar form of Moll. EMMET (Irish) is held to be of Emma. Centuries ago when as yet the terrors of the Registrar-General had not set in, family lady names were exchanged for those having no bar sinister. Nations dwelling in small groups, as Tartars, Arabs, Indians, often cherish names from a mother in preference to one of paternal origin. Curiously, the Arabs reverse the laws of onamatology by taking names from children. This applies especially to birth of a first-born son. When an heir to tent and camels is called SULEYMAN for Solomon, his father becomes ABU-SULEYMAN : father of Suleyman, and his mother OM-SULEYMAN : mother of. This OM is our better known MA, turned round as AB is PA, and is *con.* EMMA, AMEN, all of which may be rendered, faithful, nourisher. FUDLE-ALLAH : God's bounty given by, is the Arabic correspondent to NATHANIEL. ABU-FUDLE-ALLAH : father of the daughter given by God's grace. ZILL ALLAH : the shadow of God, is a title of the Shah. The former portion is absolutely identical with ZILLAH (Lamech's wife) except the *fem.* ending. ZILLAH : woman shaded (by ringlets). ZALMON : great shade, protector, comforter. How strange that a word used at the gate of Eden should still be in daily use. But fashions change less on the banks of the Euphrates than on those of the Seine. ZILTHAI for ZILTHAIAH : shaded, protected of the Almighty. AYUB said, "Let the day perish wherein I was born, and the night in which it was said, There is a *man*-child conceived." Arab wives being childless, call themselves by that name, they would give a *son* if they had one, as OM-AYUB : mother of Job. JOB, AYUB, AYOUB (Khan) : sobber, weeper = AJAX, an imitation of the *eh! ah!! oh!!!* of distress. This could only be the proper name of the man of the land of Uz by chance coincidence (which is most unlikely), by prophecy (as unlikely), or is *post mortem* from his sighing and sobbing. The true translation is JOB : sobber. Then we must record the noble Mahometan name ABU-BEKER : father of the virgin, viz., Ayesha, suggesting BETHUEL (father of Rebekah) : daughter of God, a virgin = PARTHENOS, VIRGINIUS, a pure man, *con.* BETHULIA : daughter of God, a pure woman, applied to the city besieged by Holofornes, in the sense of not violated. ABULFEDA : father of reconciliation, peacemaker = the Puritan MAKEPEACE and the monastic PACIFICO. Here AB is figurative, as in ABISHALOM : father of peace = LYSIMACHUS : looser of strife. ABU-HOREIRA : father of the cat, applied to a friend of Mahomet's who was fond of cats = the Italian GATTINA, GATTY. DEMON is a family name found in the United States, and means son of a monk, whence DEMONICO, of the Broadway, N.Y.

CHAPTER VI.

NAMES OF WOMEN.

IN remote ages when "one person, one name" was the rule, the appellations of women were as varied and independent as those of men. However, when mononysm fell out of use, their place was generally supplied by appending a feminine ending to masculine names. Christianity did much to lessen the names peculiar to women. Obeying the spirit of its teachings, the bride signifies dependence upon her husband by renouncing her maiden name and adopting the name of him who adopted her. This helped to consolidate family ties, but resulted in the loss of designations peculiar to women. By consequence, feminine names have so diminished, as to necessitate the formation of new ones, which is effected thus:— VICTOR gives VICTORIA, AUGUSTUS, AUGUSTA, and we even meet with ADAM, ADAMINA. Writers on physiology say that woman is man modified, that man is the essence of humanity, women the accident. They must answer for the truth and gallantry of such averments; yet their theory is corroborated by this specialty of philology,—words expressing *man, woman, male, female*, besides giving us proper names, more or less express sexuality. The Hebrews said, Ish: a man, Isha: a woman, a maness. From Ish the well known ISCARIOTES: man of Kirioth, not far from Bethlehem, for Judas was the only Jew proper among the apostles, the rest of the twelve being Galilean. From Isha we have ESHTON: uxorious, a woman chaser. "*Eshton* begat Beth-rapha." From Ish, JESHISHAI: descended from an aged man = BENJAMIM, SHANEGAN. Some high authorities gives ISIS (Eve, a goddess): the woman. So BAAL: lord, master, BAALATH: lady, mistress. The Greeks said *o* anthropos: a man, *e* anthropos: a woman. Anthropos: turning up the face, whereby man is differentiated from the lower animals. No cow ever views the sky, no horse sees the stars. In Latin we have VIR: a man, VIR-GO: a woman, VIRGINIUS: a pure man, VIRGINIA: a pure woman. Hence our virgin means more than maid, the latter applying to females only, the former to either sex. "For they are virgins." The Dutch say BOER: a man, MOER (ma, mater): a woman. Our MAN: one of mind, *con*. mens, "Mene." Woman is wifman, the man who weaves, in contrast with spearman. So PAIS (a boy): one led, Paiduetics: science of leading, instructing, Pusa: a girl, Pusilla: a little girl, Pusillanimous: having soul of a little girl. Lad : one led, Lad-ess, Lass. Younker: a young man. Younkster : a young woman. Former obsolete in England, though used in the United States, while latter is applied erroneously to a boy as a troublesome lad is called *vixen*, properly pertaining to a girl. *Mas.* Fox, *fem.* Vixen. In the Italian we have ZITA : a girl, ZITELLA : a little girl = Pusilla,—

" Gentle Zitella, whither away?
Love's ritornella, list while I play."

In the catalogue of Burns, Oates, & Co. we read, " Life of St. *Zita* 3*s.*"

Seeing the woman's rights section of the ladies are full sail on the franchise, they should take action on being merely nominal terminations of the rougher sex, so far as names go. In like manner the titles of women are usually formed upon those of men, as DOMINUS : a lord, DOMINA : a lady = DON, DONNA, when aged DUENNA. So our English LORD : loaf afforder, LADY. So with the Tartars, KHAN : a lord, as Cawnpore : Khan's city, Kokhan : hill country of Khan, KANHAM : a lady. RAJAH : a king, RANI : a queen, as our REX, REGINA, ROY, REINE. In respect to kin, we have Nephew, Neice, as though NEPOS (Cornelius), Neipce. Nepos gives Nepotism : favouring relatives. So also from Avus : aged, a grandfather, in which sense Nepos is also used, *con.* Ævum : an age, Cœval : living in same age. Avunculus : little grandfather, *ab.* to Uncle, *fem.* Aunt. Avus gives AVES = GAFFER (Gray) and PAPPUS, the former Latin, the latter Saxon, the last Greek. *Mas.* GAFFER, *fem.* GAMMER (Gurton): grandmother. Isha, pusa, pusilla, zita, zitella, domina, regina have *a* final in common. The classical designation of the quarters of the globe, and almost every country upon it so ends, as Europa, Asia, Africa, Australia, America, Britannia, Caledonia, Scotia, Cambria, &c. This ending is clearly derived from the Biblical *ah* wherewith most recorded names of women in Genesis end. CHAVAH : living (Hebrew form of Eve), Adah, Zillah, Sarah, Milcah, Reumah, Maachah, Rebekah, Leah, Bilhah, Zilpah, Deborah, Aholibama, Shuah. Feminine names are rarely mentioned in the Bible. There are only five female names to ninety-five of men in the Old Testament. In the New Testament the proportion is more favourable to the weaker, as though women were to be more active Christians than matriarchs and Jewesses were in making known the ancient form of worship. Who was Noah's wife, Lot's, Job's ? It is an old platform joke to say Mrs. Noah ; an old Sunday school puzzle, Who was David's mother ? We should naturally suppose that in narratives such as those of Elijah and the

Zarephath widow, Elisha and the Shunamite woman, whose
sons these prophets brought again from the dead, their names
would occur. Similarly we know the sons Mary bare to
Joseph, in the order of nature, were James, Joses, Juda, and
Simon, but who knows the names of His sisters ? Who were
the sisters of Abel and Cain ? As it is in the Bible, so it is in
every national history and in all genealogies. In the Scriptures, because woman led the van of rebellion. In secular
history, because woman is the weaker, whereas history records
the deeds of the mighty. The following illustrations will fully
exemplify what is meant by the feminine ending being in *ah,
a,* or *e.* In doing so our motto will be the form used by a
Roman matron when first entering her lord's abode—

Ubi Caius ibi Caia : where you are Master I am Mistress.

Aba (Gothic for a man, as Abbs : head) gives Ebba (queen
of S.S.) : a woman. From her, Epsom : Ebba's home.

Andromachus : fighting man, Andromache (Hector's wife).

Andromedes : commander of men, Andromeda (rock).

Angel : a messenger, celestial, Angelica, Angelina. Dan-
gerous names to give a baby of the female persuasion, as the
woman might not fit.

Agathos (pope) : good = Goode, Agatha (St.), Aggie.

Amala : unspotted, virgin = Afflick, Immacolato.

Æmilius : a worker = Emily, Amelia, Mill.

Alethius : true = Ameena (Bou), Fidus, Alethia, Letty.

Alexander : helper of man, saving in battle, Alexandra,
Alexandrina.

Alfred : counselling like an *elf,* Elfreda = Sybella.

Athel : noble, Adela, Adelina (Patti), Adelaide (queen),
Ethel, Adelgonde : noble warrioress = Matilda, Brunhilda,
Bellona,

Athelgif: noble gift, royal bounty, Ethelgiva. But Elgiva,
elf gift, beautiful as a fairy. " At the coronation of Edwy,
the king retired from the revelry of the banqueting hall and
sought the society of his wife and her mother, having espoused
Elgiva, the daughter of Ethelgiva, a lady of royal descent.
Odo urged Dunstan to bring back the king." Elgiva accurately answers to the Persian name Perizada : born of a peri,
beautiful at birth.

Appius (Claudius) : fruitful, having issue, Apphia (primitive
Christian).

Agrippa (Vipsanius) : who gave sharp (acer) pains. Agrip-
pina (Nero's mother).

Augustus (Octavianus Cæsar) : sublime, awful, majestic,
Augusta.

Bland : profoundly polite speaker, Blandina (martyr).

BRAVO: a fine man, BRAVURA: a splendid woman.
BUDD: victory, BOADICEA (Iceni): victrix = VICTORIA *fem.*
VICTOR.

CHARLES: strong man, CAROLUS (Latin), CARLOS (Span.),
CHARLOTTE, CARLOTTO, LOTTA, LOTTIE, CAROLINE, CARRY.
" *Lotta* intends to make the tour of Europe this season."

CASSANDER (Macedonian king): glorious man = CLEANDER
and ANDROCLES, CASSANDRA (daughter of Herculea). This
cass is supposed to come from the Sanscrit verb, Kash: to
shine, whence KRISHNA: glorious, CASTOR (Jupiter's son):
shining one. Hence, also, the beautiful name CASSIOPE
(Andromeda's mother): bright eyes = LAPIDOTH and HOURI.
The *Cast*alian fount of Parnassus and *Cas*pian (sea), are
thought to be from *kash*. The former gave out shining streams,
the latter phosphoric brilliancy. To *kash* we trace *Casi*teros:
tin, whence *Cassi*terides: islands producing shining metal.
Hence to Cassis: a helmet, a shining head-dress, from which
CASSIUS: helmeted, or glorious one. Probably the Scotch
GASS and the English CASH are also from this source, being
British equivalents to KRISHNA and CASSIUS. But CASCA
(gave the first blow): old = PRISCUS, not an aged person, but
of old stock.

CELESTINE (St.): heavenly minded, CELESTINA = HIMMELINA.
The well known CECILIA (sacred music) is generally given as
fem. of CECIL (Burleigh), from CŒCUS: a blind man, but it is
fem. of CAIQUILIUS: son of CAIQUIL: lord of the land =
TANAQUIL, from Stan: country, *con.* THANE: land (lord),
THANA: a lady. TANAGRA: lady of the Greeks, daughter of
Æolus. In "Juventus Mundi," Mr. Gladstone gives ÆOLUS:
patterned, variegated, tartan plaid like, referring the meaning
of name rather to dress than variation of the wind. This
view throws light on the sale of Joseph. Ancient slaves wore
one colour, freemen two, lords three, etc. One meaning the
brothers of Joseph attached to his coat was, it meant he was
more highly bred than they, the sons of concubines, Bilhah
and Zilpah. By selling him for a slave they would get one
colour a head.

CHRISTIAN: consecrated to Christ, CHRISTINA, KIRSTIE,
CHRISTIERN (Danish king): christened when that was exceptional = OSIANDER, ALLGOOD, CHRISTIANA: a christian woman,
KERSLEY: Christ's field, dedicated land. The European nations
to our north use Christian as the opposite of *demoniac*, we of
brute. In Alpine districts imbeciles are called Cretins: Christians, harmless ones. Diocletian had no objection to Nazar-
enes being termed Chrestians: followers of CHRESTUS (a
philosopher so called): liberal, gentle, kind, but made it a capital
offence to be termed Christian from CHRIST: anointed and

appointed of God. Thus war raged round a letter. Was it to be *e* or *i*? Never did so much hinge on so little. Jesus and the Sadducees contended over one word (*am*, not *was*), Matt. xxii. 32. Paul staked all on *s*, Gal. iii. 16 (seed not seeds). CHRISTOS is still common in Greece, whence CHRISTOPULOS: Christ's servant = GILCHRIST. From Christ we have CHRISTIE (M.P.), CHRISTY (minstrels). Ten years since the chief brigand of Epirus was a wretch named Christ. There are thousands of Germans named Christ, some of them American innkeepers; in their case the name was originally obtained by playing the part of our Lord in a Morality Play.

COUBA, JUBA (Negroes): Friday born, CUBINA, JUBINA.

CREON (Corinthian king): head, chief, prince, CREUSA (wife of Eneas).

DAN: a judge, DINAH (Jacobites both).

DAVID: beloved = MUNGO, VIDA, DIDO. Former modern.

DEBOR: an oracle = REID, ARISTOLBULUS, DEBORAH (prophetess) = SYBILLA.

DIOS, DIVUS: a god, *div*ine, DIANA, DIVA (prima donna), DIONE, JUNO.

DRUSUS: fruitful, as though watered with dew like Eden, DRUSILLA (wife of Felix), often given as having an eye like a dew drop, which is poetic but incorrect.

ERNE: an eagle, ARNABELLA. ARNHEIM: home on mountain frequented by eagles.

EPHRON: a roebuck, ORPAH ("kissed her"): deer-eyed = DORCAS.

ETHELBURG: noble protector, ETHELBURGA, a high favourite with Saxon ladies.

EUSEBIUS: a pious man, SABINA: a pious woman.

FAUSTUS: lucky, prosperous, FAUSTINA (wife of Antoninus).

FELIX: fortunate, successful, FELICIA (Hemans).

FELICULUS: playful as a kitten, romper, FELICULA (martyr). FELICULA differs little from GATTINA: she cat. "An Italian indictment of the Papacy by Petrucelli Della *Gattina*, M.D. of the Italian Parliament."

FLAVIUS (Josephus): yellow-haired = BOYD, SORLEY, gives FLAVIA, answering to JACINTA the *fem.* of HYACINTH.

> " His fair large front and eye sublime, declared
> Absolute rule; and *hyacinthine* locks
> Round from his parted forelock manly hung
> Clust'ring but not beneath his shoulders broad."

FULVIUS: foxy-haired = ROUSSEAU, FULVIA.

GAFFER (Gray): grandfather, GAMMER (Gurton): grandmother.

GEORGIUS: earth worker, GEORGINA. Georgium Sidus: star of King George.

HERMOSUS, for FORMOSUS: well shaped, HERMOSA = PUL-
CHERIA: good looking. The Latin *f* is represented in Spanish
by *h*, hence from Ferrum we have HERRERA: iron worker,
farrier.

HEROD: son of a hero, HERODIAS for HERODIAH.

ʹHLUDWIG: a warrior who is *loudly* spoken of, HELOISE.

HUGH: full of battle ardour, HUGHINA, like the Russian
fem. owna.

HUPATOS (from Upo: under, subordinate to the S. P. Q. R.,
Acts. xiii. 7): a deputy, HYPATIA = CONSUELIA: the consul's
lady. CONSUL: a consulter, one who *sits with*, takes part in
a sederunt.

IDAS: a son, IDA, OUIDA: no body's daughter.

IDDO: loved (son), JEDIDAH: beloved (daughter).

JAMES: heeler, becomes JACQUES, and gives JAQUELINE.

JOHN, JOHANNES: the grace of God, JANE, JOHANNAH,.
VANKA.

JEHUDI (Nethaniah's son): a Jew, JEHUDIJAH (Mered's
wife): a Jewess, JUDITH.

LARS: a *lord*, one of the *lares (et penales)*, LARTIA: a lady.

LAWRENCE: laurel crowned, LAURA, LAURETTA, LORETTO
(Our Lady of).

LORD, LAIRD, LAYARD: loaf afforder, LADY.

LATIMUS: a man of Latium, a lowlander, LAVINIA (young).

LŒTUS: joyous, she who lilts, LETITIA, LETTICE, LETTIE.

LOUIS (Hludwig): famous victor, LOUISA.

LUCRETIUS: son of Luke, LUCRETIA, LUCRECE, LUCETTA,
LUCIA, LUCY.

> " *Lucetta*, as thou lov'st me, let me have
> What thou think'st meet, and is most mannerly."

MAHLON, MALON, MAHLI: sickly, invalid, MAHLAH (Zelophehad's daughter). Probably to MAHLI should be traced *malus*,
mal, malady, me (in Megrim: disease of the cranium), as the
primitive idea of badness would be weakness.

MAC: a son (*con.* Maggot: rapid breeder), MAB: a daughter,
MABLE, MABEL, which some resolve into Ma-belle: my beauty.

MAOCH: oppressed (with troubles), MAACHAH.

MAR: a lord (*con.* Maranatha: the Lord cometh), MARTHA:
a lady.

MONICHOS: a solitaire, dwelling alone, MONICA (Augustine's
mother).

NAAMAN: handsome, NAAMAH = Ruth: fascinating.

NAARAI: a youth, NAARAH: a damsel = PUER, PUELLA.

OLYMPUS: shining, glorious, like the Olympic gods,
OLYMPIA: majestic, Junonic.

OPHELIUS (ovis): a shepherd, OPHELIA: a shepherdess =
PATTI, *con.* pastor.

8

PETER : a rock, not easily moved, PETRULLA.

PHILIP : lover of horses, good rider, PHILIPPA, FELIPPA, PHILIPPOVA.

PORCIUS : a swineherd = HOWARD : hog warden and SUARIUS, PORCIA (Cato's sister).

PRISCUS : of the old stock, aristocratic as to pedigree, PRISCILLA.

PI : a mouth, a good speaker (the Hebrew letter פ. Seen to advantage in Pi-Hahiroth, mouth : mouth of caverns), PUAH : a talkative woman. It is exactly = BOUCH (Tay Bridge), *con.* Rebuke : to shut the mouth.

SHEPHER : bright, handsome, SHIPHRAH = HERMOSA, HELEN. PUAH and SHIPHRAH were midwives, and who can conceive of a name more true to fact than for a midwife to be called PUAH : a chatter box ? PUAH neatly contrasts with PUY-PARLIER (sane lunatic) : little speaker = TACITUS (tacit), DUMAH (dummy), MOODY (mute), MUDIE, and the English bishop STILL.

QUASHEE : Sunday born. QUASHEBA (*con.* Quassia).

RAHAM : merciful, REHUMAH : compassionate lady = RUTH (when English, from Rue : to pity).

RAM : high, dignified, REUMAH : lofty dame, haughty woman.

ROBERT : famous counsellor, *cor.* to ROBIN, ROBINA.

ROSH : head, ROSHENA, ROXANA (Alexander's Persian princess).

SAID (Port) : fortunate, happy, HAIDEE = FELICIA, FAUSTINA.

SAR : a military prince = SAHIB, SARAI, SARA, SARAH.

SEPHER : a book, learned = BOOKER, BUCER, SAPPHIRA.

THEOCLES : glory of God (seen in gift of child), THECLA.

THEOS : divine, deity, God, the placer, THEIA, THIA (mother of the sun), THETA, THAIS : divine daughter.

THERON (and *Aspasia*) : harvest man, THERESA (Nostra Rex).

THOR : Asiric bull-god, TORAGA : celestial cow adored by the Hindoos, and THORA.

WENDELL : of Vandal descent, a confirmed wanderer, WENDOLINE.

WILHELM : protected of Will, WILHELMINA, MINNIE. Sometimes MINNIE : a female minnie singer, who kept old times and persons in *mind.*

ZABAD : a gift, baby boy, ZEBUDAH : a girl, ZEBEDIAH : given of Jehovah.

ZIPPOR (King of Moab) : a bird, timid = BIRD and VOGEL, ZIPPORAH : birdie, pretty and timid.

ZORAH : whose birth is like sunrise, DZOHARA (Arabian Venus) = HELEN.

The endings *i, e, ie* and *a* are identified with the Biblical *ah.* Those in *e* are rare compared with those in *a*. E was a favourite Greek ending, but *a* found favour with the Jews. ALCITHŒUS: quick runner = RHESUS, LIGHT, GALLETLY = ALCITHŒ.

ALLAN, ALLAYNE: quick runner = SWIFT—ELLEN, but HELEN: shining, glorious, shining skin through health = GRAINE: glorious for beauty, *con.* Helios: the sun, is Greek, whereas ELLEN in English from the Goths.

ANTIOPUS: against the face, antagonist, ANTIOPE (Amazonian queen). " I withstood him to the face, because he was to be blamed."

BERNICIUS: bringing victory, born at time of conquest, BERNICE.

BLANCH: white pale, blonde = BAIN—BLANCHE = BANSHEE.

HARPALYCUS (Thracian king), compounded of HARPY: ravisher, snatcher, and LYCUS: a wolf; who comes down on foe like a wolf on a flock—HARPALYCE (princess).

MEROPS (King of Cos): dim sighted = CECIL, and in some families, the Irish KEY, KEE—MEROPE (married Sisyphus).

PODARGUS (ergon, urge, urgent): swift footed (Hector's charioteer) PODARCE.

LEUCIPPUS (Daphne's lover): a white horse, LEUCIPPE.

THESSALONICA (Philip's daughter): born at time of victory over the Thessalians. In her honour the city to which Paul wrote was so called.

In addition to the Indo-Germanic feminine endings *a, e, ie,* or *y,* mere tints and shades of *ah,* we also have the Biblical ending *eth,* as shading off of our old friend *oth,* the form of the *fem.* plural. From this source our Saxon ancestors obtained *ath.* They said, *mas.* Moon, *fem.* Monath. EAD: happy = BONHEUR—EDITH = HAIDEE, FELICIA. EDGAR: lucky spear, is from same, and *con.* with *Allodial:* fee-free farm, in contrast with Feudal: subject to feu, fee. HODDER: an allodial farmer. From *ead* also EADIE = FORTUNATUS, rather than a nick-name formed from ADAM, as ADDIE. GODFREY: lover of God = AMEDEUS, THEOPHILUS—GODFRITH. LIND: a serpent. LILITH (for Lind-ith): graceful walker. "It is an old Talmudical legend, mentioned among other writers by Burton, in his 'Anatomy of Melancholy,' that a snake was transformed into a wife for Adam at first, and named LILITH; that, because her offspring turned out snakes also, she was superseded, and Chavah (Eve) created in her place; and that it was in jealousy that she resumed the serpent's form, and tempted Eve to fall."

Reu (Hebrew): to look upon, as REUBEN: look! a son— RUTH: fascinating. Rue (English): to pity, RUTH: a compassionate woman. The *ith* ending is very common in holy writ, as—HAGGAI : born at feast time, exultation of parents, HAGGITH (David's wife).

HILLEL (rabbi): praise, MAHALATH (Esau's wife): praise singer, she who lilts, whose voice is like a stringed instrument. This is *con.* with Zul: a musical instrument, whence ZULEIKA : she whose voice is like a zul, silvery toned lady. DZOHARA, ZULEIKA, and HAIDEE, *fem.* of SAID : lucky, are the three favourite names for daughters and brides through all Persia, Turkey, Arabia. ZULEIKA, MAHALATH = MELPOMENE : whose voice is sweet as song.

JUDAH : one who is praised = ÆNEAS, JUDITH (Holofernes).

NAARAI: a youth = JUNIUS, YONGE, YOUNGMAN, Naarath : a rising city. "The border went down from Janohah to Ataroth, and to *Naarath,* and came to Jericho, and went out at Jordan."

SHELOMI: a peaceful man, SHELOMITH (Zerubbabel's daughter). Applied to church.

SHIMEI : famous = CLEON, SHIMEATH = SEMIRAMIS.

SHIMRI : a watchman, SHIMRITH : a female ward.

CHARLES : strong, CHARLOTTE (Bronte), CAROLUS, CAROLINE.

HENRY : home ruler, HENRIETTA (Carrachiola, of monastic fame).

ANTOINETTE is, literally, little Antoine. So CHARLOTTE : little Charles, HENRIETTA : little Henry ; applicable to sons, daughters, or even wives of Antoine, Charles, Henry, as they are all physically less than those from whom named, when first so called. HARRY (not a form of Henry): one who *harries,* plunders, HARRIET.

ELIZA for ELIZABETH : the oath of God, she who is in covenant with God, having the assurance of His oath, gives LIZZY, LISETTE, IBBOTT, GISELLA, ELSIE, ISABELLA: beautiful Eliza, whence BELLA, BEL. Seizing on the last syllable of Elizabeth we get BETTY, BESSIE, and BET.

JOHN: the grace of God, given by, JOAN (pope), JANE, JANET, JINNY, JEANETTE : little John, JEANOT : little Jane, JUANITA, ANITA (Garibaldi), GILL for Jill ("Every Jack has his *Gill* ").

JOSEPH : He (God) shall add (another child, viz., Benjamin), *con.* ASAPH (who sang with the cymbals): gathering, gives JOSES (brother of James the less), JOSE, or JOSEY. "Lopez, wounded, was called to surrender, but refused ; then a cavalry corporal, by name JOSE DIABLO : Joseph, the Devil, killed him. Caballero was a little distance away, surrounded by the Brazilians," etc. Joseph also gives JESSOP, JAAPS, JOPSON, JEBB (Joshua), BEPPO, the Italian for JOEY, EPPS (cocoa), PEPYS (diary), and the following *fems.:*—JOSEPHINE (imperatrice), JESSIE, JESSICA (violet bank), FINETTE, GUISEPPE (the Italian form of Joseph), gives GUISEPPINA.

FRANCIS : an Italian speaking French, similar to Irish

GRIGGS (when not from (Mc) Gregor): learned in Greek, gives (San) Francisco: city of St. Francis, FRANCES, FANNY = in the Spanish PANCHITA. Hence SECCHI (Jesuit astronomer) = FRANCICELLO: little Francis.

The Celts, whether Bretons, Britons, Pictones, Picts, Gauls, Gaels, Irish, Welsh, or Manx, had no names for women formed on those of men, as Cassandra on Cassander. Instead of so forming them, they gave names of a highly poetical, but natural cast, indicating striking peculiarities of the lady as to person or manners. Such names faded away as Christianity became a living power among the Celts. A child being presented for baptism, the priest was careful that a name should be given that would consort with religious propriety. He then frowned down their beautiful appellations, urging changes on Biblical or Calendar names conveying no spark of meaning, whereby nationality and the genius of their language was discouraged. In heathen times there were as many names as women, now a score covers one half used by British women. The Celtic style being true to the heaven-implanted instincts of men, would have saved us from absurdities so common that they escape unnoticed. The idea of calling a girl Mary Robert*son*, addressing a young lady as Miss Hardman, or coolly terming a matron Mrs. Properjohn! Except such be accepted as elliptical expressions they are ridiculous. Howbeit, we cannot enjoy the use of the double name system without its drawbacks. The following is a selection of female Celtic names used before the Christian era. It is to be regretted that more have not come down to our cold utilitarian age:—

SUILGORUM: blue eyed, *con.* SULLIVAN, and Cairngorm: blue mountain = GLAUKOPIS (for a Greek lady) and GLAUKUS (killed by Ajax) for a man = our GRAY.

SUILMALDA: meek-eyed. SUILALIUN: beautiful eyed = DORCAS, ZIBIAH, CASSIOPE. LANSHUIL: full-eyed = BOPIS (bous ops): ox-eyed.

COULAVA: soft-handed, womanly, *con.* Liff, Loof: the hand.

GALAVA: milk white, *con.* Gala: milk, Galaxy = Via Lactea.

BOSMINA: soft palm, similar to Mulier: a woman from Mollis: soft.

OICHOVA: tender virgin, compassionate maid = RUTH: who rues for others.

COALMIN: soft haired, fine tresses = ZILLAH: shadow, made by ringlets.

COOLAULIN: beautiful hair = JACINTA, AURELIA: gold tressed women.

MALVINA: smoothly browed; similar to TALHIRAN: iron browed.

FLAMINA : softly mild = LENTULA. AGANDICA: snow faced = CHIONE, *con.* (C)Hiems: snow time, winter: also = the English SNOW, and BLANK (Bristol), whence Blanket : a woollen cover made by him, and sometimes = BLAKE : bleached.

EVIRCHOMI (Ossian's wife) : the tender, merciful Evir.

ROSGRANA (Fingal's first wife): a sunbeam, *con.* GRAINE, Greenock.

GAOLNANDONA : the love of men, she after whom men search.

FINELLA : white shouldered, *con.* COSTORPHINE : fair Christopher.

STRINADONA : contention, she for whom men strive. Upon a centigrade kalometer (beauty measurer) on which an aged warrioress from the ranks of the king of Dahomey's body guard would stand at zero and Venus at 100, STRINADONA would run the instrument up to 96.

BRIDGET : strong, *con.* BREE : a braw man, gives BRIDE (M') and Hebrides : islands so called from a religious house, visible from the sea, dedicated to St. Bridget.

COLLEEN BAWN: fair maid = BRITOMARTIS. From CALLAN (t): a lad, we have COLLEEN, like lad, lad-ess CALLAN becomes CULLEN = Haflin: half a man. The Bawn, *con.* Bane: white, whence Bann and Boyne : brown streams that *bleach* linen. So Bain: a bath from Bane white, because it makes white,—

> " By the clear lakes of Killarney,
>   Walk'd a youth, one fine summer morn,
> Who softly was whisp'ring blarney
>   To one whom he called *Colleen Bawn.*"

ROWENA : white skirt, *con.* Gowan (daisy): white flower.

GENEVEIVE (St.): wave-foam, whiteness of the sea = APHRODITE : froth of sea, *con.* GWYN (Nell) : white, fair (the Welsh Venus), *con.* ROWENA.

KATHLEEN (erroneously taken as a form of Catharine): beautiful eyed, *fem.* to KATHLIN : battle eyed, a man looking at his foe. CATHLIN gives CATTLE, CATT, *uncon.* with Vacca or Felis, as CODD *uncon.* the fish being from CODY for MacOdy,—

> " Kathleen Mavourneen ! the gray dawn is breaking,
>   The horn of the hunter is heard on the hill ;
> The lark from her light-wing the bright dew is shaking,
>   Kathleen Mavourneen, what ! slumbering still."

When translating grammatical feminine names, as distinguished from naturally feminine, we must refer them to their proper masculine, or embarrassing absurdities may turn up. Thus URSULA may not be made to mean *a little she bear*, nor FELICULUS : a little she cat, but they must be presented as the *fems.* of ORSON : a bear (hunter) = SU-AGROS, and FELI-CULUS : a little cat, a wonder to climb. Probably the honourable Scotch name ETTY is fashioned on EADIE, and that not from ADY from Adam but from Ed, Ead : fortunate, whereas ETTIE may be taken from any of several *fem.* endings. Some philologists claim ETTY as *con.* ITHAI (*"Itthai*, the son of Ribai, of Gibeah"), or, which is the same, ITTAI ("Ittai, the son of Ribai, out of Gibeah") : living one, vigorous, distinguished.

Owing to the small choice of female appellations, high flown dames are often at their wits' end to avoid such as are trite, as Margaret, Janet, Jessie, Sarah, Mary. Hence the array of Celestina's, Arabella's, Angelina's, Stella's, and a profusion of jingling inanities met with in fashionable circles. Another device of the upper ten is to make family names baptismal, as Wortley Montague, Dormer Stanhope, Bulwer Lytton. This is better, as names become monumental of the once departed but ever dear. If the dead were great, their name is inspirational as well as monumental. Our deathless Hood describes, as no one else can, the pangs of fashionabilities when name-hunting,—

> " Now to christen the infant Kilmansegg,
> For days and days it was quite a plague,
> To hunt the list in the Lexicon.
> And scores were tried, like coin, by the ring,
> Ere names were found just the proper thing
> For a minor rich as a Mexican.

> Then the babe was cross'd and bless'd amain,
> But instead of the Kate, or Ann, or Jane,
> Which the humbler female endorses,
> Instead of one name, as some people prefix,
> Kilmansegg went at the tail of six,
> Like a carriage of state with its horses."

Absorption of maiden names by husbands is not yet accomplished in all civilised communities. In Borrow's charming work, " The Bible in Spain," we read, " Drenched in perspiration, which fell from my brows like rain, we arrived at the door of JUAN LOPEZ, the husband of MARIA DIAZ." These are the commonest of Spanish proper names. JUAN LOPEZ = JOHN LUPSON, and MARIA DIAZ (received paternally as to DIAZ) = MARY JAMIESON. Thus we have LE LUBEZ : the Lopez, there being so many like VON ROBERT : the Robert.

Husbands and wives have different names in the Azores. The following are some of the best known lady names :—

LINDE : either a serpent or a lime tree, *con.* LINDSAY : lime tree island, a woman moving gracefully like lime branches moved by wind, or a serpent, sinuously, fascinatingly. This became so high a favourite with Germans as to become syno-

nymous with maid, as LINTRUDE: maid of truth = FIDELIA,
EMMA : amen nurse, faithful to her charge.

ADELIND : noble maid, *con.* ATHELSTAN.

FREDELINDA : peaceful maid, *con.* FREDERICK.

ROSALIND : beautiful as to face, graceful as to form.

BELINDA (bel linda). beautiful maid.

ESMERALDA : beautiful as the emerald (Spanish lady), pairs
with MARGARET: a pearl, wave-born beauty = APHRODITE.

ZEENAB, ZENOBIA : father's ornament = CLEOPATRA.

ACHSAH : an anklet, beautiful as. EUCHARIS: happy-grace,
winsome, graceful, *con.* Eucharist.

EUPHEMIA : well spoken of, *con.* POLYPHEMUS (cylop): much
spoken of.

EULALIA : good speaker, who speaks charmingly = ZULEIKA.

POLYXENA : much given to hospitality. " If she have lodged
xenoi."

TRYPHENA, TRYPHOSA: over nourished, pampered, cockered
(carefully cooked for), delicately brought up = DELILAH,
COCKER, COCKERELL.

Some writers give TRYPHOSA from Phos : light, and so thrice
brilliant = TREBELLI : very beautiful.

LAODIKE : who obtains *justice* for the *people* by intercession,
whence Laodicea, now Latikia (cigars).

SOPHIA (Santa) : wise woman, gives VYE, *con.* Sophist : pretender to wisdom.

SOPHONISBA : of a wise life, *con.* Biology : science of life.

AGNES: a maid, she who has begotten no child, chaste =
JEZEBEL : without cohabitation. AGNES takes the odd form
of NEST. In the R. C. church, AGNES is given as from Agnus :
a lamb, and stands allegorically for the triumph of innocence,
as MARGARET for triumphing by faith.

KATHARINE, CATHERINE (giving the Irish pets KATE and
KATTY) : pure, stands for intellectual devotion, while

BARBARA : a stranger = XENO, stands for artistic devotion.
Of these four by far the most prolific in supplying names is

MARGARET, which some good writers give from *mer grit :*
grit of the sea, giving MARJORY, MARJORIBANKS (the banks
and braes of Marjory Bruce), MEG, MADGE (Wildfire), MAGGIE,
GOTON, MAY, MOGGY ; hence also Magpie for Margaretspie, the
German pet name GRETCHEN, and PEGGY.

TALLMADGE : tall Margaret, son so called from mother being
born out of wedlock, gives TALMAGE = MOLLISON and MAR-
GERISON : son of Marjory.

AGNES = PARTHENIA, VIRGINIA, BETHULIA is identical with
AGNO (nymph who nursed Jupiter) : a virgin, having for
its *mas.* correspondent the builder of Amphipolis, AGNON,
VIRGINIUS, BETHUEL, PARTHENOS : men of pure life.

LUCRETIA : a spinster, for so say high authorities, but it seems better to make it a *fem.* of LUCRETIUS.

PENELOPE : a web. The former symbolises a maid, this a wife.

SINDONIA : a spinster, maker of fine linen, *con.* Sinde, the best linen coming from India = CLOTHO and Woman for wif man.

FILATRICE : a spinster, thread spinner, *con.* (rank and) file.

GISSELDA : golden Hilda, precious maid of that goddess.

HILDEGARVE : guarded of the Asir Hilda, *con.* MATILDA : Hilda's maid.

OLGAR (Russian princess) : holy, consecrated, *con.* HOSIUS, OSIANDER.

EMMA : a nurse, one cherishing, germane with AMON, AMEN, mamma, and is credited with EMMET, but that is more rationally derived from EMLY (eoch miles) : a horse soldier.

WALPURGIS (from Walburg, a fortified town) : guarded by modesty.

HIMMELINA : heavenly = CELESTINA : celestial (maid).

HIMMELTRUDA : heavenly truth = EVANGELINE.

ANGELINA : angel like = CHERUBINI : one of the cherubim.

SHAKAR-LAB (Hindoo) : sweet kisser, lit sugar lip = our SACCHARISSA, and *con.* ISSACHER : wages, sweetness. The wages of the labourer is the sweetness of his toil. " Leah said, God hath given me my *hire ;* and she called his name *Issacher.*" Our words Saccharine and Sugar are from this source. Pliny says—

" Saccharum Arabia fert, sed laudatius India,"

which in the grocer's language means : We can give a good article from Muscat, but this Calcutta sample is the best in the market.

CLARINDA, CLORINDA, CLARISSA, CLARA : clear skinned, hearts, blondes.

CLORINDA is a compound, in some cases, of Clarus : clear, and Lind : the lime, meaning fair and graceful. But CLARA has no connection with CLARENCE (duke of) that being from Clare, Suffolk, latinised Clarentia, while CLARIDGE means a rig, ridge, hill cleared of timber = CLARENDON (constitutions of).

ALICIA, ALICE : captivating = REBEKAH : a rope with a noose, a female lasso (which a lass might be), REBECCA, BECKY : fascinators cut short. These ladies may fairly be compared with MIRABEAU, BRAVO, BEAUREGARD, FORMOSUS, ARBA, HORACE : handsome aspectable men whom we like to look at.

EVANGEL : gospel preacher, from Euangello : to tell good news, gives

EVANGELINE : one who has believed = VIVIAN : revived,

regenerated Gospel : God's spell, charm, turning the cruel to be kind.

DAM, DAME : mother.   Former now limited to animals, latter to aged persons.

MADAM : my mother, being the correlative to MONSIEUR : my sire, father.

MADEMOISELLE, DAMSEL : miss, little lady = the German.

FRAU : a free woman, as Jungfrau : mountain where the young woman perished.

FRAULEIN = VIRGINIA, PARTHENIA, *con.* FREISCHUTZ : free shooter.

ROSABELLA : beautiful as a rose, an artificial name, if not an artificial flower.

ROSAN : Annie, like a rose = FLORA, BLOOMER, THALIA : all flourishing with youth and beauty, suggesting

MIRAFORA (countess) : sweet as a *thousand flowers* (mille flora).

ROSAMUND (neither *rose* of the *world* nor *pure rose) :* defended by Rhoss.

ORABELL, ARABELLA (not beautiful altar, but from Oro : I pray) : prayerful woman = the *mas.* names BEDE, GOTOBED, EUSEBIUS.

ANNABELLA : beautiful Annie, often taken from Hannibal, but no European, to say nothing of Christian, would name a child after an African idolater.

CHLOE : green herb, flourishingly juvenile, *con.* the imperial CHLOROS (Constantine), of which it is a kind of *fem.* (when Cambrian).

CORDELIA : Jewel of the sea, *con.* LEAR (king) : sea king, and LLOYD : extended, invading, as waves do the shore.

EVE (British) is from Aoiffe, daughter of Lear, whence EVELYN, from which DEVLIN : of ancient British royal stock, whence also Evesham : Aoiffe's house, as likewise EFFIE (Deans). DEVLIN is identical with Dublin by chance coincidence.

NANNY, NANCY, are from the Asir Baldur's wife.

NANNA : daring, usually given as from ANN, HANNAH.

ZIBIAH, TABITHA, DORCAS, ORPAH, ORPHAH (Ur : fire) : all Houris : had eyes like does, deers, gazelles, and moved gracefully. "In the seventh year of Jehu, Jehoash began to reign ; and forty years reigned he in Jerusalem, and his mother's name was *Zibiah* of Beersheba."

JAEL (Heber's wife) : a kid, a tender one, soft eyed.   Similar SYREN : (she who) draws, answers to the foregoing, *con.* Syringe : water drawer, Syrtes : quick (moving) sands drawing in ships.

AMANDA : one loved, amiable woman, like AMY.

EDGIVA : happy gift, *con.* Allodial, and = SAMUEL, and such.

ELGIVA : elf given, fairy like, *con.* ALFRED, ELFRIDA.

GODIVA (Coventry) : God given = DEODANDA, DOROTHY.

ANONYMA : woman without a name, a beauty without breeding.

INCOGNITA : unknown (to society), unintroduced.

PERDITA is now used in the sense of a lost woman, a charmer waltzing to *perdition*, though used by Shakespeare in another sense. The last three are rather epithets of soiled doves than names of women.

ECLECTA : chosen one (2 John 1) = NIMSHI. Some maintain that this is a name.

KURIA, CYRIA (a good *fem.* to Cyrus) : lady = MARTHA, who is the only woman that had the honour of her name being recorded in the Bible in a double form. " Martha ! Martha !! thou," etc. " The presbyter unto the *elect lady.*"

DAME : lady, DAMIAN (St. John) : son of our Lady = NOSTRO-DAMUS.

STRATONICE (wife of Antigonus) : victory of the army, born at time of triumph.

EUODIA : good journey, given by a father returning from a perilous journey when a baby daughter was presented to him.

EUNICE : good victory, *con.* NICANOR = VICTOR.

LOIS : agreeable (to look at) = RUTH, when Hebrew.

PARTHENIA : a virgin = AYESHA, AGNES, CORA, Corinna (who competed with Pindar) : *con.* Parthenon : temple of Minerva the maid.

MIRANDA : admirable woman = MIRA (star), *con.* mirror, mirage,—

> " Admired *Miranda !*
> Indeed, the top of admiration ; worth
> What's dearest to the world ! Full many a lady
> I have eyed with best regard ; and many a time
> The harmony of their tongues hath unto bondage
> Brought my too diligent ear : for several virtues
> Have I like several women : never any
> With so full soul, but some defect in her
> Did quarrel with the noblest grace she owed,
> And put it to the full. But you, O you,
> So perfect, and so peerless, are created
> Of every creaturess, best."

We may compare the designation of the Kenite JAEL : a kid, to the Spanish CABRERA : a goat. " Divine service was performed by a former Catholic priest named *Cabrera.*" Of course, *con.* Capri : goat island, Caprice : action without reason.

AHOLIBAMAH : tent on the high place, who dwells on high, not poor. " Esau took wives. . . . *Aholibamah,* the daughter of Anah." ANAH : spring discoverer, its root being En : a well, *con.* Een : eyes, circular wells are like eyes.

RIZPAH : a live coal, glowing with love, seraphic.

ZILPAH: drop of myrrh, pleasing as aroma does—MORDECAI: bruised myrrh.

PENINNAH : coral, pearl, glittering with beauty, the Biblical MARGARET.

ZERUAH : stricken (with leprosy). " Jeroboam, whose mother's name was *Zeruah*, a widow woman."

ZERUIAH : stricken of Jehovah. " Now Joab, the son of *Zeruiah*, perceived that the king's heart was towards Solomon." As her husband is not alluded to though she is often referred to, it is supposed he was, what rustics term, no better than he ought to have been. " The grey mare," etc.

NOADIAH : meeting with the Lord, one receiving revelations. " He said unto Balak, Stand here by the burnt offering, while I meet the Lord yonder." " My God, think on the prophetess *Noadiah.*"

ZERESH : a star, splendid with beauty = STELLA. " When Haman came home, he sent and called for his friends, and *Zeresh* his wife."

SHETHAR-BOZNAI : star of splendour = the Italian beauty.

ASTRIFIAMMANTE : flaming star, cometic in splendour.

ZETHAR (one of seven eunuchs of Vashti) : a star, identical with SHETHAR.

ESTHER : a star, aster. Stars being all the rage in the court of Ahasuerus, she took this Persian name in the place of HADASSAH (Hebrew) : a myrtle, conveying the same idea as MORDECAI.

ASTARTE : star goddess of the Syrians = VENUS when morning star.

VASHTI : beautiful = PULCHERIA. " To bring *Vashti*, the queen, before the king, with the crown royal, to show the people and princes her beauty, for she was fair to look upon."

PULCHERIA : fair skinned, from Pellis : the skin. Skin is identical with Schon : beautiful (by brilliancy) and shine. Beauty is either from the healthy shining of the skin or from shape, as

FORMOSA : beautifully formed, like the Medicean Venus.

VENUS : she who causes men to *come* (Venio : I come) = SYREN. CUPID : he who causes *desire*, con. cupidity : covetousness.

KEZIAH : pleasant as the odour of *cassia*.

KETURAH : pleasing like incense. A class of Eastern names suggested by the fact that fragrance, odour, aroma are proportionate to warmth of climate. The violet of Scotland is less highly scented than that of England, and the English violet less odorous than that of France.

GRACE (Darling) : she who has found favour = HANNAH.

PATROCINIO (Sor): who has obtained grace through her *patron* saint

SOR, SURR: sister. Sororcide: sister killer. Its correlative is FRA (Paoli) = FRIAR (Tuck), FREE (mason), FRATER: brother.

DOLORES: sacred to the *dolours* of the B.V.M.

AIMEE, AMY: amiable, beloved = LOVE, DEARLOVE. One of the wild women of Cambridge was *Amy Stockings*. STOCKINGS: a stocking weaver, root *stick, stitch*.

PRAXIDICE: doing justice, con. PRAXITELES: finishing perfectly, con. *practice, telos*. The acquired name of the king of. Greek sculptors.

DORA: a gift, a baby girl born when issue was much desired, sometimes used in sense of gifted, con. POLYDOR (Virgil): much gifted, like POLYHISTOR: very learned.

PANDORA: all gifts, the mythic name for "gifted EVE." DORA oddly enough corrupts to—

DOLLY.
"*Dolly* Dobson, how do you do?
Nicely, thank you, how are you?"

FULVIA: brown haired, auburn tressed, another shade of FLAVIA, Roman ladies.

PHENISSA (Dido): (Syro) Phœnician woman. That land was so called from Phoinix: a palm tree, whence the mythic bird which, growing old, took a brand from the altar and lighting its pyre, composed of aromatic plants, was burnt to ashes, when a young *phœnix* arose from its ashes, to live, like its mother, for a hundred years, when it would pass through the same process of acquiring immortality by centuries. This ideal bird is elegantly used as a sign for fire insurance associations, which guarantee that your house being burnt a new one shall arise from its char. The myth originated in young palms growing round the decaying stock of the parent plant, bird and plant having an identical or similar name, Phoinix or Phœnix.

VIOLET: little sweet (flower). Violin: sweet (music), VIOLET = the fashionable IOANTHE: violet flower.

MIGNONNETTE: little little (dear), con. Minion: a favourite, a pet, little one, one who *minis*ters to another's pleasure, identical with NINIAN (St.).

SYBEL, SYBELLA (Theosboule: giving divine counsel = THEOBULUS, of which SYBELLA is a fair *fem*.

MEDINA: lady medium, who goes in for the golden mean.

UNA: one, truth, as truth makes unity = TRUMAN, but better yet AMEENA: an amen man. The BOU in the case of the Tunisian Kroumir BOU AMEENA is a form of BEY for BASHAW, for PASHA: king's foot.

DUESSA: double-minded, contrasts with UNA.

ELISSA : deficiency, unhospitable, *con.* Ellipsis : a want, a contrast to POLYXENA.

FLORIMEL : honey flower, sweet as both = MIRAFORA. Here we have fancy names originated by Spenser and found in his " Fairy Queen." When UNA is pure Irish, it has the sad meaning of born in *famine.*

NORAH (the pride of Kildare) : of honourable birth = HONOR, HONORA.

DULCINEA : sweet one, *con.* Dulcimer : sweet (music).

DULCIBELLA : sweet and fair, good-tempered belle.

FILOMENA (filia) : daughter of the moon, fair as, child of light =

SELENA, *con.* Selenite : sparry gypsum.

PHILOMELA : love of song, applied to the nightingale. Sometimes a name is elaborated from a letter, as—

PEGGY from MARGARET (g), NINA from ANN (n), DICK from RICHARD, (d), ULICK : little WILLIAM (l), the *ick* from *ig,* from *egan* from Eoghan : young, son.

AZUBAH (queen) : forsaken, what would be called in Glasgow a *grass* widow, an expression taken from the Church granting divorces by *grace,* the husband yet living.

HEPHZIBAH (queen) : my delight is in her, EPSY.

NITOCRIS : Neith the victorious, Wisdom victrix. The Babylonian queen was named from the same goddess as Joseph's wife.

Schole : dilettante idleness, gives School : place of idlers, for so scholars were thought by muscular labourers.

SCHOLASTICUS : an idle, stupid fellow, Scholastica (nun's name) : a humble unconceited woman.

CHAPTER VII.

LOCAL NAMES.

" In *ford*, in *ham*, in *ley* and *ton*,
The most of English surnames run."

ENCHORIAL or local names are more frequent amongst the moderns and western people than amongst the ancients and, especially, the orientals. Names derived from places were rarely used by Greeks, less by Hebrews, least of all by Arabs. They are common in France, more so in Germany, most so in England. There is scarcely one city, town, village, or hamlet in all England, if built before A.D. 1200, which has not supplied proper names to several families. This simple method of naming individuals from localities was esteemed too prosaic to be fashionable with the polished Greek and the trope-loving oriental. Such appellations tell nothing of the man as sage, worshipper, or warrior; individuality is swallowed up in locality, personality in place, in a place common to noble and mean. When society was consolidating in Europe many personal names were derived from estates, which brought in the aristocratic or, at least, the laird element. Such names with an attachment as *De, Du, Van, Von,* or "*of that ilk,*" in the sense " of that same "—person or place—as Buchanan of that ilk : Buchanan of the place so-called, M'Leod of that ilk : M'Leod of the M'Leod clan, generally indicate names originating in landed property. Yet proper names of local origin were descriptive to a certain extent, and for a short time. In cases where they did not die with the first bearer, they merged into family names. Names, however simple as to origin, may be ennobled. HAMPDEN is inseparably associated with love of liberty, combined with a sacred regard for constitutional rights, and yet it means only a valley dwelling = HOVEDEN (chronicler) for HOWDEN. And TRESHAM (Nov. 5) simply means a gentleman having *three houses,* similar to the less known TOOBY (twa): two dwellings.

Local names may become lofty landmarks in a nation's history. The world will not forget Milton and Pitt any more than Homer and Pericles. The mention of Milton calls forth, as with the touch of a fairy wand, all known of the scholar, statesman, poet. Augustus does no more. Number men like street houses or cavalry horses, and some numbers rise to being symbolic equivalents for the most revered names recorded on the scroll of fame. On the other hand, let each of us bear an appellation equal to the grandest known to the most powerful nations, nearly all will be consigned to oblivion directly their late wearers are consigned to the tomb. When imperial Rome, and its vast empire, was in its decadence, such titles as PANHYPERSEBASTE : above all named Augustus, and AUGUS-TULUS : most august, were flourishing. Such bombastic appellations suffer total eclipses when bracketed with Moses or Plato. Proper names are variable exponents whose value changes with the life of its owner. No grandiloquent title merging into a name can ennoble the native little. No impersonal or unpoetic cognomen dooms the naturally great to take a lower grade than their actions assign them. Cicero complained of being known only through himself, not ancestry. Possibly had he been known by pedigree he would have been known only thereby, in which case his ancestors would have been known rather than he, and the world would have been his orations the poorer. A Roman " Lord Dundreary " would hardly reach A.D. 1883. No dandy is immortal. Men joke about him for three generations.

In this chapter, indeed throughout my work, localities giving names to persons are rarely identified, as many, *e.g.*, Milton, Newton, Walton, Fordham, Brooks, etc., are common to scores of places. To determine from which of these a family took its name is the business of the biographer or genealogist, not of the etymologian. If the translation of a Post-Office Directory teaches anything, undeniably it teaches this— primitive Europe was an affair of woods and forests. Indeed, the observation is extensible to the world as we shall soon show. The coming catalogue of names connected with trees and their undergrowth does not contain one tithe of those arrangeable under that head. Howbeit, we are necessitated to lead off with water rather than wood for reasons that will forthwith be obvious.

We have a name BECK : a small stream, taking the diminutive of BECKETT : a smaller stream, ABORN : at the burn. This name Beckett had in the middle ages and some families, the prefix *At*, shortened to *a*, thus A'BECKETT (Thomas) meant Thomas living at the little brook. This *at* and *attan*, when plural, and *a* will be found to have attached themselves to trees and streams most parasitically, thus—ATTWOOD : living at the wood. And even ATTREE. This *at* preserved names : it was a philological mordant. Poor men during the Wars of the Roses had one name. Say John. He resided in respect to a village in his vicinity *at the wood*, whereupon villagers spoke of him as *John at the wood*, which by lingual shrinkage became JOHN ATWOOD. A similar process took place in France in relation to JEAN DUBOIS = JOHN WOODS. Thus we have AKASTER : at the camp. So ADDENBROOKS ('s hospital) : at the

brook = A'BECKETT. Adden for atten. NASH for Attanash.
BIAS, TASH: at the ash = DORMER (Stanhope): of the ash =
DASHWOOD—NATTRASS: at the ash, and the DESORMEAUX
(historian), and the odd sounding ASHBASH = ASHWOOD and
TASHWOOD. So NELMES for Attanelms: at the elms, as NAPPS:
at the aspen (poplar) tree, BURNAP: trees running by poplars.
That litigious fellow John NOAKES is John at the oaks, written
NOKES, as NOCK: at the oak = BIASK and ATTACK (Samuel):
con. Lilac: lilyoak. Similarly BYACK: dwelling by an oak.
So we have AMOR for at the moor = MUIR, MOOR. The Ger-
mans have SIEBENEICHER = the English SNOOKS: seven oaks.
The Hebrew Oren: an ash, gives the Latin Ornus: an ash,
whence the French Orme.

It is not always clear whether a name is from Orme: an ash,
or from Orm (worm): the serpent of Asiric mythology. Thus
ORMESTON: town of Ormes. ORM: tree or god. ARAUNAH:
a large ash, stout tall man = PINUS, whence PINELLI. ORNAN:
great ash. "Rear an altar unto the Lord in the threshing
floor of *Araunah* the Jebusite." "Lo, David gave *Ornan* for
the place 600 shekels of gold." Both names to one man who
was of lofty port = ROWAN, with which ORNAN is identical,
gives ROUNTREE and ROUNSIWELL: a spring among rowans.
ASHBY, ASBY: dwelling among ash trees. ASHBY - DE - LA -
ZOUCH: the Ashby family, living near the stock of a
notable tree = STOCK (Simon) and TRONCHET: a trunk, *con.*
Truncheon: great trunk. Fraxinus: the ash, gives through
form frene, FREVILLE = ASHTON. DUFRESNOY, DUFRAINE:
DEFRAINE: of the ash tree. A Mr. FIVEASH died 1859.
ASCHAM (Roger): ash tree home, suggesting OCCAM (Dr.),
YOCUM: oak home = the Polish DOMBROWSKY (general) VAN
NECK: of the oak, EEKHOUT: oak wood. ACKMAN = DRYAN-
DER. DELLE ROVERE (Julius II.): of the oak (robur). ASPLEN,
for Aspling: son of the asp tree, timorous, trembling like pop-
lar leaves. "Trembling like an asp" leaf. APPS: an ash.
NAPPS = NASH. ASPINWALL: ash field, with a fountain there-
in. APSLEY (Pellat): ash field. Eddaic mythology, teaching
that Adam was made out of an ash, that tree of renown be-
came a favourite apart from its use or beauty. Thus ÆSCIN-
GAS: sons of the ash, and ASHMAN: of ancient lineage = PRISCUS.
BUSHNELL (Horace): mansion in a wood = PYBUS, BOSOM.
CHATTERTON (Bristol boy): cottages in a wood = BOYCOT (ted).
BOSCAWEN (admiral): house surrounded by alders, suggesting
TRIM (corporal): elder. Elder: tree growing to a great age.
DAUNEY: an alder. But BOSTWICK, looking so like a home in
a wood: house near a creek. EDGEWOOD (Miss): living at
edge of Epping forest as gypsies yet do = EDGE and OUTHOUT:
having an outer edge of wood in a hut. EDGECOMBE: first

9

house in the valley, suggesting INDICOTT : last house in the village. ELLWOOD, ELLENWOOD : elm wood, sacred grove. Sacred among Saxons as they held Eve was made of elm. This gleams side-light on the Israelites worshipping in groves. Sometimes ELLWOOD is a contraction of ETHELWOOD for ETHEL-WALD : noble defender. In Switzerland EDGEWOOD is UNTER-WALDEN : under the forest = UNDERWOOD : under protection of a forest, from blast. WEDGEWOOD (Etruria) : frequented by widgeons. SCROPE is scrub, whence SCRUBY : dwelling among scrubs, shrup = SCROGGIE: scrubby. SCROGGS (Giles) = STUBBS, STOBO : living where the trees have been stubbed. BROGLIE : a thicket. So BAVEY: low copse wood, whence bavins, faggots were got = BUSEMBAUM (Jesuit) : tree among scrub, under-growth, nut tree = COPSEY : living in a copse = CUTBUSH. From Kopto : I cut, wood cut at intervals. These = the Milesian MONEY : scrub land, MONEYMORE: great heather and shrub land. DRINAN : a blackthorn. But CORK = MARSH, MARSTON. The city of Cork was built on marshy soil. CORK, MARSH = VENN : a fen man = FENNER (when it does not mean hunter) = FENIAN, FENIMORE (Cooper) : a fenman. HEENAN is synony-mous with MONEY and MARSH. QUAGENBOSH : a wood on a bog, *con.* Quagmire. WODTON, VODDAM, BESOM, BOSOM (bois ham) : town in a wood = Kirjath-Jearim : Carthage in a forest. WALTON for Wald-town = WALWORTH (mayor) and WALZ, VOLTZ = WOODS, WADRAPP : wood raven. WALLENSTEIN : wood covered hill. These = the Polish OSINSKI : city among trees = WOLSKI (waldski). Ski or sky : a town, gives MARIAN-SKI : town of the B.V.M = MARAVILLA (cocoa). JABLONOWSKY (prince) : town among hazel = CALTON, *con.* Dunkeld : hazel hill = Luz, *con.* Lusitania. DEMBINSKI : town among oaks = ACTON. BOGATSKY (divine) : city of God = Theopolis, and BALTIMORE : city of the great god. Bog the Sclavonic for God gives our nursery terror, BOGIE ; hence also the name of the river Bug, the Sclavic Euphrates. BOGOSLAV : the glory of God = THEOCLES, THECLA. BOGDAN : the gift of God = THEO-DORE.

But we must away from the Poles and back to the trees. COYLE, *con.* Gael and Caledonia (Kill in composition), FEW, WALTZ, WALTERS (in some cases), FRITH (" Frith and fell :" wood and hill) = GREENWOOD, WITT, WITTY, WIDDOWS, or WETTE (de), WHIT, WHITE (in some cases), WITH, also answer closely to GREENWOOD : a plantation. " Bind me with seven green *withs,*" hazel, or ash. WITHWRONG: a winding wood. BECKWITH: brook running through a wood = WEDDERBURN. The Scotch prettily render " He who is born to be drowned will never be hanged," by " The water will nae wrang the *widdie.*" The widdie was a with twisted into a halter

WIDMORE: a great wood = GUYYON, which gives THYNNE. WHIDDEN: wooded valley = WHITCOMBE, WHITESIDE: living side of wood. WEATHERHEAD: at woodhead = WOODHEAD. WEATHERBY: dwelling in a wood = WOODS, BODDAM, BUSKED, DUGUID, ITTEM, WHITTEM, HOLTUM, HOLSTED, (Mᶜ)QUIDDY. May not GALLOWAY be from Gallovia: great forest of the Gaels? DUST (Forest, Horst, Hurst, Hust): of the wood. Miss Deeks marries Mr. Dust against her father's advice. Being ill used she came to the old house at home at two o'clock A.M. with a thud at its door. Old Mr. Deeks protruded his head from bedroom window, and replying to entreaty for entry, said, " No, no. Go back to your husband. Dust thou art, and to Dust shalt thou return." Our word Basket is from the Britons who called it Basged, of which *ged = whid*, wood. KITT is not from Christopher, being prehistoric, and means wood-dweller = KELT. FOSKETT: dyke wood. APPLEQUEST is applewood, and APPLETON = JABLONSKY: town among apple trees. LEDWITH: a wood in which there is a laid, a wear, regulating water supply. Laid is obsolete, but gives Ladle: liquid regulator. LAIDLAW: a hill on which is a laid, reserve of water. Hence that grotesque looking name, SHAKELADY: shaggy, bushy ground where there is a laid. Hence the name LADE (Bulloch & Co.): one resident near a dam.

One of the reasons we have so many names from trees is that they were objects of worship on this island till A.D. 400. Perhaps this would account for such names as BOM = TREE. The odd looking FITTS = WOODS. CARURTHEN: camp wood = CASHOW (shaw). WHITHEROW: a vagrant who sleeps in woods and preys on farm yards. Sometimes simple woodland names assume absurd forms as COCKSWOLD: a wood frequented by cocks, becomes CUCKOLD. GUITEAU (Garfield), VIDOCQUE, GUY, TANGUYE: pine wood, GUIDO: wood dwellers *con.* BALGUY = WITHHAM WOOTON, GUION (line): great Guy. BALQUIDDER: town in a woodland district. Such = GROVES, FIDDIMAN, FIDDES = WOODMAN. WITTIKIN: baby found in a wood. TORFID: Thor's wood, where the Asir hero was worshipped, becomes TRUFIT. GROVES, the French correspondent of which is AUBUSSON: at the grove, may not be simply local, as sometimes it signifies grovekeeper to a god. Sometimes NIMMO (nemus) = GROVES. In Germany we have Luther's great battle ground Wittenberg: wooden fortress = TYRWHITT, originally like those made by the Britons of newly felled trees. There lived CRANACH (Lucas) exactly = the Irish CRANNAGE and CRANNATCH, each meaning son of a tree. These are aboriginal names, suggestive of the Stone Age, when men dwelt here on artificial islands, each known as a *cranage,* because built of wood on piles.

In England we have WITNEY : wood island. ASKWITH :
ash wood. WITHER (George, poet) : wood dweller. In the
Sanscrit Vid : know, Rigveda : ruling knowledge (*con.* Rego :
I direct), is the most ancient sacred book of India. This is
our *wit* and *wood ;* it entered the Greek in Ideo : I see,
whence Idea : seen mentally. Ideo entered the Latin with
the *v,* Video : I see. The other form of its meaning gave Ida,
whereon Paris judged Venus, Juno, and Minerva ; Ida simply
meaning woody (mountain), nearly = Sinai : bushy, covered
with undergrowth and WALLENSTEIN. Vid is probably the
root of Vetus : old and wise, aged as a tree, and learned as
those who studied in nature's oldest library—the pathless
woods. Connected herewith is Liber, the inner bark of a tree,
and Liber : a book, bark made = Boc : the beech from which
our Book was made, both word and thing, gives PHARNAM-
BUCY : a ferney field in which are beech trees. Wittanagemot :
witty men's meeting, oddly corresponds to Eisteddfod : the
wood setters, Welsh forest parliament. Wittan being next
derivative from Wid, Vid : wood. VEDDER = WOODMAN.
How strange a thing is life ! knowledge is still from the tree
though evil is inseparable therefrom. But the curse was taken
away by that other Tree, so that now man shall have the
knowledge without the evil. Fid, fod, vid, wood, ket in
basket are one, *con.* Fiddle : instrument made of wood. The
t in Scot is identical with *d* in wood, meaning wood dweller =
Greek names HYLAS, HYLŒUS, HYLLUS : son of the wood =
CRANNAGE, CRANACH. WITHCRAFT : a tree progagator, and
WITCRAFT : learned in timber. Gwyet, Guit, Quid, Guy,
Guion, Gyot, Guido, Vetus, Veda, Ida, Fid, Fod, Vid, Witt,
Hout, With, all have to do with wood. HEPWITH (hips) =
HEDGES. GWYDER : a druid, learned in Celtic, the letters of
which are taken from trees. Here we have the true idea of
DRUID : leader, head of the learned, from *dre wid.* Pliny was
the first to derive DRUID from Drus : an oak, probably misled
by the word HAMADRYAD : living with an oak, as long as.
Philological bellwetherism caused him to be followed until
scholars asked how would Celts name their learned from
Greeks ? Druid as nearly corresponds to our D.D. as the
difference of circumstances can be conceived to allow.

Wit : wood gives WIDNESS : wood island = WITNEY, and the
preposition With, as " You will go *with* me," united to. Also
Withers : that part of a horse where shoulder and body unite,
suggesting WITHERS = WIDDOWS. Coyle : a wood, gives
QUILTY = WOODS, and KELLS when not from Cell of a saint.
KILLIGREW : eagle's wood, KILBURN : brook running by a
wood. Bois : a wood, gives BOISSON : great wood = Matto
Grosso : primeval forest of the Amazon = CHACEMORE, WIDMOR,

Guyon. Bushell (bois ville) = Wooton. Trenton : town
among trees. Bushel : a wooden measure in contrast with
Peck : a poke, a bag. Ambush, Ambuscade : lying wait in a
wood. Bosjesman : bush dweller = Bussman. Buoy : wooden
float. Boz, Baum, Tree, Boos, Bosh (Ten), Bushnell (Horace),
Beza, Dubois, Kells, Quilty, Busby, Boyle, Bysshe (Shelley),
De Witt = Van Houten, Withers, Widdows, Guy, Balguy,
Guido, Vidocque, are all of the woods. But Woods may be
as local as Atwood, or may be = Gwyder, Druid. If modern
the former, if ancient the latter, and greater. Bosdet, Bost,
Boscowen, Bosquet (general): a little wood. Grafton: grove
town. Bosquet is Bouquet : now flowers, formerly evergreens,
a buss, *con.* Boscobel : beautiful wood, *con.* Burbush (burg),
Burbage, Boswell, Beville (when not beau ville) = Bamber
(beamber) = Wooton, Pybus. Foulis, Foules : living where
the *foulys* do sing, as the German Vogelsang, though some
prefer it from Folium: a leaf, living among = Ramage, Raimes,
from Ramis : a branch, *con.* Ramolini (mother of Napoleon):
little branches. These lived near groves frequented by the
songsters of the wood. Sylph : a wood nymph = Silvanus,
which abbreviates to Silas. Silvis : a wood, gives Savage
(when not Irish), Sage, Savigny, Saville, all men of the
woods unless Sage, when from Sagus : wise, as in Le Sage :
the man of *sagacity.* Lignum : a wood, usually applied to
undergrowth, gives Ligny and De Ligny = Atwood. Free-
house is met with, meaning house near a notable tree = Baum:
a tree, whence *beam,* gives Bamfylde (Moore Carew) : tree
field = Woodley. Baumgarten : an orchard, Bombarson :
son of Baumgarten, Bumpstead : place of trees. Baumtree
and Attree are living names. Shaw (*con.* Shade); a little
wood. Crayshaw : wood frequented by crows. Fanshaw :
haunted by fawns, deer. Enshaw, Ensor, Hinshaw : by
herns, herons. Herne (the hunter) : heron taker, if not an
eagle. Harwood : hare wood. Scrimshaw (screen): shaw
sheltering a village, similar to Hinton (Jack): *behind* (a hill)
town.

Gladstone (W. E.) for Gladstein, from Gleed : the glider,
a hawk = Gliddon (geologist) and Falkenstein : a hill frequented by hawks, as Gladsmuir = Falkland : moor haunted
by kites, gleeds, hawks. Rubenstein (composer) : hill visited
by ravens, Arnsteen: by eagles. Falk (laws) = Hap: a hawk,
Hapsburg : hawk tower, frequented by. Forest is from Foris:
abroad, meaning outside of city, woods are *far* from busy
haunts,—

" In somer when the *shawes* be sheyne,
And leves be large and long,
Hit is fulle merry in feyre *foreste*
To hear the fouly's song."

Forest abbreviates to hurst, as LYNDHUST (lord) : lime tree
wood = LEIBNITZ and PONIATOWSKI (prince): dwelling in a
FOREST, HURST, generally applied to gamekeepers = RANGER.
BRADHURST = BRADSHAW, but not BRAIDWOOD, for *brad* applies
to that part of a stream which overflows, so becoming brad,
broad. BRADFORD : where folks fare, ford, the brad, BRADLEY.
BRADLAUGH (Charles): fields subject to flooding = NUGENT,
NOA, *con.* No : I swim, swampy, *con.* Noyades : drownings.
WALKINSHAW : wood through which a path runs. BROAD-
HURST nearly answers to BROCKLEHURST : wood by a brook.
BRADDON (Miss): hill, fort near a brad. DEWHURST : wood
frequented by deer = FANSHAW. RINGWOOD (New Forest):
king's wood. SOHO (shaw haugh): a wood in a valley.
LENNOX : elm growing district. HOLT, OLT : a wood, a hold,
place defensible = HOUT = WOODS, whence HOOD (when not a
cowl wearer), and VANHOUTEN : of the wood. HOLLINSHED :
living near head of holly grove, as AIKENHEAD : at head of
oak grove = PENCOIT : head of wood = WEATHERHEAD. AIKEN-
SIDE (Mark): side of oak grove = WHITSIDE, WHITESIDE,
WOODSIDE, and likewise SIDE, *per se :* hillsider. These range
with WALTON, BAMBERGER, and WOODSTOCK when BAMBERGER
is not forest hill (living on), or a forest shepherd. BUXTON
(Fowell): town among beaches = BUXTORF (lexicographer).
Similar in meaning is DELAFAYE, DUFAILLY, DUFOY (de fagus),
and DEBUKE, who cling to the beach. BROGLIE (general) : a
coppice = TALLIS : wood often cut. TALBOYS : wood cutter, as
TELFER : iron cutter, helmet cleaver, at full length it stands
TALLIAFERO, and *cor.* to TOLVIE.

Hope : a narrow vale formed by the bases of hills
almost meeting, leaving but a small level, gives HOPE
(John), whence " Band of Hope," not of hope. HAPGOOD,
HOPGOOD : fruitful valley = BUNCOMBE, GEHAZI : ghor of
vision, one we like to look at. HOPLEY (Susan) : field in a
hope. STANHOPE : stony dell = STANDEN. HOPPET (when
not from Hob for Robert) : little hope. LOTHROP : low lying
valley. HYSLOP, HASLOP, HISLOP : hazel-dell. DUNOYER : of
the nut tree. KIRKHOPE, KIRKUP : church on the hope =
HOBKIRK, and the Welch LANDELLS : temple or church in a
dell, *con.* SCANLAN : old church. TROLLHOPE : a hope wherein
is a hollow inside of a hill. When Trollop : slattern, from
trail ; one who trails her dress. TUDHOPE : fruitful valley =
HOPGOOD, CONEYHOPE : valley haunted by rabbits. WALLOP :
a hope with a well, spring in it = SPRINGDALE. WAUCHOPE : a
hope through which a wall, dyke, vallum, is carried, becomes
WALKUP, WACCUP. HOPETON, HOPETOWN = DALTON. HASLAM :
hazel home = EASTERHAZY (prince), originally Estord Derhazy :
eastern hazel home = the Spanish AVELANNO, the French

COWDRAY and our HAZLEWOOD = Luz. HASWELL: spring among hazel bushes. HAZLITT: hazel lot. HASLAM: home among hazel trees. From Ail: strong, Allon: an oak, strong wood, giving ALLONVILLE = ACWORTH. Worth is a defended place. HOLDSWORTH: a fortified place in a wood, from Wear, whence Ware, Ward. From Quercus: an oak, literally a fine tree, we have Chene: an oak. Oak is from Eke: to grow, to increase, so that it means a tree that grows (as to age) above others. DUCHESNE (actress), DUQUESNE (admiral): of the oak = VANNEQUE, and DELLA ROVERE (pope), *con.* ECK, ECKIUS: son of oak (or of Eck) = DARRACH. Glans meaning either fruit of tree (acorn, oakcorn), or the tree itself, gives GLANVILLE: town among oaks = GLENFIELD (starch): oak field. Glean: to gather corn, meant gathering acorns. Gland: an organ shaped like an acorn. GLANDERS: a corn gatherer for cattle. GLENFIELD = OAKLEY, but HOCKLEY: high field = AIRD, *con.* Airt: quarter whence wind blows. HOLYOAK (George Jacob): an oak growing in a monastery, the same as *Hollyhock.* ACH = OGG: an oak, HOGBEN: oak hill, OGBURN: brook running among oaks. HOLMS (M.P.): from holm oak, a formation on holy. In some cases HOLM: a river island, *con.* CHISHOLM: gravel river island. BRADDOCK (general): broad oak, or one growing near a brad. DIMMOCK: little oak. AITKEN, AIKEN: robust, oaken, strong. EICHORN (German savan): oak hill. AKROYD: oak ridden, oaks stubbed up, gives DACROY: son of Akroyd. SHORROCKS (captain): shorn of oaks, exactly = RADAX: rid of oaks. SOUTHACK: south oak, NOCK: at oak = ATTACK, but KNOCK, KNOX = HILLS, TELL (William), KNELL. SNOOKS: seven oaks, KENT, becomes SENEX = SIEBENEICHER. CHENEVIX (French), *cor.* to CHENNECKS (chene vicus) = ACTON: oak town. CHENEY (bishop), CHINIQUY (Father). DARA, ADAIR (when not from Alasdair, Alexander): an oak. Kildare: oak grove. SARON (king), SHARON (Turner), SARONY: an oak. DARROCH, DARRACH: son of an oak = SARONIDAS: a dryad = ACKMAN, DRYANDER. DE LOLME (historian): of the holm oak. CASSAGNAC: place of oaks. TRELAWNEY: oak grove town. HIGGINS, HIGGINBOTTOM: a dale where the mountain ash grows. SHOEBOTTOM (Shaw): a wood in a dale. AUCKLAND: oak land.

Dumas (novelist): of the mast, beech. DUFAILLY (general), DUFOY: of the beech. LAYFAYETTE: little beech. Fagus: the beech, from Phago: eat = Mast *con.* masticate. BEECHY (captain), for beechley: beech field. BACON: one feeding pigs on beech mast. But BEACH (Hicks) from the bee. TREFFRY (Eternal Sonship): three beeches. QUARTERFAGES (naturalist):

four beeches. CINQUALBRE: five peach trees. BEECHENHAUGH, BICHENO: haugh of beech trees, con. SOHO (shaw haugh). Haugh gives HAWES (when not from Hal, Harry)=DENMAN: valley dweller. DEGUIGNES: of the vines=VIGNOLES, con. Vignette: a little vine, a frontispiece of vine leaves. DUNOIS ("Partant pour la Syrie"): of the nut tree, gives NOISE. CORYLUS (shepherd): a filbert tree. FIGARO: a fig tree= OLYNTHUS (Gregory). DUPIN: of the pine=VON DER TANN, TANGYE=FICHTE. PINELLI, SPINOLI (Spanish general), SPINOZA (pantheist Jew), con. Spina: a thorn, and signifies dwellers in a spinny, answering to such names as STOBO, SCROGGIE, BADE-NOCH: overgrown with bushes. To these add TURNHAM (for Thorn home): dwelling among bushes=DORNER, suggesting Thorney, Cambs. But we have such living names as THORNES and SPINNER. CURZON: a vine stem, vine dresser.

LINNÆUS (Swede): a lime tree, so called from Lind: a serpent, because it waves like it. LINDSAY: lime tree island. TILLY (when not a weaver from Tela: a web): a lime. TILLOT (archbishop): little Tilly, or a growing lime. TILROYD: cleared of limes. "This unfortunate man was named Morgan *Tilroyd,* and was by trade a jeweller." LAURA (Bridgman): a bay, a laurel=DAPHNE, takes the *dim.* LORETTO (Our Lady of): little laurel grove. MORE (sometimes): a mulberry tree, a dark fruit *con.* Amaurosis: dimness, darkness of the eyes, *con.* Mauritania: the Morian's land=Soudan, Karamania, Nigritia. MOROSINI (amoroso): dim sighted=CECIL. TAMAR: a palm, literally straight, applied to a majestic woman, gives Tamarind—*ind* for India, as in Indigo: plant from India. "One daughter whose name was *Tamar.*" ITHAMAR (son of Aaron): land of the palm, born among palms. VERNET (Horace): an alder=DAUNEY.

WILLOUGHBY: dwelling place among willows=SALIGNAC (salix, sauch) and De SAULCY, *con.* AULAY: tall as a willow, Sauchiehall: house in an osiery. These *con.* SALES (Francis de: though some give his name as a form of *cells,* cloisters), SAYLE (governor), SARSFIELD (Aughrim), SAUMAREZ, SOULT (marshal), when not from Solvo: I loose, and so=FREEMAN: freed: all dwellers among the osiers. Osier: water plant, *con.* Ooze and Ouse. Willow gives Wily: river with willows on banks, whence Wilton, which gives Wiltshire, wherefrom WILSHER (cricketer). WYCHERLEY (William): witch elm, used by witches in their incantations. BIRCH (favourite Celtic tree, giving *b* of their savage alphabet): may not mean simply a tree, but a man of ancient stock. BIRCHENHAUGH: birch dale, gives BRISCO. AUBE: white wood. VANLOO: of the wood, sometimes = VANDERVELD (painter): of the field. DOUGHERTY, DOCHARTY: high dwelling among oaks=VANNEQUE.

We must cease planting and commence hewing. As European emigrants clear Minnesota and Manitoba, so were our primeval woods cleared by continental emigrants passing the Channel in coracles, or later invaders of the aborigines. Field is simply felled, so Fold, FAULD(s): *an enclosure.* When the Saxon felled trees he enclosed his land therewith. FIELD = RODEN: land ridden of timber = THWAITES, for so Norsemen called their clearings. LITTLETHWAITE: small clearing, gives LILYWHITE (batter). APPLETHWAITE: clearing planted with apples, giving HEBBLEWHITE. MICKLETHWAITE: great clearing. HOLROYD: cleared of holt, wood = GRUBB: trees grubbed up = STUBBS, wrongously fathered on Stephen. OLCOTT (colonel): cot in a holt. BLUMENRODEN: blooming field, flowery mead = BLOOMFIELD ("farmer's boy"). RODNEY: field through which a brook runs = BURNLEY. PENROD (ben rid): hill cleared of timber. NESSELRODE (diplomatist): cleared of nettles = THISTLETHWAITE, or SWAITE = DUCARDONNET: of the thistle field and CHARDON. JOELAH: removing of oaks, a man so strong he can remove oaks. "*Joelah* and ZEBADIAH, the sons of Jehoram." So the French Purlieu: purus locus. "In Henry III.'s time, the Charter de Foresta was established: so that there was much land disafforested, which has been called *purlieus* ever since." PURLIEU = CLARENDON: a hill cleared = CLARIDGE, PENROD. COLERIDGE (Samuel): cold hill = BALFOUR: cold town, exposed to winds = COLDHAM, COLLOP: cold hope. But Winthrop, that one might be excused for supposing it means windy dwelling, and so = TREWENT: windy dwelling, *con.* PENNYGANT: windy hill (Throp, a transposition of Thorp, Dorf, as APTHORP: the abbot's dwelling): winsome, beautiful dwelling = Sheen, Nain, etc., Balfour pairs with FORDYCE: cold south, one dwelling where there is southern aspect, yet cold. PURLIEU, the *op.* of RONGE (holy coat), RANKE (historian), RANCE: rank with timber. LUMM: a clump of trees. LUMSDEN (provost): a valley in which trees are in clumps, groups, nearly = WALDEN: woody valley. PARLEY (Peter): Peter's field = Peterloo, suburb of Manchester half a century since, like VANLOO, Waterloo. WOODLEY = BOUSFIELD (bois). HATFIELD: heathfield — HEDDERWICK. dwelling among heather = HATHERLEY = GARFIELD (president): gorse, furze, fern field, *con.* FARNWORTH = BRACKENBURY. CLAVERHOUSE (Dundee): clover field house = FETCHAM: home among fitches. Clover, from Cleave: to divide. Clover = Fraise: strawberry, from frango, fraga, frasa. FRASER: strawberry planter. CRESSINGHAM (betrayer): home in a cressfield. But GRESHAM (merchant prince): gross home = MEIKLEHAM: big house = CASABONI, CASAUBON: bonny house = BRIAN (O), whence

CHATEAUBRIAND : palatial castle. BRYANT (Amer. poet) and
BARNEY (thought to be from Barnabas) are therefrom ; BRAD-
BURY and INGERSOLL (*con.* Entresol: entry of hall, saloon)
also applied to palatial residences, dwellers therein. As also
HOUSE : the chief house, which assumes the form ACE, AUDUS :
old house. TETLEY : fruitful field, *con.* TUDHOPE, and *op.* of
BARLEY: bare, barren field. FELTON : town in a field. FULTON:
foul town, dirty roads = Foulmire (Cambs.), and *op.* CLINTON:
clean town. FELTON = TOWNLEY, LEIGHTON, KEMPTON and
BURLEIGH, from bury, though this last may mean a judge,
from Byrlaw : laws made by neighbours (near boors), whence
Bylaws : local regulations.

To these English may be added the French *red*, FONVEILLE
(Ulric), *con.* Foin, Fon, Fœnum : fodder hay, whence Fen-
nel, supposed favourite food of serpents. MEAD = LEE,
LEITH. CLUNY, CLUNIE, *con.* CLONES = MEADOWS. PENNY-
CUIK : cuckoo's hill. CARLYLE (Thomas): man of Carlisle :
camp (Roman) beside the trench. WITHERSPOON : grazing
place on spur of a mountain. CHAMPOLLION (Egyptologist):
field of a man named POLLION : great Paul. CHANTRAINE (*con.*
Ranunculus : little flower flourishing on wet soil where frogs
delight to dwell): living where the *chant* of *frogs* is heard. I
have been in such a place and am slow to forget it. This suggests CANTELOUP (lord): living where the howling of wolves
can be heard. DANGER : of Angers, France. FAULDS : land
enfolded. SANDYFAULDS : gravel fields. ENCLOS (Madam de):
enclosed = CLOSE, *con.* Cloisters : college enclosures. Strangely
indeed this = the Roman Cohort from Cohors : a fold enclosing
sheep. Men were put together for war like sheep in hurdles.
This throws a gleam of light on Shepherd Kings : Xerxes
numbered his soldiers by the cohort arrangement, placing them
by turns in an enclosure as did Cetewayo his Zulu warriors.
Stranger, Cohort is our word COURT (when not meaning short):
a castle, a place enclosed and defended as in HARCOURT (Sir
William) : castle of Hariald in Normandy. COURT = WORTH
(man milliner) : a place wared, warded, defended = GUISE : a
fortified position, originally with felled trees. These suggest
PALLAVICINI: living in the vicinity of *pales,* palings, enclosures,
as in the English Pale in Ireland. So also STACK : living in a
stocado, place staked = STOCKWELL (ville), STOCKS, STOKES,
STOCKER, STOKE, STOWELL (Hugh) for Stowville, abbreviates
to STEELE (Richard). BOSTOCK (bois) = Walthamstow (wald
ham stow). STOWE (David) : a place *staked* out. COMSTOCK :
dwelling in a valley. Steak (beef) : carried on a stick. COPE-
STAKES : staked out for cheap, cope, market. Though COPPER-
FIELD (David) : field where coppice, scrub, is regularly cut =
COPSEY. COPPERTHORN = CUTBUSH and COWPERTHWAITE. Such

project our thoughts to an age when England was a place of shanties, settlements, and log huts, as the name SETTLE = SEIDLITZ (powder): where an emigrant settles; so also SIEGEL, SIGEL clearly show. BARTON : strong place to receive the produce of the land, what it did *bear*. Barton Worth, Ton, Town, Fold, Fauld, Burg, Stowe, Close, and Cot, all mean enclosures in some form. Invaders and emigrants first seized, then enclosed. Byre for cows may be added, as it is from Beorgan : to protect, whence Burgh, whence Burglary : breaking into a protected place. Enclosure underlies the idea of property whether landed or personal. BYARS and BOUVERIE (Kilmarnock) = COTTON : cow enclosure, a byre, owner of one. COEVELT (Flemish painter) : cow field = Clontarf. Argos (the mother of Greek civilisation) : a clearing, thwaite, ridden, sohl, settlement. From Ergon : a work, *con*. ARGO (ship), ARGUS (100 eyes), ARGE (huntress) : sharp, active, quick = PODARGUS : swift footed. *Con.* Argives : Greeks, organ, organon : works in music or literature. Energy : putting work in. Ego : I, the doer, worker. Ergo : therefore. Argentum : silver, made white by work. Argil : potter's white clay. GEORGE : earth worker, Georgics : science of working the earth. NEIGHBOUR : near boor, is doing good work as a surname and forms a fine contrast to MALVOISINE (bishop of Glasgow) : bad neighbour, best out of the *vicinity, con.* PALLAVICINI. We also meet with HOUSENEAR and NIGH. Ton : an enclosure is germane with Ten and Tun, the former allied to number of fingers closing, the latter encloses liquids. Hundred : hand reed, red, *con*. Ratio : reason, REID : a counsellor, it gives the reason on the hand. Ton is found in a vast number of local names, as SMEATON (engineer) : smith's town = GOVAN = ZINZENDORF (count) : tinsmith's dorf, thorp, town, SMEE : small = BASSETT, BASS. But MEE : a Meath man, (Mac) NAMEE : warrior of Meath. So (Mac) NULTY : an Ulster man. LARPENT : the arpent, place to be ploughed, *con.* Aro : I ear, plough.

From that ancient word La : low lying, we have Lateo : to lie hid, Latent : lying hid. Whence Latro : one who lies hid to rob, Ladrones : isle of thieves, Larceny : theftuous act, LATONA : concealed goddess, Lagos : a hare because it lies close to the ground, hidden, Latium : low lying country, gives Latins : lowlanders = Girgashites : dwellers on clay land. LATINUS : lowland king, and our LEE, LOO, LEA, LEIGH, LAUGH (LAUGHTON = FELTON), LEWES, LESLIE, LISBURN, LISMORE, LOGAN, (Mc) LAGAN, LOWTHER, LEITH, LOTHIAN, LOUDER, Low, and that American puzzle Lo, are all persons resident on depressed meadow land, or under shelter of hills = FOOTE, PEDEN, ORISPUS, PLATT, FLAT, POGGIO : living on the flat = CAMPOBASSO and the Hebrew MAACHAH : depressed, applicable literally to one living on low ground, figuratively to any one in low spirits, and to either sex; hence we find it in some cases a man's name, in others a woman's. In the literal force it corresponds to CAVAGNAC: dwelling in a hollow= CAVAN, HOLLAND: hollow land, and Hollow: hole low. VAN-LOO is the Dutch for MEADOWS (Kenny), and PRATT (Orson), *con.* prado, paradise, prairie. PEDEN (Scottish worthy): a clear plat, an open space=PADDOCK, which abbreviates to PARK. KONIGSFELDT: king's field=KINGSLEY (Charles). But RAWLEY, RALEIGH (Sir Walter): roe field, land frequented by roes. Roe: rough deer. ROEBUCK : rough buck. And DUR-LEY (looking so like deer field): dry field, the *op.* of SOFTLEY : bog land=the cacophonic BUGG, whence BUGBEE : bog dweller =MOSHEIM: home on the moss=MARSH. NOA (chess)= NUGENT : swampy ground, from No : I swim. BUGBEE is positively *cor.* to BUGBED.

BASILEWSKY: king's town. "A grand marriage is on the horison of the French aristocratic world, between M. le Comte de Galve, brother of the Duke d'Alba, and cousin to the Empress, and the charming Madame Bravura, daughter of *Mr. Basilewski,* who is famed in St. Peterburgh as being some twenty-five times over a millionaire." No name better illustrates the vanity and fastness of that time when Eugenie was queen of the fashions. BRAVURA: finely clad lady. "The Lord will take away their *bravery.*" Bravura applies to a brilliant style of singing, but as a secondary application of the word, which belongs to the eye—Bravo! Bravo!!: Fine ! Fine !! Now finery is to look upon. Rio Bravo : fine river. BRAVO : a handsome man, BRAVURA: a beautiful woman.

VANDERKEMP (African missions): of the field. KEMPEN-FELT : an open country, champaign. A'KEMPIS (Thomas) : at the field=ATMOR, *cor.* AMOR. CAMPION : a fighter in an open field.

" His sword was in his sheath, his fingers held the pen,
    When *Kempenfelt* went down, with twice four hundred men."

ASTLEY : east field. AUDLEY : old land, grass land lately ploughed. But ALLEN : a hound, then means swift, some-times applied to a stream, when to a man=PODARGUS, LIGHT-BODY, GALLETLY : its *fem.* is ELLEN. BERKLEY, BARCLAY (brought by Normans): birch field. BRIMLEY, BRINKLEY : fields on the *brim, brink* of the sea=COSTLEY : coast leigh= the great ORELLANA : meadow reaching from mountain top to river mouth, *con.* Oros : a mountain, and Llano for Loco plano: flat country. Nearly corresponding to the Gaelic URQUHART, URKET : margin, long coast, and the Gallic LARRIEUX,

LARRIVE : Ripuarians, bank dwellers = the Saxon RIVERS, CURRANT, and the Spanish RIBAS. These suggest SORBY (Sheffield): dwelling on the shore = SANDS, when local. WINDSOR : winding shore. MERTON (and Sandford) : town on a mere or sea = SEATON, BALMERINO. HARTLEY : deer field. HURLEY, HARLEY (when English) : hare field, but HARLEY (Mc)ARLY (Irish) : a form of Charley. LESLEY, LESLIE (leesley) : meadow land = LELAND (antiquary) = HOYLE, COWAN, CAVANAGH (Bernard), all = CAVAGNAC : living on cavernous land, *con.* CAVOUR : cave dweller. MEADOWS, MEAD = PRITTY, from Mow, mead, meadow : land that is mowed. Seen to advantage in "Barley*mow*." Mow gives the comparative more, and the superlative most, as though *mow, mower, moest.* LEE, LEITH, LOO, FOGG, FOGO, and PRATT, from Pratum : a meadow, whence Prado, fashionable promenade at Madrid—DUPRE : of the meadow = GREEN, from grow, MUSPRATT : meadow on a moor. DELAFIELD (brewery) : of the field = VANDERKEMP. BANCROFT (historian) : bean croft. CROFT : cultivated with *craft*, skill. TOFTS : small farmer. " Ne toft, ne croft have I."

CALCRAFT (carnifex): kale croft, some claim it as a trade name, meaning maker of *caltrops*, to prevent advance of cavalry. In former case CALCRAFT = WORTLEY : a cabbage garden. Wort gives Wurtzel. SOFTLEY : living on bogland = NOA, NASSAU, MARSH, MARSTON, MONEYPENNY : at head (pen) of bog where peats are cut. DENOVAN (dunavon): hill by side of stream, identical with the Irish DONOVAN (Rossa). GARVON (Garrough): rapid stream. DUNDEE : hill by the Tay, Dee. WYNN : white = FINN. WENTWORTH : white dwelling made of pealed willows = CASABIANCA, *con.* DECAZES : of the cottages, houses = VAN BUREN : of the boor's (houses). Casa : a house, CHEESE, Chasuble : dress covering wearer, as cottage does a dweller. Cot is identical with coat : a cover, hence COATES : dwelling at cottages. PETICOTE : little cottage = HUTT, PYCOT : cottager (by). Cotswold (hills): shepherds' huts on the wold = SHILLINGLAW, from Wald : a forest, as the wolds were wood covered = Ida. GARTH : an enclosure (small), *con.* girth, girdle, garter, garden, yard, the last being the length of the king's girdle. GARTSHORE : part of foreshore enclosed. GARSCADDEN : enclosures used as cow pastures. APPLEGARTH : an orchard = BAUMGARTEN : beam garden. HYDE : as much as a yoke of oxen could plough in one season, called so because hidden by hedge rows. MALHERB (poet) : bad pastures, *op.* BONPLAND (companion to Humboldt): good land = DE LA VEGA : of the flourishing land, *con.* vege-table, from Vigere : to flourish. These = LYNCH and SLADE,—

> " It had been better for William a'Trent
> To have been abed with sorrow,
> Than to be that day in the greenwood *slade*
> To meet with little John's arrow."

Though Lynch applies more accurately to meadow by a stream,
as the " Links of Forth." Compare William a'Trent with
Thomas a'Becket. Sorrow for soreness of body.

Many surnames are derived from those who originally bore
them dwelling on mounds, hills, or mountains, or living in or belonging to castles which were generally built upon such places.
These carry the mind back to a time of baronial grandeur,
when castles were too often centres of tyranny, but became
the nuclei of civilization, around which the villain reared his
thatched hut and the boor tilled his garth, while constitution-
alism was dawning in our cities. Illustrative of such facts we
have ALTAMONT, MONTALTO, MOWAT, MOET (and Chandon) :
high mountain, GRAMMONT, MONTMAGNY : great mountain =
MORVEN, MONTFORT (Simon de) : strong mountain, Tel-el-
Kebir = Monte fixo, whence MUSCHET. HOHENZOLLERN
(Prussia) : high toll hill, whence black mail was levied from
travellers. Similarly TOLAND (deist), a form of Tolan, Normandy : applied to land over which if men passed they
were tolled. MONTAGUE (mount acute) : sharp mountain =
Spitzbergen = EGREMONT, and strangely inverted in ARGUMENT,
a directory name,—

> " Confessing that he himself was a *Montacute*,
> And bare the arms that I dyd quarter on my scute."

MONCUR, MONCURE (curt) : truncated hill = RAFTOR. DUNLOP
(Colin) : hill at bend of stream = BARSKIMNING, SKIMMING =
REACH, ENGSTROM : living at bend of stream. DUNDAS :
fallow deer hill. WINSLOW : battle tumulus = BARROW, CAIRNS.
LAMONT : the fortress, a baron. MONTES (Lola) : living in a
fort, a castle = TERENCE (Latin and Irish) and TYRELL (Sir
Walter), which latter becomes TRAILL. CAREY : castle dweller,
but CARUS : loved, cherished. MONTEJO (Countess de) : little
mountain, small fortress. EUGENIE is also styled Countess de
Teba. TEBA from Tebanus : a hill. TEBA translates MONTEJO.
MONTANUS = MOUNTAIN = (Mc)BEAN, gives the following *dims.*
MONTUCCIO (Chinese dictionary), MUNDELLA (M.P.), MOTT.
DELAMOTTE : of the hill = EMMONS : home on a mount.
MONTREY : royal mountain = Montreal. DYMOND for dumont :
of the mountain = DE MONTI. Battle of the Diamond, 1795.
Diamond = Orontes : a mountain stream, *con.* ORESTES : a
mountaineer. DIAMOND is from the river, and is therefore
uncon. Diamond : a form of adamant : unconquerable (as to
hardness). HELMONT (chemist) : spiral mountain, *con.* Ilissus :
helix river. MONTFAUCON : mount or castle frequented by

hawks = HAPSBURG, HAP = HAWKE. So FALKENSTEIN = GLIDDON and GLADSTONE. MONCRIEFF: frequented by crows = Criffel: crow fell. MONTEITH: fortress on the Teith. MONTEFIORE (Sir Moses): flowery mountain = BLUMENSTEIN, and nearly answering to Oregon. MONTEAGLE (lord): hill haunted by eagles. EVREMOND: mountain frequented by bears. MONT-JOY, MOUNTJOY is simply a mound topped by a guide-post, or aught indicating the whereabouts to a French traveller. As the hill from which crusaders descried Jerusalem was a *mount-joy*, the word passed into an expression for a pilgrim who had succeeded in visiting the city of David. LANGRIDGE, LANG-HORNE, LONGOMONTANUS: long hill. TICKLEPENNY: living where a hill overhangs. SCORESBY: dwelling on a scar. We have the name SCORE: a hill, a scar = TALLACH, SCAREDEVIL: villa on a scar. MARMONT (marshal): martyr's mount. CHIARMONTE (pope): clear mount = Clermont, Monte Video and Belvidere: beautiful view. But BELVIDERE, an Italian beauty, similar to BEAUREGARD: fair to look upon.

From the Erse for old, viz., Sean, Scean, Shan, we have SHAND (lord), for SHANDON (dun) = OLDCASTLE, Shantie: old tumble down places. TAM O'SHANTER: Thom of the shanties, SHANIGAN (eoghan): old man's son = BENJAMIN, SCANLAN, HANLON (oarsman), HANLAN: old church, *con.* Llanbryd: St. Bride's Church. Some Irish authorities make HANLAN: a champion. SANQUHAR: old fortress = SHAND. SANKEY (and Moody): a chronicler, he who records old tunes = VIEUXTEMPS (violinist). SEACHLAN (St.): little old man. CARRICK, CRAIG = FELL: a rock. CRACKSTONE (looking like craggy hill, is very ancient): splitter of rock helmet. Carrigheen (moss): little rock. MELROSE: projecting hill. CULROSS: back of a hill, rear of a wood = HINTON (Jack): town *behind* a hill.

ROSLIN: projecting point in a pool. VANDERBILT (*con.* bill of a bird): living on a spit of land = SPITE, *con.* Spithead. These differ little from (Mc) NEE, NESS, (Mc) NISH, NEST: living on a promontory, a peninsula, or an island near main-land, *con,* Nesos: an island, whence also the odd name NAST. NEASHAM: home on an island. GARIOCH: the rough district = BADENOCH and Trachonites, Thrace. Garry, Garone: rough river, from Car: angular, whence Carron: very crooked, and therefore rough. These *con.* Yare, Yarmouth, YAIR = GARRY, giving YARRELL (naturalist). Yare also applies to a stream dammed in various parts so as to catch fish. WEMYSS: a troglodite, cave dweller = CAVOUR (count), LAVOTTE: the vault = CAVE. WEMYSS becomes HUME, which becomes HOME, Ham, whence HAMLET (Danish king). Our home was once, though not originally, a cave. These ancient names, out-reaching the chronicles of our country = HOR, HUR of the

Hebrews. "The Horites in their mount Seir." Seir: rough with bushes, like Sin (wilderness of) and Sinai. The Horites in Seir would be living like WEMYSS and HUME in Badenoch and Garioch. CARVOSSO: a castle. TORIJOS (marshal), TORRICELLI (barometer), CASTRIOTTO (George) = TYRELL: little castle, turret = TURRETIN, TYRWHITT: wood castle. CAREW (castra eau): castle on water. TURRACREMATA (cardinal), TORQUEMADA (inquisitor): burnt castle, incremated towers. Quemadero: the place for burning heretics, Madrid. CASTELAR (orator): a native of Castile. RATICAN: head of the rath. RAT: a castle dweller. RAFFLIN: red rath. CASTLEREAGH (rath): king's castle. New Castile, Neufchatel = Newcastle. Old Castile, Torres Vedras = OLDCASTLE. TOWERS = TERENCE: castle king, a baron. ROCHE (*con.* rock): a manor house, place approaching in strength to a baronial hall. ROCHEFORT (Lanterne): fortified manor house = MAINWARING, DUROC, DE LA ROCHE: of the manor = DUROCQUE. LEMAS, DUMESNIL: manse dwellers, *con.* Maison: a house, messuage. HOLDER: living in a stronghold. STERNHOLD: stonecastle. HOLDEN (holt): wooded valley = COMSTOCK gives BOLDEN (ap): son of Holden. WILBERFORCE (emancipator): Wilburg's foss, the trench of Williamstown. LOYOLA (Ignatius) and XAVIER are named from Spanish castles. XAVIER is Moorish for glorious = CLEON. TRENCH (Chenevix): living near an entrenchment = DYKES, the Dutch VANDYKE: of the dyke, vallum, wall, and DIECKMANN. DIGBY: dyke dwelling. THIRLWALL (*con.* drill, thrill): where the Roman wall was broken through. WALLSEND: where the wall of Adrian ended. BRAND (when local): a steep brae. BANKS = HILLS, "Ye banks and braes o' bonnie Doon." But BANKIER: a banker, one exchanging at a bench = DUCANGE: of change. Bankrupt: ruptured bench. BRANTON: town on a steep = VAN BRUNT. BRUNTON: Brown's town. FINDLATER (temptingly, like *Fin:* the end, *de:* of, *la:* the, *ter:* land = Finnisterre): the white slope, *con.* FINELLA: fair Irish lady, CORSTORPHINE: fair Christopher. BLAIR: cleared of timber, plain in a hollow = RODEN, FIELD, THWAITES. VASS (when local): a valley. Consult VASA. VAUX: valleys, dalesmen. DUNS (Scotus), PENN (Pennsylvania): Penn's wood, (Mc)BEAN, COLLIS, TORR, TELL, KNEE, KNOCK, KNAGGS, KNOWLES (knolls), KNOLLYS, FELL, FALL, TULLOCH, TALLOW, RAGG, TULLY, TEBA, MONTEJO, ORESTES, MONTERO (*con.* Montana), MOTT, PECK, PEAK, AIRDE, LAW, DUNN, BARR, HOWE, TOE, TAWSE (bailie), RIGG, RUDGE (Barnaby), STEIN, STEINITZ (chess), HOCHE (general), HOOK (Theodore), HOORN, HORN (gives Cape): hill dwellers, or named in connection with heights, BIGELOW (papers), = Benmore. WINSLOW (syrup): furze hill. Tor: a hill, *con.* Taurini: hill dwellers, whence Turin: city on a hill.

Taurini = Helvetii : hillsmen, whence HELVETIUS : a Swiss. SNIVELDY : snow hill. DUNBAR : fort on a hill = HARDCASTLE. SIDDONS (Mrs.) : south hill = SIDLAW. UTTERIDGE (atridge) : living at the hill. MONTMORENCY (*con.* Sierra Morenos) : dweller on the brown (ling) hill, *cor.* to MUMMERY. DUNCAN : hillhead, gives (Mc)DONNACHIE, which becomes (Mc)CONNACHIE. DODDRIDGE (Dr.) : hill. SHADLAW (shedlaw) : a hill dividing districts = SHIERLAW. BRECKENRIDGE : bracken hill, *con.* BRACKENBURY = Fernese Braes. SHERBOURNE: a brook dividing two parishes. So SHERWOOD : boundary forest. HINSHAW : sheltered behind a wood = HINTON. WALKINSHAW(quoits): wood through which is a path. SHILLINGLAW: a hill whereon are huts, *con.* SHIEL : a hut, SCHILLER (poet) : a cottier. South Shields : huts to south. WARDLAW (Ralph) : a hill on which watch is kept = BEACONSFIELD (betoken, from teach) = FLAMESTEAD. LAUGHTON (sometimes) : town on a hill = KNOWLTON (pamphlet) = HUGTENBURGH (painter), HILTON, FELSBERG, HAMMOND (ham mound) : exactly = EMMONS. COLVILLE, DUNVILLE, DUMVILLE, all living in towns on hills. TOOGOOD (torr) : a fruitful hill. COLVILLE becomes COVILLE. HACKENBERGER : dweller on a hill covered with hedges, *con.* HAGUE : hedge dweller = HEDGES = HEADLAND : a boor dwelling near a hedge at top of field. LAMBSHEAD : head of the land. HEAD of land or wood, but sometimes physical. HOCHHEIM, HIGHAM (Ferrers), HYAM : home on high ground. YELVERTON (major): town where *yawls* come in, small harbour = SKIFFINGTON = SHIPTON (mother) : when not sheeptown. Schaffhausen : ship houses, a portage.

Every variation of hill seems to be discoverable in the London Directory. We might almost call it British geography. Thus HORSFALL : a hill for horse grazing. KNOX, KNEE, NEE, NEEDHAM : home on a hill = SCAREDEVIL, SCORESBY (captain), EMMONS, STEEPER. NEEDLES = HILLS. PINHORNE (Sir John) = HILLHEAD and *con.* PENCOIT, but PENCLUTHA : Clydehead. CLUTHA : lady of the Clyde. CRUMPECKER : round hill, *con.* GRUMBLE for CRUMBLE (crom peel) : circular tower. HARDACRE : field on a hilltop = INKPEN (Ing : a meadow). HARTSHORN : hill frequented by deer. HARLOW : high hill. PIGFAT (peak) = LANGHORN. PIGFAT *con.* FADYAN : long John. LIGHTSTONE : bright hill, noted for beautiful sunsets. RAGG gives RIGBY : hill dweller = SHELDON. TORR, TOE : a hill, TOWELL, TAWELL (quaker) : little hill. HOGGPEN : high hill = ALTAMONT. After the following names town is understood. ASTON, EASTON : east. WESSON, WESTON : west, *con.* Vast : the ocean west of the European continent. But WESTLEY (Charles), not west field, being a form of WELLESLEY (Arthur) = SPRINGFIELD. WAISTCOT : west cottage. NORTON = NORBURY. SUTTON : south = SUDBURY. DALTON : dale = THAL-

10

BERG = COMPTON, COMSTOCK : in a comb. TITCOMB (bishop) :
little valley. FANCOMBE : frequented by fawns. FRANCOMBE
(frenum) : ash tree valley. DUNCOMBE : hill in a valley.
BATTERSCOMB : Batteur's dale. BATTEUR = THRESHER. COMBE,
COOMBE, COOMBES : a valley, forms *cumb*, as Cumberland :
land of valleys. A poet of that county says,—

> " There's Cumwitton, Cumwhinton, Cumranton,
> Cumrangen, Cumrew, Cumcatch,
> And mony mair Cums i' the county,
> But nin wi' Cumdurock can match."

WELCOMBE : valley where is notable spring. BUNCOMBE (bon)
= HOPGOOD, GEHAZI : valley of visions, beautiful sights,
gives BUNKUM, whence the Americanism, Bunkum : brag.
SLOCUM (Podgers) : slough coombe, mud vale. PODGERS :
poddy, big in the body = HOGARTH. COMMISKY (looking
like a Pole, is Irish) : watered valley = DALLAS (esk), conversely, ESCOMBE. ISDALE : dale through which a burn flows.
FALLAS : a hill well watered. RANDALL, RANDLE : round valley.
FEATHERSTONHAUGH (longest English name) : town of
Frithestan, in the valley. FRITHESTAN : most free, generous,
liberal. MAXWELL : St. Maccusville = MAXTON. MACCUS : the
Mac : son, *i.e.*, first born son. HOWLAND : hill land = Kohistan.
DALHOUSIE (esk) : field at corner of water. RUSHTON, RISHTON :
town among rushes = RUSHBURY. RUSHOUT (hut) : a cottage
among sedge. KERSE : a rush, living among. "I don't care a
curse off a common." DENMAN : valley dweller. EATON,
HEATON, HATTON : on a heath, though sometimes EATON =
WATERSTON, at others a Hessian.

TWISTLETON (twa) : near boundaries of England and Scotland
= BORTHWICK, BORWICK, MARWICK (march) : border villages,
con. Vicus : a village, giving WICKS : a villain, villager, when
not local, means active, lively = QUIGG. MARQUIS : who has
charge of the marches, *con.* MARCHIONESS.

Murcia (Spain), Mercia (England), MERSEY : bounding river
= ORR, whence ORUM : home on the boundary river. MAR-
WOOD : boundary wood = SHERWOOD : dividing forest. Marcomanni : men defending the marches. BISMARCK (prince) :
end of bishop's jurisdiction, as Gravesend : where the Sheriff
of London ceases to have jurisdiction, and Denmark : Dane's
boundary. MARGRAVE : the march greve, *con.* REEVES, GRAVES,
BISLAND : bishop's glebe. TWISS : wearing a twisted sash,
ornamental belt, a warrior with his loins girded, prepared
unto battle. TWI (birth name) : a twin, *con.* TWISS and twice.
z becomes *t*, as Weiner Zeitung : Vienna Tidings, the Austrian
Times. Seen, too, in Zwibrucken : two bridges = Deux Ponts.
CAXTON (printer) : Cage's town. GRANTON : town on a green,

great, or Grant's town. If the first = FELTON, GRENVILLE ; if
second, GRANVILLE, Mecklenburgh : mickle borough. BIGHAM :
humble dwelling, home in a bigging = HUTTON.
LANGTON, LANGHAM, LONGUEVILLE, LONGWILL! : straggling,
lengthy town. NEWTON (Isaac), VILLENEUVE (admiral), NEVILLE,
NEWELL, NEWSHAM, NEWSOM, NEWSTEAD, Novgorod, Naples all
mean new city, town or habitation. ALTON (Locke) : old town
= Utica. KONIGSBERG, REGIOMONTANUS, CUNNINGHAM, VILLE-
ROY, KINGSTON : royal residences, the last sometimes meaning
king's stone (Scone), where the coronation was held. TURTON :
near a tower = WICKS. WOLLASTON (chemist) : east town on
a wold. WOOLFIELD : wold field. But WOOLARD : wearing a
hair shirt. " The *naked* truth of it is, I have no shirt, I go
woolward for penance." WOOLNOTH : bold as a wolf. WOLCOT
(Peter Pindar): cot in a wood. PANTON : town approached by a
bridge = BRIDGETON. CHATTERTON (the noble boy) : Cedda's
town. WARTON : dwelling among rank vegetation, *con.* Wort
as in Wortzel, and = RANKE. WORDIE : cultivating a little garden = TOFTS, sometimes means a boaster. MILTON (John, when
not from mill), MIDDLETON, MITTENDORF : dwelling in the
middle of the town. TOWNSEND : living at end = DULONG : of
far away up. BURKE, BROUGHS, BERRY, BERRI, in some families DUBARRY, DEWBERRY (du or de burgh): burgesses to a man
= CITTIDINI, BORGHESE, BORGIA, BURGESS, BROUGH, BRUFF,
BURROWS : persons having civic rights. But BORROWS : a
pledge, hostage = HOMER. URBAN, URBANE (its *fem.*), TOWNLEY :
refined, cultured, civic, not rustic. And DRYBROUGH, DRYFRUFF :
waterless town = DRAYTON. Civilise : to make into a citizen.
Polite : city bred, not rustic as to gait or manners. Astu : a
city = Stead, gives Astute : cunning.
METANASTE : who changes cities, an emigrant. ASTYANAX :
defender of city by intellect, its king, *con.* Senex : aged. Bury : a
city, from Beorgan : to protect, *con.* Perga, Burgos, Pergamos, from
last, Parchment. Burglar : who commits *larceny* on a protected
place. Polis : a city, from Polus : many, Police : 'city wardens.
BURDETT (Francis) = VELPEU, LYTTLETON (lord) : small towns.
GUTTENBURG (printer) : good town. WHYBROW (Wyeborough):
on the Wye. SWEDENBORG (Emanuel) : town of the Swedes =
SWEABORG. STURTON (when not on the Stour : muddy river,
stirred up), for stor town, great = MEIKLEHAM, GRESHAM.
LARGE (when Irish): dweller on a hill side = SIDE (when Norman), for De Glarges. BELLAMY, from Belesme, Normandy,
is given as *fair friend.* DEATH : for De Ath : of Ath, Nor-
mandy. Death is from Do and means *done*—it is *do-eth,* death.
So some say, " I'll do for you." ATH = FORD, ATHEY : ford of
Ae, Hugh, there slain. ATHERTON = FORDHAM = OVERTON,
OVERBURY, OVEREND (and Gurney) : part of town near ferry

Ford from Faran: to go, whence Ferry. ATHOL: rockford.
ARROL: high rock. BURFORD: ford to town famed for beer,
over the Windrush. CRAWFORD (Caerford): castle ford, mistaken for *crow ford.* STAFFORD: stream passed by help of a
leaping pole. STRATFORD (strait): narrow ford. DISBURY
from Diss, Norfolk. BECCLES (bishop): beck, brook running
through leas = BROOKLANDS. CAJETAN (cardinal): from Cajeta,
now Gaeta. CATALINE (conspirator): Catillon, on Tiber.
JANEWAY ('s tokens): man of Genoa. LUBBOCK (Sir John): of
Lubeck. LIGUORI (St.): of Liguria. BRABY, BRABNER, BRA-
BENDER : men of Brabant. NAPOLEON: of Naples. SALMASIUS
(*op.* of Milton), SEYMOUR: of Semur, for St. Maure in French
Flanders. Some have Semur (sine muros): without walls, and
get SEYMOUR from sew, whence seamer, seamstress, semmit.
SEMMET, a trade name. One may be from the place and an-
other from trade, only pedigree can decide. SOMERS: man of St.
Omers. "There is not a town in Normandy which has not
given name to some English family."

Persons were named after their residences by non-residents.
LUMNER: Londoner, used a century since by Yorkshire
dalesmen to indicate one of their number who had visited
the metropolis. What would it signify in Whitechapel!
LUMNER = LUNDIE (traitor), written in old charters de Lundie;
a Londonderry name, though its ill odour there has expelled
it therefrom. BORDELAY from Bordeaux. MARSIGLI (writer
on Hydrostatics): from Marseilles. Marseillaise (hymn):
sung by deputies from Marseilles. BRIDGES (algebra):
Bruges, *con.* our Brigton and BRIGGS. JERVIS (admiral):
Gervaise in France, gives Jarvey: a coachman. Some families
insist in deriving from Gar: a spear, and Fuss: impetuosity,
but Gervaise may be that and give name to place. TOLETUS
(Spanish ecclesiastic) from Toledo. BALBI (Spanish-Jewish):
man of Babylon, son of the captivity = ZERUBBABEL: seed of
Babylon, hence BALBOA (navigator). WURMSER (general): of
Worms = DE WORMS (Greenwich). PARRHASIUS (alchemist),
PARRIS: of Paris. But PARIS (Ida): under the protection of
Isis (goddess). CELSUS (sceptic): high, lofty, may be local or
social, PARACELSUS (alcohol): very high. DANVERS is De An-
vers: of Antwerp, and Antwerp: at wharf. LUCCHESI (sculp-
tor): Lucca. PISANO: Pisa. Gournay, Normandy, gives
GURNEY, meaning sometimes Spear new. BRIMER (Toronto):
braes of Mar, a disguised M'Gregor. CORIOLANUS: man of
Corioli.

> " Therefore be it known,
> As to us, to all the world, that Caius Marius
> Wears this war's garland: in token of which
> My noble steed, known to the camp, I give him,

With all his train belonging: and from this time,
For what he did before Corioli, call him,
With all the applause and clamour of the host,
Caius Marius *Coriolanus*."

Ilium, Troy's citadel, gives the great name IULUS (puer),
whence JULIUS. " *Julius*, a magno demissum nomen *Iulo*."
Therefrom we have Castra Julia : camp of Julius, gives
Trogilium, better known as Truxillo. JULIAN (apostate) : son
of Julius = CŒSARION. Juliodumun : fort of Julius, gives
LOUDON (Poitou), suggesting CHILHAM (Kent) : home of Julius,
nearly = FREJUR for Frejus, for Frejules, for Forum Julii :
market town of Julius. Hence also JULIEN (operatic king),
JULES (Favre), the month July, island Jersey, Gilly : flower
blooming in July, suggesting Genitans : June eating's (apples),
JULIA ending with JILL (Jack and). From Cæsar we have
Xeres, in Spain, whence Sherry. TROILUS (and Cressida) : a
thorough Trojan, compounded of Troy and Ilium, city and
citadel, so a Trojan of the Trojans. Caiapha, at the foot of
Carmel, taken by the Crusaders A.D. 1215, gave CAIAPHAS
(Joseph). " High Priest for that year." Migdol : a watch
tower, gives Magdala in the Decapolis, and the acropolis of
Theodore of Abyssinia, whence MAGDALEN (Mary). Kir : a
wall, Kirioth : walls, fortified, ISCARIOT : man of Kirioth, only
apostle not a Galilean. MAGDALEN gives MAUDLIN (college),
Maudlin : wersh and whining cant, Magdalena (river),
MAUDSLEY : field dedicated to Mary Magdalen, but MAUD
(queen) from MATILDA : maid of Hilda. JEBUS : place trodden
down = MAACHAH = the Scotch PEDEN, the English BOTTOM
(beat), the Italian IMOLA and CAMPOBASSO. Jebus and Salem :
peace, give Jerusalem. " The man would not tarry that night,
but he rose up and departed, and came over against Jebus,
which is Jerusalem." Sometimes tortured into Hierosolyma :
holy peace, at expense of history and languages. MAULE :
Thor's hammer man, applied to priest who broke the spine of
a human victim with a hammer on a blood stone (altar),
shortens to MALE, giving MELVILLE : town of Male, and that
may mean dwelling of Thor's priest. In some cases MALE : a
painter.

The Savona river gives the martyric name SAVONAROLA. Savona *con.* Savanna : a meadow, the river bank being luxuriant
= the illustrious Scotch preacher's name IRVING : a stream having verdant banks. CAIRNEY, KEARNEY (Kate, the pride of
Killarney) : a river running by a notable cairn. Cairngorm :
blue mountain, cairn shaped. " The blue mountains glow in
the sun's golden light." From Cairn the French CARNAC :
place of cairns, but the Hibernian CARNEGIE is warlike, meaning victorious. Yet PITCAIRN (Gaelic) : cairn near a quarry

=PITT=MANBY (captain): dwelling near a mine. CAMERON vibrates between local and personal. If the former: curved projection on a river, if latter: crooked nose. Cam: crooked (river), whence Cambridge, and Camel, another crooked stream. Cam also gives Akimbo (arms). *Camera:* a chamber, curved roof, whence CAMERARIUS=CHAMBERLAIN Crom: curved, gives CROMBY: crooked stream=Kishon: bow shaped. ABERCROMBY (Sir Ralph): mouth of the Crombie. CROM, CRUM (Ewing), CRAMB: stones placed in a curvilinear form for the worship of Baal, Crom, or Ti-mor: great god. Of this origin CRUMLISH, CRUMLY: Crom's field. Crum= Dura, plains of. DOUGLAS: dark gray (stream), *con.* GLASS applicable to a grey-eyed man or to a stream. KINGLASS: head of river=PENCLUTHA, PENFOUND(T), and PENGELLY. GLASHAN (Mc)=BECKET, BROOKS. KINGLASS, *con.* KINROY: red head. Water and the eye are connected physically, ideally, and as to language. En: a well, also means an eye. "Tamar put her widow's garments from her, and covered her with a veil, and wrapped herself, and set in eynim:" the place of eyen, where men cast amorous glances, sheep's eyes. Our letter O is *con.* Eau: water. The eye is Ain (Heb.), Ops (Gr.), Oculus (La.), Occhio (It.), Ojo (Sp.), Oeil (Fr.), Oin (Celtic, identical with Hebrew). Hence Og: to look, Ogle: to look boldly, which adding *go* gives Goggles: eyes on the go, rolling. GOGGLE is an actual family name. Compare Oeil and Well. Now Eye, Eau, and O are philologically one, and Well differs therefrom but little, five hundreds of years since it was spelled Oell. As we get *G* from the camels head and neck, hieroglyphically, Camel, Gimel, so we may have O from the well. Notice: No punster is allowed after reading the afore written to say O! He may say aye! But OCELLA: a man with little eyes,—

> "Loe yonder doth Erle *Douglas* come,
> His men in armour bright,
> Full twenty hundred Scottish speres
> All marching in our sight:
> All men of pleasant Tivydale
> Fast by the river Tweede.
> 'Then cease your sports,' Erle Percy said,
> 'And take your bows with spede.'"

DUFFUS: dark stream=BLACKWATER and DONOVAN, when the don is not a form of Dun. DUFFERIN (lord): dark third, a portioner of bog land. Glass may mean grey, water, a stream, GLASS: man living near it, ice, glass or grey-eyed, whence GLASSPOLE (pool). RUTHVEN: red river (*con.* DENOVAN)=Rubicon, Rio Colorado. "Lord *Ruthven*, pale and haggard from recent illness, and like a corpse in armour, followed Darnley." RIOU, RIBAS = RIVERS. Rialto: deep river. FONTARIVE : rapid flowing spring = Fontarabia.

> " Brave hearts! to Britain's pride
> Once so faithful and so true,
> On the deck of fame that died
> With the gallant good *Riou.*"

CARRUTHERS: red castle, or fort = RAFFLIN. CATHCART: strait of the Cart, where it runs between narrow banks = DETROIT. KYLE : living at straits, *con.* Calais: town on the kyles of Dover. DALZIEL, beautiful meadow = BEAUPRE, BEAULY. DALRYMPLE (Kate) : meadow by the winding pool. DE WINTON : of Winchester.

PERCY (earl) : from the Perche valley, it assumes the forms PEARSE, PIERCE. But the story of his being named from pushing a spear into a man's eye is all—but that's vulgar. He, or his ancestors, was called Percy before Alnwick Castle was founded. CHISHOLM : river island formed of gravel, living on. RODERIC DE TRIANA (first Spaniard that descried America) : Roderic of Trajan's town. Florence gives FIAN-ZUOLA (painter) : a Florentine. DACRE, thought to mean St. Jean d'Acre: St. John of Accho, is a Cumberland name, DEACRE = AGER, AGES, CLUNY, *i.e.*, of the field, like DELAFIELD. HAGUE : hedge. The Dutch Hague was the hunting ground of the Flemish nobles. It is *con.* HAAG (CARL), DE LA HAY: of the hedge, boulevards. HAYNAU (Austrian hyæna) : new hedge = QUIGLEY : a field surrounded by a quick. HAY is identical with High, and so is applicable to person or place, as is Barr and Celsus. Hence HOY : island, high above the sea = *Ogygia*, an old name of Ireland, from which also ORMOND : east Munster, DESMOND : west Munster. Deal : to divide, gives DALE : a division of the land ; in German, THAL. Thus DALBY, DOLBY = DALTON, (chemist), THALBERG. SWANTHALER (sculptor) : dale haunted of swans. SAVERTHAL (songstress) : Savannah dale, meadow valley, *con.* SAVONAROLA. DALRY : dale of the Rye—

> " Comin' through the Rye."

Rye : a run of water. Hence RYE (Miss). LILIENTHAL : lily dale, *con.* Lilac: lily oak. SCHONTHAL : beautiful VALLEY — VAUBAN (bon) = GEHAZI, HOPGOOD = JOLIVAU : pretty valley. ODELL : dale of the Ouse. SUDDEN : south valley. DUVAL (Claude) : of the valley = DELAVAL. DALKEITH (Buccleuch) : narrow dale. But KEITH: one of Catti, *con.* Caithness. Catti: warlike, *con.* CADOGAN. GLENDINNING : sheltered glen. DOL-LINER : a dalesman. NORVAL usually given as *northern vale* = NORDEN, but Norman's vale—

> My name is Norval; on the Grampian hills," etc.

GRUNDY GRUND: living on low ground = MAACHAH, LOO, THURLOW: Thor's valley. SHUFFLEBOTTOM: shaw field dale, a wood in a field in a bottom. RAMSBOTTOM: a dale in which a kind of onion flourished that was called rhom, whence the name RAM. WINTERBOTTOM, WINTERBOTHAM: winding dale = VALLETORT, SHOEBOTTOM: small wood in a valley. TWISDEN: double dale, *twa, twice, twis.* WINTERBORN: winding burn = CARRON and WINTERBACH. BOTTOM differs little from FOOTE and ORISPUS: living at foot of hills = LOWTHER and MOFFAT. FOOTHEAD: head of the valley = PERCY, PERCIVAL. BOWDEN (booth den): dwelling in a valley, *con.* BOOTH (general, S.A.), Beth, Bed, Abode, Abad, BOWERS and BOTHWELL: abode of Gaels, strangers = BALLINGALL. GALLOWS: the Gaul's or strangers' haugh. HADDEN: haugh den = BOWDEN. SWINEHOE: haugh frequented by swine = SWINFEN: hog bog. MARSDEN: marshy valley = BUGDEN ("Mrs. BUGDEN'S will"): boggy dale = SOFTLEY: where the ground sucks in = BUGG, NOA, NASSAU. TILDEN: lime tree dale, TILLINGHAST: lime tree wood. EADEN, EDEN, DENNY (eau): valley through which a stream flows = RODNEY, ISDALE, COMMISKY. But the Bible Eden: pleasure, gives ADONIS and Aden on Red Sea. The foregoing contrast with DRYDEN. HOWDEN: haugh den. HO: a haugh. SUGDEN = SWINDELL: valleys frequented by swine. DENMAN (lord): a dalesman = THAL, DEANE. But ADEAN: at the dale. CAMDEN (antiquary): where a camp has been. LAGDEN: low lying valley = LOGAN, LAGAN. WALDEN: forest in a valley. Den, Din gives DINGLE: little den,—

> "In *dingles* deep and mountains hoar,
> Oft with the bearded spear,
> They combatted the tusky boar
> And slew the angry bear."

Such a huntsman a thousand years ago was called CHACEPORC, MAHON, MAUGHAN, or MAHONEY. SELDEN (antiquary): spacious valley = Strathmore. COBDEN (corn) = PERCIVAL: head of the valley. VANNER: a valesman = VAUX, THAL, DENMAN. BRODIE (sometimes): house in a plain, a lowlander = PLATT, PEDEN (at others): an embroiderer, a subtle weaver: if Milesian, spelled BRODY: opulent = JESSE (of Bethlehem). A man might be forgiven for supposing BLANE to be local *con.* Dumblane ("Jessie the flower of") and = CLARENDON: *blank* of trees, but it is contracted from Bel Agneau (Franco-Culdee): beautiful lamb (Jesus), *con.* LAMB who carried lamb standard, whence LAMMIE. In some cases these are nurse names of endearment. BELLARMINE (theologian): of the order of knights of the *ermine*, compounded with Bell; beautiful. LUNDT, LANDT, LUND, LANDOR (Savage), LOWNDES are forms of *lands.* THWAITES,

SWAITE and Brooklyn: broken land = NEWLAND: newly cultivated, the *op.* of AUDLEY. Our Den: a valley is formed on
Stan: a country, as Belochistan: poor country, barren. Peris-
tan: fairyland, peris. Palestine: country of shepherds, Philistines. Syria is Suristan: country of Soor, Tyre, and Tyre: a
rock, Zur as ZURSHADDAI: whose rock is the Almighty. TAN-
SEIN (Stan Since): a Chinaman. " That which grows over the
musician *Tan-Sein.*" TANAGRA (daughter of Eolus), for Stan
Graii: Greek land, Helenistic lady. THANA-LARTIA (Venus):
lady owning the country. Lartia *fem.* of LARS: a landlord,
whence Byron's hero LARA, and "*Lares* et lemures." Tingitania: country about Tangiers. Lusitania (Portugal): land of
luz. Luz: the hazel. Suggests Calton: hazelnut town, Dunkeld: hill of hazel bushes = Luz where Jacob dreamed. THANE:
stan (land) holder, *con.* Thanet. FIRDUSI (Persian poet): paradise. " Firdusi, although his own name was taken from *paradise,* usually employs for it only the word *behhischt.*" Paradise:
watered garden, *con.* PRE, PRATT, PRITTY, Prairie, DUPRE.
Let us take to water again. TORRANCE (when neither from
Tor: hill, nor Turra: a tower) a torrent, a land flood, *con.* Terra:
earth, land, country = BORROMEO (St. Charles): living at the
bore = CURRANT. STORAR: great waters = *Pison, con.* STORY:
great. Storm: great rhime, Storthing: great gathering of
thinkers, for think and thing is the same thing. TYNDALE
(translator), TYNDALL (scientist): dale of the Tyne. TWEDDLE:
Tweed dale. WADDELL, WADDLE: Wear dale (Yorks). WEAR,
WEIR, WARE: a waterfall, that *wards,* guards the river from
floods, nearly like LADE, LAIDLAW. Sometimes Ware, and its
variations from De Vere, when a war name: defender, warrior
who protects = MUNTZ. But Waddle: to walk from side to
side, is from Wade: to pass through water, and that from
Weed: long grass, passing through. DROUIN DE LHUYS
(diplomatist Fr.): Drouin of the sluice. Similar to SLUSE
and GUSH. DROUIN: true win, fair conqueror. So DELES-
CLUSE (exclusa): of the sluice, that which excludes, shuts out
water. SURTEES: upon the Tees. Aufidus, a river of south
Italy, gives *Aufidius.*

> " See him pluck *Aufidius* down by the hair:
> As children from a bear, the Volces shunning him."

Sul: the south, from Sol: the sun, as Puerta del Sul = SOUTH-
GATE, gives SOLE, SOLANO (Lopez): a southron = SOUTHEY
(laureate), SOUTH = SURR, SOTHERN (Dundreary), Temanite
(from Teman, Yemen: the south, *con.* BENJAMIN). Deccan:
south (India). SOLDENE: southern lady. PLIMSOL (M.P.):
south of Plym. The wind Solano, not from Sol: the sun.
Winds are named by the people from their observed direction,

and not by philosophers observing their origin. Solano corresponds to Libecchio : Libyan wind = Africus, and means the south wind. Sul also gives SOUL, SOULE = DEAS, all southrons = SUTHER (bishop). SUTHERLAND: south of Norway. NEWSKY (Russian): town on the Neva. SUDANOWSKY: south of the Danube.

> " A multitude like which the populous north
> Pour'd never from her frozen loins, to pass
> The Rhene or *Danaw.*"

Tober, Tiber (in the Celtic): a spring, well, or stream flowing therefrom. Thus Tobermory : well of B. V. Mary = Motherwell. Tiber : a stream, a river, which was also called Albula = Elbe, from its whiteness, and Ruma, because of cattle *ruminating* on its banks, in which Ruma = Buchan, the Scotch corresponding well with Italy, Vitulii, suggestive of cattle, and much the same as Beotia, Boii. Tiber personified gives TIBERIUS (uios): son of the god TIBER, whence Tiberias : city named in honour of the emperor which gave name to lake. From RUMA the twins REMUS and ROMULUS, the latter being the *dim.* he probably was the smaller baby. We may translate their names *sons of Ruma.* The imperial word Rome : city on the Ruma (as certainly as Cambridge from the Cam) gives Roumania, Roumelia, Morea (for Romea), Erzeroum : land of the Roman, Romaic (modern Greek), Rommany (Gypsy language), Romance (language of southern France). ROUSTAN : of the Roman country.

BURNS (in some families): small streams, rivulets. BARNET (battle of), BURNET (bishop), BECKETT (A'BECKET). BARNWELL: a spring where the bairns (young men) met for gymnastic exercises. But BARNUM (showman): home near a barn, a field labourer. COBURN, COCKBURN (some authors give COCKBURN, COBURN as forms of COLBRAND), BROCKLE, GLASHAN, Donnybrook (fair), BECK, BACH, BACKIE : brook, stream or streamlet. In America we meet with BACK. VANDERBECKEN : of the brook = the Irish TULLY and FLOOD, similar to BORROMEO : living where the water occasionally rushes in, as we speak of the Bore of the Ganges. BICKERSTETH (Tatler): station at a brook. HEPBURN : hedge burn, similar to BROCKLEHURST : brook passing through a wood. BACHMAN = BROOKS = BECK, last combining to form CLUTTERBUCK : clear brook, the *op.* of Stour : stirred up, muddy, STURTON : (town on) the Stour. The Germans have Bach as GRIESBACH (biblical critic), for Grossbach = FULBROOKE. STORAR : great water. ACHENBACH : brook flowing by oaks = WALDBROOK. " Herr *Achenbach* has produced Mendelsohn's St. Paul in a dramatic form at Dusseldorf." MEERBACH : a brook running into the sea. BOLINGBROKE (sceptic): small wood (bois) near a brook. BLUMENBACH (musical composer): brook flowing through blooming meads = English, FOTHERGILL, GILFATHER, GILFEATHER: water running through fodder, cattle food, *con.* BLUM, BLOOMER (costume): living in bloom = MEAD, MEDE, MEADOWS: that which is mowed. RUSHBROOK: brook among sedge, reeds, like RIDDLE, RIDDAL: reed, rush dale = Reidvale. REUSS (professor): rushing burn. RUYS-DALE = ISDALE, RISELY: brookfield, COMMISKY (esk). OFFEN-BACH (operatic writer): rapidly running brook = FONTARIVE. SCHWARBACH (swarthy): dark water brook = DOUGLAS. BECK-FORD (millionaire): ford of brook = FORDHAM. OVERTON: ferry town. OVERING: son of Over. I knew a family so named. OVER: a ferry (man), hence Hanover.

BIRKBECK (mechanics' institute): birch tree brook = the fatal Berezina: birch river. BIRKETT (hout): birch grove. BIRKS, BIRCH: of an aboriginal stock = the Saxon ASHMAN. RISELY: field through which water rushes = REUSS, RUYSDALE. *Syke :* a run of water less than a beck, so called because it *sucks* in water from the hills, gives SYKES (Bill). TICHBORNE (claimant): de Itchen bourn: of the Itchen brook, Hants. Brook: that breaks out of the earth, BROOKS. Bourn, in the French BORNE: a boundary. LABONDE: at the boundary, brave = LAMARCK (evolutionist): at the marches, these may be called Marcommanni: men defending the coast line. " That bourn from which no traveller returns." BURNHAM: home on a stream. BURNS (when local) = Mersey, ORR, URE: bounding stream, *con.* Horos: a boundary, whence Horizon, boundary of vision.

Oros: a mountain, district divider. Some give the rivers Orr and *Eure:* cold and so *con.* BALFOUR: cold dwelling. Orontes: a mountain stream. ORISPUS (American politician): living at mountain foot. BORD (pianos): living at border = BORWICK. MICHAL: a little stream, joy giver. " The name of the younger was *Michal.*" One of the Erse words for water is GILL, giving GULLY (game chicken): a water course. GOOL, the British for a canal or channel, PICKERSGILL (painter): pike stream. Pike: spike nosed. CARGILL: camp, fort, hill by water = Crawford or thereby. Gill gives CULL, whence CULL, GOLLAND, YOLAND, GILLILAND: well watered fields. MUNCASTER (Greek brigands, taken by): mound caster, castle on a hill = GORDON: goat fortress, not to be confused with Mon-caster: monk's fortress, now Newcastle. GOULBURN (bishop): a combination of *gool* and *burn:* a dividing stream. TREGELLES (commentator): town on a stream. PENGELLY (Kent's cave): head of stream. PENCOIT: head of wood. PENCLUTHA: Clyde head, *con.* Pennygant: hill of winds = Schrekhorn: shrieking mountain. Stream in Norse words assumes the form of

Strom, as Stromness: stream island, projection into bore = Spithead. Maelstrom: mill stream. STROMIER = RIVERS, RIBAS, REIS, *con.* RACE: where waters rush. ANKARSTROM (assassin): stream in which ships anchor. GOLDENSTROM: gold flowing = Chrysorhoas. STOCKENSTROM (" Brave, if justly brave "): a stoke (place slaked out) near a stream. ENGSTROM: angle of stream. PEMBROKE (pen): a hill with brook at foot, *con.* PENNANT: head of valley = PERCIVAL. DESAIX (aqua): of waters = WATERS, *con.* *Aix-la-Chapelle:* waters of the chapel. (Mc)LACHLAN, (O)LOCHLIN, LACHLAND: lake land dwellers, sometimes applied to the natives of Norway. LEWIS (when local): lake land (island). SUTHERLAND: land south of Norway: north way, road to pole. STAMFORD, STANFORD: stony ford, stones placed to aid in fording. STANBACK: a stony brook = Abana, from Eben: a stone. RUTHERFORD: ford of the Ruther, tribe of Tweed, so called from gravel colouring = SANDFORD (and Merton). STRATFORD (le bow): street ford, old Roman road. STAFFORD: stream forded by leaping with a pole.

> " *Pembroke* and *Stafford*, you in our behalf,
> Go, levy men and make prepare for war.*"*

FORD = WADE, *con.* Invade: to go into. FINNEY (American divine): fen waters = MARSH, MARSHAM. WELLER (Sam): a gulf where the water wells, boils up. WHALLEY (M.P.): field with a spring in it. WELLHAUSEN (critic): a spring of water supplying houses = PAGAN, *con.* WELCOMBE, WALLOP. In vulgar fact these were village pumps, persons living near. Pege: a fountain (*Pedao ex ge:* leaping out of the earth), gives PEGASUS: winged horse of the Muses whose heel by a kick laid open a spring. When Christianity was making way in the cities and great centres of population, rustics still stood by the old superstition which therethrough was called Paganism from Pagani: villagers, from Pege: a well, those who gathered round the village pump. Heathen: ethnoi, nations not Jews, gauyim, strangers. PAGAN assumes the forms PAYNE, *con.* Paganism and PAINE (Tom). CHOLMONDELEY: cold mount field, *cor.* to CHUMLY = COLLOP: cold hope = CALDICOTT and BALFOUR.

By: a place, as Bye-laws: local regulations, gives KIRBY (naturalist): kirk village. CROSSBY (arithmetician): dwelling near a cross. DERBY (generally pronounced DARBY, as in Darby M'Guire): dwelling on the Derwent. CROSSLEY, CRUTCHLEY: field where a cross is erected to do stations by, *con.* CRUCIGER (reformer): cross bearer, a crusader. " Luther was accompanied by Melancthon, CRUCIGER, and Jonas." HARLECH (men of): long stone. LECKIE: stoney. AUCHINLECK: stony field, gives AFFLECK, when AFFLECK is Saxon:

immaculate, unspotted, without *a flick.* STANLEY (Penrhyn):
stone field = the great French LA PEYROUX: the stony.
PENRHYN: head of promontory = Spithead. STEEN, STEIN: a
hill, rock, stone. ARNSTEIN: eagle hill. But STONE (sometimes): blood stone, sacrificial altar. EINSTEIN: one stone
(boundary). ALSTON: old ·boundary. FRANKENSTEIN: rock
fortress of the Franks. VANDERSTEEN: of the hill = HILLS.
FOLLY, FOLI, FELL, FOLY: of the rock. FALSHAW = ROCKWOOD.
ROKESBY: dwelling on the rocks = DUHALDE: of the stronghold. VANDEMAN (island): of the mine, *con.* Manchester:
camp quarry. VALLENSTEIN: rocky valley = STANHOPE.
STANDISH (Miles): rock surrounded by water (esk), dwelling
on. AVALLANO: hazel valley. LEICHTENSTEIN: light stone.
WEISENSTEIN: white hill = WHITELAW. STAINES: stones,
living at boundary = LAMARCK. VANHOUTEN: of the wood =
BUIST, DE LA BOST. VANDEVEER: at the ferry = OVER.
VANDUZEE: dwelling by the shore = SANDS when it is local.
EEKHOUT = OAKWOOD and BOYACK.

WINK, WINKS, WINKLE: field corner, land gushet, living at
corner house = ENGELS. RIP VAN WINKLE: Rip of the corner.
RIP (from Ripa: a bank. Ripurarian (Franks): living on
Rhine banks. Arrive: to reach the bank by swimming or
sailing). BANKS: bank dweller. BENTHAM (Jeremy): bent
home, dry grass stalks. BENTLEY (lexicographer): bent field,
living in. LANGHAM, LANGTON (Steven): long straggling
village.

MARSHAM (Mrs.): home in a marsh = MOSHEIM (historian and
the *op.* of DRAYTON (Polyolbion): without wells. Polyolbion:
much about Britain. DRAYTON answers to DRYBURGH:
ill supplied with water. MOSSMAN = PETMAN, PETLEY, MOSS
(when not formed on Moses): residing on turf land. MOSS-
CROP, MOSSCRIP: turf cutter. MUSPRATT: meadow on a moss.
Moss trooper: galloper over the moss. MOSS = HEENAN, CORK
(and sometimes) ROSS, BUGG: bog brothers. DIVORTY: living
in a turf thatched hut. CESPEDES (Spanish General): resident
on uncultivated ground = the foregoing, and such as FERNEY,
FARNIE, FARNWORTH: fortified place on fern land. FURNIVAL:
ferney valley. HEATH, LING, BROOM, BROOMHEAD = MUIRHEAD
and HEDDERWICK: heather dwelling BOOTH, BOWTELL (in
some families) BATTLE: dwelling place, bothie, *con.* Bethlehem:
house of bread, DALBETH: dwelling in a dale, BOTHWELL =
BALLINGALL, Allahabad: God's dwelling, Khorsabad: Cyrus'
dwelling, Bedstead: place of. CORREGGIO (painter): king's
house (casa), *con.* CANOVA (sculptor) = NEWHAUS. LACHAISE
(pere): *the* house = HOUSE, common in England. MALTHUS
(Malthusian): malt house. BACCHUS (if local): bake house,
born in, or there dwelling. DUFFUS: pigeon cot. House forms

Hustings: little house, Hussy: house wife. HOUSE = LACH-
AISE, MAISON. HOUSEGO: house joy. Wic for Vicus: a
dwelling place, gives FENWICK : village in the fens = MARSHAM,
VENN, MARSTON, *con*. BERWICK for Aberwick : village at Tweed
mouth.

YORK (captain) YORRICK (poor): Urewick, on the Ure, and
URE : bounding stream = ORR as Orwell : dividing brook.
ORUM : home on the Orr. BEVIL (beau), when not from bois
= Bristol : bright stow = WINTHROP, SHEEN, Nain. WADS-
WORTH : among wad, where lead ore is found. WADDY
(Samuel): wad field. WORDSWORTH (Excursion): among rank
vegetation = WARTON (M.P.) and WORDIE, when not a boaster.
THORP : a village where roads intersect, whereat a cross was
erected, *con*. THWAITES : a clearing, TWYSDEN : double dale,
and CARFAX : four roads. In German, Dorf. SIBTHORP
(colonel): Sigbertsthorp. SIGBERT: glorious conqueror. CAL-
THORP : cold dwelling = the Highland BALFOUR and COLLOP.
APTHORP : abbot's house = TABBEY : at the abbey. NEWDORF
= NEWTON. ZINZENDORF (count): tin smith's town. TISCHEN-
DORF ("Codex Sinaiticus"): carpenter's village. FAIRCLOTH :
beautiful clough, pine glen = HOPGOOD. CLOUGH forms CLOW,
The Dutch form is Kloof, as BLOOMENKLOOF : flowery glen,
con. BLUMENSTEIN. MILTON, MIDDLETON = MITDORF. Midden :
a dungstead, means middle of property wherein was deposited
what was useless in the house = Trivial (tres via): three cross
roads where scraps were flung.

HAMILTON (haugh mill town): a town having a mill in a
haugh. Haugh gives HO, HAWES = DENMAN. SOHO: shaw
haugh. HAWLEY: field in a haugh. We meet with HAUGH
for HAGUE, HAAG. HEDGES = LA HAYE, but HAYMAN : a hedger
and ditcher. The Hibernian CINNAMON : old turf dwelling on
a moor = DIVORTY. MUIRHEAD = PANMURE and BROMHEAD,
con. PENCOIT : woodhead. LAMBSHEAD for lands-head. HEAD-
LAND, *cor*. HEADLAM : head of land, ploughed, applied to a
squatter who pitched his hut at the hedgerow at field top.
MOFFAT (Bosjesmans) : moor foot. MORPETH : path across the
moors.   MORLEY: moor field = HATHERLY, HEDDERWICK =
LANDELLS, when not from Lann : a church, temple, enclosure
= LANYON : little enclosure = CLOSET, *con*. Landes, on French
coast. AMOR : at the moor. MULHOLLAND : mill of the little
wood. LLOYD : grey or extended sea, living near = MORGAN,
VANDUZEE, and VON REAUMER, and BYTHESEA : a shore
foundling. But SHORE (Jane), *con*. sewer, seneschal : high
servant. SAUMAREZ : salt marsh. SHIELS (Lalor): huts
where persons are shielded. GREENSHIELDS : huts among
trees = SHELTON, SHELDON, HUTTON (algebraist) : living in a
village of huts = COATS and VAN BUREN. HAMMOND, EMMONS :

home on a hill, artificial. CHISHOLM : gravel island, in a river. On a sea island, SKERRAT, *con.* Scar, Skerries, Skerryvore (more): great rock, Hebrides. SCORE, SCORESBY : rock dweller. BARRY (sometimes): bare island, but usually a hill, *con.* Bar : a son, Chaldee, exalted. Sometimes BARRY : bare, barren hill = RISK, *con.* RISE = BRAE. BARRY (eau): head of stream = PENGELLY, *con.* POOL : a stream. CASTLEBAR : castle on the hill = HARDCASTLE (aird). BARRY (Welsh): son of Harry = PARRY, HARRIGAN. Barry gives BARROW : funeral mound. Enters France as Bar-le-Duc : the Duke's citadel. DUBARRY, DEWBERRY : of the castle. BARRIE : castle dweller = TERENCE. STYLES : at a style. PENN : a hill, gives PENNANT : living at hill foot, or head of the valley = the odd FOOTHEAD. (Mc)BEAN (Sawney): dweller on a ben = SLEVIN, ALPIN (clan), *con.* Albyn, Albion, Alps. It is Americanised out of sorts into HALPIN.

QUINCY (when local): quince tree plot = PLUMSTEAD and PLUM for plum grower. I know persons thus named. CARSTAIRS : lands attached to a caer, car, castle, *con.* DE CHAIR (middy): of the castle = AKASTER. ACQUAVIVA (general of Jesuits : running water = CURRANT, PRIDEAUX, WATERS. ANSTRUTHER : stream passing through a strath. Latter part gives STRUTHERS = DALE, *con.* STRABANE : white strath. SUMMERLEE : field sown with spring wheat. TRELAWNY (Cornish): vale grove town. TREVANNION : house in a hollow = HOYLE = CAVOUR *con.* CAVAN, germane with Cavus : hollow, and the old verb Caw : to which, arch, curve, giving Corb : a chariot, Corve : a cawed up basket, (Mᶜ)CAW : war charioteer, CORMAC: son of a chariot = ANTIOCHUS : swift as a chariot = PODARGUS : swift footed = LIGHT, LIGHTFOOT, LIGHTBODY : a swift messenger. CURRAN : a reaping hook, a scimitar, a scythe. CAVANAGH (Bernard): round hills. CAVE, VOLTA : vault dweller = WEMYSS, HUME, HOME : troglodytes all. So France supplies CAVAIGNAC : dweller in a hollow, " depression de terrain" = MAACHAH and CAMPOBASSO. ISBISTER : dwelling among ice. COTTERELL : feudal villein, holding land by paying a fee = VAN METER, TENNANT. HAVILAND : land on which oats are sown. Haversack : bag for oats, forage. Knapsack : carried by KNAPP : the knave, servant. Castra : a camp, *square* fortifications, gives Chester in Saxon counties, Cester in Danish, Caer in Welsh, and Cahir in Irish, abbreviating to CARR, KERR in Scotland, *con.* Kir (" Made bare the shield") of Palestine. KERRIDGE : camp hill = MUNCASTER. PINKERTON : town on a fortified hill. Locus : a place, bye, and Plana : flat, give Llano: a flat place, strath, whence LANDES, LANNES (marshal), combining with Oros : a mountain we have ORELLANA (eponyme of the greatest river known) : possessing a mountain side reach

ing to the edge of the sea = BRIMLEY, EVELETH, COSTLEY,
SORBY: shore dwellers = VANDUZEE.   From Llano and Magnus,
MAGELLAN (magellanic clouds): great plane.   Phao: I shine,
gives Pharos: a light house, shiner, whence Ferrol, FAIRHEAD:
headland where there is a light house, born near.   MEERS,
MERRICK (mere wick): village near mere or sea = BALMERINO,
SEATON, SAY: sea near.   When SAY is French: maker of
armour padding, *con.* Soie: silk.   DITCHEN: of the Itchen
(river) = TICHBOURNE (claimant).   POOL, PALLAS, GLASSPOLE:
living on land watered by pools.   BARRAS: living at edge of
wood, at a barrier = EDGEWOOD.   In some cases BARRAS = BER-
RYER: man at barriers taking toll = DELAPORTE: of the gate,
con. LOCKPORTE: who had charge of a city gate, and DELA-
PLACE: a freeman, having gate liberty.

SEIDLITZ (powders), SIEGEL (mother): a settler, squatter,
newly arrived emigrant = NEAL.   INGERSOLL (colonel): palatial
abode having a portico entry, *con.* Entre-sol = GRESHAM, HOUSE,
LACHAISE: the house.   Some names assume almost a comic
aspect, as PEASOOP, which is nothing more than a *hope* in which
peas are cultivated.   So ESSIP (ais, esk), which becomes ESOP:
a hope through which water runs.   PETICOTE: little cottage.
PYCOT: a hut.   RAD: living at or near a rath, to which belong
the names RAT, RATTER, RATTO: rath, castle dwellers = CAREY.
RATICAN: head of the rath = KENEALY.   RAFFIN: white rath.
RYNO, RYNN: spit of land running into sea = SPITE.   SHIL-
LINGSWORTH: fortified huts (shiel) on a meadow.

UTTERMARE: coming from beyond the sea.   From Ecclesias:
a church, we derive EAGLESHAM = KIRKHAM, ECCLES, EAGLES,
EGGLESTON, EGGS, and EELS.   Fancy EAGLES, EGGS, and EELS
meaning a church!   INCHES, the parent of many a joke =
INNIS, INCE: an islander.   BUGBEE is only bog dwelling (by).
YETT is one living near a park gate.   FANE (not from Fanum:
a temple) = BAIN: fair, giving FANEUIL (hall): little Fane.
MAXUM = MAXWELL: the abode of MACK: the son.   LONG-
WORTHY, LANGTRY (Mrs.), LONGSTREET: long straggling dwellings.   GOODENOUGH (haugh) = THOROUGHGOOD (thal-er):
fruitful valley.   FOGO, FOGG = MEADOWS, PRATT, GRŒNEVELT:
green field.

As already seen, Normandy supplies England with a large
proportion of names, as DANGERFIELD, *cor.* from D'ANGERFIELD.
ANGER: man of Anjou.   HOMER is from St. Omers, as is
SOMERS.   Blois gives BLISS (burnt).   BASKERVILLE (Norman
Irish) for BACQUEVILLE: town on a stream, *con.* Beck: a
brook, whence BECKETT, *cor.* to PICKETT.   BEWS (when not
from Hugh) is from Bayeaux.   BELLEW: beautiful waters,
gives BELLOWS.   BOYLE (philosopher), BULLIS (bois ville) =
WOOTTON.   DEVINE (Norman Irish) is from William DEVIN:

of the vines = VIGNOLES. VARDEN (Dolly), FARTHING (ver dun): GREENHILL, Vermont, VALDELOGE : strong dwelling, *cor.* to FULLALOVE, and *con.* with *lodger.* IRONS (Joseph) from Airan, in Normandy = our Govan : smiths' town. KIRK (when not Scotch) : living near an oak (quercus). MILLION is from Melin, Normandy. MONEYPENNY (magnepeine): living on land taking great pains to cultivate. MOTON (M.P.) : town on a mound, *cor.* to MOTION.

PETO : man of Poitou, whence also POINTER. PORTWINE, from Poitevin. WARBOYS (verbois) = GREENWOOD. STAGNO = POND, *cor.* to STANHOW, while POND contorts to POUNDS. TOLER : tower dweller = RAT, CAREY. HUSSEY is a directory name from HOUSE : living in the principal house = ACE, AUGE (aqua, eu) = WATERS, as BELLEW : beautiful waters, *cor.* to BELLOWS, and *contracts* to BLEW, whence BLEUETT. CARDWELL (cardon ville): thistleton = CHARDON. ECCLES : a church, DIGGLES. DIXIE ("I wish I was in Dixie") is Normanised from Diss and = DISBURY. Wesleyan ministers think the Norfolk people poor and hard. A standing conference joke when a young preacher is appointed to the Diss circuit is, "He is *dis*appointed." TARRANT, TARRY, TARR : living near a tarn, deep dark lake on a hill. Casa : a house, gives CAZNOVE, CANOVA : near house. CHEESE = MEIKLEM : great house, one living in the house of that village = HOUSE. A lady named CHEESE was presented to her Majesty at a levee, and was voted one of the *creme la creme.* ROWELL (road well) : living on road to a sacred spring. MIRRILEES : miry fields. The great MELANCTHON : black earth = PEATS, its latter part, *con.* THON = our CLAY, FIELDS. The family name BALNAVES, from Ben Nevis : mountain snow. RADSTOCK : ridden of trees and staked for culture. This Rad *con.* Rath : a fort, a place cleared of trees, with which it was fortified. Consult Tyrrwhitt. FOWNE (s gloves) : living amidst grass land. Fœnum : fodder.

In this work there is no chapter on human names derived from flowers, such not being comprehended in the less poetic one on locality or that on trades. Had we one on flowers it would have been headed by DJULEEP (Singh): the rose. SINGH : a lion. He was fair to friends, but dreadful to foes.

Flowers have but lately, in the world's history, been a powerful factor in refining men, and therefore supply few names.

11

CHAPTER VIII.

PATRONYMS OR GENTILE NAMES.

PROPRIETY suggests our making an addendum to local names by illustrating personal designations on the wider scale of nations, whereby light is not only reflected upon individual origin, but that of a people, and, at the same time, side lights are thrown upon the geographical expression by which countries are known where such nations are located, and thus new interest attaches to the study of geography, and its connection with history is seen more clearly. A woman may marry her name away, a man may change his by law, or disguise it through caprice, but nations are not subject to such vicissitudes. Witness the world honoured name Britain: in all probability given thereto by Phenician sailors. The learned generally hold that when the Tyrians were trading for tin with Cornwall and the Cassiterides, they termed the country Brittistan: the stan, country, of the Britti, whence our Britannia. On our copper coinage we have Victoria D.G. Britt. Reg. F.D. Not Brit. The *t* is doubled to indicate the implied plural form of our great empire. So also we have Lusitania for Luzistan: hazel land, from the same brave seamen. (Gen. xxviii. 19.) So, too, Phenicia: land of the Phœnix: palm tree = Palmyra. Buckowina = Buckingham: beech tree country. Grenada: pomegranate land. Pomegranate: grained apple-grain, becomes gren. No such nation as the Lusi was known, and a king so named is purely mythical. Neither invasion by Roman, Saxon, nor Norman has driven the proud old name of Britain from national nomenclature. Nay, in the Tyrian ages Brittistan covered but a fringe of our south coast, now the name Britain covers a congeries of nations unified under one tri-colour.

The names of persons derived from countries are termed Patronyms, from Patria: fatherland. The following is a selection of the more instructive and better known:—

AUSONIUS (tutor to Gratian): an Italian = VITALIAN.

BRETT: a Breton, native of Brittany = BRIS (St.) In respect thereto our country is called Great Britain.

BRITON: pretty, fine made = PRYD (Welsh), ARBA (Hebrew), OLYMPAS (Greek), BRAVO (Italian), PRETTYMAN = foregoing, HERMOSUS, FORMOSUS = ISHOD: man of glory, fine made, becomes IZOD and IZETT, generally rendered fair. But PRITTY (pratum), from the Normans and = MEADOWS.

BURGOYNE (general), BURGIN: a Burgundian. The Burgundians were named from their weapons, as were many other nations. Their name is *con.* Bore : to pierce, an allusion to their lances, and Gon : war, as GONDEMAR : glorious warrior. So then,

Burgundians: war piercers, those who break through the ranks of their enemy with lances = L'OUVERTURE (Dominican warrior) : the opener = TALLEYRAND (diplomatist) : who *cuts through ranks.*

BARBARA : of Berber descent, a stranger = GERSHOM, and L'ESTRANGE, but STRANGE is a French form of the Scotch STRANG, as though Le Strang.

LAMORICIERE, MAURICE, MORRISS : of Moorish descent. From MAURICE the isle Mauritius.

Mauritania : stan of the Moors, dark people = Nigritia : Negro land, Soudan of the Arabs = Caramania (*con.* Caracal : dark eared wild beast) = Hindostan, Hind, Sind, SINDBAD (the sailor) : a native of India, *con.* Allahabad : the abode of Allah.

From Moor *con* Amaurois: darkening of eyes, and gives Mohair, as also the Morian's land, MURILLO (painter): little Moor.

Numidia : land of nomads, graziers. Nomad : one who seeks Nome : pasture.

Palestine : stan of the Philistines, shepherds, Pales : wanderers =

Gael, Gaul : forest dweller, *con.* Coyle : a wood, whence CULYER = SAVAGE, CONGAL : brave stranger, *lit.* dog Gaul. NEAL, NEIL, were originally Nageal, Nageil, *n* answering to new, seen better in NAGLE, NIGELL : new Gael, *i.e.*, an emigrant = NEWCOME : a stranger. HY NIAL (nine hostages) = O'NEIL. NEIL assumes the odd form of NILE. Dhu : dark, whence Dun : dark ; Dee, dark river, giving Donkey : dun coloured, DUFFUS : dark water, in combination with Gael, gives DUGALL, DUGALD, DOWELL, DOUL : dark Gael. GALYON : son of a Gael, an Englishman. Half a millennium since the Irish called us Gaels : strangers, thus GALLOCHER : half Gael, half Sassenach. FINGAL (prince of Mowen): fair Gael. OGAL : young Gael, whence OGILVIE : Ogal's by, dwelling. Hence, too, GALES, GAULT, GALT, GALL (phrenologist) GALLIE, WALE, WALLACE (Elderslie) : a form of Gallois. CORNWALLIS : compounded of Kern : a foot soldier, and Gallois. Galloglasses : blue Gaels. " The Galloglass succeedeth the horseman, and he is commonly armed with a scull: shirt of mail, and a Galloglass axe. The Irish do make great account of them." To the Gaels we owe GALLOWAY, ARGYLE : high places of the Gaels, *con.* Arch, high. BOTHWELL : their bothie, dwelling = BALLINGALL. WALES (Pays de Galle): CORNWALL : promontory of

the Gaels. Waloons: continental Gaels or Gauls, Caledonia
for Galedonia, Deucaledonian sea: black sea of the Gaels,
from vessels being wrecked there. So the Turks call Pontus
Euxinus, the Black Sea. Ortegal = Argyle: cape of Gaels.
Sinigaglia, from the Galli Senones. Galatia, for Gallo-Grecia:
inhabited by Gauls and Greeks. Gallant (accent on first
syllable): brave as a Gaul, though some have it a form of
Callant, which is also claimed as the source of VALENTINE.
Gallant (accent on second syllable): polite as a Gaul. Golosh:
sabot worn by the Gauls. So Cravat from the Croats, whence
also KRATTS: a native of Croatia. Gala and Galoon are also
Gallic, telling of display, characteristic of that nation. Walnut: foreign nut. Wallflower: foreign flower. As Coyle,
Coile: a wood, gives Gael, so we derive therefrom Celt.
KELT: a wood dweller. But Kelt: an arrow head, a flint axe,
is from Celtis (Latin): a chisel. Coyle properly means cover.
Forests were that to men as they yet are to beasts. Kilt: a
cover = Quilt. Hence Celtibri: Celts on the Ebro.

Franks: free, not subjected to the Roman yoke. Ripuarian
Franks: dwelling on ripe: Rhine *banks.* RIP (Van Winkle)
was a ripuarian, where boats arrive. Frank gives Franconia,
Frankfort, France = Liberia. Enfranchise: to make free, to
put among the Frelungi. Feringees: Turkish for Europeans
not of their faith. FRANCIS: an Italian speaking French.

GASCOIGNE (judge): a native of Gascony, becomes GASKIN.
From the Vascones we have VASQUEZ: son of a Gascon. VASCO
(de Gama): a Gascon, a Basque, one living near the Bay of
Biscay. Bay, Bas-que, Vas-co, Gas-con, are essentially one:
But our BASCOME: a wooded combe, valley. Gasconade: a
boast, suggesting RODOMONT (*con.* Rota and Mons): mountain
mover, our Italian boaster's appellation, whence Rodomontade
= Gasconade. Gascon also forms the well known GASTON.
We abbreviate gasconade to gas. " That is all gas."

Goth is identical with the words God, Gott, Good (fighter)
as pugilists say, " He's a good man ; can punish heavily." GETA
(son of Severus), GŒTHE (poet): a Goth. HIDALGO is Filius:
son, De: of, Al: the, Go: Goth; a Spanish nobleman. Massa-
gœte: great Goths, or Scythians. Gothland = Catalonia for
Gotholonia. Mœso-Goths: Goths of Mœsia. Ostrogoths: eastern Goths. Visigoths: western Goths, to whom we owe the
word and name BIGOT, whence, sometimes, PIGOTT. They
were unitarian and gave neither heed nor quarter to the orthodox. France owes them Cagot (canis Goth): a dog of a Goth,.
a hypocrite. We use Goth for spoliator, ignorant, unappre-
ciative of art. The Gothic order of architecture was an imitation of their shady forest dwelling in the Caucasus.

HELVETIUS (Physician): a Swiss, a native of the hills. Hel-

vetia (so called by dwellers on lower parts of Rhine) : hill country. Helvetii, Allobroges, Hernici, Taurini : highlanders, Swiss :
sweaters = Labrador : country needing great *labour ;* so called
by trappers and fur dealers.

Huns : hounds, like Cagot. So termed by the people whose
lands they invaded because of their hound-like looks and
actions. They call themselves Magyars. HUMBOLDT (cosmos) :
bold as a Hun. HUNNIADES (conquered Amurath) : son of a
Hun. Hence, too, Hungary.

ERIGENA : native of Erin, Irish born. Erin = Hesperia :
western, and (M')INIERNIE : man from west, and *con.* Hibernia,
Juverna.

SCOTUS (Duns) : a Scotchman = SCOTT (Sir Walter). DUNS :
a hillsman, gives Dunce = (by irony) Duns Scotus.

GIRALDUS CAMBRENSIS : Gerald the Welshman = WALSH :
welch.

INGLIS, ENGLISCH (chess) = LANGLEY, LANGLOIS: the Englishman.

JARMAN, JERMYN, LALLEMAND : a German, spearman.

HOLLAND: of the hollow land = HOLE, HOYLE. Hollow: hole
low, Neath : low, NETHERBY : dwelling on low ground = LEITH,
LATHAM. OLANDER (Dr) : a Dutchman.

FIAMINGO, FLEMING, FLANDERS : of the Flemings, so called
from their fleeing after some prehistoric battle.

HATTO : a Hessian, and PRUCE : a Prussian.

DENMARK : boundary of the Danes. DENCHFIELD : Dane's
field. DENFORTH : living on the Dane's road. DANBY : Dane's
dwelling. DAGMAR (princess) : glory of the Danes, though it
looks = DZOHARA : glorious as the daybreak. DAGBROD : power
of the Danes. HALDANE : half-bred Dane. DANSKIN : of
Danish origin. DENT (Strand), DENTON : Dane's town.
CRUDEN (concordance) : slaughter of the Danes. DANA (Am.
poet) : a Dane. The force of the word *dane* or *den* is not
easily given. One view is, it is ultimately derived from

Dagh : a hill, Daghistan : hill country, as it is supposed that
when first known to civilised men they were called

Daci, Dacians : hillsmen, uncivilised mountaineers. Under
this name they fought their way from the Caucasus to the
North Sea. When they settled in the Cimbrian Chersonesus,
the land lying low, it was called

Den : down, Denmark : low lying marches.

POLIGNAC (cardinal) : a Pole. POLAND : a plain. *Cossacks :*
goat people, climbers.

FRISBY : man of Friesland.

BRABY, BRABAZON, BRABENDER : man of Brabant.

LOMBARD : long battle-axe, *con.* Halbert, Halberdiers. "The
halberts hewe on hed, the browne billes bruise the bones."

BRISBANE: bone bruiser, brown bill man. Halbert: stone broad (axe), pre-historic. From Lombard (pawn shops) the word Lumber: timber, anything in the way.

PICTS: pike men, PICTON: great pike man. Pictones: Gaulish pike men. Puy-de-dome: peak of dome-shaped hill. Poictiers and Picardy are also *con.* therewith. PICHARD (ard): piked height = EGREMONT, MONTAGUE. Sometimes PICHAUD: a beggar, from Peto: I seek, petition. Sometimes the name of PETO: a seeker after bread. PICARD: native Picardy. But PICADOR (bull fighter): gilded pike. Pict has been given: painted, stained with wood. Tatooing was resorted to (1) for protection from gnats, (2) adornment, (3) distinction of clans and classes, as plaids afterwards, (4) to terrify in battle, (5) to honour the gods by their symbols, so when God, assuring the daughter of Zion of his love, says, "I have engraven thee on the palms of my hands." As nearly all ancient nations tatooed, so doing would not *strike* legionaries as distinctive in the Picts. Their pikes might. We had Picts or Picti insular and Pictones continental. So Britons on this island, and Bretons on the continent, arguing a community of language and origin—parts of the great Celtic family.

FIFE: a Pict, autocthonal to Scotland.

Vandals: wanderers, *con.* Baino: to go, wend, wind, went, wand-er, wond-er (mental wandering). Vado: to go; invasion = anabasis, WENDELL (Philips): Vandalic, of an old stock, all more or less involve to and froism, or at least motion. Andalusia for Vandalusia.

Suevi: swayers, going to and fro(m). Sway implies a forthput of power in wielding weapons, and is allied to swing, swim, swift: manifestations of strength. It is *con.* ZWINGLE, ZUINGLIUS (latinised), SUENO, SWAYNE, SWAIN, SWING, SWISHER, SWIFT, (St.) SWITHIN: forthputters of strength, Swither: to sway mentally, Swivel: a hinge, Swap: to change hands. From the Suevi we get Suabia, Sweden.

Rossi (the) obtained their appellation from the Sclavonic word Rossica: scattering, dispersion, nearly = Sparta: scattered village, and Diaspora: Jews dispersed like seed among the Gentiles. "Will He go to the *diaspora?*" The Rossic manner of life was similar to their nomadic neighbours, the Tartars. Of course Russia is from the Rossi, while Prussia is Bo-Rossi: near the Rossi.

Turk, Turcoman: wanderers. From Turk, Dragoman: an interpreter.

Pelasgi: wanderers, *con.* Planaomi: to wander, whence Planets: wandering (stars), Pales: a shepherd, *lit.* a wanderer, gives Palestine: stan of the Pales, Philistine. Pales also gives Palatine (hill): settlement of the Pales. Hence Palace: building on the Palatine. PALESTRINA (composer): from island settled by the Pales, of the old stock = PRISCUS (Mc)ALL.

D'OYLE, DOYLE, OIL: speaking the language of Provence (the province), as distinguished from one speaking after the manner of Languedoc (lingua de oc). The former speech was Attic, the latter Doric.

Wallachia: shepherd country, wanderers = Palestina, gives WALLACH, *con.* Gaul, WALLS: a pilgrim, WALLET: pilgrim carrying a scrip: scrapbag therefrom termed a wallet.

Bulgaria from Vulgarii, tribe from the Volga.

Servia: slave country. Fugitives from Roman slavery.

Saracens: descendants of the matriarch SARAH, hence Sarcenet: made by them. Of course, in this, as in many cases else herein, the reader must take the article, as do merchants, at their own risk.

Hagarenes: of HAGAR. "The tabernacles of Edom, and the Ishmaelites; of Moab, and the Hagarenes."

Sabeans from SHEBA: a captive, a caitiff. "And the Sabeans fell upon them."

Allimans: all men, each a man emphatic, gives Allmayne, Allemand. So, too,

Illinois (American Indians): men, par excellence. Similarly Guanches (unique aborigines of the Canary Isles): men = Muysa, a nation of Central America, on Humboldt's authority. There is a tribe of Negroes calling themselves

Bubees: men, which our sailors render Boobies. There was a primitive people located near the Caspian called

Mardii: men, whence MARDONIUS (brother-in-law to Xerxes). Not far therefrom was Hyrcania, whence the surname of the Maccabean hero JOHN HYRCANUS, from his victories over the Hyrcanians, as SCIPIO

AFRICANUS: conqueror of Africa, victor at Zama. The great convert

AFRICANER, and the more classical TERENTIUS AFER: Terence, the African, are also therefrom. Europeans having offspring in South Africa, those so born are called Africanders.

ANDREW (Greek): a man emphatically = DRING, WHYTE (English). The legislators

MENU (India), MINOS, MANNUS (Asir), *con.* Mons: mind, and mean men mentally.

MAN was formerly a title of honour, as was woman among the Hebrews. "Woman! behold thy son." "In French law, *baron* and *femme* denote the same as *vir* and *femina.* And in the laws of the Salians, Allemans, and Ripuarians, *baro,* or *varus et femina* occur for a *man* and a *woman.*" Hence our name and title

BARON: a superior man. Baron, Vir, Boar, Bear: strong,

virile.   From boar, the verb Farrow: to bring forth a litter of pigs.

QUEEN: a woman of political power, QUEAN: of bodily, a virago.

Ish: a man, Isha: a woman, Isis (goddess): the woman, Eve deified.

Marcomanni: march men, similar to Ukraine Cossacks: border guards, as

MARGRAVE: border sheriff.   MARQUIS: charge of marches, MARCHIONESS, its *fem.*

BISMARCK: bishop's boundary.   MARKHAM: home on the march, MERTON.

Jutland: land of the Jutes, giants, great *eaters*, as all giants were thought to be.

TEDESCO (*con.* Theod, Teuton): Italian for an Austro-German.

AUSTRIA (our brother): eastern realm, but Australia for Austral (southern) Asia.

STRAUSS ("Leben Jesu"): an Austrian, in some cases, or *con.* Struthio: an ostrich.

Pamphylia: all tribes, a mixture of different clans.

Triphylia: three tribes, viz., Epeans, Eleans, and Arcadians.

Tribe is from Trees: three, it is Oscan, Etruscan, and Roman clans welded.

Abyssinia: a mixture, so called by Arabs, who claim being of one blood.

Falashas is the name its natives own.   This word answers to Hebrews: emigrants.   Hebrew, Falasha, NIGEL, NU (actual) convey the same idea.

Ghez, or Itopia (for Æthiopia: burnt face) is what the Abyssinians call their country.

CUSH: swarthy, black-a-vised = ÆSOP: a Cushite, Æthiop. "Can the Cushite change his skin?"

Soor, Zur: a rock, gives Syria, Suristan: the country round Tyre, for Soor, Zur, Tyre, are one word.

EPHREM SYRUS: Ephraim the Syrian, Tyrian, as

DUNS SCOTUS: Duns the Scotchman.   This Duns gives *dunce*, as folks called a fool Duns in irony.

Sicambri: strong for victory, *con.* Sig: victory, as SIGISMUND: victorious defender.

Heruli: men of the Here: army, warriors.   Zeuss and Grimm say

Cherusci: swordsmen = Saxones and Cherithites: slashers.

Teutons: numerous, *con.* Theod people, Germans who were also called

Tungri: men who gave tongue, uttered loud war cries when engaging =

Zamzumim and Zulus, who both do or did swash-buckler work.

Belgii : populous, the many, *con.* Vulgus : the common people.

Dutch : from the great Asir Tuisco. DEUTSCH, *cor.* DEITCH, does not mean Dutch, but Tuesday born, dedicated to Tuisco. DITTMARSH : Dutch boundary, DITTMAR : glorious as Tuisco.

Mexico: from worship of MEXETLA, the American Mars, and so

Mexican = Mammertine : son of MAVORS, MARS, *con.* Mors : death.

Parthians : horsemen = Achaians, *con.* EACHRAN : a horseman. From Asp, Persian for a horse, ASPIMIRTAS : lover of horses, good rider = PHILIP.

Ispahan : place of horses, as Spain from Span (Phenician) : a rabbit, and so : overrun with rabbits as certain parts of Australia are. Spain gives Hispaniola : little Spain, Spaniel : dog of Hispaniola. The Phenicians gave names to Mauritania, Tingitania (Tangiers) Lusitania, Spain and Britain.

Italy : cattle country, *con.* Vitulus : a calf, *con.* Veal. So the Boii : men of cattle and Beotia : land of oxen = Clontarf (taurus) : bull meadow = OXLEY, HUXLEY (scientist).

NORMAN: north man, native of Norway: north way, NORVAL: Norman's dale.

Sclavi: glorious = Hellenes. Conquered by the Genoese they gave us the word Slave.

SLOVACTEN (Junius, 1809): a Sclav, speaker of their language.

Helenes : shining ones, whom we call Greeks, which name they repudiate, as the natives of our western principality do being called

WELSH, WALSH : stranger. Hence Welcher, who losing makes himself strange.

Cimbri, whence *Cambria, con.* Sicambri, is what they prefer being called.

DENMARK was formerly the Cimbrian Chersonesus: peninsula of the Cimbri.

Chersonesus : golden island, having advantages of an island yet with a continental connection.

Scythians and Scoti primarily : woodmen, forest dwellers, and secondarily wanderers. "The Scythians were divided into several nations or tribes ; they had no cities, but *continually changed their habitations.*" Some of them made a raid upon Palestine, where taking Bethshan : house of the sun, the Grecised neighbours called it Scythopolis.

> " How came the Gypsies into Spain ?
> Why look you :
> They came with Hercules from Palestine,
> And hence are thieves and vagabonds, Sir Alcalde,
> As the Simoniacs from Simon Magus."

Early in the fourteenth century certain unknown wanderers appeared in Europe. Separated from the people, upon whose lands they intruded, by language and habits the learned and ignorant were equally at a loss to know whence they were. An opinion arose that Egypt was the cradle of these anonymous refugees. This theory receiving general acceptance, they were called

Gypsies (GYPSEY is an actual family name) : emigrants from Egypt. They called themselves

Zincali or Zingari, words identical to a philologist. It was observed that *in* stood for India, às *ind* does in

Dindon (D'Ind) : of India, a Turkey cock. So Indigo : Indian plant, as

INDICOPLEUSTES : who had sailed to India. The *z* proved to be a formation upon *d*, while the terminal syllable is of similar force to *er*, as in slater, swimmer. Now *cali* is just *kali*, identical with *coally*, *con*. Kalos : beautiful. KALI : black goddess, Hindoo beauty. So then

Zingari : coally men of India. Further investigation brought to light that Gypsies were fragments of Hindoo tribes driven from the peninsula by the chronic wars about the time of Genghis Khan. They are yet termed

Zingari in Turkey and Persia, Zingani in Russia, Zinguener in Germany, and Zincali in Spain. The well known

GADSBY : dwelling place near which Gypsies, gadders, encamp. Nations were generally named in relation to war. Countries, when not called from their people, usually derived their appellations from their products or appearance. Many communities were designated after the manner of our regiments, from the pet weapon used. As we have

Fusileers from the fusil, musket ; Grenadiers from the hand grenade, so

Hernicia from Hern : a sword = Sicarii : sabreurs. Thus, too, Quirites : spearmen = Dorians. The old Scotch SPIERS : a quirite, a spearman. This is not philologically *con*. with Quirinal : oak hill, as Viminal : osier hill. So likewise

Samnites : dart men. We might say DOWDS : a Samnite, SPIERS : a Quirite. We have seen that the favourite weapon of the

Burgundians was the lance. May not LAUNCE (and his dog) : a Burgundian ?

LANCELOT : little Lance, or son of a Lance, or son of a soldier =

WICKLIFFE, but not meaning little lance, as usually given. Barbarian mobility is shown in the following names :—

Numidians, Vandals, Berbers (shepherds, gave name to Barbary), Walloons, Scoti, Celti, Turcomans (or mani), Pales, Suevi,

Wends, Wallachs, Scythians, Falashas, Hebrews, Pelasgi; and to the wanderers by land we may add the sea rovers (robbers), Vikings and WALMER, the former signifying sons of the fiord, ford; the latter : wanderer of the main. We should commit shipwreck on the rock Similarity by saying

Barbarian : a native of Barbary, as Bowditch does in his work on names when he has DALBY : doll of a boy. The Greeks termed those barbarians who spoke a language unknown to them, however humane they were. " The barbarous people showed us no little kindness." Foreigners seemed to Greeks to say bar-bar, mere babbling. Thus the Dutch called an African tribe

Bosjesmans : bush men, Hottentots, for they seemed to continually say *hot* and *tot*. After a similar type the Arabs stigmatised certain Africans as

Kaffirs, Caffres : infidels, miscreants, not Mussulmen.

Caffa (in the Crimea) : city of infidels, Giaours, Feringees.

Gueber = Parsee : a fire worshipper, non-Moslem. Gueber is root of Giaour. Compare

Caffa with Istamboul (islam polis) : city of the faith.

Kaffiristan (N. E. of Afghanistan) : country of infidels.

Tyre corresponds to Soor : a rock = Selah.

Petrea, Selah : rock built city. From Said : a hunting station. Sidon (aug.) : great Said, and also Zidon, whence

Zidonians : dwellers round the fishing and hunting station. We have the Spanish historic name SIDONIA (de Medina) : a crusading man. The Tyrians called the country round Tangiers

Tingistan, which the Romans softened into Tingitania, as the Latins delighted in the terminal *a*.

OBERDANK (Irridenta): an upper Danubian.

ONDERDONK (contractor) : man of the lower Danube.

CHAPTER IX.

GERMAN MYTHOLOGICAL NAMES.

When as yet Celts roamed the wide plains of Europe, before the heroic ages of Greece had passed away, Providence cradled mighty nations in the Caucasian mountains that were destined to overflow into the fruitful fields of the west, and possess lands then held by effete or infirm aboriginal races. These were the *Ases*, ancestors of the great Anglo-Saxons, who, on account of traditionary prowess and wisdom, were deified by their warlike and politic descendants. In the language of the East, Koh means a hill, whence Kohistan : the hill country = Montana. Koh and Ases gives Caucasus : hill of the Ases. Not only do they give name to that mountain barrier, but to the fairest region of the earth, viz., Asia : land of the Ases. Certain of their tribes were known to the Hebrews, Greeks, but most to the Romans, as Scythians. Thus we have SARSECHEM : Scythian prince, Scythopolis : Scythian city, previously called Bethshan : sun house = Heliopolis. One of the earliest Asiric leaders was SIGGA: victorious, *con.* Seco: I cut, he cut in, was a slasher = SLAGG. *Sigga* enters into the composition of many personal and national names indicative of the warlike propensities of its bearer, or if not from the warrior *Sigga*, yet from the same root whence his name sprung. Such names are SIGBERT, SIGBRAND, SIGISMUND, which consult. The Ases descended from the sides of the Caucasus and invaded Asia and Europe thousands of years since, as hundreds of years ago Highland clans made raids on the lowlands, and the Circassians devastated Russia from the same stronghold. It was the Asirs who fought ancient Persia before the victorious scimetar had been wrested from Elam by the brilliant Greek. The great name CHOSROES means warrior of the Ases. Though they failed in their Persian invasion, lasting proofs of virtue were left on the field of fight. That the Ases were a primeval race is evident from the following considerations. In the Hebrew, Persian, and Arabic languages, *az* or *as* means strong. Thus AMOZ : robust = ANDREW, AZAZ, strong, strong = STALLY : strong as steel. " And Bela, the son of *Azaz*." BOAZ : in strength, never breaking down, not fainting. " Solomon set up the left pillar, and called the name thereof *Boaz*." UZZIAH : the strength of the Lord, gracious strength (is given). UZZAH (Peres): strong person. Perhaps his strength occasioned his death, he thinking a man could hold up, if strong, the ark of God. It is seen to advantage in Gaza : a fort, strong place, sometimes Gaza : a goat, strong at butting. May there not be a deeply inlaid allusion thereto in these words : "But the Philistines brought him down to Gaza," the strong man caged in a strong place ? In the Hebrew this *az* passes into *ezer, ozar:* help, for strength is the sole source of help. ABIEZER : father of help, bringer of assistance. "There was also a lot for the children of *Abiezer*." AZUR : a helper. "Hananiah, the son of *Azur*, the prophet," varies to EZRA, ESDRAS with unchanged meaning, but shines most in EBENEZER : stone of help. Now, from this *az, as* strong, we have Ases : strong ones, probably the Persian for a horse Asp : strong one, and the better known AMAZON : woman, strong, very, from AM, OM : mother, woman, *az:* strong, and *on,* an augmentative common to most languages, ancient or modern, as seen in Pison from Pi : mouth, and means river with a wide mouth, debouchement, and Salon : great hall. So that Amazon : very strong woman. The story told me at school, "They were called amazons from a : alpha privative, and maza : the breast, because these women cut off their right breast the better to draw the bow," was indeed drawing the long bow. Salverte gives Az : strong, in the Persian as derived from As of this people, but the converse is true, as Az for strength was one of the first used by men. Long after Greece had run through its splendid career in politics, war, and philosophy, the wives, sisters, and daughters of the Ases met their husbands, brothers, and sons in full retreat before the superior discipline of the iron-clad Roman legions, led by the dread Marius. Instead of receiving them to their home encampment with tears, these amazons drove them back to battle with slings and spears. Strabo in his seventh book on geography, speaks of the *A*spungi living on the shores of Palus Mœotis, sea of Azof. That lake was probably so called from the Asir race. What if Azof : sons of Ases, its shore dwellers ? Their country was Aspungitani : Asir land. The *tani* from stan, as Beloochistan : poor country, ill to cultivate. One Asiric clan was called Aspasii from Asp : a horse = Parthian. From it ГУЅ$ТАЅГЕЅ (Darius): possessing horses = ASPIRMYRTAS : rich in horses. PHARNASPES : commander of horses, or chief horseman = ARCHIPPUS, MARSHALL. Thus Aspasii may mean Ases on horseback, and ASPASIA : an amazon, whence VESPASIAN from his mother. Some centuries before the dawn of the Christian era they gathered their forces from the Asiatic slopes of the Caucasus, and moved west as far as the Tanais : the Don, which seems to have been their Rubicon. Tanais (probably): Tan Ases, Asir land, telling of its waters shutting in their country. This they passed about

200 B.C., slowly fighting their way through the Celts until they reached the Elbe A.D. 90, and the Isle of Thanet A.D. 449. While some of the Asir nations broke up the Roman empire, purifying the corrupted southern lands, others fulfilled their destiny by invading Britain and founding an empire combining that liberty with bravery and stern superiority which characterise the old Caucasian stock. They reached America A.D. 1490, for the crews of the three ships which ploughed the virgin waves of the western seas were the sons of Visigoths and Lombards of Asiric blood. One section of the Teutons won Sadowa in that *annus mirabilis*, A.D. 1866, another cabled the stormy Atlantic, so that between their nations there should be no more sea. Their last sublime act was to make an iron road from the Atlantic to that greater sea men call the Pacific, A.D. 1869. They are now about to mingle the waters of the two oceans by a ship canal. The Asir will play Colossus with a continent for his foot hold. When at the beginning of the Christian era the Caucasian braves arrived at the storm beaten shores of the Northern sea they did not blanch thereat, though the sight of ocean was quite new, but forthwith built war ships and became kings of the sea, as they had been of the land, Vikings : sons of fiords. The Gael, too, had ventured upon the perilous Deucaledonian Sea but in a tiny coracle, and rarely beyond a distance covered at starting by the eye. What can more forcibly illustrate their reckless nature than the fact that their Hoff : temple, was on an island in the bosom of the black north sea called by them Fosetisland, but by Christians since, Heligoland : holy land. Imagine the Israelites, into whose tremulous souls Hittites struck terrors, had they had their (the) temple placed in such a sea! Here the ancestors of Blakes, Cooks, and Nelsons, and the long line of our sea lions, braved ocean's fury, not of necessity. but battle gladness and the wild excitement of gamblers who love risk. Their Hoff was uncovered, as they esteemed it unlawful to worship their Asiric ancestors under men-built-roofs. Here their priest called HOFFMAN, BLOTT, BLOOD, sacrificed victims conquered in battle and rowed from the mainland. " The many blood-stones scattered over the continent and isles of Europe are blott's altars." Of their gods, Odin was first and oldest, governing all things : and though the rest of the gods were powerful, yet they served him as children serve their father.

ODIN : one = HADAD. Sometimes he was called

WODEN : from Wod : mad, furious, inspiring men with warlike fury. He was represented completely armed, and with a drawn sword. His worship here is manifested by such names as

WANSBOROUGH : Woden's town, WANSTEAD : Woden's place. WONFOR : Woden's ford. His favourite temple was called WISBY : holy dwelling, often mistaken for Ouseby : dwelling on the Ouse. Woden was also called Gautr, whence GAUTREY : his worshipper. Sometimes he was known as GRIMR : strong, terrible. Grim death is strong death, reminding us of one of David's heroes, AZMAVETH : strong as death, *con.* Mors. To this name of Woden's attribute is to be traced

GRIMM (Jacob), GRÆME (Grim's dyke), GRAHAM and GRIMBALD : bold as Grimr, whence GRIMALDI (Joey), GRIMSTONE (snuff) : altar of Grimr, besides GRIMMOND : protected by Grimr. But in the Celtic GRAHAM : sullen, morose, gloomy. Another of his titles was BROWN : fiery, impetuous, *burn*ing for the fight. He also had the titles Bulmer and Bruce, whence BULWER (Lytton) and BRUCE (Bannockburn). Odin is also known as

JULVATTER : Jul's father, in whose honour the Yule log was burned.

YUILLE : born while the Yule log was burning. One of his sons was

TUISCO : earth born, gigantic, ancient, heroic. Some claim Tuisco as identical with Theos, Deus, Dieu : divine. To him we owe the word Tuesday : Tuisco's day. On the third day human victims were sacrificed in his honour. From him the people of Holland are called Dutch.

HERTHA, our Earth, was his daughter, and the *hearth*stone was his family altar. From her we have

HARDWIDGE and HARDWICKE : Hertha's dwelling, her temple. On each shoulder of Odin sat a raven, one being termed

HUGIN : forethought, provident, whence

HOGG : thoughtful, wise, as also HUGO, HUYGHENS (astronomer), UGO (Bassi), UGOLINI, EUGENE (Aram) and EUGENIE (Imperatrice). The other raven was

MUNNIN : memory, afterthought, whence MUNNS when not a form of Edmond. The raven on Odin's shoulder was stamped on the Danish standard. Woden, Frey, and Thor constituted the Asiric triad, answering to the Hindoo Trimutri and Biblical Trinity, tri unity. The Danes rendered to Odin the hyperdulia of their service, the Norwegians gave highest honours to Thor, while the Swedes gave their supreme worship to Freya. This last was an hermaphrodite, adored as Freyer *mas.*, Freya, *fem.* To him or her we owe our word Friday, as Wednesday is due to Woden. Connected with such worship is

FREYTAG (Pictures of German Life, 2 vols.) : Friday born. The tag or dag, for day, is *con.* Dagger : flashing like *day*, used swiftly.

TAGG (when not a trade name : maker of metal tags previous to use of pins) : a daggerman = DUDGEON : great dagger.

DAGOBERT : bright as day, very glorious.

FREYA : loved one, formed from Freon : to love, whence Friend.

FREYMUTH : having the spirit of Freya, amative, a lady killer.

FRIGGA : goddess of love and marriage, the Norse Venus, from same root as is

GODFREY : lover of God, GEOFFREY, JEFFRY, in Ireland SHERRY.

FREYWOOD : grove where Freya received divine honours.

FREYMONT, FREEMONT (president) : protected by Freya. Some claim these as meaning hill frequented by fairies. The fays, in this case, were made out of the sound of the name of the goddess

FREYER : lover, according to Asir lore slew the demi-god

BELI : bawler, whence BEALES, *con.* BELCHER for bawlcher. The sacred book of this Norse mythology was called Edda : old, ancient, which gives a description of the Eddaic Pantheon, wherein Thor sat at its centre, higher than the other deified Ases, having on his left hand seven stars. Thor's chariot was drawn by two goats, and the rattle of his chariot wheels on the welkin caused thunre, thunder, Thor's noise. From him we have the name

THURSO (Caithness) : Thor's dwelling. He presided in the air generating wind, showers, or fine weather. From him Thursday, when his blood (priest) honoured the god with the blood of men. Sometimes he was represented with a hammer, instead of a sceptre, accompanied by a Wolf and a Bear, which were deified through connection with him. Newly born children were dipped in running streams and marked on the forehead with his hammer. How strange that pious Hebrews should receive a similar mark, our T, for Torah : the law, of which the letter ת represents the word Torah, meaning : *this man keeps the law.* " He called to the man clothed with linen, having the writer's inkhorn by his side : and Jehovah said unto him, Go through the midst of Jerusalem, and set a ת (*tau*) T upon the foreheads of the men that sigh and that cry for all the abominations that be done in the midst thereof." How supremely strange that every year millions of children are signed with the sign of the cross that they may be gospel observers. Thor's hammer was called

MIOLNER : the miller, crusher, whence MILNER.

MACCABEUS (Judas), MACE (Jem), MAULE (Justice), *con.* mallet, MARTEL (Charles), SCHLEGEL, all mean hammer wielder. flavoured by Thorine vim rather than as the peaceful smith,

In all likelihood the name of this god means strong, and is the root of Taurus : a bull, whence

TORO : bull tamer. As to the god himself we may say

THOR : Asir bull. From his name we have

TORAGA : celestial cow, adored by Hindoos, it is a *fem.* of Thor. " Le toit du temple du *Toraga* est orne de quatre taureaux dorés." Compare these four gilded bulls on the roof of her temple with the winged bulls in the portico of the Assyrian temple at Khorsabad. Compare Tora-*ga* from Thor with Vir-*go* from Vir. These names are mementoes of prehistoric times. Many personal appellations are allied to bull worship, as

KNATCHBULL : son of the bull, forms KNOBEL, *con.* KNIGHT, *con.* Gnatus : born =

APION (opposed Josephus) : son of Apis, the Egyptian bullgod. Thor was our bull-god and Brahm that of Hindoos.

SERAPIS : Apis hidden, the constellation Taurus, Thor : the bull-god, below the horizon of the Nile.

SERAPION : son of Serapis, of divine genealogy.

Apis, Thor, Brahm, the human-headed bull of Assyria, and the Sinaitic calf are various embodiments of one idea. Divine strength manifested through creaturehood. Thor and Theos differ in this, the former became the symbol of brute strength, the latter was essentially connected with holiness in Himself, justice towards His creatures. There are few languages of the old world not supplying their quota of taurine personal names. Howbeit, personal names are more deceptive than ordinary words, and so the name-hunter sometimes fancies he has bagged a genuine bull of Thor descent, whereas it may be only local. Such is the modern Roman

BASVECCHI (Pietro), teasingly like Vacca : a cow, yet means living near *old foundations* of Roman wall, *con.* Civita Vecchia : old city, and also *con.*

BASETTI : a dwarf, near the *base,* earth. The names

COE (captain) : a cow, COWIE, BULLEN, BOLEYN (not from Boulogne), are mysteriously *con.* with this ancient symbolic worship—serving the sign instead of the Thing signified.

THOROLD : protected of Thor's power, becomes THURTELL, TYRELL (Sir Walter), and has for its first form THORWALD, whence

THORWALDSEN (sculptor) : son of Thorwald.

THURKETTLE, KETTLE : having charge of Thor's kettle used in divination for incanting by weird women as in Macbeth.

TONER : of Thor, born on Thursday, or during thunder.

THORBURN, THOBURN : Thor's bear, *con.* BERNSTEIN : hill frequented by bears.

THURLOW : Thor's sport, good at throwing Thor's hammer.

12

THORGAR : Thor's spear, a good shot.   TORSLEFF : loved of Thor, brave fighter.

THURSTAN : the stone whereon human victims were slain on Thursday, a priest, takes forms, TUNSTAN, DUNSTAN (St.), DUNSTONE.

TORQUIL : Thor's pledge to fight, *con.* guild.

TRUFITT (fid. wid.) : Thor's wood, priest presiding over his grove = GROVES when not local.

ASTOR (library) : Asir Thor, the divine Thor.   Thursday born.   In the symbolism of the Valhalla, Thorine, strength and fire (active principle), were intimated by placing a flint on a pedestal.   In later ages, " The Flindt god was formed lyke the image of death (grim); and naked save only a sheet about him.   In his right hand he held a torch, or as they termed it, a fyre blase.   On his head a lion rested his two fore feet, standing with one of his hinder feet upon his left shoulder, and with the other in his hand, which to supporte, he lifted up as high as his shoulder."

FLINDT, FLINT : priests of that god.   The Asir of judgment was Forceti, whence

FAWCETT, no connection with hawks.   There was also a Frissian goddess, Foseta, from whom is derived

FOZIER : priest of Foseta.   She it was who gave the primitive name of Heligoland : holy island, viz., Fosetisland : sacred to Foseta.   Another member of the Caucasian Olympus was Baldur, the Apollo of the Asirs.

BALDUR : white, beautiful = FLINN, BAIN, BLAKE.

BELISARIUS : white prince (date oboli).

BALDWIN : loved of Baldur, wise.   A delusive guess makes it *bold victor.*

BALDRED : counselling like Baldur, *con.* ALFRED : counselling like an elf.

BALDREY : ruling like Baldur, a wise monarch.   Usually given by canting, as *bold king,* or soldier *girded* with *baldrick.* It is sometimes hard to tell whether certain names are from Bald : bold, *stripped* for battle, or from Baldur.   Weland was the Asiric Vulcan, whence

WAYLAND : priest of Weland.   Of the great Asir, called Will, we know little, his worship being confined to the prehistoric period, but we do know to him is due the world wide name,

WILLIAM : beloved of Will, *con.* over*whelm,* and Helmet : a head covering.   The name is often given as a form of GILD-HELM : a Teuton, who, slaying a legionary, received, medal fashion, a gilded helmet.   That guess came of the Romans having no *w,* so that, when the name is Latinised, it stood Guellimus, suggesting gold, but the old Germans went in for isen (iron).

WILLIAM varies to WILLIS, WILES, ULLIN (lord), GUILLOTIN (whence Guillotine), WILKES (democrat), WILL, WILLET, WILLIMOT, WOOLCOCK, WILHELMINA, whence MINIE (rifle), MINNIE (Gray), MINA, WILLOX, WILLOCKS: little Will = the Irish *dim.* ULRIC.

WILLING is a name now in use meaning son of Will, heroic, courageous.

WILLFRITH: loved of Will, bold.

WILFRED (patron of Ripon): counselling like Will, advising to fight, and showing how.

WILLARD (tracts): of Will's nature, brave.

WILLIMAR, WILMER: famous as Will. From him we also have VILLAR, WELLER (when not local), and VILLIERS. Then there was a demi-Asir, like Hercules, known as

MANNUS: the man, by excellence. He had three sons— INGO, ISCO, HERMINO, whence the Ingœvones, Iscœvones, and Hermiones, ancient German tribes.

INGO: the son, first born = ELAM, gives

INGRAM: Ing's raven, Danish standard bearer.

INGLE: priest of Ingo, being quite unconnected with Ignis : fire.

ISCO: the ash, son of the first man, of the old stock.

HERMINO: man of heer, her, army, warrior = HERMAN.

IRMAN: man of battle fire = BROWN: burning to be at it. Irman was the German's marching god, receiving special honours when the braves began their line of march. To him we owe the name Erming (Street). Nor may we forget the terrible Asir known as Loki. He agrees in certain attributes with

APOLLYON, SIVA: destroyer, and SATAN: adversary. To him was committed the caverns of Mount Caucasus, where those who died of age, disease, or had fainted in battle, or were wounded behind, were confined. With him was associated dread

HELA: coverer, who cast perjurers and cowards into caverns where snakes ever spurted cold poison. Hence our word hell, and the noble name

ELGIN (marbles), for Helgyn, for Hela given. Loki teased gods and men. He was a combination of Mercury and " Jack the giant killer," which latter hero is none other than an embodiment of Lokian exploits made readable. From him we have LOXTON, LOCKSTON : town of Loki, where was his temple.

LOCKHART: Lok or Loki's nature. The legend of Douglas taking Bruce's *heart locked* in a casket is as true as that

GUTHRIE is *gut three* (fishes), or NAISMITH is nail smith, or equally wrong *nae smith* ava.

LOCKMAN is not lock maker, but very fierce.

HAVELOCK: had in the care of Lok. In him the old Asiric
fire burned in full heroic glow. Had the Hindoos worshipped
Asirs instead of Punch and Judy gods, Victoria would not be
Empress of India. The Asir Neptune was Œgir, who had
charge of wind and tide, as had the sea-god of the Gaels,
Neithe, whence

ABERNETHY: mouth of Neithe's river. The Oder or Eider:
Œgir's door, where the Asiric Neptune let the sea into the
land. Of men receiving names from Œgir we have

EGAR, EGBERT: bright as Œgir, vikings, seamen brave.
Hence, too, OGRE: Œgir: like, Egg: to drive on as waves do
wood to the shore. Nor were the Asirs wanting in ladies.
Besides our old friends FREYA, FRIGGA, FOSETA, and HELA,
true amazons, they had a Norse Bellona called HILDA, a
sublimated Semiramis, Boadicea, or Joan of Arc. To her is
due the well known name

MATILDA: maid of Hilda, becomes MAUD when that is not
from Magdalen. Then we have the notable

HILDEBRAND (pope): sword of Hilda, becomes ALDROVANDO
and *cor.* to HELDENBRAND and HELLBRAND. Besides which we
have the Visigothic

ILDEFONSA, ALFONSO, ALONZO: rich in war instruments,
spears, arrows, swords, Hilda's *fund.*

CLOTHILDA: celebrated as Hilda, *called* as much as Hilda.

CHILDEBERT: bright, glorious as Hilda.

HILDEMAR: glory of Hilda = HERCULES: glory of Juno,
Hera. Hilda was so common as to become synonymous with
girl, as

BRUNHILDA: clothed in armour, a Teutonic Boadicea, *con.*

BRUNO: mail clad, from this name the famous dynasty

BRUNSWICK: Bruno's dwelling.

SWANHILDA: swan-necked girl. To this favourite amazon
we owe

HILDYARD: guarded by Hilda. In addition to these goddesses the Teutons believed in a kind of battle angels known as

VALKIRIERS: fallen electors, selecters of the fallen. They
flew about deserted battlefields, swan winged, picking out the
heroic dead for the Valhalla: *hall* of the *fallen,* shield roofed,
next Vingolfa: the Asir palace, their Pantheon. But the
Valkiriers left on the battlefield any wounded in the back, or
whose red right hand did not still grip the blood-stained spear,
for HELA and LOKI. Besides these greater gods they had less
known as

JOTUNS: giants, from the root *eat.* The Greek notion of
giant is earth born from Ge: the earth, but the Norse idea
was great eater, as is illustrated in the case of the giants Jack
killed. From eat we have

OATTS, OATTMAN : eaters, giants, *con.* Oats : that which may be eaten, edible. The same is seen only in a more gluttonous form in

SWAGEMAN : one who *assuages* at meals that he may start again. From Jotun we have

JOTURNUS (king of the Rutuli) : who appears in Virgil as TURNUS. From Jotuns, Jute, whence Jutland : country of, and

GETTINGS : son of a Jute, born of a giant. One of the grotesque Asirs was

HROSS : horse god, with three legs, whose priest was known as DREYFUSS : three feet, being in peril of passing for a Manx man. Hence in some cases

ROSS, whence ROUSE (bravo !), ROSSINI, ROSETTI, and

ROSAMOND (fair): Hross protected, *Fair rose* and *rose* of the *world* are sheer cant, guesses by sound. These Jotuns correspond to Theseus, the Cyclops, and heroes known to the infancy of all nations. Whether their biographies are purely historic, mythic, or exaggerations of traditions, founded upon facts, who shall, in all cases, tell ? Probably Asirs and Jotuns were men like Hengist and Horsa, who signalised themselves in unchronicled wars about the roots of the Caucasus. Their Œgir was an Axine (Black Sea) or Caspian pirate idealised into a god by the time they had fought their way to the Baltic. This seems the more rational, as the Germans used Anar in the sense of ancestor, whence

HANSARD (reports): Anar natured = PATROBAS : walking in his father's steps. A current M.P., 1883, is *Septimus* (Hansard) : seventh born.

ANSON : son of his Anar, as we say son of his father, chip of the old block = PATROBAS, ICILIUS.

ANLAF : left of his ancestors to fill their place in the battle array, or as Paul would say, " Baptized for the dead," to take the place of.

OLAF is a form of ANLAF, whence OLAVE (St.), giving

TIRAULAY : land dedicated to St. Olave.

TOLLIDAY : born on St. Olave's day, *con.* Tooley (street).

ANGOTT (Madam de): of divine descent, good son of his Anar = OSGOODE.

Some names are derivable from Ases in the gross, as

ASKEW (Ann) : Asir descent, giving HUSKISSON (railway), son of ASKEW. Probably the Highland (M') ASLAN, AUSLAN, AUSLAND : son of an Asir, one of heroic descent.

Anselm and Anselmo : helmeted, protected by Ases.

AASBIORN (Danish): divine bear, whence the more common OSBORN, which neither means *Ouse burn*, nor *house born* (serf).

OSWALD : shielded by Ases, under their protection.

ANTLIFF : loved of the Ases, for bravery.

OSBEORT: glory of the Ases for her beauty. The Wolf, Bear, Bull, Fox, and Raven being sacred to Woden or Thor, their names are frequently used with an Asiric force, but taken in common animal sense. As we have seen Taurus is from Thor, so Foxes receive their name from that Asir from Friesland to Spain. The Spaniards called it Thorra, which has passed into Zorra. It seems to have taken name from Thor because of colour, he being red-headed and having a foxy beard, besides, as to character, being crafty. From the Wolf-god we have a liberal supply, of which it is not easy to allocate fairly between the ancient god and the vulgar wolf. Perhaps we had better put gods and wolves into one pack, and leave some bold hand the responsibility of dividing them into divine and common.

WOLFGANG (Gœthe): whom the wolf god gangs with for protection, conversely gives

GINGOULPH is gang wolf (god), *cor.* into cockney oath " By JINGO ": by St. Gingoulph.

RUDOLF and RODOLF : famous wolf, much talked of warrior.

MONTGOLFIER (balloon): mountain frequented by wolves.

CANTELOUP (chant de loup): a settler who, from his dwelling, can hear the wolves howl. Common both in the Old World and America.

KENWOLF : made keen by the wolf-god, inspired of him.

ULPHILAS (Mæsogothic bishop): little wolf, short of stature = FILLAN (St.) whence GILFILLAN and M'PHELAN.

LYCIDAS : son of a wolf, but capable of meaning son of Luke.

GUELPH (Victoria Alexandrina): a wolf, a howler, yeller.

WOLFSTAN (archbishop) : greatest wolf, chief warrior.

LOVE, from Lupus : a wolf, LUPSON = LOPEZ (Spanish) : son of LOBOS : a wolf, whence also LOPE as LOPE DE VEGA : Lope of the champagne.

VEGA : a meadow, from Vigeo : I flourish, as grass does.

LYCAON : son of LYCUS, and as

LYCUS : a wolf, LYCAON may be the Greek answering to LOPEZ, for *Lycus* might be a man so called as our WOLFE (general).

Lycaonia may be the *kingdom of Lycaon,* or from river

Lycus : white = Elbe, from Albis white, but Lycus may mean wolf (river) as

Zab : river where wolves drank, it is *con.* ZEEB : a wolf, a hyæna, so called from the noise made. Thousands of men have been named ZAB. Xenophon in his Anabasis mentions the Zab.

Louvre (palace): she wolf, killed when foundation was being laid.

WOLSEY (cardinal): wolf's island, near Winchester, where the Welsh paid tribute in wolves' heads. Woolsey = Ulva, as SHIPPEY : sheep island, and RAMSAY (Allan): ram's island = Faroe : island of sheep.

DUPANLOUP (bishop): of the wolf's head, carried on shield.

PINCELOUP: wolf snarer, trapper, catcher, *con.* Pincers, from Prehendo : to take hold of.

WOOLNOTH : bold wolf, warrior. NOTMAN (sometimes): bold man.

LOUVOIS (statesman): wolf's wood, forest haunted by.

ASTOLPH : hasty wolf, raging for fight or prey, whence our HASTINGS (Warren). Lupus, LOVE, takes a *dim.*, LOVELL (lord) = ULPHILAS, PHELAN : little wolf.

> " He was beloved by all, and most of all by the children ;
> For he told them of the Loup-garou in the forest,
> And the goblin, that came in the night to water the horses."

Loup-garou is the remnant of a superstition that prevailed throughout Europe for three thousands of years. An old writer says, " Were-wolves (the English of Loup-garou) are certayne sorcerors, who having annoynted their bodies with an oynment which they make by the instinct of the Diuell, and putting on a certayne inchanted girdle, does not only unto the view of others, seeme as Wolues, in worrying and killing and most of humane creatures." This is what the Greeks meant by

Lycanthropy : a man becoming like a wolf. Thus Periander's son,

LYCOPHRON : wolf-minded, and notably

LYCAMBES (father of Neobule) : wolf-life, animated by a wolf.

> " Thy currish spirit
> Govern'd a wolf, who, hang'd for human slaughter
> Even from the gallows did his fell soul fleet,
> And whilst thou lay'st in thy unhallow'd dam,
> Infused itself in thee."

LYCOPHRON, LYCAMBES of the Greeks, accurately answer to WOLFMUTH (Michael) of the Germans. Each of three may be interpreted wolf-inspired.

These names and words are relics of belief in transmigration, a doctrine yet held by the major part of Adam's race. That many Jews held it is manifest from Matt. xvi. 14. " Some say thou art John the Baptist ; some Elijah : and others Jeremiah." Now, of these, two were known to be dead, John and Jeremiah. The same is plain from John ix. 2, " Did this man sin that he was born blind ?" All unconverted Jews hold it, as do the Chinese and Hindoos. The latter eschew beefsteaks lest they should be dining off a grandfather.

LUPA : she wolf = Louve. By her help we unlock the myth
of the twa bairns put out to be wet-nursed by Mrs. Wolf. In
Virgil we have her equivalent in

FLAVIA LYCORIAS : auburn-tressed Lupa. This last gives
Lupercal, where the twins were suckled, or because there
the Lycian Pan received adoration.

> " May we do so ?
> You know it is the feast of Lupercal."

GUNDULPH : war-wolf, whence GODOLPHIN (lord).

AUTOLYCUS : a wolf itself, rapacious, great robber.

BIDDULPH : commanding wolf = LYCOMEDES (king), gives
Botolfstown, contracts to BOSTON.

BARDOLPH : bear wolf, attendant on Thor, standing by the
man named from them in battle as they stood close to Thor,
contracts to BALFE (composer).

RANDOLPH : shielded by wolf-god (Ran : a shield round),
gives RALPH, ROFF, RAWLINGS, RALSTON : Ralph's town.

LYCURGUS (Spartan): wolf-guard = BERGER: flock protector,
early designations for shepherds, *con.* Lycopolis (Egypt) : wolf
city, exactly answers to our WHELPTON (pills) and LUPINOF
(actor).

WOLFSRUNA (St.) : runes, counsels, like a wolf = WOLFRAD,
con. Runnymede : council meadow, Wolverhampton is from
WOLFSRUNA.

MAIDULPH (cantingly given as *maid helper*) : mead wolf =

LYULPH (ly for lea), neither haunting mountain nor wood,
gives Maidulphsbury, whence Malmesbury (wine).

WOLSELEY (Garnet): wolf's field, place frequented by
wolves.

WOFFENDALE : valley frequented by wolves. Wolves were
at large in England till A.D. 1300. January was called "Wolf-
monat, to wit, Wolfs-month, because people are wont always
in that month to be more in danger to be devoured of wolves
than in any season els of the yeare ; for that, through the
extremity of cold and snow, the ravenous creatures could not
find of *other beastes* sufficient to feed upon." In Scotland,
where they never were numerous, though there they had
better cover, the last was slain by Sir Ewen Cameron, far on
in the seventeenth century. Rory Currah was Ireland's great
wolf-slayer. The last was killed in the Wicklow mountains
A.D. 1770. There are few Celtic personal names *con.* the
wild dog, for so the Celts called the wolf. We have

MADDEN : dog, fox, or wolf.

SKENE : a dagger, a clansman, so called for killing wolf
therewith. The worship of the wolf-god never took amongst
the Gaels, so that any names having to do with the wolf must

be disassociated from the god if met with in Scotland and of Highland origin. The king of France kept a Louvetier: wolf hound master, whence LOVET (lord).

TURPIN (Turi-lupin): wolf of Turin, a heretic. Papists so named the followers of Claude, Bishop of Turin, as he favoured the doctrines of the Vaudois. Lupin: wolf plant, earth devourer. Wolf's bane: wolf-killer, Wolf, Vulp(es), Yelp, Guelph, Golpe (O. French for a fox, made obsolete by RENARD: hard judge), are one word given to the animal for the skirl it makes.

WADDILOVE, WADLOW (truly innocent looking) are wolves in sheep's clothing, being formed on Vado and Lupus—invading wolves, warriors good at a raid across the marches. Then

FIDLER (note, not Fiddler) is fashioned on Vis de lou: visage of a wolf, hairy and scowling =

HUN: face like a hound. The German Jews revel in proper names taken from animals, as

HIRSCH = our HART, BOCK, DEER, yet it is far from correct that all their names are taken from the animal world.

GALPIN (Cassels) = FOX. The names LUPUS, LOVE, LUPA, LOBOS, LYCUS, LYCORÍAS, GUELPH, ULPH, JELF, ZEEB, and HIRPUS = WOLFE, HIRPUS, signifying literally snatcher =

HARPY: ravisher, whence HARPAGUS (general) and

HARPALYCUS: harpy wolf, ravishing wolf, ravenous robber. These names show how wide the range of the wolf has been; but we will make from wolves to gods. Teutons worshipped more by libations than did the Celts. Every bred English labourer will, when he has finished drinking his pint of beer, invert the pot so that its drainings and foam fall on to the earth. I have noticed many Irish and Scotch labourers drinking, but never saw one so do. The residuum let fall was once a libation to the Ases. From drinking religiously to the Asiric divinities we owe our drinking healths. An old Saxon would lift up his bowl of ale and say, "Here's to Thor's min": to the minding of Thor, then he would pour out the remainder as though it would be licked by Thor's bear and wolf. Through this form of worship the Germans and English drink more than most people in the world. Hindoos and Mahometans worshipping on the dry principle are more sober. The Eddaic mythology taught the immortality of all men. But those who have wounds in the front of their bodies received in combat enter Valhalla, answering to the Celtic

Flathinnis: island of the brave, where companionising with Ases they drink ale or metheglen from the skulls of conquered foes. When fou they fell into attitude and fought unto death, sleeping during the night to awaken next morning and pass through the same happy scenes. Valhalla was called Ham:

home, and a dying warrior was said to be going home. The
Teutonic Peter who kept the gate of Valhalla was called

HENRY (ham ric, ry) : home ruler. The antiquity of this
name may be inferred from the number of its derivations, viz.,
HENDRY, HENDERSON, HENRIETTA, HENDRICK, HANDRICKS,
howbeit HARRY, HARRIS, HARRISON, HAL, HARRIET, HAWES,
HERRIES, HERRICK, HALLEY, HALSEY are not from HENRY,
but an independent word, viz.,

HARRY : one who *harries*, plunders, man of war having a
weakness for expropriation = MERODE: marauder. Our ancestors
also believed in a water demon who like HROSS had three legs.
Him they called

NICK, whence NIXON : son of Nick, spiteful, giving the
metal Nickel. When the miners first discovered it they
naturally thought it was silver, but finding it to be far
inferior thereto, thought old NICK had changed its nature, and
so they termed it Nickel. This name has been generally mis-
guessed from Nicolas. The ancient Germans worshipped
neither Muses nor Graces. Greeks sought the good and adored
the beautiful, becoming like the gods they adored. Teutonic
service of the gods was often limited to bravery, whereby the
Germans became as indomitable as the Ases. Howbeit, they
were characterised by a love of freedom equal to that of their
fondness for war. In the nature of things braves cannot be
slaves. They cherished a strange fondness for home quite
contrastive with that of the Red Indians. In their march
from the Black Sea to the Baltic, unlike Greeks, Romans, or
British on the line of march, they took their home with them,
household requisites and family. Hence the Germanic stock
care much for fireside enjoyment and home pleasure more
than the Romance nations do. They take kindly to civilisation
by reason of training to labour in encampments and marches
for a thousand years. Hence they colonise with success which
no purely Celtic race does. We must not part company with
this grand old stock without adding that amongst their demi-
gods was

BILL : the moon, whence our BILL = MOHUN, and

BILLINGS (Josh) : son of Bill = BILSON. Now, as every one
knows, this name is generally given as a form of Will, but
suum cuique. BILSLAND : was land whereon was the hoff:
temple of Bill. Asiric tradition teaches that at a destined
period our earth will be destroyed by fire, which will be done
by

SURTUR : the black one, *sooty*, who sits at the end of the
earth holding a flaming sword. Hence

SUTTER (Californian captain). Till the world ends LOKI
remains fettered in his Caucasian cave. A new world is to

emerge from the ruined old, wherein the good, *i.e.*, the valiant, will be happy. Then the Ases sit in judgment condemning all cowards to dreary habitations. From the mythologies of Celt, Greek, German, and Roman, a third part of Biblical history, doctrines, and prophecies may be inferred. These nations must have had a primitive religion in common, of which their mythologies are the debris. The Teutonic Valhalla was an exaggerated memory of hunting and fighting amidst the primeval forests which the Muscovites cut down when unearthing the Circassians a few years ago. They were a remnant of the old Asir stock. From that Caucasian Olympus of the Asirs we have our love of liberty, our fortitude, our aptitude for labour, and scorn of danger. Our native mountains are loftier by far than Ossa and Pelion as, though foreshadowing days when we Anglo-Saxons would by as much excel the Greeks. Our Bible knows Baal, Milchom, Moloch, Dagon, Astarte, Jupiter, Mars, Apollo, Diana, but is ignorant of Odin, Thor, Hilda, because the cradle of our race and their western route all lay far north of Palestine. Biblical silence as to the Asirs and their warlike sons is indirect proof that Asiric worship, like Druidic, was not in the habitat of prophets and inspired penmen. Yet Paul says: " Where there is neither barbarian, *Scythian*, bond nor free." The apostle of the Gentiles had heard of our fighting ancestors. So, in the book of Maccabees we read : " Ptolemee taking the king aside into a certain gallery, as it were, to take the air, brought him to be of another mind, insomuch that he discharged Menelaus from the accusations, who, notwithstanding, was the cause of all the mischief ; and those poor men, who, if they had told their cause—yea, *before the Scythians*, should have been judged innocent, them he condemned to death." Though the Germans had only so faint a connection with the Hebrews, their knowledge of facts and doctrines clearly stated in the scriptures, is truly wonderful. According to them the first man was

ÆSC : an ash tree, being made therefrom.

EMBLA : the elm, was first woman. The sons of Hengist, who reigned hundreds of years in Kent, were called

ÆSCINGAS : sons of the ash, of the aboriginal stock = Iscevones of Germany. There is a true and deep connection beteen xylomancy, telling fortunes by trees (the Greeks called it rhabdomancy : rod divination), and the marriage of Adam and Eve. A thousand years ago, when a Saxon was smitten of Cupid he went to

ASHCONNER : who *kenned* all about the ash tree branches, and consulted him as to his bride and outcome of union. Herrick refers to this old custom when he says :—

" Of ash-heaps by the which ye see
Husbands and wives *by streaks* to chuse,
Of crackling laurel, which fire-sounds,
A plenteous harvest to your grounds."

Choosing a wife by ash streaks, was a form of consulting Adam
as to which of his daughters should be chosen. Who fails to
see a connection between this and the streaks Jacob made in
poplar, hazel, and chesnut rods? Boys now read the low
(root of lum), glour in the fire to see things to come, but men
did it thousands of years since, only the boy's fire is of sea-
coal, but our ancestors' fire was charcoal of ash or flaming
laurels. Strange to tell, men took to the ash (Adam), but
women to the elm (Eve, like to like): hence we have Witch
Elm, and the famous name

WYCHERLEY (William): his cognomen being from a field in
which such trees grew. Tree worship was not unknown to
the Celt as

(Mc)COLL: the hazel, and BEITH: the birch; not dwelling near,
made of, but original. The German word Gott now applied
solely to God was originally applied to any Asir in the sense
of good (fighter), just as a pugilist terms that person a good
man who can hit hard and is a glutton at punishment. It is
now a common directory name.

GOTT gives Gottin: goddesses, as HILDA, HELA, FRIGGA,
hence Gottingen (university): abode of the Asir goddesses =
Hildersheim: Hilda's home, suggesting THORESBY, THURSO:
Thor's home, and giving the provincial English name

HILDERSHAM.

ASHCONNER *con.* ELCORN, OLDCORN (& Garnet), forms of
aleconner: an exciseman, a guager.

CHAPTER X.

HIERONYMS—NAMES MYTHOLOGICAL.

THIS title is *con.* HIERONYMUS: called after a god, a holy
name, giving JEROME, GIRALAMO, GERONIMO. These be they
which in earlier ages were not only names but powers, mighty
powers too, and much for evil. No man now trembles at the
mention of Jove, Baal, Pluto, Thor, or Dis—gods supernal or
infernal—nevertheless, records of their supposed being and
doing are fraught with instruction, and may not be lightly
lost sight of. So antiquaries and geologists search on and
under the earth to win information for historians, despising
neither coins, barely legible, nor the rude looking stone.
Such skilful toil unveiled Herculaneum, laying bare the inner
social life of patrician and plebian as the current of life flowed
in the days of the elder Pliny. Such names tell the thoughts
and intents of heathendom when as yet it was, in its appointed
way, preparing our place on the great stage of history. The
mind Divine encompasses past, present, and to come, blending
all in one eternal Now. Man is likest God in intellect when
apprehending, to the extent of his limited powers, the history
of the past, the laws governing multiform being, whereby he
is able, though in small measure, to forecast in economics and
physics. Such being the case, what field of thought is despicable to a thinker? Even though, by reason of past study, his
mind be so richly stored with literary lore that novelty of information be impossible, still he despises not a suggestion,
knowing it may prove the means of linking thought to thought,
in the order of cause and consequence, whereby he may perfect knowledge already realised, but lacking this finishing
touch. Our chapter will be in much part, mythological, a
study as needful to the divine as alchemy to the chemist. As
light flowed by command from anterior darkness, cosmos from
chaos, so science was based on previous error. Not the less
has that error a beauty, a charm wholly its own. There was
a system, a glamour of beauty, about myths and gods to
which cultured minds ever render the tribute of admiration.
Those ancients adored their gods, we moderns admire them.
The spell that bound a son of Hellas gazing on Olympus may
be gauged by the fascination, yet hovering over his literature,
architecture, and statuary. No such beauty adorns the
grotesque gods of the East Indies and the South Sea Islands.
They lack the mystic grandeur, the harmonious adaptation of

gods to men characterising the mythology of Homeric and Virgilian lands. What comparison can there be between the six armed Siva cutting off the fifth head of Brahma and Apollo striking the lyre in the Temple of the Muses? The Greeks and their imitators the Romans divide gods into celestial, terrestial, and infernal. When praying to the last, they pointed earthwards or stamped upon the ground. Infernal is *con.* Infra : beneath, In-hera : in the earth. The di-gamma, *f* being used formatively.

HERA : earth, gives the telluric deities, earth-born gods, ARES (Mars), HER-MES (Mercury), HER-A (Juno).

Areopagus : Mars' hill, ARION (poet) : son of Ares, ARETAS (king) : martial, war-like = MARTIN, ARETINO (Guy) : warrior, ARETHUSA : virtuous, valiant, ARISTOS : best, most like Mars = BEST (beat, beater, beatest, best : who beats all).

HERA (Juno, earth-born goddess) gives HERCULES : Juno's glory, ERCOLE (Itn. form), HERODOTUS (father of history) : Juno's gift, Heraclea : city of Hercules. In the system of Berosus, the sun is called Arsa : burner, whence ARSES (son of Ochus) : son of the sun, destroyer, *con.* Ur. Therein the earth is called Aretz, whence Erzeroum : Rouman land.

EROS : love, is from Hera : earth. "The cosmogenic EROS of Hesiod is apparently a personification of the principle of attraction, on which the coherence of the material world depends." Simonides assigned him APHRRODITE : foam spring, and ARES : earth, for parents ; a mythical way of saying EROS was child of Earth and Sea.

EPAPHRAS : foam sprung, may be viewed as the masculine of APHRODITE. "*Epahras*, a servant of Christ, saluteth you."

EROS : love, *con.* ERASMUS, ERATO (presides over love songs, lyric poetry),

ERATOSTHENES (geographer) : strength of Erato. HER-O : earth sprung =

GYGES : a giant. Giant from Ge : earth, whence GAIUS (mine host), CAIUS, KAY (Shuttleworth), when not from Hugh, KEY as in Key's College. The Greek idea of giant is earth born, the German notion great eater. Consult JUTE, TURNUS, JOTUN, OATTS. Besides Hera, Ge, Terra meaning earth, we have Ops and Tellus of similar meaning, whence

OPPIUS (Cæsar's friend) : son of the earth, OPPIDIUS = TUISCO : earth born, autocthon.

Oppidium : an enclosed earth work, a city = Turra from Terra : earth which in its turn is = Tel-el-Kebir : strong earth work = Purgos, from Ge : earth.

TULLIUS, TULLY, TULLIAN, TERTULLUS (orator), TERTULLIAN (father) : earth born, indigenous, very (ter) ancient. Hera is the root of Aro : I plough, Sero : I sow, and Erian : to plough.

DEMETER (Ceres): ge meter, mother earth. DEMETRIUS, DIMITRI : worshipper of Ceres.

CERES : increaser, *con.* Cresco: I grow, whence Cress = Grass : that which grows. Ceremony : worship of Ceres, as Veneration : adoration of Venus. That CERES is to be understood of the earth is manifest from the myth making PLUTUS (god of riches), the son of Ceres, and PLUTO (god of hell), son of SATURN : sower, and OPS : earth.

PLUTUS, PLUTO, formations on Polus : much, many, meaning rich by crops, or metals got from the earth. Polus gives Poll : university degrees, Plus : more, plu in plu-perfect, full and poly as Polynesia : many islands.

PLUTARCH (biographer): chief in riches = POLYMELES (historian): many sheep, opulent (ovis) = GEMALLI: rich in camels.

DIS for Dios : divine, other name of Pluto, is root of Dives : riches got by spade, plough, or pick.

HERA also gives Germanic goddess, HERTHA = DEMETER. From Ops : earth, we have Opici : aborigines of Campania, Opaque : earthy, not to be seen through. Corroborating above,

Homo: a man, from Humus : ground, whence Humilis : low, Humility, the opposite of Hauteur: highmindedness, Humidus: moist, low lying, Humanity : becoming mankind, Homo forms Hon in French, as

PRUDHON (communist) for PRUDHOMME (" Le Journal"): prudent man, following odd fashions, antiquated. Hon forms One : a person, as : " One hardly knows what to say." To summarise, we have gods, men, principles, and common names traced to a telluric source, as ARES, HERMES, HERA, EROS, CERES, OPS, DEMETER, HERTHA, HERO, GAIUS, CAIUS, TUISCO, TULLIUS, TULLY, OPICI, giant, aro, sero, erian, homo, hon, one : all of the earth earthy.

DIOS (Jupiter) : divine, gives Dioclea : Jupiter's glory, city where his temple is, like Heraclea : where temple of Hercules, giving HERACLITUS, so former gives DIOCLETIAN (emperor) : from Dioclea in Dalmatia. He is also called

ZEUS : living, in the superior sense of life giving, *con.* Zoon : an animal, a living thing.

ZEPHYR : life bringer. ZOPYRUS (maimed his nose to take Babylon): the fire of Zeus, lightning — BARCA, LLEWELLYN.

ZEUS : living, gives DIOS, DIS, DIVUS : a god, *fem.* DIVA (Patti) : a prima donna, Divine : god like, Divination : revealing mind of god as to future. DION (Cassius) : divine, DIONYSIUS (Bacchus): dug out of Dios, gives (St.) DENNIS, which some contract to SIDNEY, but this is local, meaning south water.

DIOGENES (snarler): begotten of Dios. DIOTREPHES (preeminence) : nourished of Dios, his protege.

Dios: divine, gives the *fems.* Dione, Diana, Hence, too, Dioscuri: divine twins, Castor and Pollux. "A ship of Alexandria, whose sign (figure head) was Dioskourois."

Dioscorides (physician to Anthony): son of divine twins, their worshipper. Dios also forms Jovis, and Jovispater: Jupiter: father Jove, and the *fem.* of Jove is Juno, whence also Jovial: merry, like Jupiter or Olympus at a banquet, hence, too, Jocundis, Joke: witticisms at feast of gods. Dios forms Dii: gods, whence dies: a day, the portions of time being named from gods, as Vendredi: Venus' day, Friday, as Thursday from Thor. Dies gives Diurnal, Journal, etc.

Hermes and Aphrodite give Hermaphrodite: Mercury and Venus in one, androgyne, John and Joan.

Mercury (medius curro): middle runner, courier between earth and skies. Though some give it as *con.* Merx: merchandise, Merceo: to sell, whence Mercenary: a hireling. Alchemists applied it to Quicksilver: living, moving silver. So lead was called Saturn, and copper Mars. Phos: light, gives

Hephestus (Vulcan): fire god = Agni, called from Mulceo: I soothe, soften, from Mollis: soft, Mulciber: metal softener. Vulcan gives Volcano: workshop of the fire god. Vulcanise: to make metallic looking.

> " Nor was his name unhear'd and unadorned
> In ancient Greece; and in the Ausonian land
> Men called him *Mulciber:* and how he fell
> From heaven they fabled, thrown by angry Jove
> Sheer o'er the crystal battlements; from morn
> To noon he fell, from noon to dewy eve,
> A summer's day; and with the setting sun
> Dropt from the zenith like a fallen star
> On Lemnos, th' Ægean isle."

Estia, Vesta (the zenith) star. "The altar of the deity was in the *centre* of the house, and sacrifices commenced with her, because, as Plato says in Timœus, she was the oldest of all the gods; or rather the *pivot* on which they all turned." She was also worshipped under the form of the crescent moon. Horace calls her "Siderum regina bicornis:" the two horned queen of the stars.

Astarte: star goddess, Astrifiammante: flaming star, queen of night. Hester, Esther, Eoster, Asteria, Estelle, Stella: stars, risers, shiners.

Asterope: star faced, glorious. Astrophile (and Stella): lover of star lady. Asterion: son of a star, *con.* Æstus: the tide, *rising* waters, whence Estuary: tide way. East: point of sun *rising.* Austria: east kingdom. Yeast: barm, which makes to *rise.* Eoster is identical with Easter: when special honours were paid to the Saxon Astarte.

HESTER (when male name): Easter born, fortunate.

TYPHON (*con*. Typhoon: wind spindrifting the sea like smoke): son of smoke, volcanic agency personified.

PALLAS: brandisher, spear vibrator, *con*. Ballo: I throw. Palladium: an aerolite, said to be statue of Pallas fallen from heaven, upon which Trojan safely depended. Trial by jury is the *palladium* of British liberty. Luke says, " Ye men of Ephesus, what man is there who knoweth not how that the city of the Ephesians is temple-keeper of the great Diana and of the (aerolite) which fell down from heaven." This aeorlite was the pedestal of Artemis. To this hour there is one served in the Medjid (Temple) at Mecca, called Kaaba, which the Arabs say was white when it was the footstool of God at the time He visited Adam in Paradise, but turned black when he sinned. Thousands of hadjis will kiss it this year.

PALLAS when an English name is formed on pool and esk.

ARTEMISIA (Carian queen): daughter of Diana, ARTEMIS.

MINERVA: strong, *nervous*, *con*. NERO, NERVA: men of nerve and verve.

JANUS is a form of Eanus, from Eo: I go, alluding to change of seasons. He was Bifrons: two faced, one looking to old year, other to new, Memory and Hope, like HUGIN and MUNNIN.

JANUS, *con*. Janua: a gate, from Eo: I go, exactly = Gate, from Go, which gives gad, GADSBY—gadfly, goat, guest, PREN-DERGAST, Ghaut: the mountain gate. Janitor: gate-keeper = YATES, GATES. January: gate of the year.

ARTEMIS (Diana): whole, pure, virgin = AGNES, JEZEBEL, PARTHENOS (Sciote monk). A man may be a virgin, only a woman can be a maid. " These (144,000) are they which have not defiled themselves with women (been guilty of spiritual adultery, idolatry): for they are virgins." PARTHENOS = VIR-GINIUS. Hence ARTEMUS (Ward).

APOLLO (sun, whence sunstroke): destroyer = ARSA (Persian). APOLLYON: son of destroyer = ABADDON (symbolic king of locusts) = BALAAM. APOLLOS: dedicated to Apollo. APOLLO-DORUS (the illustrious): gift of APOLLO = MITHRIDATES. PHŒ-BUS: life light (the sun) PHŒBE (moon) *fem*. Diana. Him they armed with golden arrows, rays, her with silver.

> " Queen and huntress, chaste and fair,
>   Now the sun is laid to sleep ;
> Seated in thy silver chair,
>   State in wonted manner keep,
> *Hesperus* intreats thy light
>   Goddess excellently bright !

> " Lay thy bow of pearl apart,
>   And thy crystal shining quiver ;

13

> And give unto the flying hart,
> Space to breathe, how short so ever;
> Thou that mak'st day of night,
> Goddess excellently bright!

HESPERUS is a short form of Eosperus: light scatterer, the gloaming, gives Hesperia, Italy, so called by Greeks, the Romans said the same of Spain. It is the *op.* of Anatolia: sunrise country, the Levant, HESPERIDES (three): daughters of *Hesperus.* Vespers: evening worship, the evening star being in the west. Vespertilio (bat): evening bird. West is a form of *vast,* applied to the Atlantic, wherein the sun seemed to set to old worlders.

ATLAS: bearing much, mountains of N. A. personified. As the clouds rested on them they seemed to bear up the sky, the world,

ATLANTIADES: daughters of Atlas, Atlantic islands. That ocean is named from washing roots of Atlas mountains.

CYBELE: cube like, perfect, a cube being symbolic of perfection.

PAN: all, all the principles and powers of nature personified, gives

FAUNUS (son of Picus): a satyr, hence Fawn: young deer, Fauna: animals of a country.

> "In shadier bower
> More sacred and sequester'd, though but feign'd
> *Pan* or *Sylvanus* never slept, nor Nymph
> Nor *Faunus* haunted."

SYLVANUS, SILAS: son of the wood = SAVAGE: wood-dweller. Pan gets the credit of teaching the aborigines of Italy to make bread, whence called Panis, giving Panniers: bread baskets. After baking he took to building, and erected the first temple from which any temple is called Fanum, giving Profane: before the temple, unclean, excommunicatee. After cookery and architecture he began his military career as a lieutenant under General Bacchus, whom he served in his Indian campaign. He won no star-medal but scared the enemy, whence Panic: fright caused by Pan. He was worshipped at the Phials of the Jordan, where a city was built to his honour, called Paneas or BANIAS: son of Pan. PANDORA: all gifts. The Graces were

AGLAIA: splendid, THALIA: flourishing, EUPHROSYNE: merry girl, making of a joyful mind, nearly = Euphrates and PHRYNE: rich in mental endowments. The Hours were

EUNOMIA: good law, DICE: justice, IRENE: peace.

> " Universal *Pan*
> Knit with the *Graces* and the *Hours* in dance,
> Led on th' eternal spring."

CLOTHO (the Fates): cloth worker, spinster = FILATRICE: thread spinner.

ATROPOS: not to be turned, inexorable, unmoved by prayers. LACHESIS: allotter, who give mortals their lot. When happiness was to be a man's portion, they span a white thread, but black if his undertakings were to be disastrous. CLOTHO held the distaff, LACHESIS spun the thread, ATROPOS cut it. FATES from Fari: to speak = WEIRD (Sisters), from Word.

The Muses were

CALLIOPE (1): beautiful voiced, *con.* KALI: beautiful, and ZULEIKA: music voiced. -

CLIO (2): proclaimer, caller out, *con.* CLYTUS: renowned = POLYPHEMUS: much spoken about. CLESIDES (painter): son of Clio, famous man. CLISTHENES (invented ostracism): strength of Clio, illustrious.

MELPOMENE (3): cantatrice, songstress, *con.* PHILOMELA: lover of song, giving FILOMEL. Melodious: pleasing as song, Melodeon: giver of melody.

EUTERPE (4): turning well, moving gracefully, *con.* Trophy victorious *turning-point* in battle, Tropics: sun's turning-point, EUTROPIUS (historian): Euterpe's son, polished man.

ERATO (5): amiable, *con.* ERATOSTHENES (librarian): Erato's strength, an admirable man.

TERPSICHORE (6): turning gracefully in the dance, fascinating danseuse. Choir was anciently dancers. CHORAGUS: dance leader = CORYPHEUS.

URANIA (7): heavenly muse = CELESTINA, HIMMELINA, *con.* Uranus: distant planet.

THALIA (8): blooming with youth and beauty. May take it as *fem.* of THALES (of seven wise men) and = BLOOMER, FLORENCE, FLORA and Flora: the vegetation of a country. THALES = FLORUS. THALPIUS (Helen's suitor): Thalia's son, handsome fellow, *p* formative = TANTALUS (Lydian king), gives Tantalise: to tease.

> " They ferry over this Lethean sound
> Both to and fro, their sorrow to augment,
> And wish and struggle, as they pass, to reach,
> The tempting stream, with one small drop to lose
> In sweet forgetfulness all pain and woe,
> All in a moment, and so near the brink;
> But Fate withstands, and to oppose th' attempt
> Medusa with Gorgonian terror guards
> The ford, and of itself the water flies
> All taste of living wight, as once it fled
> The lips of *Tantalus.*"

POLYMNIA: full of hymns, tuneful, *con.* POLYBIUS (Corinthian king): long lived, patriarchal = GERYON: aged, who governs.

Museum: temple of the Muses. Musa: a song, Music: the science of song. Amuse: to sing to. Muses: singers.

Antiope (Amazonian queen): beholder, large eyed, con. Optics: science of vision = Europa: ox eyed (bull's back). From her we are supposed to have the word Europe: landing place of Europa. These names are the op. of Myotis: she who shuts her eyes in a pretty playful manner.

Amphitrite (ocean personified as a woman): rolling round. Brontes: thunderer, hammersmen = Thor. Cyclops (forms Cocles, Horatius): whirler of forehammer, alluding to sledge hammers, describing segments of circles, con. Encyclical: circular letter, sent all round. Briareus: strong = Forbes. Cottus (Titan): smiter = Smith, and giving Cotta (Aurelius).

Britomartis (Cretan goddess): sweet maid. Cranaus (of Athens): head, chief, con. Cranium: the head, Creon, fem. Creusa, Crœsus (rich): governor, Cressida: royal daughter. Scylla: rockhead, identical with Scull: hard part of head.

Calypso (Oceanide): hidden, covered, con. Apocalypse: uncovered, as

Latona, Leto: *latent* ones, being maids they were Alamoth: hidden in harems, or by veils.

Cacus (robber): bad, con. Cacodemon: fiend, devil. Demons, like other spirits, were good or bad.

Gorgon: terrible. Demogorgon: terrible demon. Desdemona: demon bound, afraid of ghosts, superstitious.

> "And the cannibals, that each other eat,
> The Anthropophagi, and men whose heads
> Do grow beneath their shoulders. These things to hear
> Would *Desdemona* seriously incline."

Stheno (Gorgon 1): strong one, as Sthenelaus (Mycenian king): strength of the people = Demosthenes, Folkhardt.

Euryale (2): wide sea, con. Euripus (strait): wide flowing, whence Euripides (tragedian): son of Euripus, changing like its tide, fickle. Eurynome (mother of Graces): wide ruling. Nomos: law.

Medusa (3): commandress. This and Medea (sorceress) may be taken as *fems.* of Medon: commander.

Æolus: variable, as the wind. Æolian lyre: harp played by the wind.

Esculapius (Egyptian god): man dog, man of wisdom, dog for vigilance.

Galatea (thea): milk-white goddess, con. Galaxy: milky way.

Gallio (deputy): brought up on milk by hand = Achilles: without the lip.

Lactantius (apologist): son of milk, con. Via lactea: milky way = Foster.

Leucothea: white goddess, the dawn personified.

> " Meanwhile,
> To re-salute the world with sacred light,
> *Leucothea* waked, and with fresh dews embalm'd
> The Earth."

Hebe: youth. Ganymede: joy commanding, *con.* Oregon: mountain joy, that covers the hills with flowers.

Eden, Aden: pleasure, gives Adonis: pleasure giver. "*Adonis* symbolised the quickly fading flower of youth—of all that flourishes luxuriantly and perishes rapidly; and the festivals which bore his name, the celebration of which was accompanied by the lamentations of women, were amongst those in which the ancients had reference to the decay of nature." The Syrians called Adonis,

Thammuz: hidden, not to be found = Calypso, Latona, Leto,—

> " *Thammuz* came next behind,
> Whose annual wound in Lebanon allured
> The Syrian damsels to lament his fate
> In amorous ditties all a summer's day;
> While smooth *Adonis* from his native rock
> Ran purple to the sea, supposed with blood
> Of *Thammuz* yearly wounded."

Adonis (the river): red, *con.* Adam: red earth, Edom: red-bodied, so called from carrying down sand and red ochre after heavy rains. Adonis was favourite of Venus, who mourned his loss when he was fatally wounded by a boar.

Venus from Venio: I come, that which brings, love by which comes life, Ventus: wind, which comes and goes, Veneor: to hunt, *come* after.

Iris (rainbow): *uniter*, link of beauty between earth and sky, *con.*

Irene (empress): peacemaker. Iridescent: coloured like a rainbow.

Ireneus (father): peaceful = Pacificus (frater), Solomon.

Iris was daughter of Thaumas: wonder, admiration, *con.*

Thaumaturgus: miracle worker, and Electra: brightness, *con.* Electricity: light from amber.

Meleager: land lover. Morpheus: shaper, former, *con.* Formosa. A god who prevented sleep being monotonous by varying it with dissolving views, commonly called dreams. Milton, with a charm all his own, describes his industry, but calls him Fancy for Phantasy, from Phainomai: to appear. It is to be distinguished from Imagination: the act of making mental *imagery*,—

> " In the soul
> Are many lesser faculties, that serve
> Reason as chief, among these Fancy next

> Her office holds. Of all external things
> Which the five watchful senses represent,
> *The forms, imaginations, aery shapes*
> Which Reason joining or disjoining, frames
> All what we affirm, or what deny, and call
> Our knowledge or opinion ; then retires
> Into her private cell when Nature rests,
> Oft in her absence *mimic Fancy* makes
> To imitate her ; but by joining *shapes*
> Wild work produces oft, and most in dreams."

MORPHE, also *con.* Morphia : sleep producing drug, Forma : shape, gives

FIRMIUS (conquered by Aurelian): well framed = BEAUREGARD, ARBA, TETRANDER.

NEMESIS (goddess of vengeance): distributor, retribution bringer, *con.* Nomos : law. Anti-nomian : law opposer.

OMPHALE (Lydian queen): the navel, *con.* Umbo, Umbilical, a name of mystic meaning, *con.* worship, derived from Egypt, and =

Delphi : the womb (of the world), *con.* Adelphos : a brother, one from the same womb.

NEPTUNE : washer (of the shore). POSIDEON : footbinder, salt waters difficult to walk in.

PELOPS : dark faced, swarthy visaged = SWARTZ, ÆSOP, DEE, DUFF, DARNLEY, *con.* APELLES = PHIN : fair.

PELEUS : black-a-vised, giving PELOPIDAS (Theban): son of Pelops, Peloponnesus : island of Pelops, now Morea for Romea : Rouman territory.

SISYPHUS : very wise, *con.* SOPHIA : wise woman. Sophist : having semblance of wisdom.

NIOBE (daughter of Tantalus): new life, *con.* Biography : life description.

BIAS (of seven): full of life = WICKS. The rivers of Hell were

Lethe : forgetfulness, *con.* LETO : hidden, as drinking of it *hid* former life.

Phlegethon : burning, *con.* PHLEGON : fiery temper. Phlogiston : burning gas, phlegm : viscid matter from *inflammation.*

Acheron : *ache run,* flowing with pain, *con.* ACHAN : troubler. Cocytus : wailing.

ULYSSES : anger (of his grandfather). Odyssey : ode of *Ulysses,* song of his wanderings.

OSIRIS : much eye, the Sun, Egyptian Apollo.

ISIS : the eye, the Moon, the Egyptian Diana. Some excellent writers give

ISIS as formed upon Isha : a woman, Eve deified.

BAAL, some give as *lord,* others derive from OBEL : serpent of God, greatest, *con.* Ophis : a serpent, whence Ophiusa : serpent isle.

OPHIUCHA : SERPENTARIUS : serpent holder. OPHION : great serpent = OBEL.

PYTHON : stretcher, great expander, said to have sprung from the slime of the Deucalian (Noachian ?) flood, being slain by Apollo, the Pythian games were instituted in commemoration.

> " Dreadful was the din
> Of hissing through the hall, thick swarming now
> With complicated monsters, head and tail,
> Scorpion, and Asp, and Amphisbœna dire,
> Cerastes horn'd, Hydra, and Elops drear,
> And Dipsas (not so thick swarm'd once the soil
> Bedrop't with blood of *Gorgon*, or the isle
> Ophiusa) ; but still greatest he the midst,
> Now Dragon grown, larger than whom the sun
> Engendered in the *Pythian* vale on slime.
> Huge *Python.* . . . . .
> And fabled how the Serpent, whom they call'd
> *Ophion* with *Eurynome*, the wide
> Encroaching, Eve perhaps."

Scorpion : scatterer (of poison). Asp : a shield. Amphisbœna : going either way.

Ceraste : horned. Hydra : water snake. Elops : glider.

Dipsas : thirst (producer), *con.* Dipsomania : madness for drink. "As we went to prayer a certain damsel possessed with a *pythonic* spirit met us." Pythonised men inflated themselves as though receiving an *afflatus* (consult Flamen) from the deity, which was like serpent swelling, or leather bottles filling. That the Jews were guilty of ophiolatria is plain from their use of the word Ophel, identical with Obel : the serpent of God = Ophion. "Manasseh compassed Ophel, and raised it up a very great height." The Medians were serpent worshippers also, as their names show.

ASTYAGES : dragon, flying serpent, DEJOCES : biting snake. No civilised people, free from ophiolatria, would take names for great men from reptiles. OBEL forms

BAAL, BEL, is the root of LARS : lord, LARA (Byron), Lares, household gods, LARTIUS : son of a lord = HERRING.

> " With these came they, who from the bord'ring flood
> Of old Euphrates to the brook that parts
> Egypt from Syrian ground, had general names
> Of *Baalim* and *Ashtaroth ;* those male,
> These feminine ; for spirits when they please
> Can either sex assume."

BAAL gives BELUS : son of BAAL, BELIAL : useless. This is one of the most expressive in the entire Bible. It implies that a wicked man can do no good, must be useless, for " without *me* ye can do nothing." BAAL answers to APOLLO, MITHRAS, ARSA, HADAD, names under which the sun was worshipped, while ASTARTE, VENUS, DIANA, URANIA corresponds to worship of star or moon.

ASHBEL : august, fire of Baal. "The sons of Benjamin were Belah, Becker, and *Ashbel.*"

BALADAN (Baal adon): Baal is lord, the opponent of ADONIJAH : Jehovah is Lord.

BELSHAZZAR : Bel most glorious. BELTESHAZZAR : Bel's prince, the ruler Bel favours, nearly = HANNIBAL. That name must have been an abomination to the great slave Daniel. Gabriel does not say, O Belteshazzar ! but "O Daniel."

ESHBAAL is identical with ASHBEL. "Saul begat *Eshbaal.*" He was also called

ISH-BOSHETH : man of shame = ÆSCHYLUS. Bosheth: shame, confusion of face, is from Baal, whose worship brought shame. Some hold that Baal gives Balah : to destroy, to ruin, whence

BALAAM : destroyer of people (am), but BAALAM : of a strange people, a foreigner.

MEPHIBOSHETH : exterminating Baal. MERIB-BAAL : contending against Baal. Saul might have named these his sons in a spirit of antagonism to his worship, but as Hebrews were forbidden to mention gods, it would have looked healthier had there been no allusion to Baal in the names of the royal family.

JERUBAAL : let Baal plead. A surname of Gideon, "But the name clave not to him."

BALTHAZAR : king protected by Baal. Baal gave name to Baalbec and Arbela, cities wherein his sacrificial flame was kept burning. Beyrout is Baalberith : lord of the covenant. There are several places mentioned in the Old Testament from this god, as Baal-gad : lord of fortune, Baal-hamon : lord of the people, Baal-hazor : lord of Hazor. "Absalom had sheepshearers in Baal-hazor." Baal so commonly combined with the names of localities that it came to mean simply a place, as

Baal-perazim : place of breaches. Baal-tamar : place of palms. It takes two forms, *fem.,* to wit, Baalah, Baalath. "The border was drawn to Baalah, which is Kirjath-jearim." Solomon built Baalath and Tadmor in the wilderness." Philistia served

BAALZEBUB, BAALZEBUL : fly lord = Jupiter Muscarius : the fly-dispelling Jove. In course of time this deified "Papier Moure" came into use with a contemptuous force, so that in apostolic times it was synonymous with Satan. Zebub: a fly = Tetze, S. African bull slayer, from Ze : noise made = Musca, from muzzing, for Muzca. Our Fly: that flees. Zebub, Tetze, Musca = Buz : to drone.

BAAL-PEOR, BAAL-PHEGOR : lord of the dead. Jesus contrasts Jehovah with it. " Jehovah is not a god of the dead, but (God) of the living." " They joined themselves unto Baal-Peor, and ate the sacrifices of the dead," *i.e.*, of the lord of the dead.

ADHERBAL (slain by Jugurtha): greatness of Baal. ASDRU-BAL (son of Hamilcar): of the seed of Baal, *con.* Zoroaster: fire seed, begotten of the fire god.

HAMILCAR is from the Sidonian Hercules, written in Punic, Ha-Melk-Art: the great king, *con.* ARTAPHERNES: great shepherd, leader.

HANNIBAL (Alps) = BAAL-HANAN: grace of Baal, born by. Latter very ancient.

BELEPHANTES: Baal's priest. When Alexander entered Babylon he foretold his visit would be fatal.

METHUMBALLES (Carthaginian noble): man of Baal, *con.* METHUSELAH: man of the dart.

CASSIVELAUNUS is the Roman form of CASSIBELAN, from the Cassi tribe in composition with Bel.

> " He was carried
> From off our coast, twice beaten: and his shipping
> (Poor ignorant baubles) on our terrible seas,
> Like egg-shells mov'd upon their surges crack'd
> As easily against our rocks   For joy whereof
> The famed *Cassibelan*, who was once at point
> (O, giglot fortune!) to master Cæsar's sword,
> Made Lud's town with rejoicing fires bright,
> And Britons strut with courage."

May was called by the aboriginal British Beltaen: the fire of Baal, as then the sacred fire was renewed on his altar in honour of the sun beginning to put forth power. The old custom of maying and dancing round the maypole is *con.* therewith. The dance symbolised the sun god circling through the sky. Baal was worshipped conjointly with Nebo, the star god. " Bel boweth, Nebo stoopeth."

NEBO: interpreter, foreteller, *con.* Naib, Nebi: a prophet = Weird: who speaks the word. NEBO was the Chaldean Mercury, by whose passage through the sky seasons were forecasted. So

KRONOS (Saturn) for Chronos: time, time being measured thereby.

NEBUSHASBAN: worshipper of Nebo = HERMODULUS: servant of Mercury.

NEBUCHADNEZZAR: Nebo is the god of fire. NEBUZAR-ADAN: Nebo's lord or leader = HERMIANAX. " *Nebuchadnezzar*, king of Babylon, gave charge concerning Jeremiah to *Nebuzaradan*, the captain of the guard."

NABOPOLASSAR: a compound of Nebo and Asar, a form of

Asshur, the progenitor of the Assyrians, and to whom they owe their national designation. In return they deified him. So TIGLATHPILESER is composed of Tarkat (mother of gods = Ops) and Asar of Asshur.

ESARHADDON (Asar adon): lord of Assur, a name so accurately describing his office that it deserves being called a title. Assur combines with local names, as Telassar : hill of Assar, the mound where was his altar. " We do sacrifice unto God since the days of Esarhaddon, king of Assur."

> " Eden stretched her line
> From Auran eastward to the royal towers
> Of great Seleucia, built by Grecian kings,
> Or where the sons of Eden long before
> Dwelt in *Telassar.*"

Tel : a hill, mound, earthwork, runs through many languages. SHAREZER: prince of fire, *con.* Sarah. NERGAL-SHAREZER: Nergal is prince of fire.

NERGAL : rolling light, revolving star, *con.* Galilee, applied to a cock which crows at returning light. "The word of the Lord came unto Zechariah, when they had sent into the house of God *Sharezer* and Regem-Melech and their men, to pray before the Lord." Parallel to the cruelty of naming Daniel Belteshazzar was that of calling Zerubbabel

SHESHBAZZAR : fire worshipper. "All these did *Sheshbazzar* bring up with the captivity, they were brought up from Babylon to Jerusalem."

ZERUBBABEL : seed of Babylon, *con.* ZOROASTER and answer to

BALBI, BALBOA (Spanish Jews): man from Babylon.

ASENATH : belonging to Neith, the Egyptian Minerva, a wise person.

ZAPHENATH : he who receives Neith, wisdom, is divinely taught.

NITOCRIS (Babylonian queen): victory of Neith, wisdom wins.

PAANEAH : he who flies pollution, an allusion to Joseph from his mistress.

POTIPHAH and POTIPHERAH differ as Joses and Joseph, each meaning priest of the sun = HELIOPHANTES and the mad emperor

HELIOGABALUS, whose original name was GABALUS, from the Gabellus, tributary to the Po, which was changed when he became priest to the sun in Phœnicia.

RAM : ("of the kindred of"): high, gives RIMMON : very high, applied to the pomegranate in a mystical sense,—

> " *Rimmon*, whose delightful seat
> Was fair Damascus on the fertile banks
> Of Abana and Pharpar, lucid streams."

TABRIMMON: Rimmon's goodness. TOBIAH: goodness of Jehovah, gives TOBIAS, TOBY (uncle). TOOBY (usually given from it): double dwelling, big house. Tob: good fertile soil = Aleppo: fat. "The elders of Gilead went to fetch Jephthah out of the land of TOB."

HADAD for Ad ad: one one, the one, most eminent, double first, applied to the sun.

BENHADAD: son of the sun = ONION (temple of) from On: the sun.

HADADEZER: whose help is Hadad. "David smote also *Hadadezer.*"

DAGON: great fish, literally = grampus, megalicthus, the emblem of fecundity from Dag: a fish, whence Tagus: fish river = Great Fish River of South Africa.

NUN, NON: a fish, the letter ɔ, he who is prolific. "The children of Israel were fruitful, and increased like fishes." Dagon was a merman,—

> " Then came one
> Who mourn'd in earnest, when the captive ark
> Maim'd his brute image, head and hands lopp'd off
> In his own temple, on the ground edge
> Where he fell flat, and sham'd his worshippers:
> *Dagon* his name, sea-monster, upward man
> And downward fish."

DOEG (the Edomite): a fisherman. But DOIG (Scotch): a dog, a gallant fighter.

THOTH (Egyptian god): divine, *con.* Theos, Ti, Tu in Tuisco, gives

THOTHMETHES: Thoth's man, *con.* METHUSELAH. According to some authorities he was worshipped by the Teutons under the name of Tot, whence

TOTTENHAM: home of Tot, built upon a site sacred to Tot. "Tottenham in his boots." This sobriquet was acquired by Charles Tottenham, Esq. of Wexford, and a member of the Irish Parliament. Tot became DODD, giving

DODDRIDGE (divine): hill where Tot received divine honours = TUTTLE for Tot's hill. The Egyptians were Caucasian, and in the pre-historic period swarmed from that hive of nations, tho valleys of the Caucasus, long before the Teutons started for the Dofrafields. Hence German and Egyptians had *bull* and *serpent* worship in common; besides words, ideas, and objects of adoration. The Egyptian for God is

TEUT, nearly identical with the Asir, TIEU, whence Tuesday: God's day, literally.

TEUCER (progenitor of Trojans): a divine man, son of a god.

SIBYL (theosboule): giving the counsel of God = FABIUS, from Fari: to speak, *con.* Fable.

Nabi: who gives the word of God, *con.* NABOTH (garden) = THEOPHRASTUS: who speaks the words of God.

TIMOR (Tieu and More: great): great god, whence name, title, and place,

BALTIMORE: city of the great good. TIMOR, BAEL, and CROM were the aboriginal tri-mutri of Britain.

CROM, CRUM: curved, the moon in crescent. CROMWELL: spring where Crom was worshipped =

(S)CALDWELL: fountain where scalds sang to gods. Bal: a town or village, as in BALMERINO = SEATON. Baltimore = Theopolis =

BOGATSKY: city of God. The Welsh had a god who came across the sea on a pig's back. Him they called

COLL: the hazel, probably he used the sacred wand to guide his porcine charger, whence

COLE (old king) and GALL (St.). We have seen that SHEM: a name, and ARAM: high, whence Arimathea = HYAM, gives

SEMIRAMIS: exalted name, famous, whence SEMIRAMIDE daughter of Semiramis, but savans say it also gives

SEMELE (mother of Bacchus). " In the festival of the wine-press, the torch-bearer cried out to the people Kaleite Theou:" call ye upon God, and they answered " Semele Iaache plouto dota." As Semele admits of no grammatical construction in this sentence, and is connected with the Hebrew Jah, Dr. Hales deems that it denotes the Hebrew Shemali: hearken to me, as in Lev. xxvi. 21. This would give consistency to the popular response, as it would signify " Hearken to me, O Jah, thou giver of wealth." Forgetting, if ever knowing, the meaning of SHEMALI: hearken to me, the Greeks metamorphosed it into a woman,

SEMELE, supposed to have expired at the sight of Jove arrayed in all the terrors of his glory, as the people feared they would at Sinai. This origin contradicts the Greek tradition that Iacchus was the son of Ceres and Proserpine. Yet this conjecture is supported by the fact that a number of Hebrew words and phrases were used in the ceremony of the Grecian festivals.

JESSE: wealthy = GEMALLI: camel possessor is from Jah, as also is

Iacche, which with Bar: a son, supplies us with BACCHUS: son of Jah, the wealth giver, if so JESSE and BACCHUS are, nominally, near a kin. Yea or nay, BACCHUS gives

Debauch: to make in a bacchanalian state. SHEM varies to SEMI(RAMIS), SEM(ELE), SIM(EON), ISHMA(EL), SHIMEI(M).

CHAPTER XI.

NAMES DERIVED FROM ANIMALS.

No few personal names are referable to animal origin. Those that are ancient generally originate in the fact that the persons so designated displayed some qualities of the animal from which they obtain their name. Others, more ancient, are traced to mystic connections between the original nominee and idolatry, he adopting or receiving the name of and symbolising the god he worshipped in such animal. A large proportion of more recent names are mementoes of the Crusades being obtained by persons who bore representations of animals on their shield. Such as are allied to worship must be looked at from the altar standpoint, being thereby clothed with august value. In the worship of God, humble birds were offered, whence there was a scape sparrow (Levi. xiv. 53) as well as a scape goat. To this Jesus possibly alludes when saying, "Not a sparrow falls to the ground without the will of your Father." Moses records minute details of Judaic ritual, but other religions, gay or cruel, older than it, have left few memorials of existence besides stones and names. In view of such facts we regard

SPARROW not necessarily as a sparrow-catcher, breeder, birdseller, as sparrows as well as doves were sacred to Venus, as swans were to Juno. In olden times people clothed animals with imagined attributes as boys now do robins, calling each God's bird. We lose sight of symbolism in these utilitarian days, the outcome of ancient communion with the glorious East. Religious considerations throw mystic light over many names, investing them with the charm of antiquity more pleasing than accurate knowledge of common-place matters. Thus it was men reverenced the great name,

AUGUSTUS, from Augur: who foretold by avispection, looking into birds offered sacrificially. Avis: a bird, Specio: I see.

August: awful, sublime, grand. "My *august* master, the emperor." Hence August: the month so called in compliment to Augustus Cæsar. Hence, too, AUGUSTINE, AUSTIN, AGOSTINO, AUGUSTULUS (last Roman emperor): most august =

SEBASTE: worshipful, honourable, whence Sebastopol = Augsburg. From SEBASTE,

(St.) SEBASTIAN: son of SEBASTE, BASTIEN (germs). English would be impoverished by the loss of AUGUSTUS; but such name could only be had through worship, true or false. The unknown always affects more deeply than the known. AUGUSTUS corresponds to the Persian Arta: the sacrificial flame of the fire worshippers, as seen in ARTABANUS. Each answers to the Celtic

BOYD: fulvous headed, auburn tressed, Thorine haired. The tint cannot be exactly given, as it means hair coloured like the altar fire, which varied from bright yellow to a ruddy glow. Akin to it,

BOWIE: for whom a propitiation has been made, the Gaelic for

PIUS, PIO. Happy the Celtic mother or German matron who had a son with hair of this sort, as she had ocular proof the gods favoured her. We look at heads either æsthetically or phrenologically, considering whether they are winsome or promise ability, whereas the ancients looked at them in relation to the gods. Knowing history casts awe over even stones, and dignifies what the ignorant think common into sublimity. Augustus is synonymous with the German

WERTER (sorrows of), from the root *worth* upon which we form *worship*. The following are a selection of personal names illustrating the foregone views:—

RACHEL: a sheep, one fondly tended.

BREBISSON: great sheep. "In a work upon the useful grasses *M. de Brebisson*, that botanist says," etc.

OVID: little sheep, darling, nurse name = LAMB,

OVIEDO (Spanish historian). Ovation: triumph when a sheep was offered.

WEDDERS: a weather sheep.

CHERAN: a lamb. "The sons of Dishon, (were) Amram, Eshbon, Ithran, and *Cheran.*" Cheran from Kar: a lamb, giving Karnos, dropping the initial Arnos, whence

ARNOBIUS (African): lamb lived, exactly = our AGNEW =

SEELY: silly, sheep like. A silly sheep means an innocent one, does not butt ram-like. These =

DILKE (Sir C.): a sucking lamb, a little dear = LAMMIE.

ALECTRYON (watched *Apollo* by order of *Mars*, a myth, meaning *soldiers* should be watchful till *sun*-rise): a cock, literally means *not bed* = the Hebrew,

NERGAL: a cock, *lit.* rolling light, *con.* Gal: rolling. Galeed: heap of witness, they rolled stones to it. Doubled in Gilgal: rolling away completely. "This day have I gilgal-ed the reproach of Egypt." Gal gives Globus: any round thing. Globe: that may be rolled. Golal: a tombstone. Mark xvi. 3. From same source Golgotha, Galilee. "The men of Cush (Ethiopians) made Nergal," designation of Mars.

NERGAL-SHAREZER: prince helped by Mars, *con.* Sarah and Ebenezer.

BERNARD (Dr.): of a bear's nature, strong to fight, varies

to BERNHARDT, BARNARD, BAREND, BERNADOTTE (king), NADAUD, BARENTZ (navigator). Ursa: the bear, from Ur! Ur!: grunter, gives
ORSON, ORSINO, ORSINI, the *fem.* URSULA and HORSENAIL !! BASS, VASS: a bear, BASHAM: home, whence bears can be seen. Wolves were extirpated from Britain long before bears were, as they kept more out of our way. Tradition says bruin put in an occasional appearance up to two centuries since when the last of his race was knocked out of time on a Leicestershire hill called therefrom Bardon =
BARLOW (Billy): bear law. Sometimes Barlow for barr law, hill top. Bears appear never to have flourished in Scotland, although they had more cover than in England. The only Celtic names *con.* this brute are supposed to be
MATHER, (Mc)MAHON (marshal), MAHONEY, MAUGHAN, which are probably =
SUAGROS: bear hunter. But MACMATH = DE MATTOS and MATHWIN, all sons of Matthew. The Greeks called the Bear Su, the Romans Ur-sa, both from noise made by it. So the former called a Sow, the same word, (H)us, but in a converse order, which gave the Latins Sus (like Hudor: water into Sudor: sweat) and us Hyœna: the bristler. SUAGROS, *con.* SUIDAS: son of, and AGRESTES: a huntsman = SAID, SIDETES, HUNT, HUNTER, and *con.* Onager: a wild ass. "Ishmael shall be an *onager.*" MATHERS assumes the form of
MAVORS, or MAVOR, but the Roman
MAVORS, MARS, MORS: death, *con.* Morgue: place of dead. Bulls are, nominally, as prolific as bears. Hence
TURNBULL, TRUMBULL, TREMBLE: said to be given to one Ruel, because he turned a bull which was threatening to gore Robert Bruce in Stirling Park. But the name is older than that period and simply means good at driving the cattle of England into Scotland, Kaffir style. AGATHOS: good, is from Ago: I drive, and means first-rate cattle thief. From the same animal we also have
BOLEYN, BULLEN. A Saxon thane who rode a bull when going to confer with William the Conqueror was called
BULLSTRODE: bull straddler.
PAINBŒUF (French soldier): bull's head on shield.
TORELLI = BULLOCK. Thor gives Taurus, whence
TORRERO, TORREADOR: Spanish bull fighters.
COLDETOR: bull necked, strong = Bull, *con.* Colporteur: carrier on neck. "Here also we find the celebrated group known as the Toro Farnese: or Farnese Bull."
METCALFE, MEDCALF: meadow calf, heifer = STURROCKS (steer, stirk).
BUDD = foregoing three. A butt of leather is the hide of a Budd.

MOSCHUS (Syracusan poet): a calf = VITELLIUS, *con.* veal.

GALBA : fat calf = EGLON, *con.* Aleppo, Haleb : fat soil, giving LIPPO (Memmi): a stoutly built man.

LEPORELLA : a little hare leveret, one very timid.

DAMARIS : a heifer = EGLAH. "The sixth Ithream, by *Eglah* David's wife." "A woman named *Damaris.*"

DAMARIS : broken into the yoke, *con.* DOMITIAN, *con.* the Persian,

DAMASPIA : horse breaker. "If ye had not ploughed with my heifer."

VITALIAN (emperor) from Vitulus : a calf, *con.* Italus.

Italia : the country producing kine, as

Achaia : horse producing country,

Spain : rabbits, and = Beotia and Bohemia : home of the Boii : cattle tenders. Italy, Beotia, Bohemia fairly answer to Buchanan.

Ravens were to Norsemen what eagles were to the Romans. To them death under the dusky wing of the raven insured entrance into Valhalla.

BRANDUBH (king of Leinster): raven black, *con.* Dublin = Black pool.

RAPP (general), RAPIN (historian): a raven.

BERTRAM, BERTRAND : bright raven, brilliant fighter.

WIGRAM : victorious raven, *con.* WIGMORE : great conqueror = MEGANICES, and *con.* Wigan : place of victory

RABY : carrier of the Dane's raven standard = CORAX.

ROYSTON : hooded crow (corvus cornix). Corvus, corax, crow, forms of Craw ! noise made.

CORBETT, CORBYN : a crow. CORBETT and RIDDLE are the oldest Scottish surnames.

VALERIUS CORVUS : Valerius who was helped by a crow in fight with a Gaul.

STERN : a raven = RAVEN = HIRPUS, HARPY : snatcher, ravisher.

CROW is ancient, but whether *con.* war, religion, or nature it is too late to say.

CRAWFORD (looking so like crow ford): camp ford.

CROYLAND (abbey): frequented by crows, agricultural. Next are of war.

BRENNUS (Gallic king): a raven, as BRAND giving BRANDAN (St.), BRANIGAN : son of Brand or of the raven. Hence, too, BRAIN, (Mᶜ)BRAYNE. As ravens eat the dead, they symbolised complete victory.

OREB (Midian): a raven, *con.* EREBUS : dark as the raven's wing. Orbim : dark ones, Bedouin. "And the *orbim* brought him bread and flesh in the morning." Eagles had admirers, but not to the same extent, for the obvious reason they were less known.

ÆTION (father of Andromache): great eagle = NISROCH.

NINUS (whence Nineveh), CARCAS (chamberlain), ÆTIUS (stabbed Valentinian),

NARSES (fought the Goths) all = AQUILA (Priscilla): an eagle. Aquila is a form of Acuila, from acus, whence Acute: sharp, meaning sharp flier, literally = swift (bird), SWIFT (dean): who runs swiftly. Aquilone: wind rushing like an eagle = Boreas: wind from the Thracian mountains, from Oros: a mountain. Aquiline: shaped like an eagle's beak. Some give

AJAX: an eagle, but it is = JOB: weeper.

ORL (Russian): an eagle, ORLOFF (count): son of Orl.

ERNE, HERNE: an eagle, ERNEST (king) = FIACRE: an eagle. Cabs taking persons to St. Fiacre's church, Paris, came to be called Fiacre: a hackney coach. From this source ARNOT: son of Erne = Orloff.

ARNOLD, ARNAUD (marshal): eagle power. St. Arnold, *cor.* to STERNHOLD (and Hopkins), if not *stone hold.*

ARNHILDA: Hilda's eagle, Valkirier name.

KIRCKULE: church haunted by owls, becomes CHURCHILL (poet) =

HAPSBURG (house of): hawks tower, born in. Hap: a hawk, which *haves*, grips. Havock: to slay men as hawks do sparrows.

HIERAX (Antiochus): the hawk, gripper, grabber, robber.

HOWLET may be little owl, but most likely is *dim.* of Howe, or even of Howell.

EULE: an owl. EULENBURG: town frequented by owls = HAPSBURG.

KORE: a partridge, it is *qra*, the noise it makes, like saws wanting grease. Enkakore: the *well* of him who *cried* with a dry throat. " *Kore* of the sons of Asaph." This Hebrew name exactly answers the Italian

QUAGLIA, as that is *quacklia*: noise of bird. " The holy father was accompanied by Cardinals QUAGLIA and PANEBIANCO."

PANEBIANCO = WHITBREAD: eating white bread, others eating coarse brown, and so well bred.

HOGLAH (daughter of Zelophehad): a partridge, one plump and pretty.

BUFFON (naturalist): great owl, with mystic significance.

RACINE (dramatist): carrying on shield *rat* and *swan* (rat cygne).

SWAN, from Wan: pale, gives SWANN, Asiric and heraldic.

GENSERIC (Vandal): wild gander, passing from land to land.

GANS, GOES, GOSCHEN: a goose, a wanderer, GOSLING: son of GOES.

COOTE, COOT: water fowl, like a moor hen.

14

LUN (Sally): great northern diver. LUNHUNTER: sea bird
catcher.

LIVERMORE from a bird called Liver which frequented *meres*
and pools, whence by some Liverpool: marsh lands frequented
by the Liver.

POUSSIN (painter): a cock, gives the Franco-Irish name
POSSINET: young Poussin. HUSS (reformer): a goose. HAG-
GAR, HAGGIS: untrained hawks, wild. MILVIUS, NISAS (Eury-
alus): hawks both.

JONAH, JONAS, JEMIMA (Job's daughter), LIVIA: doves all,
though some give JEMIMA: handsome as the day, the sight of
her being as dawn to the benighted. Similarly, from Turtur:
a dove, *tur, tur*: cooer, we have

TOVEY, TURTLE, TORTOLA (Spanish lady). "Thou art fair,
thou hast doves' eyes."

TABITHA, DORCAS: gazelle-eyed = LAPIDOTH: lamps.

STORKS (recorder) from the Stork: natural affection, for
which the bird was noted.

COLUMBUS: a dove or pigeon, one dear = POMBAL (premier),
for Palumba. Columbia (Hail!) = Fredonia: the confederated
S. of A. Icolmkill (Inch Columba): island in which is *cell* of
Columbus.

COLUMBINE is a kind of *fem.* to COLUMBUS, and so lady-dove
for lady-love = TORTOLA.

CALLUM(M'): a dove. MACCALLUMMORE: the great Maccallum.

KNOTTE, from a bird called after King Canute. Crane:
aged (bird) because lives to a great age, gives

CRANE, who bore one on shield. Crane identical with
GERON and GERYON =

SENECA: aged, in these cases as in the English names EARL
(from Ere: before), AULD, PRESBYTER, is not to be taken in the
sense of having simply scored so many years. Age giving
experience, the first kings were patriarchs, whose sceptre was
their walking-stick. Thus

ANAX: a king is *con.* Senex: aged, and our well-known

ALDERMAN is literally an elderly man though he may be in
his prime. So, then, GERON, GERYON, SENECA, are flavoured
with authority, and are to be honoured as governors. In keeping herewith it is famous that Major: greater, and Minor: less,
are applied to age. "He is in his minority." "Not having
attained to his majority." So, too, the titles

SEIGNIOR and EXCELLENCY, simply mean older, excelling by
years. "With the ancient is wisdom, and in length of days
understanding." Consult *Gaffer*, GAMMER, AVES, LAVEAU,
MAXIMUS.

CRANMER (martyr): lake frequented by cranes, CRANSTON:
town.

LOCHEIL (chief): bird lake = LIVERMORE.

MERLE (Aubigne): a blackbird. PINNOCK: little feathers = SPARROW though Sparrow: speaker, chatterer, chirper.

SPINK, PINK, FINCH: all chaffinches, being imitation of note Fink! Fink!!

SHELDRICK: shiel-drake, water bird.

STRUTHERS: an ostrich, soldier of high renown. "Amongst the far fetched conceits of the middle ages, many devices may be found more obscure and fantastical than an *ostrich* feather, assumed in allusion to the bearer's appetite for, or mastery over, iron and steel." In the German it stands as

STRAUSS (rationalist), which anciently signified " a fight, a combat or a scuffle," though now obsolete in that sense. Hence " Ich dien," with feathers, mean I serve as a soldier, having an appetite for cold steel as the ostrich is supposed to have. In some cases STRAUSS means an Austrian, and the Scotch STRUTHERS is local, *con.* Strath.

HENGIST (hertogh): a stallion. HORSA: the mare, devotees to Hross.

HENCHMAN: mounted servant, ENCKE (comet), HENGLER: a horseman.

JOKELL: horse warrior. The Saxons engraved a horse in the green sward of the Valley of the White Horse, where their descendants will renew it this summer. Hippus (flying feet): a horse.

GULIPPUS: gold coloured horse. Gul is gold, *d* formative.

XANTIPPUS: sorrel coloured horse = BAYARD (knight): bay-horse rider, *fem.*, XANTIPPE (scold). " The chariots in Homer were drawn, for the most part, by two horses coupled; that of Achilles had no more—the names of his horses being Xanthus and Balius."

XANTHUS: sord, sorrel, bay, applied to men through colour of hair.

BALIUS: thrower out of legs, galloper, *con.* Balena: a whale that throws up water, from Ballo: I throw, whence Balearic (isles): place of slingers, DIABOLOS: who casts fiery darts of accusations, DIAVOLO (Fra).

FLAMSTEED (astronomer): flame coloured horse = XANTIPPUS. Some have it from Flamstead: place of beacon fire =

BEACONSFIELD: Beacon for betoken, and token from teach.

HIPPONAX: chief horseman = PHARNASPES: commander of horse =

MARSHALL (mare schall) = ARCHIPPUS. MELANIPPUS: black horse, rider of a.

EVIPPUS: good horseman = HORSEMAN and PHILIP.

HIPPOLYTUS (and his times): horse leader, looser = GROOM.

HIPPOCRATES (whence Hippocras: wine mingled after his

recipe): having power over a horse = HIPPODAMUS: horse breaker, tamer.

HOTSPUR: swift rider, as was he who rode BUCEPHALUS: bull-headed horse.

D'ORSEY (count) is given by some as De horsey, but is from Theodosius.

Philip (Macedon) whence Philippi (city) and Philippic: discourse full of invective: horse lover, good seat, whence PHIPPS, PHELPS, PHILPOT: little Philip = FILKIN, PHILLIMORE, FILMORE, FILMER: great Philip. The Italians shape it IPPOFILO, whence LEPSIUS and SIPPEL. LIPTON: Philip's town.

MACKILLOP: son of Philip. Asp: the horse was sacred in Persia. Either the king or high priest rode forth at daybreak in a chariot drawn by horses dedicated to

MITHRAS: mother of light, whence MITHRIDATES: sun gift = APOLLODORUS. TIRIDATES: gift of Mercury. This king fought Rome.

ASHPENAZ: horse nose, he who snorts, easily rages = APPAIM. "The king spake unto *Ashpenaz*, the master of the eunuchs."

ASPATHA (son of Haman): strength of a horse, horse tamer = HIPPODAMUS. The Hebrews were not supposed to keep horses, hence it does not say, "Thou shalt not covet thy neighbour's horse." So, too, we account for no Jew being named in connection with a horse, except it be

RECHAB (Rechabites): a charioteer = (Mc)ARA, (Mc)CAW. When the Jews were brought under the Chaldees and Persians, whose strength lie in cavalry, the sacred books forthwith show it by the names of their masters. An undesigned coincidence confirming a student's faith in the veracity of the Scriptures. Saul was not on horseback when the Lord met him on the way. Asp (in the Greek): a serpent, from Aspis: a shield, like to which is the coil of a snake.

CHRYSASPIS: golden shield, princely warrior. Horse and bull are used by us in the sense of great, rough, strong. Horse-radish: strong root. Horseplay: romping. Bulwarks (boulevards): strong works, giving

BOLLAND (Bollandists): land near fortifications, boulevards = WARK: living near the bulwarks, outskirts of a town. Bulrush: rush growing strong and quickly. Bullfinch: strong finch. Wolves, bears, ravens, hawks, and horses must make way for the king of the wilderness,

LEO (pope), LEON (Arragon), LYON: lions three.

LEONIDAS (Thermopylœ): son of a lion, or of Leon = LEONATUS.

LEONRIC: lion king = LEARCHUS: lion chief = ARSLAN BEY: the lion like Pasha.

LEANDER (Hero): lion man = CŒUR DE LION: lion-hearted, or, who tore out the lion's heart, Samson fashion.

> " Before Angiers well met, brave Austria,
> Arthur, that great fore-runner of thy blood,
> Richard, that robb'd the lion of his heart,
> And fought the holy wars in Palestine."

LOWE: a lion. LOCOCK: little Lowe, or little lion = LOBEL, whence *lobelia*. The microscopists name LEUWENHOCK also = LOCOCK.

LEONARD, LEONARDO, LEOTARD (acrobat): lion natured, LENNIE: little Leonard.

BRANCALEONE (blank): white lion. There are persons named BLANKLION, the English equivalent to the Italian name.

COLLEONE: lion necked, locks hanging round the neck like a mane.

TIMOLEON: lion souled.

> " High o'er the rest Epaminondas stood:
> *Timoleon*, glorious in his brother's blood."

The nations amongst whom the foregoing leonine names were current knew lions rather by history, heraldry, or tradition than by personal conflict, though the king of the wilderness was driven out of Europe in the historic period. The royal beast was common in Thessaly B.C. 600. The following designations are nearer his present habitat:—

ARIOCH (from Ar: a lion): great lion = LEONI, a mystical name of Jerusalem, also applied to a tune 'that has been sung 3000 years. "*Arioch* brought in Daniel before the king."

ARELI: son of a lion, probably one seen about time of his birth. " Of *Areli* the family of the Arelites."

ARIEL: lion of God, greatest lion, figurative for Jerusalem, whose altar destroyed more sheep than did the lions = ASSAD ALLAH: the first standard-bearer of Islam. Assodnagur: lion's fort. E. I. " Woe to *Ariel*, the city where David dwelt."

OTHNIEL: lion of God, great warrior. " Caleb said, he that smiteth Kirjath-sepher, and taketh it, to him will I give Achsah, my daughter, to wife. And *Othniel*, the son of Kenaz, took it."

LIB: a lion, as Lib Judah gives LEBBŒUS (apostle): son of a lion.

LAISH: an old lion. " But Saul had given Michal to Phalti, the son of *Laish*." It compares with LEOSTHENES: strong as a lion.

SINGH: a lion, amongst Hindoos, as Singapore: lion's city = Leontupolis. Ceylon, termed Taprobana by Ptolemy, is known to the natives as Cinghala: lion's home, and their language is Cinghalese.

RUNJEET SINGH (rajah): Runjeet the lion.

AMARASINHA: immortal lion, the Hindoo Achilles. " The

palm Borassus flabelli formis (characteristically termed by
Amarasinha, a king of grasses) is," etc. Compare it with
Amaritza : well of immortality, the Sikh Zemzem, and Ama-
ranth : immortal flower, and with Mors : death. Etymologi-
cally, much of the Indo Germanic language, of which these
words are fragments, is what it was when the cotton clad
troops of King Porus received the shock of battle from the
brass armoured phalanx of Alexander on the banks of the
Indus. The Turks have

ALP-ARSLAN : valiant lion, *con.* ARIEL. Dandelion: lion's
tooth. Chameleon : ground lion. We thus see that many
nations adopted the royal beast as an eponyme for their
bravest. It has been fashionable to do so from the reign of
Arioch, king of Ellasar to now. The less taking Aper: a boar,
gives

HEBER (bishop), OBERLIN (papa), PERRIN, PARRAN and
PERRY, when not from Peter. These =

VERRES (enemy to Cicero) : a boar pig, a pig sticker.
Compare Vir and Verres, each mean strong. Hence also

VERY and EVERY : strong as a boar. Names that have
posed many.

EVERARD, EWART (Gladstone) : of the nature of a boar,
strong fighter.

EVERETT : little Heber. The Celtic for a boar is Cullach,
whence

(M') CULLOCH : boar (slayer) = the Irish (M') TURK. Can-
turk (town) : boar's head.

OLIVANT, OLIPHANT : elephant on shield ; though some give
it from Oliver.

CASSELS : castle bearer. So also PUL : an elephant,
"Menahem gave Pul a thousand talents."

SARDANAPALUS : Sardan, son of Pul, *con.* Sar: a prince,
SARDAN : prince judge.

BARRUS (proud of his beauty) : an elephant, from Baros :
weight, Barometer ; weight measurer.

CÆSAR : an elephant in the Punic by mere chance coincidence. Some say he was so called through some of the *gens.*
Julii keeping an elephant.

SHUAL : a fox, a crafty man. "The sons of Zophah, Suah,
and Harnepha, and *Shual.*" "Go and tell that fox Herod."

TODD : the slayer, killer, applicable to warrior or poultry
worrier.

TODHUNTER (algebra) : fox hunter. VULPIUS, ULPIAN,
VOSS, VOCE, FOUCHE (detective), FUSCH (whence Fuschia),
GALPIN, GUPPY (Mrs), and ZORRA are all foxes or their sons.
RENAUD (wine) : not therefrom, but from REYNARD : stern
judge, applied to fox judging what fowl he will take. Golpe :
yelper, is his correct French designation = GUELPH.

ALOPEX : a fox, Alopecia : baldness, like a mangy fox losing his coat.

VOLPICELLI, VALPY (grammatist), ZORILLA (Ruiz) : a little fox.

DRACO : a dragon, sharp sighted, Draconian : severe like *Draco.*

UTHER PENDRAGON : Uther of the dragon's head, Uther the dragoon carrying standard emblazoned with dragon's head, *con.*

PINDAR (poet), Pundit : men of head. PENNY, PINNEY : head of, chief.

PENNEFATHER : head father, patriarch, sept head, *uncon.* with money. But

PINDAR : cattle *pounder*, puts them in a pen.

PENGELLY (Kent's cavern): head of stream = KINEAR, KING-LASS, *con.* PENRYHN : head of spit land running into the sea.

GRIFFEN : griffon carrier on shield. Griffon : great grips, gripers, claws. The hold that serpent worship (ophiolatria) had upon nations, and, for the matter of that, yet has, is clear from the study of personal names : though a portion of such names must be allowed for symbolism falling short of worship, as when a serpent is used to signify renewal of life and health, as the snake sloughing, or as a sign of eternity when it forms a circle.

NAHASH (Ammonite) : a serpent, a hisser, giving NAASHON : ophiomant, diviner by snakes.

SARAPH (same as Seraph) : burning, causing inflammation by bite = Dipsas : thirst producer. " *Saraph* had dominion over Moab." " And Jehovah sent sarapim among the people."

ACHAN : a serpent, changed to ACHAR : troubler, pain or ache giver. " *Achan*, the son of Carmi, took of the anathematised thing." " The son of Carmi, the troubler of Israel who transgressed in the thing accursed." *Con.* Achos : pain, whence Ache : to suffer pain. Acheron : ache run, flowing with pain,—

> " Sad Acheron of sorrow, black and deep."

SHEPHUPHAN, SHUPHAM : serpent called by Greeks Cerastes (keras, cornu): horned snake. " Dan shall be *shephiphon* by the way, an adder in the path." " Gera and *Shephuphan.*" " Of *Shupham*, the family of the Shuphamites."

PITHON : stretcher, large serpent. Here is our Python, from the killing of which Phœbus became the Pythian Apollo.

PYTHON was a common Greek name. " A certain damsel possessed with a *pythonic* spirit," a pythoness. " The sons of Micah were *Pithon* and Melech."

DEJOCES : a snake. ASTYAGES (Median): biting snake, a

dragon. The Medees were ophiolatrians. One of the generic words for a serpent is ob, oub, ouph, iph, Ophis: that which blows out its body, like the Puff-adder, *con.* Obh: a bottle, Oboth: bottles. "They departed from Pimon and pitched in Oboth." The rainy season came on and the bottles of heaven were opened.

OBI: Negro ogre, whence Obeah: a charm. The inspired or pythonised person was inflated like a leather bottle when full.

IPHICRATES: strong as a python, snake killer.

IPHIDAMUS: serpent master, snake charmer.

IPHINOUS (one of Centaurs), *fem.* IPHINOE: serpent minded, subtle.

IPHIGENIA: daughter of Iphis, serpent born, offspring of the Pythian Apollo.

IPHIS: a serpent, one so named king of Argos. The ancient Germans worshipped

ORM, our worm,—

"O Eve! in evil hour thou did'st give ear
To that false *worm.*"

ORMSBY: Orms dwelling, where worshipped, sometimes from Orm: an elm, at others from Orne: an ash.

GUTHRAM is Goth-Orm: serpent god of the Goths, changes into

GOODMAN. But the widely known name

GUTHRIE: Goth ruler, in Irish it means king's voice, one used to obedience. Another generic word used by Germans for a serpent was

LIND (Jenny), referring only to motion of, and so *con.* Lind: a lime tree, *con.* Lithe: bending freely. Unterlinden: under limes. Leipsic: dwelling among limes. Supplies many lady names because suggestive of graceful motion.

ADELINDE (athel): noble as to birth, graceful as to manner, becomes ADELINE.

ROSALIND: beautiful as a rose, graceful as a serpent.

BELINDA: graceful walker. Thus Lind came to mean simply lady, as

LINTRUDE: lady true, woman keeping troth. From Lind,

LINDSAY: lime tree island. After being entangled so as hardly able to tell a serpent from a lime tree or a lady, we make for

AROD: onager: a wild ass, a man who is fleet and untameable. "Of *Arod* the family of the Arodites." Takes form of ARAD.

IRAD: the braying onager, nearly = PIRAM: swift wild ass. "*Piram* king of Jarmuth."

TASSO (Jerusalem): taxus: badger, hard biter, fighter =

Brock : bone breaker, and Grey : a huntsman. Greyhound : dog-hunting Gre : the badger. But Gray : glass, grey-eyed. " By and bye, came the cry of the dogs, and the tall *grehound* of Wales merging from the bosky dells."

Gray is claimed as De Croy : of Croy, by those desirous of being accounted of Norman descent, but it means as given.

Philomela : lover of *melody*, the nightingale = Rossignol.

Zibiah : female gazelle, beautiful eyes = Tabitha, becomes Tabby, and ultimately applied to a cat.

Roebuck : rough buck, a huntsman. Some derive it from Rabeck : rough brook.

Dishon, Dishan : a wild goat, good climber. " *Dishon*, and Ezer, and *Dishan* : they are the dukes of the Horites." Horite dukes : mountaineer leaders. Very appropriate.

Jael : wild goat's kid, little runaway. " Howbeit, Sisera fled away on his feet to the tent of Jael."

Sisera : crane and crow, symbols of vigilance and perspecuity.

Aran : wild goat, high climber, *con.* Heron : high flying bird, *con.* Hay and Hoy, which see. " The children of *Dishon* are these : Uz and *Aran*." What a wild family !

Aran is *con.* Hor : a mountain, whence the Greek Oros, giving

Oregon : mountain joy, plant there found. Ganos : joy.

Ganymede (Olympic cup bearer) : joy commanding.

Uz : strong, also applied to a goat, very appropriate for a highlander. Caper : a goat is from Carpo : I crop, gives Caprera, Caprea,

Cabral (Spanish) = Chievers, Ægeus (last king of Athens), who is said to have given name to the Ægean Sea.

Egis : shield of Minerva, made of goat's skin. Ægeade : Greeks, sons of Ægeus, not goat people. Daniel symbolises the Greeks by a goat. Kid : young goat, but

Kidd : son, by pre-eminence, gives Kidston (Ferniegair) : town of Kidd.

Azazel : goat that went from God, the escape goat, from Gnes : a goat, Azal : to go, first written Gnazazel. It is *con.* Gaza : strong city. Elegantly applied by Milton to the standard-bearer of the apostate angels. He was too scholarly to have Azazel in heaven.

> " Then straight commands, that at the warlike sound
> Of trumpets loud and clarions be uprear'd
> His mighty standard ; that proud honour claim'd
> *Azazel* as his right, a cherub tall."

Ægon : a goat, sheep and goatherd in love with

Melibœus : care of oxen = Bowman when it means taking care of cattle.

GORDON : goat's fort, to which only a goat could climb =
MINTO(r): kid's hill.   (M')GUIRE, GOWER: goat-like climbers,
mountaineers = ARAN, DISHAN.   (M')GOURLAY : Gower's field,
living in.   KILGOUR : goat's wood, frequented by.
Goat is from go, and means animal that goes about, not sub-
ject to the human will.   It is not gregarious like the sheep.
Figuratively used for the wicked, the self-willed, the unsocial.
Goat is identical with *gad* in gadfly.

VESPUCCI (Amerigo) : a little wasp, irritable = the Irish
BROGAN : son of a broc, badger : snappy = Cynic : snarler,
from Cuon : a dog.   It is hardly to be expected that fishes
should give names to men, yet we have

PHOCAS (emperor) : a seal = MORSE (telegraphist) from Mere:
the sea, and Horse, and thus nearly = Walrus : whale horse,
evidently meaning seal fisher.   But AMER : a form of AMOR :
at moor.   Some good authors derive from Phocis : a seal, the
next, but it is local.

PHOCAS : Phocian man, and gives PHOCION : son of PHOCAS.
DELFINO (doge) : a dolphin, swift swimmer.

MOUCH (spy on Huguenots) : a fly, *con.* Mosquito : little fly,
philologically identical with the firearm known as Musket,
which was light as a fly compared with the ponderous arque-
buse which it superseded.   From that man MOUCH the French
derive their word for a spy, Mouchard.

HOGSMOUTH was the name of a cleric elected A.D. 844, to
wear the Tiara.   Now as that was not a taking name to call
the head of the church, he changed it to Sergius, and was called
Sergius II.   From thence it became a rule to change the name
of any elected to the pontificate, they exchanging their proper
designation for that of some preceding pope.   I have met with
a man belonging to a family named

HEIFER = STURROCKS.   Have : to possess, is the etymon of
the word.   As goods and chattels : good things and cattle, so
Heifer is put for part of your *havers :* possessions.   Cattle,
chattels, is from Capitalia : heads of cattle, Caput.   Thus from
Pecus : cattle, Peculium : your own cattle, as compared with a
neighbour's feeding on the same common, whence Peculiar :
all my own, Pecunia : money, metal stamped with the image
of the animal it would buy.

KNATCHBULL: servant of Thor, the bull god, *cor.* to KNOBELL.
Havers : foolish talk, speaking like lawyers in court, who
keep repeating technicalities mixed with the word havers.

BUCHAN : land whereon cattle are fed = Italia, Bohemia.
BUCHANAN : such land as above through which a stream
flows, *con.* ANNAN : quiet river = Arar, the Saone.

COCKS, which might be thought *con.* the fowl, is a form of
COX : a soldier wearing cuishes.

HARENC: the herring is a true name. Perhaps = POISSON: fish (catcher).

The science of names, onamatology, constructs a second Noah's ark, a huge menagerie wherein are animals clean and unclean, especially the unclean. Menagerie is from Menage: a family. The ark contained a menage and a menagerie. It seems pitiful that the family of man is so menagerie like, containing an unclean majority, but that it does the study of names clearly shows. My reader will wonder I have not welcomed man's faithful companion the dog into our menagerie. Strange to say, all names derived from dogs connect themselves with war, and will therefore be presented under the head including such as have to do with fighting.

CHAPTER XII.

WAR NAMES.

THE study of personal names corroborates an idea poets delight to dwell upon—that in the primeval age there was no war. In the records of the two first millennia we meet with only one name of a warrior cast :—METHUSELAH : man of the dart, missile, the latter being *con.* SHILOH, Siloam : sent. However, after reading the chronicles of the Flood, we forthwith find NIMROD : rebel, *con.* Mar : bitter, indicating bitterness of spirit towards ruler. Then follows narrative of confusion (Babel), striving of herdsmen, battles of kings, seizing captives, and pursuit of retreating raiders, whereby was brought into human history for better or worse two sciences—war and politics. From that era personal and national appellations accurately reflect the altered condition of society. Even MELCHIZEDECK : righteous king, also king of Salem : peace(ful city), argues such name or title was exceptional, to urge nothing as to MELECH : a fighter, who mauls, drives (pell) mell. The aborigines of Hellas, who founded cities and taught sciences, had few war names, but in the succeeding heroic age a freshet of them is lead off by BELLEROPHON : murderer of Beller, HERCULES : glory of Hera, Juno, giving that Italian favourite ERCOLE, who were the forerunners of the "Argonantic expedition" and the "Trojan war." By the latter era, war names formed a heavy percentage of all in use among the Greeks. Roman, French, and English names contrast with the Antediluvians and Greeks in this respect,—these latter histories begin with records of doughty warriors whose names indicate prowess like those of the Greeks flourishing in the heroic age. And these things are so for this obvious reason, the three modern nations were composite, the outcome of many national wars, entering upon the historic stage after Mars and Mors had wielded their sceptres for ages. Of all known nations the Jewish possess a nomenclature freest from war names. In their history, extending from the Abrahamic age till the current, they have produced a race of braves only on three occasions,—the time of Joshua, David's reign, and the Maccabean leadership. Israel yet sends forth statesmen, artificers, savans, and men rich in whatever refines or adorns humanity, but marshals or admirals seldom come of the Abrahamic stock. A Jew soldier is just thinkable. In the late Russo-Turkish war a battalion entirely consisting of Jews were

present at the siege of Plevna, being the first body of Jews
organised for fighting purposes since Titus besieged Jerusalem.
But who can imagine a Blake or Nelson, of the stock of
Israel? Such a people could truly say, when entering
Palestine, "Not unto us." "He giveth us the victory."
"Judas, the eldest son of Mattathias, succeeded his father in
command of the army (B.C. 163), in which he was assisted by
his four brothers, especially by Simon, the eldest of them, who
was a man of remarkable prudence. The motto of his
standard was Exodus xvi. ii., "Who is like unto Thee among
the Gods, O Jehovah?" The Hebrew being MI Camoka
Baalim Jehovah. From these initials was derived the word
MACCABEE, which became the surname of the Asmonean
family. The same thought is involved in MICHAEL: who
like God, and MICAH for MICAIAH: who like Jehovah. But
the best authorities give MACCABEE: hammerer = MARTEL,
MACE, MAUL, with greater probability of correctness, as the
former origin is too cabalistic to be practicable.

Most likely the first weapons would be missive—dart, spear,
arrow: where skill in throwing took the place of pluck and
muscle. The first known so to have done was, as given,
METHUSELAH: man of the dart = the Milesian name DOWDS.
Saxon families were divided into *spear* and *spindle* sides, boys
belonging to former, girls to latter. The spear was with our
forefathers what the assegai is with Caffres, their reliable
weapon. Swords took the place of spears after many ages.
Spears were originally stone tipped. Saxum: a rock, gives
Seco: I cut (with prepared flint), whence Seax: a sword,
giving Saxones: swordsmen, sabreurs = Sicarii: dagger
carriers, poignard men, skene armed. Hence we have

SAXE (marshal): a Saxon, or swordsman. Undoubtedly of
the stone period we have

HALGIER, ALGAR, ELGER (brave earl): stone spear, old spear,
giving

ALGERNON (Sidney), HALLWARD, ALLARD: stone guard.

GEIRSTEIN (Anne of): stone spear. ANSCAR, ANSCHARIUS:
divine spear, Ans for Ases, char for gar.

GARVEY (wig to vey): war spear. Ancient names carrying
the mind into neolithic periods when Europeans were roaming
savages.

Gar: a spear, gives War: spear fighting, as Spit: a spear, does
Spite: spit fighting. Hence, too, the French Guerre: gar
combat, whence

DAGUERRE (daguerreotype): the soldier, spearman, as also
the French

TIGER, from Theod: people, Gar: a spear, spear of the
people, their defender =

NORDENSKJOLD (arctic): northern shield, he who protects the north.

GARRIBALDI (Guiseppe): spear bold, brave spear man, inverted to

BOLGER: bold spear, which two = these two, GARBETT (bold), GARNET (Noth: bold). Gar also gives the progenitor of many a Cockney joke, VINEGAR, WINEGAR (Win: love): friendly spear, who comes to help of GARLIC: good at spear practice.

To this class belongs the animal like name

BADGER: strong javelin = FALSTAFF: full staff, big, and so needing a strong wielder.

GERMAN: spearman = GARCILASSO, GERARD, GIRADIN, GARRATT, GEROLD, JERROLD, GIRALDI: all shook the glittering spear or launched the fatal lance.

EDGAR, ODGERS: happy spear, good spear man, *con.* Allodial.

LEDGER (leod gar): spear of the people = TIGER.

GORMAN (major O): spear man = HASTY, GORE (house) = SPEIRS. A bull *gores* like a warrior going at his foe with *gar.* He acts *hastily* who does as the Hasta: spear, moves.

QUIRINUS, CYRENIUS: spear man, whence Quirites = Germans.

GERRAM, JERRAM, JEROME (Prague): spear raven. These suggest Will

SHAKESPEARE = PALLAS: she who brandishes the spear, *con.* Ball =

GERTRUDE: spear maiden, an amazon. These correspond to WAGSTAFF (wag *con.* wage, in wage war), BICKERSTAFF ("Tattler") who *bickers*, fights spear armed.

BREAKSPEAR (Adrian IV.): breaker of enemy's staff. Spike gives pike, whence

PICTON (general): great pike = FALSTAFF. Pike: spike nosed fish. The Picts here and the Pictones across the sea giving name to Picard and Poictiers = Germans. But Pike = SPEIRS.

ROCKET: spear blunted for jousting, as lancer's ball does lances when off duty. "We shall be at Saynt Ingylbertes, in the marches of Calays, the twenty day of the moneth of May next commyng, and there contynewe thirty dayes complete, the Fridayes onely excepte, and to deliuer all manner of Knightes and squyers, gentlemen, strangers of any manner of nacyon. whatsoever they be, that wyll come thyder, for the *breakynge* of fyve *speares*, outher *rockettes*, or sharp, at their pleasure."

ROCKET = SPON (Jacob) for ESPON, a form of Espadon: great sword, claymore, *con.*

SPADA: swordsman, giving ESPIE or ESPEE, *con.* Spade (at

cards), originally a sword. Rocket (fireworks), so called from gliding through the air like a spear.

Rocket : stone-tipped spear = Axe, from Saxum : a rock, like HACK, HACO (king) : stone axe bearer = Halbardier : carrier of broad rock axe.

SPON = PICKLES : little pike. Add to this great company of spearmen

RUDIGER : famous spearman = DORYCLUS : glorious spearman, gives RUGGIERO, RODGER, ROGERS, and by a Saxonic twist, HODGE, HODGES : a countryman, as RODGER : a fiddler.

BERANGER (poet) : *bearing gar*, spearman, BERENGARIUS = SPIKE, PIKE (Early Piety).

ATHELGAR, ADELGAR, AUGEREAU : noble spear, who uses it cleverly = GARLIC.

LEODIGARIUS : people's spear man = TIGER, gives LEGER (St.) and *con.* (Mc)LEOD.

WIGHTGAR : strong spear man = WAGSTAFF and FALSTAFF.

WISGAR, WHISKER, WHISKIN : wise at spear, wielding it scientifically.

SINGER (sewing) for ISENGAR : iron spear, as ISEMBARD : iron sword, as

ISENMANN : iron man, worker. Names pointing to introduction of metal. But

SANGSTER (umbrella) : a singer, chorister, correctly applied to a woman.

WITGAR (Wid : wood) : using a wooden spear charred to harden it.

SPROTT, SPRATT, SPROUT are formed on spear, and mean spearmen.

ARGAR : brass spear, transitional between stone and iron.

HASTIFRAGA : spear breaker = BREAKSPEAR (Nicolas). By some

PILATE : man of pila, dart = DOWDS. Shave, to make smooth, gives Shaft : shaven.

SHAFTO (Adair) : who fights with a polished spear, a Paris carpet knight.

SHAFTESBURY : town of Shafto, Gar : a spear, gives Gorse : prickly plant, Gooseberry is gorseberry, Garlic : spear onion (leek). War, then, meant with Germans, French, Spanish, and Italians fighting with the spear ; what was its Greek meaning ? its Roman ?

Polemos : war, is from Palame : the hand, our palm, a tree was so called because its leaves were hand-shaped, while its fruit was called Date : the finger. Polemos was a *hand-to-hand* combat, a line of pugilistic encounters =

Bellum for Duellum, from Duo : two, simultaneous duels along the line, all.

PALEMON, POLEMON (teetotaller), PTOLEMY : warriors all, polemical men in a non-theological sense.

HANLON (Irish): champion = CAMPION, KEMPER : fighters on the *champagne.*

THOMAS A'KEMPIS : Thomas of the field.

NEOPTOLEMOS (son of Achilles) : recruit, tyro, new soldier = CADOGAN, SIGOURNEY (Mrs.), *con.* SIGGA, *ney for new.* No two words can more accurately answer to each other than NEOPTOLEMOS (Neos : new) of the Greeks and SIGOURNEY of the Germans. CADOGAN for Cath: war, and Eogan: son, young, new. These = INCHBALD: bold son, and INGREY (Ing: son, Heer, Her : army) : son of the army, a brave warrior.

BELLONA : bellatrix, amazon = HILDA, NANNI, TORA, *fem.* of Thor.

BASH (*con.* push), PASHLER, BRASH (*con.* bray) : strikers with such force as to break to pieces =

OSMAN (pacha), OTHMAN, OTTOMAN (empire), Osmanli (troops) =

Ossifrage and Osprey : birds breaking the bones =

BRISBANE : bruise bones, crusher, a Saxon foot-soldier, *con.* with Milesian,

(O)BRISLAINE : sword breaker (Briseur = PASH, BASH, *con.* debris), *con.*

(O)LAINE, LANEY : an Irish swordsman. Lanista : a fencing master, who drills gladiators. "Stands colossus-wise, waving his beam upon the *pashed* corses." "Bray a fool in a mortar." Bread : brayed between stones. From Here : a band of above thirty-five, we derive names of places and persons, as

HEREWARD (last of Saxons) : army guard. Hereford : army ford. Harwick : army station.

HERMAN, HARMER (vir) : army man, gives ARMINIUS : a soldier.

OTTER : army terror. LUDERS (general) : army famous, talk of the camp.

WALTER : powerful warrior, becomes VOLTAIRE, GUALTERIO, WAT, WATTS, (Mc)OUAT.

RENIER, RAYNER (*con.* rego) : army ruler = HORROX, HORROCKS (cotton).

HERIMAR : glory of the army, answering to the Greek war name STRATOCLES.

HERIOT : furniture provider for army. HARGRAVES : army steward, commissary.

HAROLD (herewald) : generalissimo = PHICOL, ARCHIMEDES.

ARIOVISTUS : army prince, *con.* Herring : fish going in armies, shoals, schools.

PUNCHION (Rev.) : a swordsman, *con.* Poignard, but sometimes a form of

PUNSHON : living at or near sign of *punchion*, barrel.

CHRYSAOR (Chimœra's father) : golden sword, wearing an ornamented = BRANDAUR.

DUDGEON : large dagger = Claymore (glaive mor), great offence, one easily huffed.

SOFUK (Persian) : a swordsman = CLINGING, *con.* sabre, sepoy, sabaoth. " He threw himself upon *Sofuk*, and clinging to his neck covered his cheek and beard with kisses."

MEEK : a swordsman, *con.* Mece : a sword, *con.* Machomai : I fight, varies to

MECHI (model farm), MEEKING : son of Meek, M'Micking : son of Meeking.

METON (metonic cycle) : a swordsman = COLGAN. In some families

BRAND : a sword, then applied to user, from it, Brandish : to flash as though burning. In this sense Brand = Dagger : flashing like day. In some cases

BRAND : a brander of herring barrels.

SWORD : a swordsman = SEFI, SIGGA : sabreur.

MARTEL (Charles) : a hammer, breaker through ranks of foes = LOUVERTURE (Toussaint) : the opener = MACCABEUS (Judas), HELEM, MAULE. " The sons of his brother HELEM."

TALLEYRAND (diplomatist) : who *cuts* through *ranks* of the enemy.

COX : *cuish* wearer, thigh armour, *con.* QUIXOTE (Don). But Box : box maker,—

> " I saw young Harry with his beaver on,
> His *cuisses* on his thighs, gallantly armed."

YEOMAN : yew bowman, YEMANS, HEMANS (Felicia), EMMINGS.

LARCHER : the archer = (Mc)Iver and SHADBOLT : who sheds arrows from a cross bow.

Bolt : an arrow, from Ballo : I throw. Bolt upright, straight as an arrow.

ALABASTER (arcu balister) : throws arrows by a machine, bow, medieval artillery man. This *cor.* to BOLSTER.

Artillery from Arcus : a bow, *arc* shaped, Telum : a dart, from Tele : distant. "Jonathan gave his artillery unto his lad."

TELEMACHUS : fighting at a distance, unlike Nelson, who gave signal for close action.

BENBOW (admiral) looks *bendbow* = TOXICRATE : powerful at bow = STRONGBOW, but is Italian, being

BEMBO (bene) = BONIFACE : well doing, beneficent = DUGUID the *op.* of

MALVOLIO : evil visaged, *malevolent.* Sometimes the name is local when

15

BEMBO (pen, ben): peaks of hills where cows are grazed.

SAKER: an artillerist working a gun called *saker* from a bird of the hawk kind.

LAURENCE: laurel crowned = BAYS, LORENZO, RIENZI (last tribune), RENZONI (great), (Mc)LAREN, MACLAURIN, LARKINS, LARRY, LAWRIE, LORETTO (little). LAWRENCE =

STEPHEN, STEPHANUS: a crown, primarily a hill top, *con.* Steep: a brae. Step: by which we surmount. STEEPLE: a spire hill high. So Arabic Tag, Dagh means either a crown or a hill top. Daghistan: hill country, *con.* Dacian, Dane. In French names Bre answers to our Bray, Brae as in BREBŒUF (missioner): cattle hill, suggesting HORSFALL.

TAG MAHAL: crown of the harem, queen of beauty. STEPHEN gives ESTEBAN, STEVENS, Stepney: Stephenshithe, hide, harbour where ships hide from storms = Hoff, Haff.

KRON, CRONE, CRANTZ: crowned, ROSENCRANTZ: rose crowned,—

> " Welcome, dear ROSENCRANTZ and GUILDENSTERN!
> Moreover that we much did long to see you,
> The need we have to use you did provoke
> Our hasty sending."

GUILDENSTERN: golden star, a crusader carrying on his shield a star in memory of the Bethlehem one appearing to wise men. But

OXENSTIERN: carrying a *bull's head* and *raven* on shield.

STERN: a raven, *con.* Stare: to look closely, STARLING: staring (bird).

OLIVER: crowned with *olive*, Olympic victor, one of *cales-ephanoi*. By some this gives OLIVANT, OLIPHANT.

OLIVAREZ: son of Oliver = BOLIVAR (Ben Oliver), whence Bolivia, S.A. These =

BELL (when not Norman from La Bel: the handsome): who carries off the bell, prize. This bell figures largely on sign-boards. Many rustic signs are copies of armorial bearings whose reason for being lies in the inability of the masses to read. A lion on a shield meant: *I fought like a lion in the holy wars;* a cross: *I bore arms as a crusader.*

ROTHSCHILD: red shield: *I was wounded.* So public house signs, a horse: *travellers accommodated with stabling;* a bunch of grapes: *Here we sell wine.* Some can read writing, more can read printing, all can read painting.

RAND, RANDLE, RANCE (*con.* round): a shield—VANDER-CHILD: of the shield = CHILDS for SHIELDS.

BORD (when English): big shield bearer, *con.* broad = SKEY, *con.* Sky: a cover.

TORQUATUS (Manlius): wearing *torque*, allied to contortion, it was wreath work for the neck.

LYSANDER (admiral): loosed man = FREEMAN = PRIAM (Troy): ransomed = LIBERIUS (pope).

RANSOM (plough): *sum rendered* for a captive, *con.* Rent: rendered for place hired =
PADON: redeemed, bought back (*d* euphonic). "The children of *Padon* were Nethinim."

HASSAN (favourite in Arabia, Persia, Turkey): slasher, slaughter, *con.* Assassinate: to slay in fight, now means murder = SLAGG, SLOGG.

ROADMAN (Ruad: noised, of whom a row, noise is made): a glorious man = CLEANDER and LUDOVIC.

ROLAND for HRUODLAND: the country's glory, becomes ORLANDO, as
ORLANDO FURIOSO: Roland the raging. Its English is ROWLAND. "A Roland for his Oliver" = "Tit for tat."

ROLAND = PATROCLUS, CLEOPATRA.

LAMBERT (Simnel): land brightness, country's hope.

CHRISTOPHER: Christ carrier, not as Ignatius was surnamed
THEOPHORUS: God bringer, subjectively, but bearer of standard emblazoned with image of Christ. It gives COSTOR-PHINE, CHRYSTIE, CHRYSTAL, CRISTOVAL, STOFFEL, STOFFLET, TUFF, TUFFIL (when not from Teufel), KIT (tanner), KITTS (St.), KEATS (poet), KITTO, unless that dates to the Phenician times (tin), meaning *cassia* seller.

VANE (when not from Bane) (Sir Harry): a standard bearer = ALIGHIERI (Dante) and
ALAFIERI (poet): bearer of standard with *wing* on it, Ala gero = ala fero.

BANNERMAN: a warrior under a *ban*, curse, if he forsook his standard, sacramentum.

PENNANT (when not local): pennon bearer, Pendo: I hang, Pennon: a steamer.

PANTALEONE is a terrific name, the Pan as in Panther: very wild beast (*pan* in sense of *peri*), and so means very lion like. There is a church in Rome dedicated to *St. Pantaleone*. It is given as *lion planter*, a Venetian soldier carrying the standard of St. Mark, but the name is far older than the republic of San Marco. An actor in a pantomime is called the Pantaloon from wearing a caricature of the breeks of the saint or the soldier,—

> " Bring out his mallard, and eft-soons
> Beshake his shaggy *pantaloons.*"

From this word the Yankees call each lady wearing the Bloomer costume a *pantalunatic.*

DERMOT (Mc), DIARMID (Mc), DERMID: a troop, then troopleader = GAD.

GUNN : war, a man of war, gives GONZALES (salus) : saved in combat, GUNTER, GONZALO, but Gun is a form of engine, and GUNTON, *cor.* form of Gunn-stein : war stone, jewel of a fighter. But

BRIMSTONE is a form of BERNSTEIN : a mountain frequented by bears, living on.

CUNDEL : war bold. GUMPRECHT, GOMPERTZ : war bright = CLEOMACHUS: glorious fighter. And the odd name GUMBOIL is formed on GUMBOLD : bold in war. Hence, too, GUNDY : a man of war = CHATTO, HATTO, HATT, *con.* Chad, Cath : war as in CATHIE, CATHLIN and CADOGAN, soldiers three. CADELL, CATTLE : war-like.

CASSWALLAWN : defence of tribe, in Latinised form CASIVELAUNUS. The Romans had a harmless habit of softening hard names.

CATHLIN : war eyed, sparkling eyed, CAHILL, KATHLEEN (mavourneen).

STITT, STEAD, STEADY, STOTT, STOUT : steady in battle array, unmoved by the foe charging.

NOTH : bold, audacious, NUTT (commodore), NUTTER, warriors both.

WOOLNOTH : bold wolf, courageous Saxon warrior.

HEGISTRATUS, STRATEGUS : army leader = HERTOGH, *con.* Stratagem : plan to *lead* an *army* out of a difficulty.

DUKE, DUCE, DUCK, DOUCE : a leader, DUCKETT : young Duke or leader. Ducat : ducal money.

SATRAP (Persian), this name or title from CHATRAPA : umbrella lord, shade of state. The *cha* for *shah.*

" Leotychides, being desired by a Samian to wage war against the Persians, enquired his name : the Samian replied that it was *Hegistratus.*' Then Leotychides answered, 'I embrace the omen of Hegistratus.'" This is a species of fortune telling called Onomantia: finding the future by names. It was common throughout Greece and the East (and still is in the latter) where a chance spoken name decided deliberations. " The historian Ferishta relates that Homayoon, being one day on a hunting party, told several of his nobles that he was uneasy in his mind regarding Hindostan. One of those who were in favour of the enterprise (renewal of invasion) observed that there was an old method of divination, by sending a person forward who should ask the names of three individuals whom he first met, by which a conclusion, good or bad, might be drawn. The king being naturally superstitious, humoured the fancy, and sent three horsemen in front with directions to come back and communicate to him the answers they should receive. The first horseman who returned said he met a traveller named

DOWLAT : empire; the second met a man who called himself
MOORAD : good fortune; and the third was saluted by a
villager who bore the no less encouraging appellation of
SAADUT : the object of desire. Thus cheered by Fate,
Homayoon assembled his forces, which amounted to no less
than 15,000 horse, and being immediately joined by large
numbers of the inhabitants of the Punjaub, he carried every-
thing before him."

LEOTYCHIDES : son of LEOTYCHUS : *con.* EUTYCHUS, and
means one who has the luck of a lion, *i.e.,* gets his prey.

FERISHTA for Faristan : a native of Fars.

MOORAD is better known by MURAD, MURAT, AMURATH =
SAID, GLUCK, JAMIN, GAD, EUTYCHUS, FELIX, LONG (when
Chinese) and FORTUNATUS.

MURAT (in some cases) : who won a *mural* crown made of
grass of a city besieged.

"Sefi, king of Persia, was unfortunate in all his undertakings;
his country suffered from pestilence, treading on the heels of
famine. His mollahs thought it advisable to counsel a change
of name from
SEFI : a sabre, to that of Solyman. He was then crowned
as though Sefi was dead, which royal fiction was carried out
by destroying all seals and deeds of office in the name of the
late king."

SOLYMAN : peaceful = SALEM (Bey), with a traditional flavour
of the glory of Solomon. To retreat from east to west, Cath,
Cad : war, gives
CATTANACH : a warrior, CALGACH : fierce warrior, Latinised
GALGACUS.

CADWALADYR: glory of the army = STRATOCLES, CLEOSTRATUS.

CATERAN : a robber, harrier, as HARRY, MERODE, Katrine
Loch: lake frequented by robbers = Axine.

CAT, CASEY (corporal) are from Cath, and mean a soldier.

ALPHEUS : a leader, strong as a bull, from A, Greek, whence
alphabet, A B, and Elephant : first animal as to size.

BEITH : the birch, B of the Celtic alphabet.

COLL : the hazel, C of Celts.

LABDA (daughter of Amphion) : from Λ of Greeks, she bore
CYPSELUS : a chest, *con.* Apocalypse : uncovering the ark.
So called because hidden in a chest from assassins.

NUN, NON from the Hebrew נ, whose sign was a fish, symbolising fruitfulness.

PUAH, *fem.* of פ : a mouth, awfully talkative woman ; the
Greek is Π, from the Hebrew.

ROSH, in Hebrew ר (our *r*), in Greek P, the dog's letter,
means a head, gives RASHI (rabbi), and in geography Rosetta :
capital of Delta, Ras : a cape. Its *fem.* is the beautiful

ROXANA, ROSHENA (bride of Alexander): SARA, MARTHA, CREUSA, "O Gog, rosh of Meschech and Tubal." From Caph (כ), Egyptian and Hebrew, K of the Greek, our K, the symbol of power, represented by an arm (" To whom is the *arm* of the Lord revealed"), gives

CEPHEUS (king of Ethiopia): powerful. Such names all mean of high antiquity, of an ancient and presumably honourable stock, as the old Erse.

(St.) ELMO, from the elm answering to our A, being spelled *ailm*.

GWYDER : wooder, learned in Celtic, taken from trees. We now leave letters to come back to soldiers.

AGESILAUS : people's leader = MENELAUS : people's strength = the deathless,

DEMOSTHENES, FOLKHART : hardness of the folk = the Roman stump orator,

PUBLICOLA : *cul*tivator of *pub*lic good. ARISTODEMUS : an *aris*tocrat, best of the people.

DEMAS (sometimes viewed as a *cor.* of DEMETRIUS): a plebian = FOLKS, DODDS, LADDS, VOKES.

LEWIS (British) from Llew : lux, light-giving.

LLEWEL : who uses his sword like lightning, whence LLEW-ELLYN (king).

CHLODOWIG, LUDOVIC : famous victor, literal meaning, *loud* about his *vic*tories, gives LOUIS, LOUISA, CLOVIS, LOYS, LOYSON (Pere Hyacinth): son of Louis, or from Eligius. CHLODOWIG also gives LUTHER, LOTHARIO (the gay), CLOTAIRE, LORRAINE : kingdom of LOTHARIUS.

CASIMIR (king): celebrated warrior. ENGELMAN = young warrior = CADOGAN.

ARCHIBALD, usually taken to mean *bold archer*, is a form of ERCHENBOLD : free, open, sincere, fearless.

SIGBRAND (seco) : conquering sword, SIBBALD : conquering prince.

SICKMAN : victorious man in a combat.

Gildan : to pay dues, Guildhall : where paid, gives

GILES (when not a goat): a pledged warrior = GAGE, WAGER, WAGES : engaged to fight. The Scandinavian pledge being in silver, he who gave it was called

SILVERSIDE or WHITESIDE (white money), to this class add HANDYSIDE.

GILBERT : glorious warrior, whence GILPIN (John), GIBBON (great), GIPP ('s land).

STURMER, STARMER : who *storms*, violently attacks =

GERVAS (gar fuss): eager to fight, JERVIS, JARVEY. Fuss meant impetuosity.

SCRYMGEOUR : skirmisher, good in a scrimmage

ALEXANDER : man helper, saving in battle = SOTER, SOZO-MON : saviour, gives ALICK, ALLEY (Sloper), ALISON (M‘)ALIS-TER, CALLISTER, SANDERSON (last four : son of Alexander), HALLACK, ALASDAIR, ADAIR when not an oak) SAUNDERS, SANDY, SCANDERBEG : bey Alexander, ISKANDER, ALESSANDRO (Gavazzi).

ALEXIS : a helper, ALEXIUS : son of Alexis, Russo-Greek, suggests

EPICURUS (epicurean) : a helper = BŒTHIUS (Consolations of Philosophy).

ONOSANDER : man helper = SOSTHENES : strong saviour = SOCRATES : a strong one saving another as he did Alcibiades.

RAYMOND, RAYMENT (*con.* Rince : to cleanse) MUNTZ (M.P.) : pure, protector.

CONCOBHAR, CONNOR (ancient Irish) : helping warriors.

EDMUND : happy defender, EDMONDS, MUNCY, MUNNS.

BERMUDA (islands) for BERMUNDA : pure protector = RAY-MOND. Ber corresponds to Greek Peri and Latin Verus : true.

AHIEZER : brother of help, aid bringer, EZRA, ESDRAS : helper.

MERODE (Fr. statesman) : a marauder, invader, raider = HARRY, whence HARRIGAN : young Harry.

HERAPATH (Here : an army, and pad, as though padded for fight) : mailed.

ALBEMARLE, AUMALE : white mail, contrasts with Black Prince, who wore dark.

"Now, God be praised, the day is ours ! Mayenne hath turn'd his rein,
D'Aumale hath cried for quarter, the Flemish count is slain."

(MACK)HARNESS (bishop) : harness wearer, armour, from Orno : I adorn. "Let not him that putteth on the *harness* boast." Hence "*harnish* plaid."

BEAUHARNOIS (Josephine) : beautiful armour wearer.

ALDHELM : old helmet, veteran. BRIGHTHELM : burnished helmet, young soldier, gives Brighthelmstone (town), Brighton.

CRONHELM : crested helmet. Helm : to cover, Helmet : a covering. Overwhelm : to cover completely. COLLARD : high helmet.

LEUCASPIS : white shield, silver buckler. ROTHSCHILD : red shield. Though this is a German Jewish name, the Jew, as such, knows no such appellation. Such names were adopted to veil origin and evade persecution. Thus

MORTARA (Edgar, boy) : polony maker, from Morta : dead flesh. No Jew ever worked thereat. The word *polony* is from Bologna.

PEVENSEY (Norman chief) : little shield (parvis), hence bold, taking little shelter.

SKIOLDING, SCOLDING : son of a shield, brave defender. When the aboriginal warriors went into action they smote their ˙shield with their sword and cried aloud. This was *scolding.* If not followed by bravery was called swashbucklering. So SKEY (*con.* Sky: that covers): a shield. ÆGIDIUS: son of the goatskin shield of Minerva, under her protection. FORTESCUE: strong shield. SCUDAMORE: shield of love = ALEXANDER, CONNOR.

SQUIRES, ESQUIRE: scutifer, shield bearer to a knight.

BERNICIUS, BERNICE: bringing victory = NICEPHORUS: who coming up the battle is won.

SOPHRONICUS: conquering by generalship. SOPHONISBA: of a wise life.

SOPHIA (St.), SOFY: wisdom. Philosophy: love of wisdom, *con.*

SOPHRON, SEMPRONIUS: sound minded, *con.* EUPHROSYNE, PHRYNE, phrensy.

EUNICE, *fem.* of EUNICIUS: good victory = GOODWIN, GODWIN (sands).

NICOCLES, CLEONICUS: glorious victory, great and unexpected = SIGBERT.

ALMANZOR: the victorious, ANICETUS: invincible = UNWIN: not to be won. The pythoness at Delphi said to Alexander, " Ei anicetus:" thou art unconquerable.

NICIAS: victorious = SIGGA, VICTOR (Hugo), ALCUIN (taught Charlemagne): all win, POLYNICES: many victories, EUPOLEMOS: good fighter.

EDWIN (*con. od* in allodial): happy victor, giving OUDIN (conjurer), OUDINOT (general): little Edwin.

EDWARD: happy guard, successful defender, becomes EDART, NED, NEDDY: an ass, TED, YEDDIE, PEDDIE (Dick, when not formed on PEED). DUARTE (king) and EDOUART (Exeter Hall fame), these =

SIGISMUND, SIMMONDS, SISMEY: victorious defender, wrongfully given *victorious mouth, i.e.,* persuading in council = PYTHAGORAS.

VINCENT, VINCENZIO, CHUNE, NICANOR, SIGGA, SICKMAN: victorious. SYCAMORE (more: great): great conqueror.

THRASONICUS: bold conqueror, who shouts and fights, hence Thrasonical: boastful.

BALL (John, mad priest), BALLS, THRASEUS, HARD, HARDY: bold, a variation of Bald: stripped for battle.

HARDTMUTH: high spirited, of a bold nature = ARCHIBALD.

HARDICANUTE: Canute the bold. BALLARD: of a bold nature.

MUSTARD (Betsy): of a strong constitution, a game fighter, *con.* May: power: Must.

LEOPOLD (leod): bold people; so DYBALL, RUMBOLD: famous for bravery (rumour).

MEROVEUS (mer, mor and veus for wig) : great conqueror.
THRASYMACHUS (pupil of Plato) : bold fighter = BARNACLE.
NICOLAS, NICHOLAS : conqueror of the people, gives Nico-
laitanes : followers of Nicolas of Antioch, COLE, COLET,
COLLETTE (when not acolyte), COLENZO, NICOT (Nicotin :
one so named introduced tobacco into France), NIX (bishop of
Norwich), from it, while the following are his sons—COULSON,
COLLINGS, CLAUSEWITZ. To these we may add the children's
pet,
SANTA KLAUS : saint Nicholas, if not KLAUS : enclosed, a
hermit. And add we must the Dutchman, Mynheer CLOSH.
NICODEMUS : conqueror of the people. Laos and Demos
differ in, the latter implying the confederation of the people,
from Deo : I bind, whereas Laos is people without reference
to politics, giving Lay, Laity : non clerics, Lewd : vulgar.
CALIGULA (emperor) : buskin wearer = LEDDERHOSE : leather
leggings, *con.*
MACLEHOSE : much, muckle hose, baggy leggings. Gallipoli :
Caligula's city.
CARACALLA (casa). " The *caracalla* was a long garment
like the habit of a modern monk, sometimes with and some-
times without a cowl." Suggests
PATCH : wearing party coloured clothing = MOTLEY (historian).
" Patch was the court name of a fool kept by Cardinal Wolsey.
He has had the honour of transmitting his name to a numerous
body of descendants, he being a notable fool in his time."
PEPLOE : wearing the *peplum* as of divine or royal descent
= PORPHYRY. Peplomania : madness for dress. But we must
get nearer war ; so then the following mean chevalier, trooper,
or knight, viz. :—
HOTSPUR : rough rider. SPOHR (Hail, smiling morn) : spur
user =
HORSMAN : But HIPPIAS : charioteer, though, literally, *son
of a horse.*
CHEVAL, CAPEL (when not from chapel), PHILIP : good rider.
ENCKE (comet) HENCHMAN : riding servant, HENGLER, *con.*
HENGIST : a stallion, stall horse, from Hang : to depend.
HORSA, a mare.
EACHRAN, EGHMILY : horse soldier (miles), gives EMLY =
JOCKELL.
ACHAIUS : son of a horse, good rider (each), Achaia : horse
country, as Italy : cattle country, Spain : rabbit country.
CABALLERO (Brazilian general), EPEUS (Trojan horse maker),
ROSS (when not local),
RUTTER, RYDER, RUYTER (De), RITTER (Carl) : riders all.
RECHAB (Rechabites) : a charioteer = CORMACK : son of the
chariot, CAW, who with

(O) HARA and (M‘) ARA were British chariot drivers, Essedi: sitters in chariot. BEVERIDGE: a knight, so termed from wearing Beaver, so called from Bibo : I drink, as horsemen in the *heat* of battle drank thereout.

REMBRANDT VAN RHYN : Rembrandt of the Rhine.

REMBRANDT : king's sword, royal champion = KEMP, CAMPION.

EUPOLEMOS : good warrior = CALIMACHUS : beautiful fighter, handling weapons scientifically.

ANDROMACHUS (burnt by Samaritans) : a man in fight, *fem.*, ANDROMACHE (Hector's wife).

ANDROCLES : Andrew's glory. Andrew : a man of heroic mould, giving ANDY, ANDERSON, and = MANNUS, BRAVO, BEAUREGARD, WIGHT, IZOD, ARBA, ISHI.

HARBONAH (eunuch) : warlike = Martin : Mars-like, gives LAMMARTINE, MARTYN, as also Martinico, Martinique : islands so called.

LAHMI : a warrior, *con.* CHERDOLAOMER : servant of Lahmi the war god of the Susanim. "Elhanan slew *Lahmi* the brother of Goliath."

DOLABELLA (consul) : battle axe bearer = HACO, HACKE, HACKING : son of either.

MEDON : a commander, *fem.*, MEDUSA (head).

PALAMEDES (invented dice) : old commander, veteran leader.

DIOMEDES : Jupiter's commander, best generalissimo.

EUDES (count) : binding well (deo), thoroughly conquering = BINDER.

VICTOR : who binds, from Vieo : I bind, Victim : one bound, Vimen : a with, Mons. Viminalis : osier hill, at Rome. From EUDES, Odo (bishops), ODILLON : great, ODY, OTHO, OTTO (when not from octo), ODETTE, OTHELLO : little, Otho, son of.

HUDIBRAS (*con.* brace) : conquering arm. FLAMBARD (bishop) : a firebrand, flaming sword = BEOR and CHAKA.

FLUGEL (lexicographer) : leader of wing of an army = AHALA, *con.* ala,

ALIGHIERI : wing bearer, *con.* Aisle : of a church.

DUMNORIX (Æduan) : possessor of many hills (*con.* dun).

ORGETORIX (Helvetian) : ruler of a hundred hills (*con.* rego).

HOGAN, HAGAN (O) : high protection, God guarded, but though so given they seem to come of Eogan in the sense of high bred, a son.

OSCAR : bounding warrior, leaping to the fight, gives (Mc)CUSKER.

LABOUCHERE (and Bradlaugh) : the butcher. Norman title of a general who slew his thousands.

BOUCHER (Maid of Kent), BUTCHER : a warrior from beat,

bat, a slasher, slayer = HASSAN. The trade word conveys a modernised sense of it. Butcher, Bottom, each from beat.

DHU : black, dark, gives DUNCAN : dark head, brown haired, the same as the Hibernian.

(THE O)DONAGHUE, DUNPHY, DONOVAN (Rossa): black white (brain) former, hair latter skin, also DUNN, DUFF, DOVE DEE, DUFFY, (Mc)HAFFIE, DOUGAN : young DHU, or DOW.

DUGALD : dark Gael, *op.* of FINGAL : fair Gael or stranger.

KEAN : head chief = ROSH. CANMORE (Malcolm): great head, bodily. KENNY (Meadows : head of the island).

(Mc)CANN : head, an Irish hero who did by his late foe what David did to Goliath. Cantankerous : head full of fight.

(Mc)KINNON, CANNON : fair haired = FLAVIUS, SORLEY, SAURIN.

KENMARE (nun): sea head, KINEALY : head of wall fort. Cantyre : head land = RAS.

KINLOCH : LOCHHEAD. KINNAIRD : Hillhead, may mean chief commander = PHICOL.

KENNETH : head of sept, varies to KENNEDY, (Mc)KENZIE, KINCAID : rock head.

KENTIGERN : head chief, as VORTIGERN (mor): great chief.

RATICAN : living at Rathhead = KINEALY.

KINGLASS : head of stream, *con.* GLASSE, GLASSFORD = PENGELLY.

FATICAN = LONGHEAD, *con.* FADYAN : long John. The tendency to corrupt names can scarcely be better illustrated than in the case of

RADBET [*con.* Ruad : famous (row) and Bid : to send]: a first class messenger, scout, becoming RABBITS.

SIGVALLADUR : conquering power.

GURNEY (which some make from Gourney): gar new, going into battle fresh with his spear, *con.* SIGOURNEY.

CHILPERIC (a great name) is *help rich,* able to sustain an ally.

FREDERICK : peace rich, who by complete conquest of foe gives a long rest to his country.

MANFRED (may main): powerful peace, long peace bringer by punishing foe so that he cannot rally.

KRIGA : war maker = CREEK, CRICK : the war whoop giver, who cries as he enters battle = GROGAN. Cricket proper is of the current century, and hence many have been posed as to how it could supply the widely spread names, CRICKET, CRICKETT, CRICKITT. The solution is, these are formations on CREEK, and mean either son of CREEK, or son of war, *i.e.,* a brave. But Cricket (on the hearth): creaking insect.

CRICKMORE, CRICKMER : great at making war, planning a campaign, cleverly.

FINIGUERRA (French): finished warrior, perfect soldier.

SLY, SLIMAN: who slays his enemy when off guard, and yet not unfairly, Ulyssian type, *con., slay, slit, slot, Slight:* to hurt one's feelings.

MILLS (when not local): a medieval title from Miles: a soldier, from Mille: a thousand. The minimum Roman army was a thousand men, the Teutonic was thirty-five and upwards. The former tells of tactics, the latter of pluck.

MILES: one of the thousand. From Mille our Mile: a thousand paces of the legionary soldier.

SCALIGER (Joseph): ladder bearer, who scaled the enemy's battlements.

MURAT (cavalry king): mural crown receiver. The first who entered a besieged place was crowned with plaited grass that had grown therein while beleagured ; after the campaign with a gold crown wall-shaped.

An astonishing number of warriors derive their names from the dog. Now, as the dog is the symbol of contempt with us, the fact of its being in high repute formerly deserves special attention. The aborigines of many countries were greatly aided by dogs in clearing the primeval woods of wild animals; evidently the dog was one of the first creatures subjected to the human will. Had Abel a collie ? Those early nations observing the pluck of a dog in attacking wild beasts when encouraged by the voice of its master, and admiring its bottom in keeping up the fight against killing odds, generally applied the term dog to their most valiant heroes. The Celts termed it *cu, con, col,* the HEBREWS *caleb,* the Greeks *cuon,* the Latins *canis,* the French *chein.* Hence we have

CUMARA: sea dog, heroic sailor, a regular Blake. So likewise

CON (of 100 battles): a dog, whence hundreds of honourable names with a currish look, as

CONNEL (O), COILEAN, CONGAN, CUNNIAN, CHANNING, CANNING, CUNLIFFE, CONON, CUILLEAN (king), shortened to CULLEN (cardinal), COLIN (Campbell), COLQUHOUN, CALHOUN, CONAN, primarily meant son of dog, *i.e.,* of warlike descent, and so = HERRING, FINGUEROLA, WICKLIFFE, HEROD, SCOLDING. " Blow for blow, as *Conan* said to the Devil." Hence, too,

COOLEY, COLLY (when Irish), COWLEY: Ulster warrior, dog of Ulster, *con.*

NULTY (Mac): an Ulster man. CONCOBHAR, CONNOR: helping warriors. Collie (shepherd's mate) is just Doggie. *Con, col* also gives

QUAIN (anatomy), identical with Cuon: a dog, hence QUIN, and

CONROY : redheaded Con, like REDMOND : red Edmond.

COWIE, COVEY : meadow hound, reminding of LYULPH : meadow wolf.

QUEEN (Mc), QUINLIVAN : young Quin, MULQUEEN : bald headed Con, *con.*

MULYON : son of bald head. To this breed add (Mac)ONIE : son of a dog.

CONNEL forms CONVILLE, which is in peril of being entangled with the *ville* gentry.

CONNAL (Glasgow, S.B.) is Highland, meaning shoresman, one living where roaring waves, polyphloisbon, great noise of the sea, comes.

CUCHULLIN (Ossian's hero) : dog of Ulster = COOLEY, COLLY, COWLEY. Hence, too,

CUSIN for Cu Sionna : hound of the Shannon, bravest on the river.

The successor of Joshua ben Nun is generally translated man of heart, lion like, as though the Cœur de Lion of the Bible, because it was thought intolerable to associate a Hebrew leader with the despicable dog, so it was crowded out of Lib : a lion, whence

LEBBEUS : lion like, but David called his son by about the same. " His second (son) was CHILEAB, of Abigail," and he would not degrade a member of his family by calling him after a mere dog.

CHILEAB : howler, a dog = CALEB = CATO (noble Roman) : a whelp, howler, whence

CATULUS : son of a dog, warrior born = CANNING. CANE (Venetian doge) : a dog =

CHEYNE (Mc), which with many similar names usually given as connected with the oak signify a primitive warrior who fought gamely against odds, as dogs do against wild beasts.

CAGNOLA (canicula) exactly corresponds to CATULUS, which means young and brave.

DURANT, DURANTE : lasting in the fight, game to the last. So the Norman

TALBOT, the Scotch DOIG, and the English DOGGETT (coat and badge) · who gave a dogged resistance to the foe. Thorough John Bull names.

DOGGART : of a dog's nature, plucky, determinate, take no denial.

DODGE is also a form of dog, meaning game fighter.

TOKE : raging for fight like a tyke, dog held back. *Con.* the last is the great

TYCHO (Brahe) : a dog, generally given as *con.* TUCK : a cloth worker, but it is a war name.

CYNOSURA (Jupiter's nurse): dog's tail she was changed to a star in the constellation Cuon. Sailors accurately observed it, whence one attracting attention is called a Cynosure. The dog days are when the dogstar is above the horizon of the Nile.

BORROWS (Bible in Spain) BORROWMAN : a hostage, borrowed by the enemy, a pledge to be returned = HOMER.

MONSABRE (Pere), a name we might be pardoned for supposing meant *my sword*, *i.e.*, a soldier, he who lives by his sabre, really means living on a *salubrioas mount*, healthy hill.

Let our rear be brought up by a Russian poet:—PUSHKIN : an artillery man = ALABASTER, taken from noise guns make when going off, similar to Tic-tick-boo: a gun, so called by Polynesians. Thus we call a man a *tinker* from the tinkling he makes.

CHAPTER XIII.

NAMES DERIVED FROM TRADES OR TITLES.

MANY personal names, especially in modern civilised communities, are traceable to some craft, profession, or official title of the first persons who bore them. No few trades supplying such names have ceased to be followed, hence the names preserving the knowledge of them have historic value, as they give a clearer insight into the past. Moderns are emphasised, because the ancients took ill to trade-names, not through want of appreciating the dignity of labour on the part of Greek or Jew, but because they were unwilling to change a name suggesting family honours, sacred relationships, or glorious deeds, for one that only levelled them with a workman. Moreover, they were affected by the obvious fact that trade names are indefinite. Only one man could literally be called Jacob, while millions might be named Smith. As might be expected, appellatives of this kind are more prevalent amongst western nations, where utilitarianism prevails, than with the imaginative sons of the east. Hence trade-names are common in countries peopled by the Germanic stock, but rare among Arabs, Persians, and Jews. Besides, the original one-name system was unfavourable to the introduction of trade-names, as each man had his name before working at a craft. When the primitive usage failed by reason of popular increase, the two-name system came in like a flood. This occurred in our country mostly in the 13th and 14th centuries, being introduced thus. A boy received his name when christened, and this distinguished him from neighbouring boys; but nearing manhood, he came into contact with a wide circle of fellow mortals, of whom several had the same name as himself. His name getting inconveinently mixed with others, in order to distinguish him from them, a trade name was added. Say the boy was called John, which would be distinctive round the door; as he nears manhood, he meets with others rejoicing in the same designation, and his neighbours, knowing he is apprenticed to make clothes, call him John the Tailor, but as vulgarity is generally laconic, he has to content himself with John TAYLOR, whereby he is distinguished from a neighbour's son also named John; but he being employed in healing (covering) houses, is known as John HULYER : John the slater.

A Greek infant, when nine days old, was called ARISTOCLES: the glory of Aristos. He growing in years, his back grew in breadth to an unusual degree, and he was called PLATO: broad (backed), nearly = the French PETION : broad chested. Plato, *con. plat, flat, platane* (trees).

Amongst the ancients the second name rarely existed with the first, but took its place. " Call me not NAOMI (pleasant to look upon, *con.* Nain: pleasantly situated): call me MARY " (bitter, born amidst bitter trials, same as MIRIAM, MARIA, and the great MIRIAMNE). Observe, she was not called Naomi Mara, nor he Aristocles Plato, whereas our trade names were parasitical upon what is termed Christian names. The following names are a selection of those, the exposition of which may be found instructive and interesting.

AGRICOLA (who first sailed round Britain): a ploughman, from Ager: a field, an *acre*, and Colo: I cultivate, whence *culture, clown, colony, colonel, colonial.* Acre, *con. Aceldama* (acre of blood, field bought by blood money). ACRES (Bob): living in a field. LINACRE: flax farmer. AGERICUS: a fieldman, anglicised to AIRY (astronomer), and AGER, a well known English name. Any of these = HICKMAN, AIKMAN, ACKERMAN and WINKLEMAN for SWINKLELMAN: who sweats through toil = SUE (Eugene) from Sudor: sweat, from Hudor: water, as our sweat is formed on wet. Switzerland: land of sweaters, labourers = Labrador. HOFFMAN : a field labourer, whence HOVEY. VANDERHOFF: of the farm, a labourer.

PEACE (Charles), which has so peaceful a look, means a landholder, a farmer. It was originally PIECE, an elliptical expression for a piece of land. It is so found in documents granting land and charters dating back to the eighth century. BUTTERS: a farmer cultivating meadow land, yielding butter. The Irish for a farmer is SCULLY, as Scullabogue : a barn, the farmer's building. BOWMAN sometimes means an archer, at others, is a form of Boorman : who bores the earth. Boor = Clown, for colone from colo, whence COLON (Christopher): a *cul*-tivator. Thence also BOWERS, BAUER, NIEBUHR (historian) = Neighbour: near boor, so BURLY: like a boor. BORLAND: town land belonging to boors = BURLEIGH (lord).

VAN BUREN: of the cottages = COATES and COTBY. BORDMAN : cottier farmer. Sul: a plough, in the Saxon, gives SILLIMAN : a ploughman = (Mc)GREAGH = TILLMAN : who toils, tills. HAECKEL (evolutionist): a field labourer who howks and harrows = HARROWER. PLEWS: he who ploughs = LAMPLOUGH : land plougher. FARMER is con-*firm*-arius : confirmed in his holding by title. FARM is common. FRANKLIN: a freehold farmer = FREYHOFFER (spectrum analysis). BOND is of Swedish origin, and synonymous with LANFRANC: the free of

the land = FREEMAN : freed man, enfranchised = COLBERT for
con. libertus, who attained liberty with another = HODDER
(and Staughton): a farmer holding allodial land. FREMANTLE
(frumentum): a corn growing farmer, not a grazier. TRAVIL:
a labourer working with travail. Travel: to journey on bad
roads. CARABŒUF : who drives a bullock cart = the classic
BOOTES : ox driver. HIND, HINE, DAY : day labourers. HYND-
MAN = TRAVIL. HINSON : son of Hind, but HINTON (Jack):
town behind a hill. From Amal : work, the historic ÆMILIUS:
a worker, giving AMELIA and EMILY (not Emma), but AMERY
(Pott & N.Y.), EMERY and AMERIGO (Vespucci) are from AMAL-
RICH : exalted ruler (ric), as also IMRIE, its abbreviated
form. When IMRIE is Gaelic it means butter, supplying king
therewith. GRANGER : grain grower. CHANGARNIER (general)
for champgarnier: raising grain on champagne land. GARNER :
grain storer, granary keeper becomes garner. DRABLE (*de-*
arable) = FREMANTLE, METARIUS, MYERS, one who *metes* fields,
land surveyor = LANDSEER = RAPER from Rap : rope, as in
Stirrup : rope to rise by, one measuring land with a cord.
But ROPER : rober, and WARDROP : who had charge of the
king's wardrobe. METAYER (anarchist) is the continent correspondent to MYERS. LEPAILLEUR (Little Sisters of Poor):
straw seller. Pallet : a straw bed. HARDMAN : earth man,
soil worker = GARDINER, GARDNER, JARDINE, though the root
idea in these is Gird, whence yard, girdle, garter, garth, Gars-
cube, Garscadden. JARDINE = HORTENSIUS, HORTENSE (Reine),
ORTON : town among gardens = ORVILLE (awful Gardiner).
Ortolan : a garden bird, but ORTOLAN : a gardener = GINNE-
THON. "Daniel, *Ginnethon,* Baruch," were sealed. From
Gen : a garden, whence also En-gannim : garden well, fountain.
Genesareth : prince's garden, very fruitful. Similarly the
Irish GARRY : a garden, as GARRYOWEN : Owen's garden, like
Tyrone : Owen's land. ANDROGEOS, AGESO, GEORGE : worker
in earth = HARDMAN. "I am the vine, and my Father is the
georgos." Hence Georgics : rural poems. JOURY (Crimean
prince), JOURISEN : son of George, GIORGONE (Italian), are
formations on George.

HUSBAND : house bond, a farmer, who in the Lothians had a
farm of fixed dimensions. SERVICE or FAIRSERVICE is a farmer
holding land for a service rendered to the king. Wife: a weaver.
Spinster: daughter who spun. WIFE is a living family name, of
course means a weaver. The name and title BARON : a strong
man, then husband, gives BIRON (marshal), BYRON (poet),
BARONIUS (historian), son of Baron. SPURIUS: a sower, who
scatters. Sporades: scattered isles, Sparta : scattered town, not
built in streets. SERRANUS, SERRANO (Spanish): a sower, allied
to Serene : weather favourable for sowing, whence serenade.

16

Singing does not go off well in a storm. SERENO: a watchman who calls out serene weather. SATURN (agricultural god whence Saturnalia: rustic festival): a sower = SEJI, whence SEJANUS (favourite of Tiberius). CYAMITAS: bean-planter. CICERO from Cicer: a vetch, field-pea, is generally given as = FITCH or VETCH. "Doth not he cast abroad the *fitches?*" But the orator was named from having a pea-like excrescence, wart, on his nose as had Oliver Cromwell. BATTEUR: corn beater = THRESHER and TASKER, giving BATTERSCOMB: Batteur's dale, from a Norman family. FAUCHEUR: hay maker, working with a *falk:* scythe, *con.* Falchion: a great sword = Claymore: great glaive. CURRAN (orator): a reaping hook which an Irishman quickly improvises into a scimitar. ALDER, ELDER, ANAX, ALDERMAN = SEIGNOR: seniors, senators, elderly men. ALDRIC: aged ruler, whence Aldersgate. But ALDO (Aldine press): audax, audacious, bold. ALDRIC = ARCHON from Arche: chief by seniority, gives TARQUIN (king). OLRIC, ULRIC, ALARIC are forms of ATHELRIC: noble ruler = REGINMAR, REIMER, RAUMER, REIMARUS: famous ruler. ERIC (king of Norway): aye ric, ever king. Ric *con.* Rego: I rule, RAJAH, MARAJAH (magnus rex): great king = ARTA-XERXES from XERXES: a fighting king. Ric is cognate with REE: a king, as in RENE (roy natus): of royal birth, and IMRIE. So MACREE (widow): son of a king. RICE, REECE, RICHARD (richard): stern ruler, giving RICKETT, RICARDO, Riccarton: Richard's town, CLANRICARDE, RITCHIE, DICK, DIXON: son of Dick, DICKENS, DEEKS, PRITCHARD: son of Richard, as BRICE or BRYCE and PRICE: son of Rice. Rego also gives REGULUS (ambassador to Carthage): little king, as also RULE, WREN (Christopher) and Wren, the little king of birds. As Kingfisher: king of fishers, because of its beauty, the wren was reckoned king of birds from its prettiness and littleness.

KING, KONIG, and CONGER: men who ken, know, are cunning. Conger-eel: king of eels. REX gives RAIKES (Sabbath School): a ruler, and ROY gives ROYLE, RYLE (Liverpool). KONIGSBERG = Kingston. But LEROY: head of a corporation, while the too well known LEFROY: the cool, frigid. VOR-TIGERN: excellent chief = SAPOR (Persian king) for shah-poor: great king. PASHA, BASHAW: king's foot. Officers of the Shah named from his members as Vizier, called his eye. From Shah, SHEIK: petty king. Chess, Check: king. Check-mate: dead king. Chess: game of kings. Ric conjoined with Theod: people, gives the dread THEODERIC: ruler of the people, whence THIERY, TERRY, DERRICK, DIACK. DYBALL: of a bold people, brave. But RODERICK: famous ruler, giving RORY (of the hills), Cuidad RODERIGO: city of Roderic. These must not be confused with THEODOSIUS: gift of God, whence THEODORE and TUDOR (house of), as also D'ORSEY (Count). THEODOSIUS transposed gives DOROTHY, DOLLY (Dobson). THEODORUS, DOROTHY, THEODOSIA, THEODOTUS, DEODANDA, apply to children earnestly desired, and so = DESIDERIUS: desiderated = SAMUEL: asked of God, SAUL: asked (of God). Theod: people, gives THEOBALD: of a bold people, *ab.* to DYBALL, which *cor.* to DIBBLE. TIDYMAN, TIDY: of the people = FOLKS, FFOULKES, FOUCHE, forms of vulgus, and allied to Belgii: populous, giving Belgium. PUBLIUS: son of the people. PUBLICOLA: who *cul*tivates the good will of the people. Theod also gives Teuton or Teutones: multitudinous = Belgii. DODD, DODDS, DIETZ (Ella): one of the Theod. DODDRELL: Dodd of the hill. Doddington: town of his descendants. Diet: popular assembly. So the Danish (Mc)LEOD: one of the people. LEATHERHEAD (which has puzzled thousands) is from Leod: people, and Rede: council, being a thousand years since a popular consultation spot like Wittanagemot: witty man's meeting. REGINALD: the power of judgment, giving REYNOLDS, RENOLF, RONALD, CLANRANALD, RENNIE. From Kratos: power, KRAFT: powerful. Craft: ability to follow a trade.

DESPOTES: foot binder, having power to put in fetters, governing without consulting governed, a despot. POSIDEON (Neptune): same reversed, as sea water binds the feet, *impedes* motion. DESPOTES = KURIOS: lord, from Kir: a city, meaning city king. From Kurios we have Kirk: house (oikos) of the Lord. SELKIRK: great church = TEMPLEMORE. KIRKE: living near a church, or having charge of one = IGLESIAS (& Montero) our ECCLES. CYRUS: lord, CYRIA: a lady (ii John 1.) CID (Spanish): lord of city. CALIPH: an Aleph: first man = ALPHEUS = PRINCE: princeps, primus capio, who takes first place. BRETWALD: wide ruling, wielding = EURYNOME. BASILEUS: basis of the laity, foundation of the people, a king, BASIL (St.), and Basle (city) are contractions of it. Basilisk = Regulus: little king, crowned snake, whence Fascinate: to catch the eye as serpents do. Basilicon: royal house, cathedral. TYRANNUS (a castle governor, *con.* Turra): a king. Tyrant and Despot now used only in a bad sense, but not so originally. "Disputing daily in the school of one *Tyrannus*" = discussing in Mr. King's school-room. (Luke ii. 29): "Despot, now Thou lettest Thy servant depart in peace." LISTER, LIST: preparer of lists,—

" Be Mowbray's sins so heavy in his bosom
That they may break his foaming courser's back,
And throw the rider headlong in the *lists*."

But LITSTER : a dyer, who puts clothes in *ley, lith.* BUTTRESS, BUTT (Isaac): setters up of butts, targets. Butt: hide of a budd. SOURBUTTS: who scars the butts with his arrow, a good archer. Target: a shield, from Tergum: a hide, from Tego: I cover. BUDD = METCALF, MEDCALF: meadow calf = STURROCKS, from steer, stirk. VERSTEGAN: keeper of a stronghold = HOLDER, HOLDEN. HOLDING: son of HOLDER, BOLDEN: son of Holden. ARK (*con.* Archives: documents kept in an ark like the decalogue). ARKWRIGHT: chestmaker = KISTNER: chestner, made meal chests. BYNG (admiral): bing maker. THROWER: thread maker = LIMEWEAVER. Thread: throwed in making. BACON (Roger) = BEECHER: fed hogs on beech nuts, GLANDER did on acorns = LARDNER, PORCHER. The latter unconnected with Poacher: game pocketer. Pocket: a little poke. Pucker: to make pokes. Peck: a bag. But PECK, PEEK: living on a hill = AIRD and PICKWITH (peak vicus) = HILTON: town on a hill. HAYWARD, HOWARD are forms of Hogwarden: charge of all hogs in a forest. HOWARD becomes HOAD, as in HOADLY (bishop): Howard's field, living in. PORCHER = PORCIUS (Festus) and SUARIUS: sow keeper, SUAREZ: his son. The original Porcher was probably swineherd in the New Forest, while the first Porcius possibly kept hogs in the Pontine Marshes. *Fem.* PORCIA (Cato's sister, who perished by swallowing burning coals). SWAIN: swineherd, as SUARIUS. SWAINLAND: frequented by swine. SWINDELL: swine dale = SUGDEN: frequented by sows. BUCKLAND: beech-tree land = Buckowina (Austria).

COPELAND: a quay, fair, where merchants deposit wares = COPESTAKES: land staked out for merchandise. Copenhagen: merchants' haven. These *con.* cheap, whence Chepstow: market place, Chap: a fellow, a hawker = CHAPMAN: a huckster = DICKERMAN, CHAFF, CHAFFEY, COFFIN, KAUFMAN (general). But CHAFFIE: baldheaded = MOULE, and *con.* CHAUVIN. CLEVELAND: cliff land = GARIOCH and FOLLY from Fell: a rock, as in Goatsfell. So RAGLAN: rough land, the opposite of SMITHFIELD: smooth field = SNODGRASS: smoothly cut grass. SNODGRASS compares well with SNYDER: cutter, tailor, and Snap: to cut off short. FALKLAND: frequented by hawks. CROYLAND: by crows. STRICKLAND (Agnes): stirk, sturrock land = Cowmeadow = CLONTARF, and HUXLEY for OXLEY. "They go into college stirks, and come out asses." BACKLER: a janitor = DORMAN and OSTORIUS: a door keeper, *cor.* to USHER, whence LUSHER (le usher) and LUSH. LUSHINGTON: the town of the son of Lush. DURWARD (Quintin): door ward, tyler = KÖSTER (Lawrence), COSTER, CUSTANCE: door custodian. YATES, GATES, YETT: gate keeper. HATCH: had charge of a

gate for deer, not going with hinge, but taken off by a *hitch.*
SALMON : saloon keeper, hall door. CALMAN (caul man), ladies'
hairdresser. (Is. iii. 13.) Gaylor is a form of jailer. CUSH-
MAN : cowman, cheese maker. BARBOUR : beard trimmer, *con.*
BAREBONES: beard bonny, fine bearded. KEPLER (astronomer):
tanner working *kipps* = PELLETAN : skin tanner. PELLISSIER
(marshal): furrier. BARKER : who works in *bark* tan =
TANNER (faster),—

> " What craftsman art thou, said the king,
>   I pray thee tell me, trowe?
> I am a *barker*, sir, to my trade ;
>   Now tell me what art thou ? "

BAYLE, BAILLY, BAILEY : a bailiff, meant a protector, from
Beorgan : to protect, whence Burgh : a walled town, *con. bal*
in such names as BALMERINO : town on the sea = SETON. Out
on *bail* is out under court protection. HAUSMAN (Baron):
house bailiff = VOGHT. BAINES, BANNISTER (Jack): charge of
a bath. Having its root in Bain : white, a bath makes white,
so Ban, Boyne,—

> " No more I do my murthis fayne,
>   But in gladness I swym and *baine*."

The ending *ster* denotes *fem. gen.* Trades to which it is
affixed were divided into branches, at the lighter of which
women worked. When through the progress of refinement
men took their place such branches retained old designations.
BAKER : batch cooker. BAXTER : female baker = CRACKNELL :
cake baker. " Take with thee ten loaves and cracknels."
FLANNER : pastry baker = WATEAU. MAZARIN (cardinal) is
con. Macaroni, and means the same as WATEAU and VATEL.
COKE (lawyer), COCK, KOCH (Paul de): a cook, whence
COCKER (arithmetician): one pampered by delicate cookery.
(Mc)DADE : kneader. BAKER = the Roman PISTORIUS (Joseph),
Italian FORNARIUS : man of the furnace, and the Normans
had BULLINGER (Reformer): a baker, whence PULLINGER.
BREWER : *con. brose, broth, breweth,* gives BREWSTER =
M'GROUTHER : the king's brewer to a Celtic king. CHALONER :
woollen weaver, *con.* Chalons-sur-Marne. WEAVER, WEBER
(Der Freischutz). WEBB give WEBSTER (Daniel): weaver of
light goods. WHIB, WHIPPS, WHIPPERMAN : a weaver, *whips*
the shuttle from side to side. WHIBLEY : the weavers' field.
There being no heavy department to spinning, we have no
man named Spinner, and as surnames of women are absorbed
in those of their husband's, no woman can be named Spinster,
that being generic for a maid, but we have CLOTHO (Fates):
spinner, *con. cloth* ; and WIFE is a family name. In the Irish
we find SHEDDY, SHEDDEN : silk weavers. The same ancient

language supplies us with COGHILL : net weaver. SLEEMAN
(Thugs): slaie maker = REEDMAN : weaver's reed maker.
LINGARD (D.D.) : worker of lingerie, napery, linen. LANYER :
wool worker, *con.* Lanimer Fair. TILLEY : a first rate weaver,
con. Subtile : cleverly done under the loom. BLACKER
(Stewart): bleacher = WHITSTER : who makes white. BECKNER
(Volney), BUCER (reformer), BOOKER : writer on *beech*wood,
learned, a book worm = SCRIBONIUS, SCRIVENER, SCHREVALIUS:
scribes. SAPHIR (Rev.) : man of books. Sepharvaim : city of
books. We not only have BOOKER but BOOKLESS. The
less in this name is *con.* LACY : learned, so that, instead
of meaning minus books, BOOKLESS : book learned ; but
librarian. ORDERS : who hoards, a treasurer = HOARD and
as Boc : a beech, BOOKLESS strangely answers to GWYDER :
learned in wood. Consult GWYDER. BOCHART : book herd,
KAMMERER. PORTEOUS : made manuals, books *por*table by
hand. PATERNOSTER (common in Bedfordshire): made
rosaries, rows of beads on which they bid the Lord's prayer.
The trade was formerly strong in Paternoster Row. BIDDLE,
BOODLE, BEDELL : prayer men who told their beads often.
BEDE (venerable). BADMAN, MONBODDO : men of beads. Bid
now means to command, then to pray, BADMAN, BONOMI,
BONHAM (bonus homo) = GOTHER (bishop), GOODMAN, GOTH-
MAN, HOLYBAD, and GOODCHILD. But HORATIO, HORACE,
often given as meaning prayerful, from Oro : I pray, whence
Adore : to kiss, as adoration was putting mouth to object
of worship, is from Oratos : aspectable, men to whom we
look as having marks of superiority, like BEAUREGARD, MIRA-
BEAU. Yet ARABELLA is undoubtedly a form of ORABELLA :
a female religeuse. The poet Horace had a mistress whom
he called GLYCERA (*con.* Glycerine): sweet one = SACCHA-
RISSA. BIDWELL : sacred spring where prayer was wont to
be made = (S)CALDWELL : fountains where the Scalds sang to
gods on harps, the memory of which passing away with the
inbringing of Christianity, folk guessed the word meant *cold
spring.* CALDWELL assumes the forms COLWELL and the
better known CAUDLE. (S)CALDWELL of the Druidical period
= HOLYWELL of the Medieval. GOTOBED : worshipper of God
= THEOSEBES. BADMAN = EUSEBES : worshipping well, very
religious, whence EUSEBIUS (historian): son of Eusebes, of
pious ancestry = DE SANCTIS, DE SANTOS : of the saints = DE
FOE : of the faith = RASSELAS : of apostolic descent.

HOSIUS (president) : holy, dedicated = ENOCH. The Glasgow
St. ENOCH is from Thenaw, the mother of St. Kentigern.
OSIANDER : holy man, devotee = ALLGOOD : hallowed, baptised
and blessed when that was rare. MALE, MAHLMANN : a
painter = PINTO of the Spanish. PARGITER : a painter or

plasterer. "Fifty and six pargits." ESILMAN : an ass driver = ASINIUS. EASEL : the painter's ass, bearing his arm as an ass does its burden.

Bugan : to bend gives Buxom : bending, yielding, and BOGUE : bow bender, archer, BIGGAR, BIGGS : bower builder, edifier in the wattle and dab style, like hurdles filled in with clay. BOGUE gives the vulgar sounding BUGG. Howbeit BOIG is a form of BOG (dweller) = MARSH, MOSS, as DOIG is formed from Dog. Big : artificially large. Great (from grow) : naturally large. Big house, great tree. DODMAN, DADMAN : dud seller, old clothes' man. " He is a dude," *i.e.*, a dressy man. BLINKHORN (blend corn) : farrago seller, he mixed wheat with rye. PEPPER CORN : a Saxon farmer paying a pepper corn, nominal rent = PENNY : farmer of poor soil, called penny land. Jews said, " A grain of mustard seed" for something small, but Saxons, " A pepper corn." Now PEPPER (patent ghost) : grocer, spice seller, of which pepper was one. It is = SPICER : epicier. " Within Coneyhope Lane standeth the Grocer's Hall, which company was of old called pepperers." FROMANT : corn salesman (frumentum), *con. frumenty*, which our country cousins persist in calling frummerty, *con.* FREMANTLE. Fomentara (island) : fruitful in corn = Java.

BUBIER, BOOTES, BOURBON : cattle driver or dealer, neat herd = NOTMAN. BOUVERIE : an ox stall, cow byre = COTTON (admiral) : cow town, enclosure for kine. COE (captain) : cow. COWLEY (when English) : cow field = COEVELT. COWARD = STODDART : stott herd = (Mc)CULLOCH : cattle tender. Coward : one who cowers, stoops to escape a blow, similar to CRAVEN : one who beaten craved his life. HYRDE, HURD, HURDIS : herdsman each. COWARD = BUBULCUS and BOUKOLOS, whence Bucolics : pastoral poetry. In some cases BOWMAN : stock keeper. WHYMAN : having charge of kye, cows. EGON : goat herd, *con.* Ægis : shield of Minerva covered with goatskin, and = CABRERA, *con.* Caprera : goat island. Phernes : a shepherd, gives ARTAPHERNES : great shepherd, men ruler. HOLOFERNES (Judith) : chief shepherd. From Far : a sheep, Faroe : sheep island, and FARRAR (canon) : a shepherd.

PHARNASPES : commander of horse = HIPPARCHUS (astronomer). CHEFFER, CHAFFER, SCHAFFER, SHAPFER : a shepherd, *con.* Shapfells, sheep hills. SMALL, SMALLMAN : who saw after lambs and kids : "Thou hast brought me no *small* cattle of thy burnt offering." TWENTYMAN : having charge of *two winter* cattle. CALVERT : having charge of *calves.* Sometimes CALVERT : a fish curer. HUMAN : an experienced shepherd having care of ewes. POLYMELES (historian) : many sheep. MELEAGER : active with sheep, folding quickly, *con.* acer. MELIBŒUS : charge of sheep and cattle. PATTI (diva) :

shepherdess, *con.* Pastor: a feeder. PATTI answers well to OPHELIA, from Ovis: a sheep, whence ovation.

KIDDER: a travelling HUCKSTER: carrying goods for sale on his *hocks*, provincially applied to shoulders = Colporteur: collar porter. KIDMAN = CHAPMAN: man selling cheap, a cheap Jack. Cheapside: near market. Chipping Norton: market at the north town. Huckster is a form of Hockster, and HAWKER is its brief form. KAUFFMAN (Turkestan), COFFIN (Tom) = COWPER: who *coups,* sells: proper spelling, COUPER, and sometimes *cor.* to COOPER.

DOBLER (Herr): dish maker = TISCHENMAKER, and TURENNE: tureen maker, who made earthen vessels, Terra = ARTHMAN. KISS (sculptor): *cush*ion maker. HANDEL (oratorio): seller by hand. BODGER: cooper,*con.* boat,boot, bottom (of land or hemp), implying hollowness. BUTTMAN: butt maker, formerly wrought in budd's hides, as Hogshead = ox hide. BUTLER: charge of butts or bottles. Bottle: little butt, as Pottle: a little pot. BUTLER = KELLERMAN (marshal): cellar man.

HOOPER (judicious), COOPER (novelist), CUVIER (naturalist): who caves wood = TUPPER (poet): tubber. The great Italian name ZOPPI is simply soup plate maker = TURENNE and CHOPIN of the French. These made wooden goods, amongst others, sabots, trenchers, bowls, corresponding to COGHIE: cog maker of the Scotch. But COOPER (Astley and that kith): a form of COPARIUS: cup bearer to king of France. CADMAN: maker of cades, casks. Caddy: a little cade. Casket: a little cask. TUPMAN: sheep (tups) breeder. POTT, POTTER, TOPFER, EULER (mathematician): potters all. The last seen to advantage in Olla Podrida: pot of putrid things, a miscellany. Olla: a pot, from Olere: to grow, whence redolent, adolescence, means a kale pot. VASARI (Giorgo): earthen vessel maker. CROKER, CROKE: crock maker, whence Crockery: pots. KRUGER (boer), KROGG: keeping a roadside public house where beer was sold out of a *crock* = SCHENKE, and INMAN (liner). So our AYLWARD and WIN-SHIP: ale and wine shop. MOST (editor): wine maker, brewed *must.*

POTTS: living near a well, spring = TWELLS: at the wells = PAGAN, from PEGE: a fountain, springing out of the (ge) earth, *con.* Pegasus. Pagan was applied to those who used the same village pump. Citizens receiving Christianity before rustics, those living in villages were termed Pagani, which became synonymous with Heathen, Gauyim: not of the Jewish religion. Takes the diminutive form PAGANINI (violinist) and gives PAINE: a villain, a villager, one of the paynim. PAYSON for Paysan: a peasant becomes PHEASANT. Civic superiority is farther illustrated by URBAN (pope), URBANE: astute, polite = TOWNLY: town like = CURTIS (gunpowder): courteous.

To return to wells. ATWELL = DELAFONTAINE : of the fountain
= FAUNT and SPRING (Tom). POZZO = VANDEPUT and POTTS,
con. Puteoli : wells stinking (through sulphur) = Fontenoy :
noxious fountain. PITT : living near a quarry. PITMAN
(phonographer) : miner, quarry worker = QUARRIER : stone
squarer, becomes WHARRIE. Some have QUARRIER : warrior.
I take it to be a trade name. QUARLES (emblems) : shot game
with a *square* headed arrow. PITT = MOLIERE (play-wright) :
millstone quarry. BOTTOM (weaver) : when not local means
worker at bottom of pit shaft, when local = DELLAR : dale er,
living in. SHANKS : pit shanker, sinker of shaft, if local,
living on projection of a hill = SPITE, *con.* Spithead. Now
for more pots. POTTINGER (of Indian fame) : pot maker = TASS,
TASSY, TASMAN (whence Tasmania) : cup maker. POTTINGER,
also old name for Druggist : *dried* herb seller. BURRAGE :
gathered *borrage* to mix with wine. SPURGE : gathered herbs
to *purge* wine, hence SPURGEON (C. H.) : son of Spurge.
BALMER (Berwick) : herbalist selling balsam, balm. PARGITER :
a plasterer or painter,—

> " Gold was the *parget :* and the seeling bright
> Did shine all scaly with great plates of gold."

CAMBYSES (Persian) : sacerdotal bard = BAIRD (Scotch), SCALD
(Norse), KEEN (Irish). Mourning for dead is known as keen-
ing, *con.* Kinnor : a harp, *con.* Cinneroth : wailing sounds
made by wind, reeds, and water. The orthodox Irish for a
poet is THADY, giving TEAGUE = PAT, from St. Patrick, and
TADDY. VIGNOLES : a vine dresser = CARMI. Carmel : vineyard of God, very fruitful. " Achan, the son of Carmi, took
of the anathematized thing." LAMBRUSCHINI (pope) : a wild
vine, unmanageable.

CARPENTER : car maker = CARTWRIGHT, now generically
applied to wood worker. CARIOLI (Italian) = CHARETTE
(French) : car driver. CARABŒUF : bullock cart driver = ARABI
(when Turkish). FABRICIUS : *fabric* maker, an ouvrir, opera-
tive, gives FABER, FAVRE (Jules), LEFEBVRE (marshal) LEFEVRE,
LEFEVER : workmen all. SLOPER (Ally) : slop maker = SMOKER :
smock-frock maker. PATON : maker of *patons,* clogs. Pattern :
like a *pad* of the foot, a vestige. WRIGHT : *wrought* at any
trade in wood, as CARTWRIGHT, PLOUGHWRIGHT, WAINWRIGHT :
waggon maker, vehicle for the *way*, road. WHEELER : branch
of last making only, wheels. ZIMMERMAN (on solitude) : timber man, materialist, *i.e.*, worker in *matter*, timber. Matter
from Mater : mother, it being mother of all, formed thereof.
Madeira (isle) : of timber. Matto Grosso : gross with timber,
primeval forest of the Amazons ; about = BUISSON (French
savan) : great wood, and CHACEMORE. STUHLMAN : stool

maker. TIGELLINUS (Nero's friend): beam fixer, tabernacle maker = the German SHURMER, SCHIRMANN: tent, umbrella, or shadow maker = TELLWRIGHT: tilt manufacturer = COPERNICUS: cover maker, hut builder. This Danish name = our Franco England MAISON, MASON : messuage builder, mansion erecter. BRACCIOLINI (Poggio): worker in *breccia* stone. PONCE (de Leon): pumice stone worker. JENNER (vaccination): a joiner. TISCHENDORF (Constantine): joiner's village. CARTER : a carman = CHARRON (French author = WAGNER (German) = HARMODIUS : charioteer, drove yoked horses = HIPPIAS. But WAYMAN : wain man, so WENMAN, WHIGMORE (Ely, 1660). "From a word, *whiggam*, used in driving their horses; all that drove were called whiggamors, and shorter, whigs." Whig, *con.* wide, for quick, living, active. QUICK (Rev. R. H.), WICKS, GRADY (O), VIVIAN, VIAL, VITALIS, VITUS (St.), each mean quick, active, GRADGRIND: quick grinder. But VIVIAN (Gray) means more than physical vitality, properly meaning one rev*iv*ed, and so = the Puritan name, RENOVATA : renewed, implies one regenerated, entering a higher life.

WAITMAN : huntsman, who waits, watches game. CASE : cottage builder, *con.* Chez: at the house of; CHIESE, CHEESE, and ACE (Jessie): the house. Casino, CASSINO (Boston): small house near a theatre, Chasuble: house-like garment = COAT : covering like a cottage. COATES : living at the cottages = VAN BUREN. CASABIANCA (gallant boy): white house = WENTWORTH, *con.* Gwen: white, as in NELL GWYNE: Ellen White, and CENWIN: white head, WHITEHEAD. CASANOVA, CANOVA = NEWHAUS. CAZVINE (Zakaria): vine clad cottage. CATCHPOLE: catch pooler. " In mining, the ore is passed from reservoir to reservoir, each constructed to retain portions of metal. He who had charge of a pool where metal was so *caught* was thus called." Also nickname for bailiff who carried a staff, profanely styled by the vulgar a pole. Names identical as to form, but differing as to sense, originate at divers periods and under different circumstances. Thus TURNER : wood worker, TURNER (terra noir): black castle = SCHWARTZENBURG (cardinal), TURNER : one who took place of an absentee at a *tourn*ament, an at*torn*ey, who engaged for another = WAGER. GAGE (whence greengage): engaged to fight, pledged to an ordeal.

TURNARELLI (of the wreath) = TORRICELLI (barometer): little castle. POOLE : near a pool, its *dim.* in some cases POLLOCK, in others it is *dim.* of PAUL. WALPOLE (wald pool): wood near water, GLASSPOLE : water running into a pool. DABBS = DUBBS: decorator, dabs on ornaments. CHANCELLOR : who cancelled government debts = KANZLER (general). CANGE (Du): money banker, of change. DRUDGE : fisherman, whose work was drudgery, dragging his net = DARG : pitman working by darg, what is dragged along and up. CHABOT : fisher off the French coast, whence CABOT (Sebastian) : POISSONIER, FISHER, FISK, HOOKER, LANGELIER, PITCHERS (pecheur), DOEG (Edomite) : fishermen every one. DOEG comes from Dag : a fish, whence Dagon : great fish (god), *con.* Tagus = Fish River. GEDDES (stool): pike fisher. POISSON (mathematician): French fisherman. FROSCHAMMER : frog fisher. PRIDE : pryde catcher, river fish like lampreys. CONDER, CONDOR : conductor of Cornish fishermen, who watched on a rock top, signalling the whereabouts of shoals (schools) of fishes.

DELCAMBRE, CHAMBERS, CHALMERS, CHAMBERLAIN (from Cam: crooked, arched roof): charge of king's chamber = eunuch sometimes means treasurer. "Erastus the chamberlain (economist) of the city, saluteth you." Eunuch had charge of bed, Chamberlain of room, Economist of house. STEWARD (stowe ward): charge of a *stowe*, whence stowed, stead, steady : keeping in one place. Bedstead : place of bed. STUART is its form in France, there being no *w* in French. STOWE (David): an enclosed place. BUMPSTEAD : place of beams, a wood = BAMPTON (lectures). The name BAUM is *cor.* to BUMM.

NUSSBAUM : walnut tree. CHANDLER : candle seller. COKE (upon Lyttleton): a cook. COCKER (according to): to cook up for, to pamper, to bring up delicately = TYRPHENA, TRYPHOSA : nourished = DELILAH : delicate, tender. COCKER takes the *dim.* COCKERELL. TODHUNTER (algebra) : fox hunter. PURCHASE : living *per chase*, by hunting = JAGER, FENIAN, BERNERS, BARNES, VENUA, VENARD, VENANTIUS, VENTRIS : men of venery, who took venison. To these add the Hindoo name VEDAH, *con.* Veddas: wooders, the aborigines of Ceylon. This word *vedda* is identical with the name of the sacred book of the Goths, Edda: old, it is literally a *vet*-eran book. Vedda, Edda, *vet*-us (old): wid, wit, Ida (mount), are variations of one ancient word used in Sanscrit, Greek, Latin, English, etc. In another aspect VEDAH = COYLE, GAEL, KELT : woodmen three. GROSVENOR : great hunter, Duke of Normandy's head huntsman, *con.* venison, and BERNERS (Street). CYNEGIRUS (brother of Æschylus) : dog driver = HUNT, HUNTER : hound (driver). Hun (whence Hungary): a dog. That nation migrated from the border of China, and having Tartar like, dog like faces, the people of invaded countries called them Huns: hounds. Howbeit they call themselves Magyars. Similarly Cagot (canis Goth): a dog of a Goth, a hypocrite. To the above huntsmen add JAGG (when not from JAGO : James), JAGGARD, and SHILLACKER, the two former being Germans, the third a Gael; as also the Spanish MONTERO : a mountain hunter.

The following are veritable sons of Crispin, viz. : CHAU-

CHARD, CHAUCER (father of English poetry), HOSIER, formed
on last. Hosen is now woven, but half a millennium since
was leather, as gaiters, leggings, buskins. GRACY : brogue
maker. SANDS (George) : sandal maker. SAVATON : sabot
maker. SCHUMMACKER, SOUTER (sutor) : shoemakers a(w)ll.
SOUTER = SEYMOUR : a seamer, sower, *con.* Semmet : sowed
garment. Sometimes SEYMOUR is from St. Maur, Normandy,
which is said to be a form of Sine muros : without walls.
CLARK, CLERK : learned, one of clerical order. During the
middle ages, only the clergy possessed the means of studying
books, and so they alone could be learned. In certain criminal
cases a convict had the Psalter placed before him with a re-
quest that he would read the king of the penitential psalms
(li.) to signify his sorrow and claim the immunity known as
benefit of clergy. If he read " Have mercy upon me, O God,
according to thy loving kindness : according to the multitude
of thy tender mercies, blot out my transgressions" in a toler-
able style, the court officer cried, " He reads like a clerk," and
he was released.

BEAUCLERK (Henry) : beautiful scholar, translated Æsop's
Fables. LECLERC : the learned = GRAMMATICUS (Saxo) : the
grammarian = SEPHER, SAPHIR : book man, *fem.* SAPPHIRA.
LACY (Evans de) is the Irish for learned, from which language
we have SANKEY : a chronicler. The Hindoo correspondent is
SURAT = Sephervaim : place of books. The Druidical correspondent is GWYDER : wooder, learned by study of Celtic, the
letters of which were taken from trees. B for Beith : the birch.
C for Coll : the hazel. Calton : town built where hazels grew.
McALL for MacCOLL : son of the hazel, one of an old stock =
PRISCUS, *fem.* PRISCILLA, not meaning old personally, but of
noble descent. Hazel rods were used in divination, rhabdomancy, and so may be termed a religious plant, like hyssop
and misletoe. COLKITTOCH : left-handed Coll.

TOZER : flax comber, from Tow : to pull, whence teeth, team,
tame, tough, teasel (used to card wool), and Tassel : head of the
teasel. TEAZLE (Mrs) : worker with teasels,—

> " By stinking nettles, pricking *teasels*,
> Raising blisters like the meazels."

TOZER = SCOTCHER : scutcher (scart, scratch) with a heckle
= FLAXMAN (sculptor) : worker in flax = KEMP, *fem.* KEMPSTER,
but KAMES (Lord) : local, KEMP : a field, campus, whence
CAMPION, KEMPER : champions fighting in the open champagne,—

> " His wife sat near him teasing matted wool,
> While from the twin *cards*, tooth'd with glittering wire,
> He fed the spindle of his youngest child."

This card from Carduus : a thistle, but other card from Charta : paper. Teasels and thistles are parents to the complicated machinery of our cotton mills. CAIRD : an artificer, applied to a tinker = CALDERON. TOOTH (ritualist) : is sometimes given as iron tooth maker, but is personal, a man of prominent teeth, being = MORDAUNT, which was originally MORDENT : great teeth. COHEN : a priest. All Cohens claim descent from Aaron. COHEN, *cor.* to CHON. LAOCOON : people's priest = BLOTT, BLOOD (colonel, stole crown jewels) : shed blood of victims. November was called Blotmonat, because cattle were then slaughtered and salted. GOODBLOOD : noble priest. HOFFMAN (sometimes) : man of the hoff, temple. SAGGARS, HAGGART, HAGGARTY, TAGGART (sogarth aroon) : druidical priests, since applied to Christian. FLAMINIUS (consul) : the flamen who received the *afflatus* of the god, his inspiration.

PRIEST (for Prestare) : who *stands before* others by reason of superiority = ANTISTES : pre-excellent. FABIUS (Roman heathen priest) : who spoke (fari) the divine mind. PRIESTLY (oxygen): glebe land. CANON (when not from (M')Kinnon) : a priest from canonicus. PRESTON : priest's town. TEMPLE (Palmerston) : a druidical crom turned into a church. TEMPLEMORE : great church = SELKIRK. CAMILLUS (delivered Rome) : a form of Casmillus, servant of the temple, gives CAMILLE (Desmoulins) = HOFFMAN and ARTABANUS : great sacrificer. ABDUL-MEDJID : servant of the temple. The original CAMILLUS would likely serve in Etruria, Hoffman in Heligoland, and Abul-Medjid at Medina. PASSAVANT (pursuivant) : a follower, retainer, servant. PARSONS : pre-eminent person of parish, gives (M')PHERSON. COSSER : horse flesh dealer, a knacker, *con.* corpse, corse. RUNCIMAN : a horsemonger. COLMAN, charcoal burner. Charcoal so called to distinguish it from pit-coal. COLLEY (Cibber) : dark a-vised man, what a spaewife would call a spade, nickname for swarthy person. The German KOHLER = COLLIER : coalworker. COMTE (positivism) : count, king's companion, whence CONTARINA (Fleming) : cognate with Constable : companion of the stable = MARSHALL (from mare), MARESCHALK : king's servant over cavalry = PHARNASPES. COMYN (Rev.), CUMMING : a count ; but CONDE . living near a confluence = Coblentz : confluence, whence CONDILLAC, CONDORCET, also local French names. VISCONTI : vice count as Viceroy : instead of a king, *con.* Vicarious : for another.

BUONCOMPAGNE, BONAPARTE (It.) : good companion = LEDRU (Rollin) : gay companion = our GOODFELLOW (Robin). It is instructive to see the literal meaning of words implying companionship. They are Comes (cum : with, eo : I go) : *one who goes with you.* Sodalis (whence sodality) from sedeo : I sit :

one who sits with you. Contubernalis, cum: with, taberna: a tavern, *one who frequents the same tavern.* Socius (whence sociable, society) from sun: with and oikos: a house, *living in the same house.* Consort, cum: with, sors: a lot, *sharing lot with.* Crony, from chronos: time, *con.* crone, croon: to sing like an old nurse, *one known of a long time.* Chum, *con.* camera: a chamber, cemetry: a sleeping-place, means *sleeping in the same room.* Mate: one who often *meets* you. Companion, is from cum: with and panis: bread: a messmate, *one who eats bread with you.*

BENEDICT, BENOIT, BENET: cleric giving benediction. Since clergy were forbidden to marry it came, in course of time, to signify a bachelor, and so = BACHELOR and FELLOWS. CAPEL (monsignor), CHAPLIN (M.P.), KEPPELL (de capella): chaplains all, chapel men. SARDOU (Paris politician) is a form of Sacerdos: a priest. PROCTOR, for PROCURATOR (procuratorcy, proxy): having charge for another, a locum tenens, *con.* CURIUS (Dentatus): full of cares. COURVOISIER (corium osier): made coracles of hides and withs = the Gaelic (M')CURRICH, which, in some cases, gives CURRY. From Corium: a hide CURRIER: hide dresser. Cortina, Curtain: bulls' hides hanging, a defence as used in the siege of Gibraltar. But (M') CURRIE, CORRY, CORY, whence CORIGAN: young CORY, mean a deep hollow in the side of a mountain, a ravine. Hence CORYDON (Irish): corrie dweller. Now CORYDON (Virgilian): a lark; while COURIER: a runner = MASSINGER (PHILIP): running footman = TROTTER, BODY: one *bid*den. LIGHTBODY: quick-footed messenger, an old English Mercury. So SANDEMAN: man sent = SANDS (George) when not local. These = FOOTE (when not for foot of hill), LEGGAT: sent on a *legation* To such add BOWD, BOTTE (Peter), TRUEBODY: trusty messenger, GOLIGHTLY, which in Scotland gets disguised into GALLETLY. TRUEBODY suggests the beautiful LIPTROT (lippen true); one in whom we may truly lippen, trust.

CRESSET: carried signal fire on night marches in shape of a cross. CLEAVER (clavier): key-bearer, Peter's two = CROSSKEY: carried papal banner emblazoned with crosskeys. The verb *cross* is from Corsian: to imprecate with the sign of the cross, whence *curse.* CROSSAN: little cross, carrying one on shield in crusades. CRIB: sieve maker = SIEBER: siever, CREBILLON: great CRIB. CROKER (Allen): crocus planter, saffron grower. FRASER: strawberry planter, *con.* Fragrant: odour like a strawberry plant, *con.* Frango: I break, alluding to fractures of leaves. ŽUCCA: gourd planter, *lit.* sweet, *con.* ISSACHER, which consult. " Among his figures Zucca usually placed one with a common gourd at his wrist, in allusion to his name." DAMON, DAMO: ruler, governor = ROY when that does not mean red (headed). RIGG (Irish): a king, whence REGAN: son of a king, or young RIGG. When local RIGG = HILLS. DOMITIAN: conqueror, tamer. DAMARIS: a heifer, one broke into the yoke, a wife. "If ye had not ploughed with my heifer." "A woman named *Damaris* believed." From Damao: I subdue, Adamant or diamond: indomitable stone. DEMPSTER: who *deems*, judges = TERRIS: *terri*torial judge = DAY: a daysman, he who appointed a day on which he would deliver judgment after taking the case *avizandum.* Sometimes DAY: a day labourer = journeyman. RICHTER (Jean Paul): who *recks*, thinks. Reckless: thoughtless. Reckon: to think carefully.

> " But little he'll *reck*, if they let him sleep on,
> In the grave where a Briton has laid him."

CRITO (Socrates' disciple): judge, critic = SHAPHAT, whence Suffetes: Carthaginian judges. DESCARTES (cartesian philosophy): having charge of governmental *charts* = PANCHARD: all charts. "John Bouchet, in the third part of his Annels of Aquitaine, marulleth at an old *pan chart*, or record, which he had seen." CHARTERIS: of the Charter House, Carthusian monastery. LASCELLES: charge of state *seals*. Its Milesian correspondent is the well known SHELLY.

MAUND and MAUNDRELL (traveller): made maunds, willow baskets, especially used for dispensing charity on Maunday Thursday. LIPMAN: a basket maker. "Moses was preserved in a leep of segg:" sedge basket. We also meet with the family name *Bauskett:* a willow worker. ESPARTERO (general): broom maker, ex spartum. Spartum: scattered plant, spread like heather, *con.* Sparta, Sporades. This sonorous Spaniard only = the English LING: ling broom maker, BROOM: heather broom maker, or FERN. But PLANTAGENET (planta genista: *plant* reaching to *Genu:* the knee): wearing broom in helmet as penance. Genu, *con.* Genoa: knee bend of Italian coast = Ancona: crooked spot of coast, *con.* ANCUS (Martius) = CROOK: walking with a stoop, and Anchor: crooked iron gripper.

DOMINUS: a lord, a judge from Dan, from Adon, though some derive it from Domus: a house, and so make it = HENRY, HEINERICH: home ruler. DOMINUS *ab.* to DOM and DON in Spain, DON PEDRO: lord Peter, DON JUAN: lord John. Hence, too, DONIZETTI, DONATELLO: lordlings. Adon, Dan, enter Hindoo names as DAR, thus ZEMINDAR: seed lord (semen), a farmer. From that and Hai: howler, the tiger, we get HYDER ALI: Ali the tiger lord (slayer). So the military titles Jemin*dar*, Jullin*dar*. From Here: an army, HERR: a lord, HERRING (painter): son of a lord, son of a soldier, warlike. MYNHEER: my lord = MONSIEUR: my sire, father. Before the Norman invasion we had no title DUKE (dux):

leader, its place being occupied by EARL, from Ere: before, whence EARLY: before, superior by age = MAXIMUS, MASSIMO. Early: before (daybreak). EARL gives ARLOTTE (family). We also had HERTOGH (tug), HERZOG: army leader, whence Herzegovina: formerly a dukedom or duchy. DUKE gives DUCKETT, DOUCE, DUCE, as also the title DOGE and the coin Ducat: money issued by a duke. Hence, too, we actually have the family name DUCK and DUX: head of class.

HERR: he who arranges the here. Here: an army, Hereford: ford of the army, HERMAN, HARMAN, ARMINIUS (arminian): a soldier, answering to Hindoo title SAHIB: sabre man, sir, lord, from Sab: an army, Sabaoth armies. Jehovah Sabaoth: lord of armies. Sabaism: worship of *host* of heaven. Sabre: *the* army weapon. From May: power, whence might and main, MAY: strong man (sometimes May-born), MAYOR: powerful officially. Le MAIRE (straits): from *le maire du palais*. The Teutons had a magistrate styled MORD-DAME: murder judge (deem). Mord, *con.* mors, mortal, Mars, mat (in matador), mate (in chess), murrain, and with the Hebrew Mav: death, as ISHMAVETH: man of death, doomed, Jesus on the crucifixion morn. Doomsday (till): judgment day, but Doomsday Book is from Domus Dei: house of God, Winchester Cathedral, where it was kept. PHARAMOND: travelled protector, of which Don Quixote was the caricature. FARRANT, FARREN, FARRAR, FARR (when last two do not mean shepherd): one who fares from place to place. We meet with SEAFART: one who goes to sea, a sailor. Faran: to go, gives fear, which makes one go, fare, fieldfare (bird), ferry, ford, be-*fore*, *far*-ther, *fir*-st, *for*-est: wood far from town, Fardel: a travelling pack. "Who would fardels bear?" Fear accurately corresponds to Metus: motion to get out of danger. FARRAGUT (admiral): one who has been *far agate*, travelled much. FORREST, FORRESTER, FORSTER DE WARRENNE: charge of forest = WOODGRAVE, *con.* GRAFF, GRAEFFE, GRAVES: governors all. BOSCHER (bois): had charge of wood, game = PARKER, PARK, from PADDOCK, PARROCK. SAVAGE: wood dweller, game keeper, from Sylvis: a wood, whence Transylvania: beyond the forest. The following are also wood dwellers: SILVANUS, SILAS, SATYRUS, Satyr: sylvan god. The *Doric* form of SATYRUS is TITYRUS (Virgil). ISABELLA SAVAGE is transformed into La Belle Sauvage: the forest beauty. WALKER, WAT, WATTS, from Wald: a wood, whence WALDEGRAVE becomes WOODRUFFE, WOODROW, VODREY ("Dublin Directory") = WOODWARD, MUSGRAVE: charge of the *mews*, stables and hawks. But FOSTER, FOISTER: foodster, nourished, adopted.

> "And in gret reverence and charitee
> Hire olde powere fader *fostered* shee."

Fader and fostered both find their root in feed. Father: he
who feeds. NORRIS: a nurse, nourisher, sometimes formation
on NORROY (heraldry): north king, as SURRY: south king,
POMEROY: head king. But SURREY: south of river (Thames),
though some have it south kingdom, corresponding to Sussex:
south Saxons. FALCONER (shipwreck): hawk tamer, man of
the mews. Gerfalcon: hawk flying in gyres. FLETCHER:
arrow maker. STRINGER: string the bow, but ASTRINGER:
great hawk keeper. ARROWSMITH: made the iron point. "The
fletcher draweth a feather when he hath but one swappe
(sweep) at it with his knife, and then playneth it a little with
rubbing it over his knife." Cognate with fleet, flit, flutter,
FLETCHER = HARROWER. Sometimes BOWS: bow maker =
BOWYER (Dundalk).

FROBISHER: furbisher, polisher of metal. "Furbish the
spears, put on the brigandines." FULLER: who thickens
and whitens cloth. "His raiment became shining, exceeding white, as snow, so that no fuller on earth can white
them." FULJAMBE: thick leg. FULLER = WHITE, whence
WHITSTER: laundress, blancheuse = LAVENDER, LANDER
(Africa), from Lavo: I wash, lave, lavish. The plant *lavender*
was so called because used in baths. "Robert Bruce stopped
his army when on the march, in circumstances of pressing
difficulty in the Ulster campaign, because a poor *lavendere*
was taken with pains of childbirth, and must have been left,
had they proceeded, to the mercy of the Kerns." TREDGET:
who trudges, a traveller. "Marry, as I told you before, John,
and Robert, be ready hard by in the brewhouse, and when I
suddenly call you, come forth, and take this basket on your
shoulders; that done, trudge with it in all haste and carry it
among the *whitsters* in Datchet mead." Trudge = drudge,
from drag, see DREDGE. WALKER: cloth cleaner, from
Welcian: to wallow, *con*. Whale: sea wallower, Wheel: that
which rolls. Wheel = the Hebrew Golal: a tomb stone.
"Who shall roll us away the stone?" *Con*. nergal, Galilee,
globus. Welkin: the circle of the heavens. GHIRLANDIS
(Italian poet): GIRLING: garland maker, *con*. Gyrus: a circle,
Gerfalcon and Gyr: provincial Scotch for a hoop, which is
identical with Year: a circle of time.

KRUMMACHER (Elijah): crown maker. PULVERMACHER:
powder maker. SCHLEIRMACHER (theologian): veil maker.
SCHEPLER: chaplet maker. HALMONEUS: seaman, as are
the following names, PELAGIUS, MORGAN, PONTIUS (son of
Pontus: the sea), HALCYON (son of the sea), FLATMAN (man of
fleet), ABIJAM (father of the sea), M'NAMARA (son of the sea),
CARRACHIOLI (sailing in a carrack), LONG (when Celtic),
FORLONG (fear, vir), PLEIONE: (*con*. INDICOPLEUSTES: he who

17

sailed to India), RUMBELOW (old English for a sailor, like
Tally Ho! for a huntsman), MARNER, MORGAN, and PELAGIUS:
mariners every one. Pelagianism : system of Pelagius. Gla-
morgan : Morgan's country, or near the sea = Pomerania,
Attica (shore lands) = Pontus. Halys: salt river = Rio Salado.
Halcyon : king fisher, supposed to hatch near the sea in calms.
Halcyon days: quiet times. HALLE : place of saltmines. Mor
in MORGAN, *con.* Mar: bitter, whence Mare : bitter waters,
the undrinkable sea. Connemara : indentations of the sea.
Loch Long : ship lake, *con.* London, which is Longdon or
Latinised Londunum : ship fort. SKIPPER : skiff sailer.
Schaffhausen : skiff, ship houses where boats taken out of
Rhine to avoid falls, portages. To these add SEAMANS,
SIEMANS, SEAFART : sailor's all. KHAN (*con.* canoe and Cane :
hollow reed) : a boatman = BATEMAN, BATES; when latter not
from Bartholomew, and BOATMAN.

KINCH, KINK : bleachfield worker, *con.* Kink : to run into
knots. HARRIDELLE : dealer in rough ponies. HOLZMAN,
HOLMAN (Hunt) : holt, woodman, dweller in, or worker in
= XYLANDER, which it translates as PELAGIUS does MORGAN.
HOLTUM : home in a wood. TALBOYS : wood cutter = BAVISTER
(Jack) : bavin gatherer, a woman's trade. " Then took he
certain *bavins,* or small faggots of brushwood." BOSCH (Ten):
wood dweller = HOLTUM, whence Bosh : the waste of wood, as
we call bad persons *faggots,* and I have heard negroes in South
Carolina calling folks they disliked *trash,* from Trencher : to
cut, applied to useless parts of sugar cane to be cut off.
HORNER (little Jack): spoon, cup, and comb maker of horn.
Common trade before this iron age set in. HORN (Cape) : a
hill. Schreckhorn : shrieking mountain, where gales howl =
our Pennygant: windyhill. CAUGHIE: Highland cooper made
cogs, plates and bowls for supping porridge as CHOPIN = ZOPPI :
souppy, soup plate maker, but more closely answering to the
English KNUCKLER: maker of noggins. HURAI: linen worker
= LINGARD. " *Hurai* of the brooks of Gaash."

SCRINE: charge of shrine = SEXTON: sacristan, charge of sacred
things = DEWAR and DEUCHAR. CHALLIS: charge of calyx,
sacramental cup, chalice = CALIXTUS (pope). MESMER (mes-
merism) : had charge of vessels used in celebrating mass.
CHANTREY (sculptor) : of that part of chapel where chanting
was practised. SANGSTER : a chorister, applied to a lady
singer. GINGLE (general) : a man singer. KIRCHER (father) :
charge of whole kirk, IGLESIAS, KIRK, CHURCHMAN. LATIMER
(martyr) : latiner, an interpreter between English and Welsh.
Then all unknown languages were called Latin. But LATNER:
latten maker, a compound of copper and lead. Latten (the
word) is from *lead.* LEADBETTER : lead beater. Churches and

castles were supplied with sheets of lead beaten by hammers before rolling by machinery came in. FRANCIS: an Italian speaking French. So the Irish GRIGG (Murtagh): learned in Greek. XENOPHON (Attic bee): knowing the voice, language, of strangers, *con.* Telephone: distant voice, sound. DRAGO-MAN: an interpreter = MUFTI, from Moftah: a key. " Ye have taken away the key of knowledge." " Pity you were not *dragoman* at Babel." LAVOISIER (chemist): osier worker = MAUND, SPURINA: basket maker = BAUSKETT. " They took up of the broken meat that was left seven baskets (spuridas) full." " The ides are at last come, *Spurina.*" SPIRIDION (Greek hermit) = SAUSSURE (Genevese savan): osier seller, basket maker. OUSELEY: osier field, ground much under water. Before metals came into use osier was in high demand. The Britons made willow gods, boats, and gates (wickets). Charon's boat is a coracle if he has not, since the days of Eneas, invested spiritual oboli, got by ferrying souls over Styx, in a a more Searle-like craft.

HONEYMAN: bee-keeper, aparian = ABELARD (Heloise), BEACH (Hicks), and BEEMAN: all bee keepers. BEBEE, BEBY: dwelling among bees. Before sugar was introduced, honey was in great demand. LEECH, LEACH, (Mc)LAY, HICKS (Irish), HICKIE, HICKMAN: medical doctors. The first three attend the Litch: body, that which *lies.* LITCHFIELD: field of dead bodies, old battle ground. HICKHOCK is a form of HICKOG: son of the doctor, answering with precision to MACLAY. GUERICKE, GUERRERO, HELOISE (Abelard), HOELAND (Saxon for Christ): healer = JASON. " The Jews assaulted the house of *Jason.*" MEDICI (Venus de): a physician. As the great Florentine family did a little in the money lending line as well as the *medical,* they killed two birds with one stone by hoisting three golden pills or balls, whence pawnbroking insignia. LEMON (Mark), LEMOINE, LEMAN: dwelling alone, a monk. Sometimes LEMAN: love man. These = MONICHOS, *fem.* MONICA (Augustine's mother). DELMONICO (N.Y.): son of the monk. MUNCHAUSEN (baron): monks' houses. OLSHAUSEN (commentator): houses in the wood, in contrast with STIN-TON = STONEHOUSE. Ecclesiastics married till we reach the year 1000. Had clericals always been celibates, such names as foregoing and following would not be. LEMPRIERE (myth-ologian): the prior, some make it descended illegitimately from the emperor, but it is = PRYOR, FOREMAN, the latter for-merly restricted to religious houses. COUSINS, though literally consanguineous, related by blood, was applied to monk or nun. NEWCOMEN (engineer), NEWCOME, NEWMAN, NEW (African missionary).

NOVATIAN (heretic): novice, new arrival in a religious

house, in some cases newly arrived emigrants = NEAL. But
NEWCOMBE: newly cultivated valley. CONVERS, CONYERS:
medieval Jewish *converts*. ABBA: father, ABBOTT (Jacob).
From it the Hindoo BABA: a gentleman (non military) = SIRE,
SIR, SORR, SURR. (Mc)NAB, a form of Abbot. (A)Bushire:
father city. We say Metropolis: mother city. WATERS, WATTERS,
if not local = VATTA, PATER. LAVATER (savan): the father. From
Vatta we have ATTA, whence ATTILA (the Hun). Feed, food,
fodder, fat, fader, fother, vatta. FATHER: he who feeds.
Father assumes form of Fare, as FAREBROTHER (father's
bróther): an uncle. PATER: father, from Pasco: I feed,
PATTI: sheep feeder, PADRE, PATRON. LAVATER = Biblical
ABI: my father. POPE: a father. All bishops were once so
called except the bishop of Rome. PEPIN, POPP, PAPPIUS,
PAPE (I met with one in Toronto), PAPPA (Demetrius): each
mean father. So, too, PATRICK, PATRICIAN, PAPIRIUS (consul):
father's conscript. Sometimes PAT and PADDY, not from
PATRICK but PALLADIUS (St.): son of Pallas, defended by the
Palladium: shield of god. This is met with in the bare form St.
Paddy. Battersea: Patrick's island. SIRE: father, applied to
crowned head. MONSIEUR: my sire. MONSIGNORE: my senior,
lord = MYNHEER. MADAM: my dame, mother. DAMIAN: son
of the dame, B.V.M.

   BISCOB: bishop, episcopos. = RAMMER, old Scotch, alluding
to the crosier he carried, *con.* RAIMES, RAMAGE, Ramus: a branch.
GILLESPIE: bishop's servant. BISMARCK (prince): bishop's
mark, boundary of jurisdiction. BISLAND: bishop's glebe.
Gravesend: where sheriff of London ceased to have jurisdiction. So Denmark: Dane's boundary. MARWICK: border
village = BORTHWICK, BORWICK. LORIMER: thong cutter,
bridle maker. MENAGE: steward, manager. Menage is
also Glasgow provincialism for a saving club. MERCATOR,
MERCIER, MERCER: men of commerce, merchants. CHATER:
caterer, he purveyed for a nobleman's family = SPENCER,
SPENS: dispenser, and PURVIS for purveyor, in some cases.
METELLUS (conquered Jugurtha): mercenary soldier, fighting
for pay, *misthos*. METZLER: received mill fees, took *grist*,
emolument = MUTER, MUTERER: a mutterer, receiving mill toll,
but MUTTER: he who stutters. GRIST: grindest. MULLER
(Bristol), MOLINOS, MILLER, MULLEN, (Mc)MILLEN were men
of the mill. SEMY (simila): miller making very fine flour.
MOLYNEUX: mill on water (Seine) = MUHLWASSER: mill water
= Maelstrom: whirlpool like a mill stream. Molindinar
(burn): mill on the brook = MILLBROOK (George Barnwell).
DESMOULINS: of the mill. All akin to Mola: a mill. Molars:
grinders. Immolate: to sprinkle meal and sacrifice. Emolument (ex mola): gain from mill. Mollis: soft as meal.

Mollusca, mulier (a woman), mole, mullet: all mean soft bodied.

MILO (athlete): crusher = MILNER: wielding Thor's hammer, crushing hammer = FROISSARD (chronicler): crusher, who *frizzled* up his enemy = BRISBANE, OSMAN: bone breakers. GRADGRIND (hard times): quick grinder, *con.* GRADY. FARINA (Jean Maria): maker of *farinaceous* food, a miller. NAPIER (logarithms): Scottish king's officer providing table cloth (nappa) and other napery. Common folk had no table cloth, thus our phrase, " Bed and board," eaten off a. " Meal time : " time for eating meal, porridge, pottage. Mappa: cloth used in starting horse races, gives Map: cloth picture of a country, Napkin: little cloth, (N)apron: cloth hung in front of a person. Napery: lingerie, house linen. WARDROP: had charge of royal wardrope. VOGEL, OGLE: bird catcher = FOWLER, BIRD and JOKSHAN, "She bare him Zimram and *Jokshan.*" KISH (asses): bird snarer (*con.* Kishon: very crooked) = LOWRIE: bird allurer. TRIPP TRIPPNER, TRIPPEN-MAKER: maker of jackets and shorgons (short gowns). PAR-MENTER: apparelmenter, clothes preparer = ROPER: a rober.

PFEIFFER (Ida) = PIPER, FIFE: who puffs. Sometimes FYFE: native of Fife. In old times pipers were called whifflers, as in Italy, pifferari. TYTLER: tootler, who toots. HORNE (Tooke): horn player. " Sir William Littlebury, *alias* Horne (for so King Edward IV. surnamed him because he was a most ex-cellent blower in a horn); he was a slater by craft." AULETES (Ptolemy): Flute player, from Aula: a pipe, Hydraulics: water pipes. VAN TROMP (admiral): the trumpeter. CYTH-ŒRON: guitar, gittern, lyre player = ZITTAU (oath). Hence CYTHERIS (courtezan of Antony): she who allures with lyre and voice, a syren. BARD = HARPER. HARPERTZOON (Martin): harper's son. Musical name his: Martin Harpertzoon Van Tromp. CROWTHER (black bishop), CROWDER: cruth, or croud player, like a fiddle :

> " The pipe, the tabor, and the trembling *croud,*
> The *sawtry,* pipe and hautboy's noisey band."

SAUTREE (Rev.): psaltry player. LUTZ (savan): lute player and SPIELMAN : musician. Tho Highland correspondent for these fiddlers three is (M')GREUSICH. WAITS: watchman playing at Christide, waiting for Christmas. MINSTREL : minnie singer who kept the heroic dead in *mind.*

POINTON, TAGG: tag maker, fastenings for dresses before the invention of pins. Tag from Tug: which tows, pulls together. In families of German descent, TAGG: born at day break. PONT: a bridge, one taking pontage = BRIDGES, BRIGGS when these are not local. PONTIFF and PONTIFEX: bridge maker.

VIPEND (vetus pons): old bridge, usually VIPOND: resident
near old brig.   MANTO (*con.* maniac): a prophet, a seer.
" Blind Tiresias was led up and down by his daughter *Manto.*"
SEER: one who sees things veiled to others.   DIOPHANTUS
(algebraist): shower of divine things.   HIEROPHANTUS: showed
sacred things = SCRINE and BEDELL.   From Pellis: a skin, we
have POLLIO (Roman) = SKINNER.   PEEL, SLOSS: castle partly
defended by bull's hides, as Gibraltar was against the combined
fleets of France and Spain.

> " The frightened flocks and herds were spent
> Beneath the *peel's* rude battlement."

PILCHER: great coat maker from skins.   " After heat cometh
cold.   No man casteth his *pylch* away."   Pellis: skin, also
gives Pilis: hair growing on skin, *vel*vet, *feel*, Pileus: a hairy
cap.   Mons Pilatus: mountain *capped* (with clouds).   " Yonder
Pilatus soars with its dark brow up towards the sky, and with
its *cap* of clouds looks gloomy enough to be in keeping with
the idle tradition of the place, that hither the governor of
Judea was banished, a conscience stricken wanderer through
these desolate regions, where he put an end to his existence
by plunging into the lake at its summit."   PILATE: hairy
skinned = CANUTIUS (Antony's enemy): white haired = the
French CHANZY.   COSSUS: rough hairy man = SEIR takes *fem.*,
COSSUTIA (Cæsar's wife), and gives KOSSUTH (Louis).   SEIR
answers well to HIRTIUS (consul): hirsute, goat like.   " The
first came out red all over, like a goatskin garment."   EDOM:
red, *con.* Dam: blood, ADAM: of red earth, sandy soil.   PILIS:
a hair, likewise gives Capillary: hair sized tubes, Vilis, vile:
of no value, not worth a hair.   BEAUPOIL (Louis): beautiful
hair = HARFAGER (Harold): hair fair.   " He made a vow to
his mistress to neglect his precious curls till he had completed
the conquest of Norway."   COLFAX (president): coal coloured
hair = BLACKLOCK.   FAIRFAX: fair hair, but CARFAX, four
roads, as CARBARNS: four barns.

RABSHAKEH: great cup bearer = BECHMAN: carried beaker
to king.   Beaker: bowl made of beech wood.   RABBI (*con.*
former): great (teacher).   REID, REDDIE (M') CREDIE, READ,
RATTE, RADETZKY (marshal) RATO: counsellors all, who rendered *ratio*, reason.   *Con.* Reichs-rath, and Hundred for hand
rede.   The Scandinavians called Rath (an assembly where you
rendered your reasons) a THING (meeting where what you
think is told): a sort of primitive M.P., a member of the thing
= the French PARLOR, PARLIOR: speakers, those who parleyed.
Hence TINGAY: who addressed the *thing*, an orator = PALE-
ARIUS (Aonius): who spoke to the parliament.   Storthing:
great assembly, *con.* Storm: great rime.

CONRAD (ken rad): knowing counsellor = ALFRED. LAMOUR (Irish): an orator. EUBULUS: good counsellor. TANCRED (thank rede): counsel received with thanks. Thankerton : Tancred's town. LEATHERHEAD : people's counsel. ETHELRED : noble counsellor. RHADEGUND (Gon: war): who advises to fight. ALFRED (elf rede): counsels like a fairy. Elf: albis: white = Banshee, from Bain : white. Bain : a bath, that makes white. ALFRED forms ALFORD (dean) and ALVA (butcher), whence ALVAREZ : son of Alfred. ROBERT (rath bert): bright in council = RADBERT. Robert gives RUPERT, RUPERTINO, CANROBERT (general) for VONROBERT : the Robert, HOBBS (hoby-de-hoy : a hafflin : half grown man), HOBSON ('s choice), BOB, ROB, RAB, ROBB, ROBIN (Adair), DOBBIE : little Robert, DOBYN, Dobbin : an ass, PROBART : son of Robert = ROBERTSON. Sometimes ROBERT is cantingly given as meaning red beard = BARBAROSSA (pirate). Canting is being guided by sound, as LOCKHART : *heart lock*ed in casquet and carried into battle, then applied to mythic bearer. So, too, CUTHBERT : cut beard, whereas this name means famous for knowledge, being *con*. Uncouth : not knowing. From CUTHBERT we have Cuddy = Dobbin = Neddy, so that we have three terms for an ass respectively from the names Cuthbert, Robert, Edward. METICHE : he who *moots*, brings a question before a *meet*ing. Witenagemote : *meet*ing of *wits*, folk rath.

ARISTOBULUS : best counsellor. PISISTRATUS : persuader of the army. PYTHAGORAS : persuader of the assembly = EUPHRASTUS : good speaker, who *phrases* well, and *con*. THEOPHRASTUS : who *phrased* divinely. "It is the voice of a god." These = CHRYSOSTOM (John) : golden mouth, CHRYSOLOGUS : golden discourser. UZ (land of) and JEUZ (son of Shaharaim): a counsellor. REMIGIUS (gave names to Rheims): a rower, galley slave, *con*. Regatta : a rowing match, gives REMEY (pisiculturist). REMINGTON : town of Remey's descendants, resident in. SECKER : sawyer. Sedge : cutting plant. Section: part cut off. BRETSCHNEIDER : board cutter = SECKER (archbishop). Bret, board, broad are identical. (Mc)SPORRAN : maker of pouch, purse, pocket.

SPARRMAN : sparr, rafter, cutter = LATTO : lathmaker, lattice manufacturer. SAYERS : assayer, metal prover. SALINATOR, SALTER, SALT : meat preservers. CALVERT (sometimes) : fish pickler. Calvered salmon is pickled. SEWARD : sea guard = NEARCHUS : ship chief = HALOCRATES : sea power, admiral = MURTOUGH (Milesian), MURDOCH (Gaelic) becomes MUDDOCKS in England, and gives MURCHISON, but MURCH : mischievous. SELL, SELLARS, SELLERS = SADLIER : a saddler. See: seat (of a bishop). Saddle : horse seat, abbreviates to Sell,—

> " Yet was the force so furious and fell,
> That horse and man it made to reele asyde ;
> Nath'lesse the prince would not forsake his *sell*,
> For well of yore he had learned to ryde."

SIZAR : scholar whose rations of bread and butter were cut of a fixed size. So for Cambridge but Oxford has BATELL : baited in college. Bate from bite = morsel from Mordeo : I bite, mordant. BATTLE : from Battle, Sussex, and that from BOOTH (bothie): a dwelling of a lowly type. TASCHER (Rose), TASKER (poet) : gathered ecclesiastical first fruits. TAYLOR : (cloth) cutter = SCHROETER (astronomer), SCHRADER, SCHNEIDER (danseuse). To these add TUCK (friar), and likewise TUCKER (Dan): cloth workers, *con.* Tuck : sacred to milliners. SHARMAN, SHERMAN : who shears cloth = SHEARER. COZIER : man who sewed cloth which TAYLOR or SCHNEIDER had cut out, he stitched only. TAVERNIER : tavern keeper = CAFFARELLI : cafe keeper, where coffee was first sold. The two last are two of our latest names. HULYER : slater, house healer = SLATER, SCLATER. Heal : to cover. " I was naked and ye *healed* me not." TEGULARIUS = TYLER (Wat), TECK. Tegula : a tile, from Tego : I cover, whence Tectus : a roof, pro*tect*ion, Texas is so called from decked boats navigating its rivers. Tego gives Deck : ship cover, without which an open boat. Tuileries : tile kiln. WAT, TYLER : Walter the thatcher, paid his poll tax on the poll of the collector with thatching hammer. DECK, DECKER : thatcher. Tego, deck, thack, thatcher, THACKERAY : thatched rath. Rath : Danish fort in Ireland. Cape Wrath : headland with rath upon it. CASTLEREAGH (premier): castle rath. RATSEY : rath on an island. SHERIDAN : commanding six raths, holding land of. Some give it as living on a hill frequented by fairies. RATTRAY : smooth rath. RATTICAN : living at rath head. TINTORETTO (Venetian) = DYER or LITSTER : female dyer working in *ley*, *lith.* Tent : coloured (wine). Tench : coloured (fish). Taint : to discolour and so render impure. But Tinto : fire (mount), though sometimes given for Tintock : misty hill. It is *con.* Beltane : May fire of Bel, Baal, as sacrificial fires were burned thereon. TOLLER, TOLLNER = toll collector = BERRUYER (French Jesuit) : toll taker at barriers = SOUTHGATE : receive custom as south gate, so NORGATE (and Williams). These = ABIASAPH : father of gathering, GABBAI : tribute collector. " After him *Gabbai,* Sallai, 928." Zollverein : united as to toll. HOHENZOLLERN (house of): high toll, castle on hill top from which black mail was enforced from travellers.

TYERMAN (Luke): maker of ornaments for head, tires, tiaras = CALMAN (caul) : ladies' hairdresser. " Jezebel tired (attired) her head, and looked out of a window" (wind-door).

Con. Tiara: fillet keeping hair out of eyes = Diadem: bound round (head). These became ensigns of royalty. " His eyes as a flash of fire, and on His head many diadems." CROZIER: charge of bishop's staff, like shepherd's crook = RODMAN: carried rood. Holyrood: sacred cross. COPE (Johnny): cope wearer, having charge of one amongst *vest*ments in *vest*ry. VERGER (virgulta): man carrying a rod. " The same day was a goodly procession, in which the lord abbot went with his mitre and *crosier*, and a great number of *copses* of gold, with the *vergers.*" VICKERS, VICARS (Hedley): a vicar, *con.* vice in Viceroy: instead of a king. But VICKERY: living in a vicarage, manse. VINTER (for vintner): wine seller, becomes WINTERS = FENNER for vinour. In some cases FENNER: a huntsman = FENIAN and BERNERS: man of venery. Berner's Street, Oxford Street. But in some families FENNER = VENN (Richard): fen man, living among bogs = MONEY. SUMMER, SUMMERS, SUMPTER: ostlers,—

> " Return with her ?
> Persuade me rather to be a slave and *sumpter*
> To this detested groome."

In certain cases SUMMERS = SUMNER: summoner, sheriff and officer. GROOM: servant. Bridegroom: servant of the bride. OSTLER was no menial in medieval times. It is a form of Hospitaller: a host over a religious house who showed hospitality, part of which was taking care of horses of guests. We have remainders and reminders thereof in Hospital giving Hotel, and in OASTLER (M.P.): hospitaller. SPITTLE: settled on the Knights Hospitaller's land when they lost them by papal bull. XENO: a guest, or an enemy = Hostis: a stranger, a gau, who might be an enemy, whence hostile. GUEST: he who goes while we stay. From Go also Gang: that go together. XENOS takes the *fem.* XENIA (pet princess of the Russians). POLYXENA: hospitable, who takes in many strangers = LIEBGAST: love guest = XENOPHILUS: fond of strangers. " Be not forgetful to be *philoxenists.*" " When saw we thee *xenon.*" Euxine: good for strangers, safe to sail on, first called Axine: not for strangers (because of pirates), now Black Sea, so named by Turks because Russians, wrecks and North winds come thereby. FRANGIPANI (scent maker): bread breaker = LORD: loaf afforder, bread giver, whence LAIRD, LAYARD (Nineveh). When LORD is French it is applied to a heavy, slow person. In the Irish TOY: a lord, and TOOLE: lordly, aristocratic. WARNER (warrener): charge of rabbit cover. WARREN (Hastings): living on a CONYBEARE for conygare: where the conies go. SPELMAN (antiquary): a labourer who works by spells = IND and HYNDMAN. Some-

times SPELLMAN : hall keeper = SALMON.   SPILLMAN : spindle
maker.
GRAVES (for ge reves, as ge leap gives gallop, and ge win
gain) : a sheriff.   Gravesend : sheriffs' end, cessation of jurisdiction.   REVES, REVELL, from root Reave : to tear, to take
by violence, whence robber, rover, rogue : all rapacious
animals.   PALGRAVE : palace steward.   But PALFREY : having
charge of a little horse.   CONGREVE (matches) : cunning
steward, like him in parable who was commended for clever-
ness by his lord.   MUSGRAVE : over mews.   CENTGRAVE :
magistrates over a canton, centum, hundred.   Chaucer lookéd
on a *reve* preaching as reasonable as a cobbler turning sailor
or doctor,—

> "The Devil made a *reve* for to preche,
> Or of a *souter*, a shipman, or a *leche.*"

REVELY : the reve's field.   MULLGRAVE : reve having charge
of mills as to grist, fees to be paid for grinding.   STADHOLDER
(stead) : place defender = GRAVES, STEWARD : stowe ward =
BYE, as in Bylaws : local laws.   GLASHIER (observatory) :
glass worker, a glazier.   *Con.* Glacies : ice.   ARBUCKLE : brass
buckler maker.   Buckler : buckled on the arm.   ARMOUR :
form of armourer,—

> "From whence came SMITH, all be he knight or squire,
> But from the smith that forgeth at the fire ? "

SMITHS are numerous.   From 1838 to 1854, 286,037 of that
name were recorded by the Registrar-General as having been
born, died, or married.   I knew a family so named living on
a flat with a SMITH straight below, and another directly above.
The floor Smith was so tormented with messages, parcels, letters,
that he fled, flitted in self-defence.   SMYTHE, SMITH : he who
smoothes metal by *smiting*, he who smiteth.   Nearly synonymous with FORGEUR : forger, feigner, fashioner, who makes
like to by fire.   SMITHS are numerous because generic, covering
all branches of hammer work.   We have no BLACKSMITH, it
being covered by SMITH, but we have WHITESMITH : who
polished his worker and so nearly = FROBISHER : furbisher.
SIXSMITH : sickle maker, giving SICKLES, *i.e.*, maker of.
ARROWSMITH : made iron part.
     ARSMITH : brass smiter, or moulder = BRASSEY (Peto).
BRAZIER : brass worker.   Ar : brass, *con.* Es, eris : brass,
whence Arma : arms, which were originally brazen.   " He had
greaves of brass on his legs."   BROWNSMITH : brown bill
maker.   Used by Saxons at Hastings.   BROWNBILL (common
in Lancashire) : a Saxon foot soldier = BRISBANE.   FIELD-
SMITH ; sharpened picks for the field, pit, mine.   GOLDSMID,
GOLDSCHMID, ORFEVER, ORFEVRE (faber) = our GOLDSMITH

(Oliver). KALTSCHMID: cold smith, wrought metal without fire. CALDERON (Spaniard): a tinker, mended kettles and *caldrons* = CAIRD. Tinker: one who tinks, tinks with his hammer. CHALCAS (priest of Apollo), CHALCUS (governed Cyzicus): brass or copper worker. The Greeks used brass before discovering iron. They called it Chalkos. When iron superseded the old metal, tradesmen in the harder material were still termed Chalcus, though literally a blacksmith should have been called Chalybeus or Sidericus. " Alexander the *Chalcus*, did me much harm." Chalcedon (whence Chalcedony : stone there discovered) : so named from its metals, now Scutari.

MESSER, MESSERSCHMID: cutler = WHITTLE (Harvey): who whets, sharpens metals. NAYLOR: nail maker. SCHMIDBRECHT = WHITESMITH : who polishes his work. DACIER (F., savan) : pairs with WHITTLE, being from Acuo : I sharpen, make acute = COUTTS (Burdett): army cutler, weapon sharpener. STAHL (George), STAEL (Madame de), STEELE, STILICHO (general) : steel armed, cuirassiers (corium), armed cap-a-pie (from head to foot), all human iron clads = ISENMAN : iron man. In some cases last = next, STAHLMAN: steel worker. But STALLYMAN, STALLY : strong as steel. STALLYBRASS: steel arm = ARMSTRONG. Brass, here, *con.* brace in Embrace : to take in arms. FAIRBRASS : iron arm (ferrum). HUDIBRAS : victorious arm. In Wales Mr. Smith figures as GOUGH (lord) or GOFF. In Scotland he becomes GOW, (Mc)GOWAN, (Mc)GOWN, COWAN. But Gowan (a daisy): white (flower) from Gwyn : white, whence Gown: white dress. GOVAN: smiths' town. In Cornwall Smith becomes ANGOWE. Celts, whether Highland or Hibernian, took ill to trade names, preferring personal, local, or patronymical designations, still we have (Mc)INTYRE, (Mc)TEER : a carpenter. In Wallachia KOVACS : a smith. Smith put in an early appearance, whence we have " The sons of Dedan were Ashurim, *Letushim,* and Leummim." Letushim : hammersmen. It is supposed that the hammer head was used a thousand years before the haft was invented.

To the above add LOCKER, LOCKYER (when not Asiric): locksmith. FERRACINO (Bartholomew), FERAND (Gonsalvo), FERRARI (Milan), FERRARS (Higham), FERRETTI (Pio Nono): iron workers, farriers. From this prolific Ferrum: iron, we also have FARIE : iron worker. A family so named has been located in Rutherglen (near Glasgow) for full six hundred years, as hinted at in this rhyme,—

> " Nae man can tell, nae man has seen
> When the *Fairies* haena in Ruglen been."

To this great company of ironworkers we may fairly add

CLOUD (St.) : nail (maker), *con.* Clef (clavis) : a key. The old key was a mere nail. CLOUD would be = NAISMITH if it meant nail smith, but it does not. TELFER, TALFORD (judge) : iron cutter, who cleaves an iron helmet. TELFER *con.* TALBOYS : wood cutter. MINISTER (from Minus : less) : correlative of MASTERS from Magnus : great, sometimes written MARSTERS and MAISTERS (de), whence MAGNUS (king of Norway), whence (Mc)MANUS. MASTERS = LEMAITRE. Magnus : great gives MAGISTER : greater (than other), presumably by age, and so able to teach. MAXIMUS, MAXIMIN (emperor), MASSIMO : oldest, greatest. RABBI : great (teacher). RABBONI : greatest (teacher). This title only given to seven of Hebrew instructors.

BRUTUS : a fugitive slave = PHYGELLUS, *con.* Fugio : I flee, whence refugee = FLEMMING, FLEMING from root flee. Tradition says the Flemish ran from some pre-historic battle field. BRUTUS is sometimes given as stupid, brute like, but the balance of evidence is unfavourable thereto, it means a fugitive slave. ORIGEN (Adamantus) ; home born slave = VERNA, VERNET (Horace), *con.* Vernaculus : impudent, giving back-talk as slaves to masters. Vernacular : demotic, language of the untaught people. " Not answering again." Some give VERNET = DELAUNNAY : of the alder plantation ; similar to LAYBOULAYE : of the birchgrove = BIRKETT.

ABEDNEGO : servant of Nebo. ABDALLAH, ABDIEL, ABDEEL = GOTTESCHALCUS (sacraments) : God's servant. " The king commanded Shelemiah, the son of *Abdeel,* to take Jeremiah."

> " *Servant of God,* well done ; well hast thou fought
> The better fight, who single hast maintain'd
> Against revolted multitudes, the cause
> Of truth, in word mightier than they in arms."

GOTTESCHALCUS assumes the grotesque forms GODSELL and GODSHALL. ABDASTARTUS (Tyrian prince) : of Astarte. ABDALRAHMAN (king of Moors) : of the mercy of God. ABDUL-AZIZ : of the precious One, one of the 99 titles of God. ABDUL-KADER (Arab chief) : of the Kadi, judge. ABDOLONYMUS (Sidonian king) : of the name (of God), HIERONYMUS : holy name, becomes JEROME, GIROLAMO, GERONIMO.

ABDI(el) : servant (of God). "Kish the son of *Abdi.*" Here a form of EBED : servant, slave. "The son of *Ebed* said, who is Abimelech that we should *ebed* him ? " ZEBUL (who thrust out Gaal) : a fly, buzzer, a component part of BAALZEBUL, BELZEBUB : the fly dispeller. EBEDMELCH (Ethiopian) : king's servant = GILDEROY. OMRI, OMRIAH : who obeys the command of God, *con.* EMIR : who gives word. EMIR-AL-OMRI : commander of commanders = PHICOL : mouth

of all, whose *mouth all* obey. ALMIRAL, ADMIRAL: the commander. OBED is the participial form of ABDON, whence
OBED-EDOM: Edom's servant. "Edom is slave (obed) under
tribute." OBEDIAH (Puritan favourite): of Jehovah, *cor.* to
NOBBS. Its Hindoo correspondent is DHAS DASA: a coolie,
servant, slave, coming into English as DASS. GANGADASA:
servant of the river god Ganga, from whom we get the name
of his son GANGES = TIBERIUS: son of the river God Tiber.
KALI (goddess): coally, black beauty, *con.* Kalos: beautiful.
Our *coal* is philologically identical with Kali and kalos, each
meaning beautiful. KALIDASA: servant of Kali, a thug.
Cutta(ck): a temple. Calcutta: temple of KALI, the Hindoo
Venus. "*Kalidasa*, the celebrated author of Sacontala, represents with a master hand the influence which the aspect of
nature exercises on the minds and feelings of lovers."
GOSSALADASA: servant of Gossala, an avatar (incarnation) of
Krishna. AGNIDASA: servant of the fire god Agni, *con.* ignis
and Agag, which consult. The names of the well known
Brahmin convert, Narayan Sheshadri, are analysed thus.
NARAYAN: he that treadeth the waters, the Hindoo Neptune,
devoted to. SHESHADRI, is from Shesh: the great serpent,
which, in the cosmogony of the Hindoos, bears the world,
and ADRI: safe (therefrom) in a mountain. BRAHMIN: born
of Brahm, the first person in the Hindoo Trimutri.

DUILIUS (consul): servant, slave—Dulia et latria: service
and worship. KNIGHT, usually given as meaning servant,
knitted, attached, really means offspring, son of high degree,
hence *con.* GNATUS: born. VAVASOUR: vassal, thane of inferior order, *con.* Volvo: I roll, boundaries being termed in
medieval Latin Valvas: doors (of the kingdom) which the
vavasour had to defend, similarly to a MARQUESS: march
defender. It was originally written Valvasour, which makes
the valves plainer.

ESQUIRE, SQUIRES (scutifer) ARMIGER: shield bearer, knight's
servant. SCUDAMORE: shield of love, one saving another =
ALEXANDER, SOCRATES, FORTESCUE: strong shield, powerful
escutcheon. EGEDE (Hans): goatskin shield bearer, *con.*
Ægis. Egedesmind (Greenland): built in memory (mind) of
the apostle of Greenlanders. GILES (sometimes): a goat =
CHEEVERS. KMETY (Austrian): a serf. Lackey is from Lag:
to remain behind, as servants do after master. LACHMAN
(Mc) LATCHIE (*con.* lackey): servants to a lord.

SERJEANT is form of servant = SERVETUS: one who received
quarter in battle, pre*served* as a slave to his victor, binder.
ANCELL: a servant, *con.* ancillary = HELFMANN (Nihilist):
man helper = SKEELS, *con.* SCALD: servant of the gods, served
them by song. GODSAL (lieutenant), GOTTESCHALCUS: servant

of God. KNAPP: servant = *Knave.* " I Paul, the knave of
Jesus Christ." Knapsack: bag carried by a servant. We
meet with BELKNAP: honest, good servant. ANCELL: *con.* the
Gaelic word GILL: servant or boy, whence GILLIE (Queen's):
servant, used not only of servitude, but patronymically, as
BAIN: white, fair (M') ILWAIN: Bain's servant or son. So
DHU, DOW, DUFF, DOVE, DEE: swarthy, dark a-vised.
M'INDOE: Dhu's Dow's Duff's or Dove's boy. ROY: red
(headed): gives (M') ILROY: Roy's lad. GILMORE, GILMER:
great servant = SENESCHALL (*con.* senior and scald), becomes
also GILMOUR. But GILMAIR: B. V. Mary's servant, as Kirrie-
muir: Mary's kirk. GILROY: Roy's lad, *ab.* to (M') ILROY.
GILDEROY: servant of the kirk. CULDEE: servant of God.
GILLIS, GELASIUS (pope), GILLIES, GILDAS (historian): servant
of Jesus = the Arabic ABDALISSU, Abyssinian BARCA-YASSOUS:
slave of Jesus. So GILCHRIST: servant of, devoted to,
Christ.

GILFILLAN (George): of St. Fillan = (M') CLELLAN, whence
CLELAND, GILDART: of Arthur. GILLANDER: of St. Andrew.
GILLIBRED, GILLEVROY, GILLEBRED: of St. Bride, Bridget.
Gillebred applied to a coast bird. From Bride, Hebrides:
island whereon was church of St. Bridget. But GILBERT:
bright, glorious warrior. GILES: pledged to a ordeal = WAGER
(captain), *con.* Guild: a pledged confraternity, and GUILD: a
member of it = FRATER. GILBERT answers to GUMPRECHT:
war bright. M'LEAN is a form of MACGILLIAN: son of John's
servant. GILLON, GILLAN (Gill Oin): servant of John.
M'LURE, *ab.* form of MacGill Cabhair: son of the servant of
the book (Bible or breviary), clerk's son. GALBRAITH (*con.*
Brehon): judge's son, judicious, discreet.

Many Celtic names are formed of Maol: bald (by tonsure),
shaving away hair to commemorate our Lord wearing thorn
crown. Hair so cut was dedicated to some saint whose name
the devotee adopted. Anciently slaves were forbidden long
hair as prisoners now. Part of Gaul was called Gallia
Comata: the long-haired Gauls. Short hair or bald head
become a symbol of servitude. "This is the priest all *shaven*
and *shorn,* that married the man all tattered and torn." As
masters of old made slaves uncover in their presence to show
they were their inferiors, we lift our hat to a superior and
enter the house of God uncovered. As wearing shoe or sandal
in the East signified right to walk over land, and therefore
landowner, Ruth iv. 8., every son of the Orient enters God's
house barefoot to signify poverty before the all possessing
King. In the case of the wasteful son, " Put shoes on his
feet," meant restore to him his forfeited patrimony. MALLOCH:
bald to Luke. Eglismaol Luach: church of bald Luke,

Lanarkshire. "The original name of the poet was MALLOCH, which, after his removal to London and his intimacy with the great, he changed to MALLET. He wrote 'William and Mary,'—

> " 'Twas at the silent, solemn hour,
> When night and morning met;
> In glided Margaret's grimly ghost,
> And stood at William's feet."

MALISE : bald to Jesus = GILLIS. MILLIGAN (Scotch) : servant of Luke, but MULLIGAN : son of the bald headed man. MALCOLM : bald to St. Columb. MALACHY (king of Meath) : bald to Maodhog, first bishop of Ferns. Often confused with MALACHI : my messenger, angel, but one is Milesian, the other Hebrew. MULLEN (made Oin) : bald to John = McLEAN, GILLON. MILROY : ecclesiastical servant to king, as GILDEROY was king's civil servant. Maol also gives MOULE = CALVIN, CHAUVIN, KORAH (Dathan and Abiram) : all bald heads. Thence also Moult, which gives Mews : aviary for hawks. Meuse Lane. Mull of Cantyre : bare rocks of Cantyre : head land. The severe climate of Russia suggested a compromise between razor and curling tongs. Instead of shaving, the Muscovites cut their hair crosswise, using this prayer : "Give thy blessing to this thy servant who is now to offer these his first fruits, the tonsure of his head. The servant of God is shorn in the name of the Father, and of the Son, and of the Holy Ghost, now and for ever, even unto the ages of ages. Amen." If his hair is dedicated to no particular saint he is simply called ISCHIN : a servant, but if to one, that saint's name becomes his with *ischin* affixed. Thus Russia has the sneezing names, MATUIISCHEN : servant of Matthew, SENTS-CHISCHIN : of Simeon. Compare such cases with the *per contra* one of Samson and the Nazarite vow. The English name CALLOW (from Calvus) and the Welsh VOYLE also mean bald. The Tartar word for servanti is Kouli, as KOULI KHAN : khan's slave, lord's *coolie*. Cawnpore : khan's city. COOLIE : serf, slave. "By the last advice from China we learn that 500 Coolies, who had been entrapped into a factory at Macao under false pretences, broke down the door, and in spite of their keepers, effected their escape." HERSCHELL (herr schall) of the German corresponds to KOULI KHAN. SWAIN (*con.* sway, involving the idea of strength) : a young man, a servant. BOATSWAIN : boat servant. GARCON : a boy, a servant, *con.* GOSS, GOSSETT, GOSPATRICK, COSPATRICK : boy, servant of Patrick. PAGE : a servant, now restricted to boy menials, gives the well-known Paget (Dr.) Pageant : grand display of servants. PAXTON : Page's town. But PAXMAN : one driving a pack horse. GUISCARD, WISHART, WISEMAN : a conjuror, *lit.* a wise nature. DREW : a conjuror, druid, whence DRUIFF : son of Drew = DRUGAN. MAGO (Carthaginian, from whom Mahon in Minorca), MAGUS (Simon): a magician, one practising magic — PERSIS, ELYMAS: of Elymais, from Elam: Persian: from OLAM, ULAM : first-born The Persians came next the Chaldees in the art of divination. These = HACHMONI : very wise. " He (Pharaoh) sent and called for the *hachmonim* of Egypt." TRISMEGISTUS (Mercury): threefold magician, greatest trickster. Mega : great, as Omega : great O, gives MAGUS : great (man) = Rabbi, whence Magister, Magnate, Magistrate. From Per : through : Ager : a field, acre, we have PILGRIM, PELL, PRINGLE, PEREGRIN (Pickle): all Pilgrims. HOP PRINGLE : son of the pilgrim.

PILLSBURY, PELHAM, PETTY : pilgrims' dwellings. The first martyr to Christianity in Rome was burned, and is referred to by Lucian in his Dialogues, was PEREGINO. PELLETT: little Pel gives the well known PALEY : Pell's field. ROME, ROMEO (and Juliet), ROMAINE (Rev.), ROMERO : pilgrims to Rome. SAINTEY : been to Saint Terre : holy land, whence Saunter : to wander like pilgrims. SANTA CROCE (admiral): holy cross, whose ancestors had the credit of bringing Vera Cruz : the true cross to Europe. ERMETE (Dr.) = Bedowee : desert dweller, solitaire. WALLS, WALLER, WALLACH (when not Wallachia) : pilgrims, *con.* Gael, a stranger. Wallet : provision bag carried by pilgrim = Scrip : for holding scraps. WANTMAN, WANT : wenders, goers about. RAINEY (principal): who *ran* through divers lands. In some families this means sea rover = WALMER : marine wanderer, viking. COCKLE : pilgrim who had crossed the sea to shrine of St. James Compostella, and so wore a cockle shell cap.

> " How should I your true love know
> From another one ?
> By his *cockle* hat and *staff*,
> And his sandal shoon."

This staff was made crutch-wise, and called *bourdonne*, whence BURDEN and CROSS : pilgrims twain. His sandals suggest DISCALZEADO (Boston firm) : discalceated friar, bare feet, meaning poverty. FRIAR, FRASER, FRERE (Bartle), FRA (Diavolo) and Free in freemason, all mean brother. DISCALZEADO = BAREFOOT, which consult. BALMER : brought palm branch from Holy Land, whence PALMERSTON : town frequented by pilgrims = PELHAM : home of. The French have LA PAUME : the pilgrim. In Snodland church-yard, Kent, is the following epitaph in memory of one Palmer of Oxford,—

> " Palmers all our Faders were,
> I a Palmer lingered here,
> And trauyl'd still, till worn with age,
> I ended this world's pilgrimage
> On the blyst Assention day,
> In the cheerful month of May,
> A thousand with four hundred seuen
> And took my journey hense to Heuen."

Much of the beauty of this lies in the distinction that palmer differed from other pilgrims, such ceasing to be pilgrims after visiting places they had vowed to worship at, whereas once a palmer always a palmer. To these add WANDS: who *wends* his way from land to land. The Germans simply call pilgrims wanderers. The generic word in the East for a pilgrim is HADJAI, *con.* HAGAR. From Gur, Gar, or Gau, the Hebrew for a stranger, a pilgrim, as " I am the son of *gur*, an Amalakite;" hence Gauyim: strangers, aliens, foreigners, Gentiles, as in the clearest prophecy uttered as to the restoration of the Jews. " For Jehovah will have mercy on Jacob, and will yet choose Israel, and set them in their own land, and *gauyim* shall be joined with them." AGEE: a fugitive, answers to PHYGELLUS. AGUR (" The words of "): a stranger, a pilgrim. Unlikely as it may seem, there is an English equivalent to this, SOJOURNER (Charleston), one who tarries with you for a day. GERSHOM (*om* for Am: people): a strange people. For he said, " I have been a stranger in a strange land." The idea is nearly that of OTTEMARE (ultra): beyond the sea, *con.* LAMMERMOOR : moor reaching to the sea. GERA (a Benjamite, a man left handed): a stranger = L'ESTRANGE. From Shem : name, famous, SHAMGAR (" the son of Anath ") : an aristocratic stranger. In the New Testament we meet with Gergesenes = Gauyim : foreigners, non Abrahamic people. Let a German bring up the rear in this array of pilgrims, WUNDER: he who wends, wanders = WANDS.

We also meet with the Italian BEZANCIO, BESANT (Annie) : a crusading pilgrim, who, visiting Byzantium, brought therefrom circular pieces of bullion without any impression, called from the city, *bezants*. By Shakespeare's time bezant became tantamount to valueless.

BUCKMASTER : master of buck hounds, but BUCK, BOX : bucks, gay fellows. " Box and Cox." COX: *cuish* maker, thigh plate. CRAMER: stall keeper. BULLAR: stamper in a stannary office, *con.* Bulla: papal seal, which, stamping a document, became a *bull.* STANNERS, STANNERY: worker in a tin mine, a tinsmith. ROSE : rose grower = ROSBAUM : rose tree grower, sometimes means rosy, ruddy = RUDD, and suggesting RHODA, *con.* Rhododendron : rose tree, literally = ROSBAUM. MOSS (when not formed on Moses): dwelling on a

18

moor, muir, bogland = Irish names MOONEY, MONEY, as in
MONEYMORE: great bog. MOSSCROP, MOSSCRIP: turf digger,
labourer on a moor. CROP, that which is *gathered, con.* Creep:
to gather, a worm gathers itself to creep. So crop of a bird
consists in what it has gathered. *Con.* this root, KRUPP
(guns): a cripple, one who creeps along.
    NACHMANN: night watcher. The French have MUNZER:
money maker, printer. SCALES and KLINKSCALES: medieval
nicknames for salesmen, which in Hindostan is WALLAH, to
which add SELLER, when not meaning SADDLER. BRAZIER:
brass worker answers to the medieval Persian SOFFAR, from
whom the dynasty Soffarides, who reigned over Khorassan
(873-907). Khorassan: sun country, sunny land, with which
some connect CYRUS (Koreish): the sun = Samson, from
Shemesh: the sun, but the balance of probability favours
CYRUS: kurios, lord. The French DELAPORT: of the gate,
DELAPLACE: of the city, DELARUE: of the street, were sometimes applied to tollmen = SOUTHGATE: toll taker there, but
at others meant burgesses, freemen; allied to Rue : a row,
street, PEREZ DE LA RUA (he gave name to Peru): Pierson
of *the street, i.e.,* main street. GREGORY (Gregorian chant,
calendar): a watchman, gives GORY, GOY, GOR (HAM), *con.*
LYCURGUS (king): wolf watcher, a shepherd = BERGER.
    LACORDAIRE: wearing cord of St. Francis, sometimes peace-
maker, who gets people into *accord.* ARDGOUR: Goat hill =
GORDON. KILGOUR (coyle): wood frequented by goats.
COYLE: a wood, Kelvin (avon): wooded river. HALLEY,
guarded hall = ROCHEFORT. AUBE: white wood. OLTRAMARE,
DOUTREMER: a foreigner from beyond the sea. PAINVIN:
holding land for which homage is rendered in *bread* and *wine.*
ANNAN (avon, of which *an* is *dim.*): rivulet. ANNANDALE =
COMMISKY (combe esk). CLIVE (India): CLEE: living among
cliffs; CLEVELAND = FOLLY, FOLI, and Du HALDE. But CLING
for KLING: a sword(sman). HELLER : sea cave entered by
tide, aboriginal troglodyte = WEMYSS, CAVE. CONNAL (S.B.G.):
raging flood = SORBEY: shore dweller. The royal name
BRUNSWICK: Bruno's cattle shed = BYARS, BOUVERIE, suggesting BEMBO (pen): cattle hill.
    SEIDLITZ (powders): is our SETTLE: living on a clearing, an
emigrant. MURILLO (painter): little walled town = LYTTLETON,
VELPEU, BURDETT, *con.* MURAT. SHEE (O): living where
fairies meet. DE SOTO: of the Grove = GROVES. TRAVEL:
to go beyond (trans) the wall (vallum), a traveller. WITLEY
(Liverpool): white meadow = WHITEFIELD. From Pre: before,
Eo: to go, we get PRETORIUS: a magistrate, one who takes
the precedency. "And the soldiers led Him away into the
hall called Prætorium."

Of recent names are PENMAN QUILLMAN, SCHREIBER, SCRIBE = the classic SCHREVALIUS. SATCHELL: a little sack, means a bag maker = (Mᶜ) SPORRAN. COSTARD (whence Custard: the outcome of cream and good cookery, was originally baked apples): an apple grower, then seller, whence the well known Costermonger: costard, apple, salesman. BRASCHI (Pope Pius VI.): cauliflower planter, market gardener. BUTTON (Billy): is a button maker. WASSERBOHR: a well borer, and WASSER- MAN: waterman, travelling by, but WASS: bold, *con.* VASA and WASHINGTON.

BACHELOR: staff winner, the last man of the poll won a wooden spoon. So also BELL: who carried off the bell. BACHELOR, *con.* Imbecile: leaning on a staff, feeble. ALCONER, ELKORN, OLDCORN (G. P.): ale conner, an exciseman who ken- ned, examined ale. ARLISS: one bound by *arles, i.e.,* earnest money to serve a year. Arles is from year, and that from gyre, gur. HALFHEAD (puzzled many): a poor farmer, one having but *half* a *hide* of land to cultivate, a hyde being what a yoke of bullocks could plough in one season. It was called a hide from being hedged, hidden. The name is *cor.* from HALFHYDE, which is rare compared with HYDE. A yet more comic contortion is ONYBRAINS from Onibyrne: John Bran or Braine. PARDON(er): a priest, but PURDON (for pure dun): a hill cleared of trees = CLARENDON, CLARIDGE, suggesting ORRIDGE: farm on a hill, and ORBY (Shipley): dwelling on a farm. Or or Orr: an enclosure, boundary, usually a water. HOARE(formerly Oore): ore raiser = PITMAN, suggesting IRETON: iron town, place where iron ore is dug. ANSER (a form of answer, for *and swear*): a scale maker, as the goods and weights had to answer, balance each other. BROGGER is the medieval English form of broker = BROKER. COULTER (*con.,* Colo: I cultivate): a smith who made iron part of plough = PLOWWRIGHT. PRUDENCE (same word as PROVIDENCE: He who pro-vides: sees and prepares before hand): a morality play character, then a Puritan name. DRAPER (*con.,* DRAP: cloth. Trap: to adorn with cloth, Drab: a ₁colour): a cloth salesman.

CHAPTER XIV.

PATRONYMICS.

It was formerly customary to receive names from ancestors by compounding their name with a word indicating filial relationship. Names so compounded were termed *patronymics,* from Pater: father, and Onoma: a name—father being used in the sense of ancestor. When personal names merged into family appellations, patronymics became obsolete ; or, more correctly, ceased to be formed. Before this change was effected, in case a man was called DENNIS : born on the day of St. Dennis, sometimes his eldest son would be called DENNISON, which, in some cases, became TENNYSON, and a man from a village in which was a church dedicated to St. Dennis was called DENNISTOUN. After the period in which descriptive names flourished, each of his children, whether male or female, would be called DENNIS, so that this became literally a patronymic, inasmuch as it was a name received from a father. Howbeit, only those names that were taken from a parent when such was not the rule are called patronymics. Personal names lead the van as to all others, and are the basis of half their successors. Long after personal names were almost as widely diffused as persons, we find patronymics coming into use—the offspring of necessity arising out of multiplicity. The hero of the valley of Elah is known as David, the son of Jesse, whence we infer there were others named David. This is the more probable, because DAVID : beloved, is a nurse name, and had doubtless often been given by fond mothers to newly born boys previously to B.C. 1085. Had he lived in the first or second millennium of history, he would simply have been called David. Names follow a regular progression parallel to history, beginning with a single personal appellation, and pass on to patronymical, and then to two, three, four, or more names being used, the final stage being the stereotyping of names as they are all over Christendom, and have been, at least, from the era of the Reformation. Nothing we know of Onamatology : the science of names, a branch of philology, favours the idea of man's antiquity stretching back into ten times the period recognised by the Usherian chronology. Had man inhabited this globe 100,000 years since, single names would not have been in use so lately as the days of Adam. As in the Old Testament we have David, the son of Jesse, so in the era of the New Testament we meet with CAIAPHAS,

Joseph : Caiaphas, the son of Joseph, which easily becomes Joseph Caiaphas. Yet earlier we have John HYRCANUS :, who conquered the Hyrcanians, dwellers near the sea now known as the Caspian. Such names approach very nearly to our present nomenclature, which is not a result of chance, but the natural outcome of human language, which is the outcome of human nature, which is the offspring of God. The first name looking like a patronymic is antediluvian, viz., TUBAL-CAIN : flowing out from Cain, as though O'Cain, given to intimate pride in relationship to Cain. During the Israelitish theocracy, Gentile patronymics were in common use, as Hittites from Heth, but those personal came in later. As soon, however, as the New Testament opens we meet with Bar-Jonah, Bar-Abbas, names received from fathers in the conventional patronymical sense. It is, therefore, manifest that the chronology of patronymics, the period of their formation, lies about midway between the primitive ages and time current.

THE SAXON PATRONYMIC

was formed by adding *ing* to ancestor's name, as

ÆLFREDING : Alfred's son, *plu.* Ælfredingas : Alfredites, like Frelungi (second order of Saxon society): sons of the free, *con.* FREW, JUNGFRAU : young free, FREEMAN = LIBERIUS, ELEUTHERIUS (popes) and LYSANDER ; men *loos*ened.

BEORMING : descendants of Beorm, BIRMINGHAM : home of his sons.

BRUMMAGEM (a name applied to inferior goods made in Birmingham) is an actual family name. A member of the BEORMINGHAM family who emigrated to Ireland was named Pierce, which was Hibernianised into Macioris, which became Macjore, which assumed the form of

MACGEORGE, a fact that should make men thankful they are not living in Irish medieval times.

Another Saxon chief was named FOTHER : feeder, provider, father, from him,

FOTHERINGHAM : home of the descendants of Fother, *con.* Fotheringay and FOTHERGILL.

WATLING for Watlingas : the sons of Wetla. Watling Street, through their settlement.

WETLA : he of the sharp sword, *con.* Whet : to sharpen, WHITTLE (Harvey). The Goths supplied the Saxons with this form, hence the dynastic patronymics,

Merovingians : descendants of Meroveus, Carlovingians : of Carloman.

CARLING (from him Carlingford): son of Charles = M'ARLE. The Danes were called

Skioldungians : of SKIOLD (Sigge's fifth son) : a shield, good
at using it, like

TORDENSKIOLD : thunder shield, thundering on shield of
enemy.

NORDENSKJOLD (navigator) : shield of the North.   SKIOLD-
= Milesian SKEY, *con.* Sky : a cover, SKIDMORE : shield of love.

SKIOLDING : son of a shield, brave, *cor.* to SCOLDING : noise
made by sword on shield, now by one tongue on another.
" How are the mighty fallen."

WELLINGTON : town of descendants of Weale. So from
WASS : keen, bold, we have

WASHINGTON.   As also WARE : a defender = EPAMNON, gives
WARRINGTON (from Ware, Herts).   WADE : he who invades,
bold at attack,

WADING : son of Wade, whence WADINGTON.   BANN, from
Bana : a slayer, *con.* Henbane : hay poison, wolfsbane, we get

BANHAM : BANN'S home.   Sometimes a form of BONHOMME :
a monk.

GOSLING *(bona fide)* : of GOSS, but Gosling : little goose.

GUNNING : son of a warrior = WICKLIFFE, from GUNN : war, as
Gonfalon : war standard, GUNTER : *the* warrior of the army.

SEEKINGS : son of Sack.   SACK : one given to plunder =
MERODE, HARRY.

MEEKING : son of Mece.   MECE : a sword, he who uses it,
MEEK, MECHI (model farm).

KLINGING : son of a sword, sabreur, from KLING : a blade,
he who uses, *con.* Clang : to make a noise.

GETTINGS : son of a Jute, giant.   BEHRING (straits), BARING :
son of Thor's bear, good fighter.

MERLING : son of the illustrious ; MAR : famous = SHEM.

MANNING (cardinal) : son of the Asir Mannus.   MANNERING
(Guy) : of MANNERS, HERMAN inverted.

CUMMING, COMYN : son of a count, *con.* Comes : a companion.

ATHELING (Edgar) : of noble descent, gives EDLIN, *con.*
ADLER : a German aristocrat.   This patronymical ending is
met with in names of the most frequent occurrence, as

JENNINGS : of John, STUBBINGS : of Stephen, RAWLINGS :
Ralph, RALSTON : Ralph's town.

COPPING : Jacob.   COLLINGS : Nichols.   From *ing* : son, we
have *ing* : little, thus

DARLING (Darlington : Darling's town) : son of Dear, or
little dear,

CARRACCI (Carus : dear) answers to latter.   Fatling : little
fat (animal), Gosling : little goose, are *dims.* of *pats.*, as most
dims. are.

WHITING (nothing to do with fish) : son of White.   WHITE :
a man, emphatic, but

WHITWORTH : white dwelling = WENTWORTH, CASABIANCA.
CHIESE from Casa : a house, is now domesticated in England. Had CHIESE invaded our coast five hundred years since he would have turned to CHEESE.
WIGGIN(G)S (weather prophet) : son of war, a soldier = the better known WICKLIFFE.
When *ing* is neither a *dim.* nor a *pat.* its used in the sense of contempt as witling, lordling, where, of course, it means little. The Saxon *pat.* was less common among our ancestors than

THE ENGLISH PATRONYMIC,

which is exceedingly common with ourselves. It is indicated by affixing *son* to the name of a progenitor, and is incapable of being used in a plural form or in the generic sense. The examples are so numerous and so well understood that one is embarrassed in making a selection fit for the occasion.
ADDISON : son of Ady, for Adam. EDISON (electric) : of Eadie, of Ed.
ANDERSON : Andrew = ANDREZ. HARRIS (when not local), for HARRISON = HARRIGAN, BARRY, PARRY.
ANSON (commander) : John = BEVAN. ALISON : Alic for Alexander = SANDERSON.
MADDISON, MADISON : of Matthew = MACMATH, DE MATTOS, sometimes becomes DYSON.
COULSON : Cole for Nicholas. TOLSON : Bartholomew.
GIBSON : Gibbs, for Gilbert. GILSON : Giles, or Gill, in latter case = MACGILL.
GIMSON : of James = JAMIESON : of JAMIE : little James.
HINSON : Hind, which becomes HINES, IND (and Cope).
HODGSON : of Hodge for Roger.
HOBSON ('s choice, this or none) : Hob, for Robert = ROBERTSON, DOBSON, ROBINSON, PROBART, ROBSON.
HODGSON : Hodge, for Roger. HUDSON : Hood. HOOD : a monk wearing one.
HUSKISSON (Board of Trade) : Askew. 'LUPSON : LOVE : lupus : a wolf = LOPEZ, LUBEZ.
IVES : an archer = YEAMANS (HEMANS) : YEOMAN, *con.* yew (tree), ISON = MACIVER.
MUNSON : Munns, for Edmund. NELSON : Nell (Ellen) or Neal, when = MACNEIL, NELIGAN.
MACKANELLY, from MacNeil. PEARSON : of Peter = PEDREZ.
PILSON of PELL : a Pilgrim = HOP PRINGLE.
PORSON (Cambridge) and POLSON (flour) ; Paul = MACPHAIL.
PATTERSON : of Patrick = GOSPATRICK (*con.* garcon). RITSON : Rider, Ritter = DE RUYTER.

SAMPSON : Samuel.   SIMSON, SIMPSON : Simms = MACSHIMES :
of Simon, MONAD from Simon, as
   STIMPSON, STIMSON, STEVENS : Stephen.   TONSON : of Tony
for Antony = DE ANTONIO, DANTON.
   WATSON : Wat for Walter = MACOUAT, MACWALTER.   NILL-
SON (madame) from Corneille.
   It is more easy than desirable to enlarge this catalogue.
We, therefore, pass to the germane subject of

DIMINUTIVES.

   The following are the most prevalent forms in our language :
—*ullus, ucci, je, ie, ing, in, kin, ot, otte, otti, ell, elle, enne, et,
ette, etti, etto, ach, och, eogan, egan, an, een, ad, un, ig, cock,* and *y.*
Before considering the part played by diminutives, we should
premise that, as a rule, final *s* in personal names makes no
difference as to meaning, being generally only phonetic or
formative.   Thus HAWKIN, *con.* HAL for Harry, tends to
HAWKINS, as Edward glides into EDWARDS.   Some hold *s* in
such words as EDWARDS to be a genetive form as though
EDWARDS : son of Edward, but it is mostly formative.   Yet in
some cases the terminal *s* does indicate *son,* and so may be
termed a patronymical form.   Is a man called George Peter ?
The ear is unsatisfied until that becomes George *Peters.*   On
this principle Will assumes the forms WILLIS, WILES.—In the
subscribed examples understand either *son* or *little* after the
original name.
   LUCULLUS (conquered Tigranes) : Luke = LUCIAN, if that
does not mean born at daybreak.
   LUKE : man of Lucania, south Italy, given, also, as shining,
brilliant.
   MARCELLUS (slew Viridomarus) : Mark.   FAUSTULUS (shep-
herd) : *Faustus* (Dr.), FESTUS : lucky.
   VERUCCI : VERUS : true = TRUMAN, LIPROT, and AMEN.
But VERON, VERRON : man of Verona, VERONICA : true image
(of Christ).
   BRAMMETJE : little Abraham = MABBOT.   EPJE : Joseph, *con.*
JAAP, JEBB.
   JANTJE :   John = SHONEEN,   ATKINS :   Arthur.   DAKINS,
DAWKINS, DEAKINS, DAVITT : for David.
   DONKIN, DONALDSON, English for MACDONALD, the Irish for
it being DONEGAN, and the Lowland MACWHANNELL.
   EKIN is derivable from Edward, Edmund, Edgar, or Eadie.
HANKIN : Hans : John = HANSOM (son).
   JIFKIN : little Joseph = EPJE, former English, latter Dutch,
each = JOWETT (professor).

Fergus gives FORGIE, as Ronald does RENNIE, and Gabriel gives GEBBIE.

JUST: born on St. Just's day, gives JOSCELIN, JOSSELYN. Lawrence gives LAKIN, LARKINS, LARRY, LAWRIE, LAWSON. Oliver supplies NOLL, NOLLEKINS. Isaac becomes NYE, NYKIN = MACKISSOCK, also giving IKE.

RANKIN is of Randall, while from Simon we derive SIMPKINS, SIMKINS, SIMCOX. As Simkins shapes into Simpkins, so Simcox grows to SIMPCOX.

GLOUCESTER: " What's thine own name?
SIMPCOX: Saunder *Simpcox*, an' if it please you, master.
GLOUCESTER: Then Saunder, sit there, the lyingest knave in Christendom."

QUAGLIENNE: little Quaglia, which consult. ADCOCK, ADY (Joseph): from Adam. Thousands of children have been named from Adam, in the belief such would attain to a great age. " Old as Adam." The Jews viewing him as the first rebel, and he being no Jew, name no child after him.

ALCOCK from Hal, for Harry. ARNOT from Arnold. BIRKETT from BURKE (from BURY), when not *birch wood.* [*]

BADCOCK is from Bartholomew, whence also BARTLETT, and BATTY (equestrian); but BAD: good, from Bid: to pray.

PIUS (Pio: I atone for): who has made an atonement, a religeuse, PYAT (red), BIOT, BIOTI, BIAGOTTI..

BUON for Bon: good, from Bonus, gives the great name BUONAROTTI = GOODY, *con.* with

BUONAFEDE (wrote "Political Chronology"): truce observer, faith keeper, identical with *bonafide* = AMON, AMNON: amen, men. These answer to

FIDELIA: keeping her tryst = BEAUFOY: good faith. BOSSUET (the learned), BOSSUE: boss shouldered, gibbous.

PAGET (M.D.) may mean little page, or son of PAGE, *con.* Pageantry: great show of many servants.

BUFFET (corps legislatif): waiter on the buffet, sideboard. Beefeater (Tower): buffetier = PAGE.

BARRELL, BARRETT, from BARRY or BARRIE from BARR: a hill, or Barry: bare island.

LAWCOCK: little hill = KNOWLES, or little LAW: a hill. In keeping with former view,

BRAES: living on a hill, *con.* BRANT: living on a steep. BRANTON = HILTON, *con.*

TANNAHILL (Paisley): a hill whether heather perishes from heat, *con.* Beltane, but

TANNOCK for TANNEROCK: young TANNER (faster): worker in oak tan = BARKER.

BERNADOTTE (Sweden), NADAUD: from Bernard. BURNET (bishop) from BROWN or Burn: a boundary =

BECKETT: little beck, *con.* BECCLES (bishop): brook running through meadow (lees).   But BECKEY from Rebecca.

CORBET from Corvus : a crow (on shield), one of the oldest surnames in Scotland.

COBBET (Preston), COPPOCK, COB (father) : from Jacob. DIDEROT (cyclopedist) from DESIDERIUS : desiderated.

DORRIT (little), DOLLY : from Dorothy.   ELLIOTT, from ELLIS, for Elias, for Elijah.

FONTINELLE from FONTAINE = FOUNTAIN = TIBER (father), SPRING.

GUIZOT (statesman), WHYATT, GIOTTO (O) from Guy.   GILLOT (pens) : Giles or Gill.

WILMET, GUILMETTE, GUILLOTIN, WILLIMOTT, WILMOT, WOOLCOCK, WILLIE (We have missed you), WILKIE, ULLIN (lord).   ULLICK : young or little William.

GROCOCK from Gregory, whence GORHAM : where is church of St. Gregory.

HIGGS : a wild ash, gives HIGGINS, HIGGOT, HIGNET.   HERBELOT (orientalist), formed on Herbert.

QUINET : from Jacques, for James, and so = JAMIE, JIMMY. HANCOCK : Hans : John = VAN HAHN.

HITCHCOCK (geology and religion) : from Richard.   GLASS : a stream, as Glassford ; GLASSCOCK = MACGLASHAN.

BROGAN : little badger, biter.   CROSSAN : little cross (on shield).   HOPPET, HOPKINS : Hob for Robert.

HEWITT, HEWETT, HEWSON (old), HUESSEN, HUIE : sons of Hugh, or little Hughs.

IVETT from Ives.   JEWETT, JEWELL : from Jew : from Judah. MORELL (H. M. I.) : from Moor or MORE : dark, *con.* MORISON.

MARCET (Mrs.), MURCUTT, from Mark = MARCELLUS, whence MARCELLINUS (pope).

MARTINET (disciplinarian) : from Martin.   NICOT (tobacco) : Nicholas.

OTHELLO, ODETTE : Otho.   PELLATT (Apsley) : from Pell : Pilgrim.   TIPPET : from Theobald.

PERKINS (and Barclay), PARKIN, PARNELL (Land League), PERUCCI, PETRUCCHIO (and Catherine), PERROTT, PIRRIE, PIRIE, PIRRET, PERRY (when not trade name : maker of perry from pear), PIEROTTI, PARROTT : are all formations on Peter the apostle, prolific of names.

DONIZETTI : formed on Dominus : a lord, and so = TOOLE : of lordly descent.

TIMKINS : from Timothy.   TONKIN, TONY, ANTONELLI (non-possumus) : formed on Anthony.

THOMASSEAU, THOMASSEN (son) = TOMMY and THOMSON.

MOLOCH and MOLLOCH are living family names from Maol, Mul : bald, and each means little baldheaded man.

DE and MAC.

From the Latin DE: of, we get a patronymical sign common to French, Italian, and even German names. Thus

DELUC: of Luke. DE MATTOS: of Matthew = MACMATH, MADDISON, MADISON.

DEARLE: of Earl. DE RUYTER: son of a knight = RITSON, MACKNIGHT.

DWIGHT (theologian): of Wight. DANTON (red, very): of Antoine = DANTE (poet),

DURANTE: lasting (as to fame) is given as its source, but DURANTE, DURANT: lasting (in fight) = CONSTANT.

DANDO (English), DANDY (Scotch), TANDY (Napper) = DANTON (French), Dante (Italian) on Andrew.

D'ISRAELI: of Israel = SCOBELOFF (general): son of Jacob, *con.* KOPINSKI: James' town, and SCOBIE.

DE SANTOS: of the saints, from Sanctus: holy, SANG, SANCHO (Pansa). Sanctus: holy, from Sanguis: blood (of sacrificial victim), hence Sanction. D'EREMAO (Dr.): of a hermit.

DE FOE: of the faith. DELMONICO (hotel): of the monk. When local, *la* is added, as

DE LA CROIX: of the cross = CROSBY: dwelling near a cross. CROSSLEY, CRUTCHLY: cross field.

DE LA RUE: of the row, street = ROWE, and Italian, STRADUARIUS (violins). In German, STROSS, whence STROSSMAYER (bold bishop): street mayor, burgh officer. The South American town Callao: the street = Main Street, High Street.

DE LA MARCHE: of the border, as BONDY = DELAWAR (whence Delaware), DEWAR: of the ward, part guarded. From the Latin ending *acius*, the French derive *ac*, used• locally or patronymically, as

POLIGNAC (cardinal): of Poligny, and that from a Pole.

BALZAC (author): of BALE, for BASIL, from BASILEUS: a king.

LUSSAC (Guy): of Luke = DELUC. MARTIGNAC: of MARTIGNY: Martin's dwelling.

ESPAGNAC (general): of Spain. RAVAILLAC (Henry 4th): of RAVIUS: son of RAPP: a raven.

COLIGNY (admiral): for Colignac: of the hill district = COLLIS, HILLS.

FITZ.

The more general patronymic indulged in by our Gallic neighbours is *fitz* for Filius: a son, received through the Normans. "Robert, son of King Henry 1st, having proposed

marriage to Osboorht, daughter of Baron Fitz Hamon, she
politely declined, for said she,—

> "It were to me a great shame
> To have a lord withouten his twa name."

His father came to the rescue, and made him eligible for
husbandship by styling his pet "Robert FITZROY :" son of a
king = (En)FAUNTLEROY : king's infant = CREE for MacRee,
BASILOWITZ and RENE (roy natus). Her name OSBEORHT :
glory, brightness, of the Ases (for her beauty). One name,
and that monosyllabic, or, at most, of two syllables, was the
rule for the poor and slaves in Greece, Rome, England, and
America. To marry a one-named man then would forfeit
aristocratic position. Demosthenes, in his imperishable
oration, "The Crown" accuses Æschines of violating that law.
" He is not such a man as you may meet every day, but one of
those execrable to the people. For lately—lately, did I say ?
—ay, yesterday, and no longer ago, he became at once a citizen
and orator, and adding two syllables to his father's name, he
changed it from Tromes to Atrometus." In giving the word
of command a long name is harder to be uttered than one that
is short. Hence Oppian advises that dogs have short names,—

> " Lest at the huntsman's call they trace in vain,
> And run with open cry confus'dly o'er the plain."

In Sweden the poor still have but one name, and that a short
one. Second names are useful in fixing a first. Before the
Reformation men changed names as expeditiously as jail birds
yet do. Then persons were often baptized in one name,
married in a second, and buried with a third, as then a
Registrar-General and a Postman were unthought of. So
lately as 1760 the Poles passed from one name to another at
a bound. Priests named an entire estate of serfs Peter, and
another, under a different noble, John. Their surname alone
prevented confusion. To return to *fitz* or *filius*. This became
fitt in certain families, as PARFITT: good son. Sometimes
filius assumes the form *iff* as DRUIFF = DRUGAN : son of Drew.

VAN, VON.

Corresponding more or less closely with *de, ac,* is the Dutch
van, usually applied with the force *of the,* as VANDERSTEEN :
of the stone, hill = FOLLI, FELL, KNOX. VAN OSTERZEE
(divine): of the eastern sea, living on the Baltic shore. Baltic:
belted, land locked = Mediterranean, which does not mean
in the *middle of the earth.* So Zuyder Zee : south sea,
Zealand : sea land, island. South from Seethe : to boil, to be

hot = HAM : a temanite, southron, man of hot climate. VAN-
DELEUR : of the Eure valley, a Norman name. VANDERVELDE
(painter) : of the field = VANLOO. VAN METER (Rome) : living
on hired land, carefully measured, paying a feu, the *op.* of
TENNANT and HODDER (and Stoughton) : holding allo*d*ial
land = FRANKLIN : free from feus. VANDEVEER : of the ferry
= OVEREND = OVERTON : town where people pass over : Over-
newtown: the new town at the ferry. Partick : a portage,a ferry.
VAN BUREN : of the cottages, boors' houses. Sometimes Van
slips into position as a veritable patronymic as VAN HAHN =
JOHNSON. It passes into *von* with an emphatic force, as VON-
ROBERT : the Robert, becomes CANROBERT (Crimea). VON DER
TANN (general) : of the pines = DU PIN and *con.* TANGYE : pine
wood. VON REAUMER : of the sea, a shoresman = CONNAL.
A living leading politician in Belgium is VANDENPEEREBOOM:
of the pear tree.

THE WELSH PATRONYMIC

is a form of the Celtic *mac*, which the Cambrian people made
mab or *map*, and shortening it to a letter *b*, *p*, or its cognate
f, gave it work to do as a patronymical prefix, thus :
 PROBART : son of Robert. PROBYN, PROVAN : of Robin.
BLAKE (mighty) : Lake.
 BARRY, PARRY (captain) : Harry. BEVAN : of Evan : John,
varies to
 BIFFIN (Miss), BAFFIN ('s Bay). BOWEN : Owen. BOYD
(when not Gaelic) : Lloyd.
 BETHEL (attorney-general) : of Ithell, an ancient Welsh
name. BEWS, PUGH, PUE, PYE : of Hugh.
 PRICE : Rheese, or RICE : king (rex), ruler, so that it =
MACHREE and CRESSIDAS.
 PRIDDLE : Riddle. PRITCHARD : Richard, POWELL, BOWELL,
BOWELLS : Howell = MACHALE. In old English Powell is a
form of Paul. So Chaucer speaks of the words, " Of Christ,
John and *Powell*."
 PROGERS : Rogers. PRIGG : Rigg = KNOWLES, KNOLLS,
KNOLYS, HILLS. PROWSE (Jeffray) : Rouse.
 FLUELLEN : Lewellyn : " Captain *Fluellen*, you must come
presently to the mines : the Duke of Gloster would speak
with you."
 FOWELL (Buxton) : Howell. FLACK, BLACK : Lake = BLAKE.
When, however,
 BLACK is not Welsh it means dark = NIGER, HAM. FEW
(when not local) : son of Hugh. The Welsh are ridiculed for
their much use of *ap* for *mab* in pedigrees. Beaufoy says,
cheese is " Adam's own cousin-german by its birth, ap Curds,

ap Milk, ap Cow, ap Grass, ap Earth." From the ancient
family of EYNION : just = SADOC, we have

ONION, whence the immortal dreamer BUNYAN : Mab Onion.
At one period of English history it seemed probable that *mab*
would become as common throughout Britain as *mac* in the
Highlands, in the form of *hop*, for *ap*, for *mab* ; thus

HOP PRINGLE : son of the pilgrim. HOP CORNELL ; son of
Cornwall. The popular vote put the veto on *hop* as a patronymical sign soon after the Reformation, but left us

APPS, UPP, HOPPS : beloved son, only son = MACCUS (from
whom Maxwell, the spring of St. Maccus), MACK (general).
IDAS, IFF, FAUNT, EGAN, GOSS, KIDD, KYD, INGO (whence
INGLE), ZOON, ENFANT, MAPPS (Oxonian professor), and
MAPPIN (of razor fame) : all son *par excellence.* Sometimes
loved one is used in the sense of son, as

WICKLIFFE (wig : war, Liffe : life, loved one) : son of war, a
warrior = CADOGAN. After analysis of the Cambrian ancestral
sign we reach the

MILESIAN PATRONYMIC.

> " By Mac and O you'll surely know
> True Irishmen, they say :
> But, if they lack both " O " and " Mac,"
> No Irishmen are they."

A free rendering this of

> " Per O, atque Mac, veras cognoscis Hibernos ;
> His duobus demptis, nullus Hibernus adest."

Favour, reader, by being sceptical hereabout as more than
half the orthodox Irish names have neither Mac nor O. The
Highlanders, Irish, and Welsh hold mac in common, but, as
we have seen, the Cambro Britons delight to have it in the
forms *mab, map, ap, hop, b, p, f.* In Irish names *mac* tends
towards *mag, ma,* and *c.* Howbeit, Hibernia did not take to
mac as lovingly as did Caledonia. The Milesians found a
greater charm in Eoghan : a son, forming *ua,* and that used as
O in the sense of eldest son, for he only was allowed to use it.
The Irish developed a patronymic out of their Erse treasury
more elastic and poetic than the Gaelic *mac.* The Celtic for
young, offspring son, is, as above given, *eoghan,* whence

EGAN (Pierce) for Hugh, eoghan : son of Hugh = BEWS, PYE,
PUGH, FEW, EWING, HUESSEN, HEWSON. This *eoghan,* abbreviated to *a,* is then used as a patronymical affix, thus, Ach :
a horse, Achaia : horse producing country = Parthia.

ECHEGAN : son of a horse = HORSMAN, PHILIP, answering
closely to HIPPIAS. By prefixing *mac* changed to *mag,* to the
foregiven we have

MAGEOGHEGAN (historian) : son of ECHEGAN. CONGAN : son of a dog, great fighter.

DONEGAN, DUGGAN : son of DUNN : brown haired = MAC-DONALD.

FLANEGAN : son of FLAN : ruddy, whence LYNN (when not local from Lin : a lake),

FLANEGAN = MACKLIN. FINIGAN (M.P.) : fair young man, *con.* FINGAL ('s cave).

HARRIGAN : Harry = BARRY, PARRY. MULLIGAN : son of the miller.

GILLIGAN : Gill = MACGILL, GILSON. COSTIGAN : COSTA (leader) : KOSTER : doorkeeper.

TALLIGAN : little hill, is the exact Hibernian equivalent for TULLOCH. Sometimes *og* only was used in name-making, as HICKOG : doctor's son, becomes HICKHOCK, suggesting when we said,—

> " Hic, hœc, hoc : lay him on the block,
> Dives : riches : pull down his breeches,
> Qui, que, quod : lay on the rod."

CRANNAGE (N.Y. Dr.) : son of Crann : a tree = WOODHOUSE, BAMBER (beam burg), living in a log hut, resident on an artificial island of wood, a lake dweller. These names are more than 3000 years old, antedating Irish history. Sometimes the last part of *eoghan, an,* was used patronymically or as a diminutive, as

CASHAN : little Cash, or son of Cash. Cash is a directory name, *uncon.* money.

ADAMNAN (St.) : little Adam. CROSSAN, CROSSON : a small cross. In theology the cross removes the curse, but, sad to say, in philology, it is its root. From *cross* we derive the Saxon verb Corsian : to curse by reversal of cross, hence Curse : to imprecate.

COBHAN : little Jacob. GRANAHAN : little Graine. Now GRAINE (*con.* the sun) : light, joy, loved one = HAUSSCHEIN, gives GREENE, to be distinguished from GREEN : living on a = FIELDS and DUPREE.

OSSIAN : a little deer, a fawn, graceful as Apollo Belvidere.

CUNNIAN : son of a dog, a bold warrior = CANNING, CHANNING, which consult.

CLANAHAN : formed from Lean by *mac* before, and *eoghan* behind = MACLEAN, LENNIE.

GALLYON : son of the Gall, stranger. Englishmen were so called by the Irish seven centuries since. This *an* frequently changes to *on, oon,* but more usually to *een,* in which forms it supplies a good *dim.* to our language.

> " Kathleen, mavourneen, the grey dawn is breaking."

AVOURNEEN : little dear, darling. MAVOURNEEN : my darling =

CARRACHIOLI: little cherished one = JESHURUN. *M, ma, mo,* signify *my* in half a dozen languages.

CARRIGAN, carigheen (moss) : little rock, *con.* Carrick, crag, SHONEEN : little Shane, rude boy =

GOSSOON (*garcon*): little Goss, *con.* COSPATRICK : son or servant of Patrick. SQUIREEN = SQUEERS : little squire.

RUSKIN (art critic): little wood, from Ross : a wood, giving ROSSA (DONOVAN) = WOODS, QUIDDY is

KILLEEN : little wood, formed on COYLE : a wood. Our college for ladies,

GURTON (GAMMER: grandmother) is Celtic, being GORTEEN : little meadow =

CLUNY (MacPherson), *con.* Clontarf : bull meadow = HUXLEY: OXLEY = Butt Green = Geshur, from gor, ghor, ghau, and Shur : an ox. In such favour is *een* with Milesians that they intermingle it with English names, marrying their words, as they do their girls, to the hated Saxon. Hence

Smithereens : smitten to small pieces.

Potcheen: pot stilled whiskey. Shebeen: small wayside inn.

Camptine : little camp becomes Cantine = CAMPALETTO.

Velveteen: small quantity of velvet. GOMBEEN: small money lender. Poreen : small path. Ballyporeen : road.

Buttereen, etc. Besides *eoghan*, they used *mac, gos, cos,* and *gil,* so that Irishman have no grievance as to lack of patronymics. A Fenian would say : "Small thanks to the Crown for that. And sure we got them from our own tongue." Here it seems proper to trace a name through some of its multitudinous ramifications, a word originative with the Celts, but used half over Christendom. Aodh, the Celtic for fire, *con.* the Persian Arta: high, the sacrificial flame, and Ara, (an altar) : that which flames,

HUGH : ardent, fiery, easily incensed, ready for battle, whence HUGHES,

HUGGINS, MOGUE: my Hugh = HUGHIE. GUZZI is its Italian *dim.* Hugh becomes KAY, which, in non Celtic names, is a form of

CAIUS for Gaius (Kay Shuttleworth), M'KAY, EUING, EWING.

HEWITT: little Hugh = WHEWELL (Trin. Coll., Cam.). Found without aspirate we have the less known

EWELL. HOUSTON : Hugh's town. Hugh varies to HUTCHAN (eoghan) : son of Hugh = Thus we get

HUTCHESON, HUTCHINGS, HUTCHEON. Philologically, HOUSton = Hutchesontown.

MACKAY, MACKIE, EGAN, EUING, EWING, PUGH, BEWS, FEW, PYE, are some few of its varied forms, as are

MACGEE (MacHugh), GEE, MAHEW (London poor), HEWSON, HUTCHAN; and the well known Glasgow names

HUTCHESON, AITCHISON: sons of Hugh, and, crowning all, the double patronymic M‘HUTCHESON.

GUINNESS (Dublin) stands for M‘Geeinnis: M‘Gee's island, a native of.

(M‘) EVOY is compounded of Hugh and Boyd: fair-haired Hugh. This supplies high proof of the great antiquity of the name. Moreover, half his offspring is not here presented. By the study of Hugh our mind is carried back to, at least, when Samuel slew Agag.

THE GALLIC PATRONMYIC

is *mac:* a son, used as a prefix, *nick:* a daughter, now obsolete, and *O* from *eoghan*, for a first, born son. *Mac, mab, mag* (for they are one) is *con.*, MAGGOT: breeder, meaning one who is bred of another, a son, offspring. It is an actual name. MAB (queen) is dream breeder. Probably to this source is to be traced Midge: (insect) breeder. The Gaels also had a patronymical affix derived from *eoghan*, viz., *ach, och*, the source of our *ock*, as seen in Hillock: little hill = *Felloch*. All *dims.* were first *pats.* This corresponds to the Hebrew *i*, for *im*, as Moabim: one of the people of Moab, the Greek *idas*, the English *ite* and the Irish *egan*. Thus MURROCH: a Maryite, devotee to the B. V. M. = MURISON when not a form of MORISON, nor of MUIR. TOSH: a leader = HANLON, gives TOSHACH: son of Tosh = MACINTOSH: son of the leader. WALL: a pilgrim, gives WALLACH = HOP PRINGLE; son of the pilgrim SKEACH: son of Sky. STOACH: of Story. CATTANACH (*con.*, Cath: war): son of a warrior, then a marauder.

FINACH: son of the fair man = the Irish FINNIGAN. DARROCH: son of Drew, or of an oak, robust.

GREIG: rough, uncouth, GREGALACH (L formative) M‘GREGOR: a Gregorite, where *ach* = *ite* and *mac*,—

> "The moon's on the lake, and the mist's on the brae,
> And the clan has a name that is nameless by day;
> Our signal for fight, which from monarchs we drew,
> Must be heard but my night in our vengeful halloo—
> Then halloo, halloo, halloo, Gregalach!
> If they rob us of name, and pursue us with beagles,
> Give their roofs to the flames and their flesh to the eagles,
> Then gather, gather, gather!
> While there's leaves in the forest, and foam on the river,
> Macgregor, despite them, shall flourish for ever."

DOMHNUALLOCH: a MacDonaldite, or if Lowland, a Mac-Whannellite.

ALBANACH: a Highlander, son of the mountain = MACALPINE: 19

son of ALBYN, *con.* Albion. The McAlpines are almost as aboriginal as heather; hence the proverb: "Evils and hills and the McAlpines." They pair well with LAMONT: a hillsman, highlander, or castle man.

EIRINEACH: a son of Erin, an Erinite = the soft sounding ERIGENA: Irish born. From that ancient root Caw: to turn, to curve, we have Curvus: crooked, Cavus: hollow, Cavan = Holland: hollow land = LOGAN and HOLE: From Caw we have Corve: a basket (hollowed), Cawb.

CAW: a chariot (whose wheels caw), a charioteer = McARÁ. Hence, too,

CORMAC: son of a chariot, swift as the scythed war chariot = ANTIOCHUS giving Antioch. In this and similar names *anti* is used with the force *instead of*, as ANTIPAS ("my martyr"), ANTIPATER: in his father's place, nearly answering to BARABBAS, PATROBAS, ICILIUS.

OCHUS (Darius): moving like a chariot. The double patronymic

McCORMACK arose when the meaning of CORMAC began to be lost sight of.

CAWLIFFE: son of a chariot, identical with CORMAC, sometimes son of Caw, his life, his love.

TOSHACH = to an inversion of McTOSH, TOSH: first, leader. MACINTOSH: son of the leader. In few national names are political and social changes more deeply engraven than in those of the Celts. Some proscribed clansman disguised Gaelic origin by letting fall their characteristic *mac*, doffed their kilt, and gave the body of their name a lowland twist. Such happened when certain of the McGregor's left their country for their country's good, over the Colquhoun business, and found an asylum in Ireland. Once there they became

GRIERS, GREERS, GRIGGS, or took the name of their native place, as

BRIMER, from the braes of Mar. So the Græmes or Grahams made for Wales, and there gave name GROOMSPORT: harbour of Graham.

GRIMES is a Cambrianised form of Graham, which name hunters tangle with those from the Asir Grimr. The McKinnon's emigrated from the Isle of Skye to that of Saints, becoming

McCANNON, or naked CANNON, under which designation their descendants are there found.

M'KINNON is formed upon Finn on a famous saint. FINNON (*on* for *an* from eoghan): son of the fair, a blonde = BAIN, FINGAL, BLAKE when that means bleached.

McNAB: son of the abbot, was absorbed into the unrecognisable names

MᶜNEICE, NENEES, MUNNIS, MONIES. Many a cognomen has been disguised through servility as MALLOCH to MALLET. Others have been barbarised through the Sassanach being ignorant of Gaelic, and so transcribing by ear the copy bearing so faint a resemblance to its original that there was little enough to swear by, as

MᶜEACHRAN into COCHRANE, MᶜDOUGALL, MᶜDOWELL into DOLE, MʻARTHUR, into ARTER.

Yet the Celt has no more to grumble about than the Sassenach and the German, when OESTMAN, STERLING: man from the east = KEDEMAH, CADMUS is distorted into OYSTERMAN and OSTRICH, which is actually the case.

MACALLISTER into CALLISTER, while the Irishman MACODY collapses to CODY.

MACEOCHALL: son of a horseman = DE RUYTER, shrunk into KEOGH. So that COCHRANE precisely = KEOGH. Then we have

MACHREE (widow): king's son, into CREE. MACWADE becomes QUAID (Mick Mac). In such cases *mac* shrivels to a letter *m*, *c*, or *k*. Thus

MᶜCROBIE: son of Robert, where *c* belongs to *mac*. So ANDERS: Andrew's son, becomes

MANDERS (menagerie) as KENDRICK; from Hendry, for Henry, becomes MᶜKENDRICK = HENDERSON.

MᶜKINLAY forms on Finlay. Now FINLAY: fair hair = HARFAGER (Harold), so that

FINLAYSON exactly corresponds to MʻKINLAY. The popular names

MᶜOMISH, MᶜTAVISH, MᶜTAUSE, MᶜCOMB (giving MᶜCUMBER) are contortions of the Biblical Thomas, and so =

THOMSON, THOMPSON, COMBKIN. RAE: prosperous = LUCKIE, GLUCK, FELIX, LONG (when Chinese).

BONHEUR (Rosa): good hour, born when some such star as Jupiter was rising, gives

RAITH, MʻILRAITH (*il* for *gil*, but mere phonetic padding), and MACRAE, which becomes

MᶜCRAW (Jock), thought to be origin of the Irish MᶜGRATH.

CALLUM, for COLUMBA: a dove, gives (Mc)CALLAM, CALMON, COLMAN (O'Lochlin).

MACCALLUMMORE: the great Macallum (Argyll). Some Celts make

CULLOCH: folder of cattle = STODDART, COWARD, others have it boar slayer, gives

MACCULLOCH: son of. MᶜHARG: red (headed) son = ROY, and *con.* Dearg Lough.

MᶜILROY, looks as though Roy's servant, but *il* is added to prevent its becoming MᶜROY, which colloquially glides into CROY. So that

McILROY : son of Roy = ROGAN, REGAN (Roy eoghan). When Norman,

ROY : a king = CONIG, whence CONIGSBY : king's dwelling = CUNNINGHAM. The late author of the novel Coningsby, wrote LOTHAIR, *con.* LUTHER, as it was to do anti-papal work.

ROY takes the forms REE, RAE, but RAESIDE : living at rath side. We are pretty safe in allocating names in ROY as red headed.

ROE is the form it came out in among the Irish, as O'CONNOR ROE : eldest son of red headed Connor.

ROWE is its English form, which tangles with those from Rue : a street.

> " King James the First, Roy of this Regioun,
> Said David was ane sair sanct to the crown."

The change of a letter or two gives a new look to a name, as

DROOD (Edwin), for Druid = DREW. So we have ADJAI for HADJI : a pilgrim, as "The Right Rev. Samuel *Adjai* Crowther, the black bishop."

So SMALLBACK (beck) = BURNET : little brook. MIRA becomes MYRA ; GAUNT (ge want, waned) : thus, CAUNT ; MOLLER is but MILLER, and EGEN is EGAN : son of Hugh. So corresponding words puzzle from other countries, as the German KLEIN = SHORT ; ZIEGLER = TYLER ; ZAHN = TOOTH.

MADGE (Wildfire), MATTY (meddlesome), formed on Margaret. So again,

YEDDIE and PEDDIE upon NEDDIE for Edward. VOKES, upon FFOULKS : for folks : vulgus, demos = DEMAS : a demotic person, vulgarite. Such names, coming of artifice rather than spontaniety, suggest

CALIBAN (Shakespeare), a formation upon *Cannibal :* a Carib (bean sea). This reading names backward after the anagram style, which is somewhat Hebraic, supplies many a *nom de plume :* pen name, disguising an author's true designation. Thus the father of Voltaire was AROUET, a *dim.* of Aroux, formed from ARNULF (heerulph wulph) : army wolf, *i.e.,* slashing fighter. Of course Voltaire was Arouet junior, in French *Arouet le jeune,* and as *u* and *v* were interchangable, as were *i* and *j,* the great deist anagrammatised it into VOLTAIRE. Some give that as a form of Walter.

MACNAIR : son of heir (of estate) becomes MACAIRE. English equivalents are

EYRE, AYRE. But the well known

HAIR is a form of (O') Hara. BANE, BAIN : white, fair, gives VANE (O Sir Harry), and SULLIVAN : fair eyed, blue eyed. We should not say

MACVAIN : son of the white (man), as that held good only once, *i.e.,* when borne by its first wearer, but should say

MacVain: son of Vain. Bane⸗White, though in some cases White for Wight: a strong man, but in sense here given it supplies

Whiting for Whitting, (as): sons of White, then Whittington (Dick): town of, etc. Dhu: dark, as Roderick Dhu: Roderick the swarthy, gives

Duff (Dr.), Duffy, which, bisected, give Fie, MacPhee, Macfie,

MacDuff = the Muscovite name, Karakoff: son of dark (man), *con.*, Caracal: black eared (wild beast). Karadagh the Russian, *confor.*, Montenegro.

Karatheodory: swarthy Theodore. From Darn: dark. Tarn: dark waters (by reason of depth). Tarnish: to darken.

Darncombe: dark valley = Valesneri: shaded by trees and hills.

Darnley: dark visaged. Duffy gives, by Milesian variation, M'Haffie, M'Guffie, and, oddly enough, Cuffe, changing to Coffee (king).

> " Sinful *Macduff*,
> They were all struck down for thee! naught that I am,
> Not for their own demerits, but for mine
> Fell slaughter on their souls! Heaven rest them now."

(M') Gowan, (M') Gavin: a smith. Govan: smith's town. Gavigan: young smith = *Gowanlock* = Macgowan, which *cor.* to *M'Goun.*

MacShimmes, M'Immey, M'Kim = Simson, Simpson. John gives

MacInnes (when local, from Innis: an island = Lisles), MacOwen,

MacShane, MacGeoch, MacKean (when not from Kean: head) = Johnson.

MacFadyan: son of tall John, which becomes Fadden. Some authorities give

MacInnes as a form of Angus. The Highland nomenclature supplies few trade names. Of those few the most prominent are (M') Intyre: the carpenter, shades off to (M') Tear (diamonds), which bereft of *mac* stands bare Teer, (M') Growther: brewer (to king) = Brewster. The Celts had neither public brewer nor baker, as the Saxons had. Their nearest approach was (M') Dade: kneader = Baxter.

(M') Naughtan (Pictish king): a bull, strong as, perhaps *con.* worship of Thor. Naughtan abbreviates to Neat: a bullock, as " Neat's foot oil." Hence

Natman: neat herd = Culloch, and Notman when Not is not from Noth: bold, audacious, then Notman: brave, man of audacity. By an intolerable Gaelic twist M'Naughtan becomes

M‘CRACKEN, whom he resembles as young Adam would an aged clansman.

M‘NAUGHT, which any poor Saxon might be pardoned for thinking it to be a form of

M‘NAUGHTAN, is a modification of M‘KNIGHT=RITSON. Such Gaelic eccentricities are paralleled by M‘DOUGALL, forming

M‘DOWALL, DOLE, M‘HOUL, and M‘OWL. Variation of this type are due to Gaels living in non Celtic localities, where the unskilled natives fell upon Highlanders by lip and pen till they hardly knew their own address.

M‘GUIRE disfigures in some families into M‘QUARRY, and that goes into WHARRY.

MACFARLANE is from PARLANE, for Bartholomew. (M‘) TOSH = ALPHŒUS.

(Mc)INTOSH : the first (of his clan). Fin : fair, gives FINNACH, FINIGAN, FINGAL,

(Mc)PHIN, (Mc)PHUN : who were what ladies call blondes, and fortune tellers, hearts.

FINELLA : fair Irish lady = Welsh Venus, NEL GWYN : Ellen White.

(Mc)KELLAR may easily be taken as akin to KELLARMAN : cellar man, a butler, but is formed on *cell, kil,* as KILPATRICK : Patrick's cell or church, so KELLAR : superior of monastery = FOREMAN, PRYOR.

KELLOCH : son of the cell, hermit, forms McKILLOCH, *uncon.* McKILLOP : son of Philip.

LEWIS (when local), from island, literally meaning land of lakes, shades into McLISE (David) and LEECE. Worthy members of the *sans culotte* nationality, when reading the Book of Maccabees, viz., "For Ptolemeus, that was called Macron, choosing rather to do justice unto the Jews for the wrong he had done unto them, endeavoured to continue peace with them," straightway pushed their *macs* almost into the Bible, in the belief that Maccabees, Macron, were members of the *mac* sodality. Such is not quite the case.

PTOLEMEUS MACRON : Ptolemy the tall, similar to Edward LONGSHANKS, suggesting

SHEEPSHANKS (picture collector): thin legged, quick footed, the *op.* of FULJAMBE, TARDIEU. Macron is met with as a Christian name in the form of

MACRO, but shines best in ALMAGRO (conquistador): the thin, spare = LONGMAN (bookseller), LONGFELLOW.

PIZARRO (his fellow soldier)=SLATER, SCLATER, LATTA, HULYER.

MACKISSACK : son of Isaac. Certain Highlanders affirm Hebrew is misspelled Gaelic.

MACGAULEY is the Irish form of MACAULAY (Babington) :

son of Aulay, varies to McGARLIE. The original Aulay was the Earl of Lennox's son, who flourished in the 14th century.

CAHILL, CADDLE, CATTLE, CATHAL : battle eye, gives McGAUL or MacALL, which latter transmutes into ALMACK(S) of terpsichorian fame.

From Lind : a lime tree (sometimes a snake), LINDSAY : lime tree island, gallicised into

McLINTOCK (Arctic voyager). Some conception may be formed of variations by misspelling from the fact that

MAINWARING : a strong built manor house, is spelled in 130 different ways.

(Mc)MURROCH (Hibernian): sea commander, becomes (Mc)MORRAN, MORROW.

McQUILLAN = WILSON, is from Will of Asiric celebrity, but (Mc)QUILKIN is a form of Wilkins, and so = MACQUILKIN = WILKINSON. Highlanders having no *w* are in the fix fastened on Italians by the Cockneys. "They can't spell *waggon.*" Whenever Celtic names begin with *w* we know they are Saxon corruptions, as

McWEE, a form of McVey, a case deserving the attention of Captain McAll. The same observation applies to McQUADE, formed on MacWade.

McQUAKER is not a friend once in drab who has taken to kilts, but a form of McVICAR = McPHERSON.

MACLARTY (Mrs), MACLAREN (Edinburgh) are from Laurence, and = LARKINS.

MACKENZIE, MACKINNEY, MACMINN are from Kenneth (Pictish king).

MACLYMONT is a form of the almost indigenous LAMONT : the mountaineer = (Mc)BEAN, (Mc)VEAN (from Ben). Lamont is credited with giving name Lomond to Loch and Ben.

(Mc)LERIE is the Milesian synonym for Clerk. The same nation stands accused of distorting good looking Duncan into the unrecognisable

(Mc)CONNACHIE, so that MacConnachie = DUNCANSON. If possible, the Irish did worse—actually made McLeod into MACELLIGOT. But their conviction did not tarry. A learned Highlander brought it pat home to Pat.

(Mc)INALLY is also Hibernian, meaning a teacher, a doctor of learning. Each or Ach : a horse, gives the widely spread

(Mc)EACHRAIN : a horseman, whence McKECHNIE, the *k* of which is the *c* of *mac*. Probably we find the root of Auriga : a charioteer, in

(Mc)ARA : a footman, charioteer = COR, thoroughly British of an age when the *essede* (war chariot) was used in battle on this island, ARA and COR would leap off, fight, jump on again, retire. From (Mc)ARA, HAIR, and (O')HARA we get also

McKERROW. Though the next three names be not *macs*, they are too thoroughly Albanach to be torn from their confreres.

LOCHIEL (head of Camerons): bird lake, living near a loch frequented by migratory birds =

CRANMER: mere frequented by cranes, *con.* CRANSTON: crane's town.

LOCHABER, LOCHINVAR: living at confluence of lochs, loch mouth, *con.* KINLOCH,—

> "There was mounting 'mong Græmes of the Netherby clan,
> Forsters, Fenwicks, and Musgraves, they rode and they ran ;
> There was racing and chasing on Canobie Lea,
> But the lost bride of Netherby ne'er did they see.
> So daring in love, and so dauntless in war,
> Have ye e'er heard of gallant like young *Lochinvar ?* "

KINLOCH: head of lake, as KENMUIR: head of moor. But BALLOCH: a gap, pass = Hindoo Ghaut, and Hebrew Abar (im), and the English SLAPP.

GLENGARRY: rough glen, *con.* GARRIOCH: rough district = BADENOCH.

FENWICK: dwelling place on a moor, fen = MORTON, when that does not mean great town = Granton.

PANMURE (pen): hill on a moor, *con.* PENGELLY, and = DUNMURE.

> "I saw our chief come o'er the hill
> Wi' Drummond and *Glengarry,*
> And through the pass came brave *Lochiel,*
> *Panmure,* and gallant Murray.
> Macdonald's men, Clanronald's men,
> Mackenzie's men, Macgilvray's men,
> O' Callendar, and Airley."

Ben: a hill, mountain (Mc)BEAN: a hillsman, gives (Mc)VEAN, (Mc)VÉY.

Pen : a hill, PENDER: oak hills, PINKERTON (caer): fortified town on a hill.

(Mc)SWEEN is formed on Sweyn (Danish king), the McSWEENS claim high northern descent.

(Mc)GIBBON is Sassenach in "the garb of old Gaul." We have seen

GILBERT : pledged to fight in an ordeal, giving GIBBS, GIBB, GIBBON : great Gilbert, in the garb of old Gaul it stands

MACGIBBON = GIBSON (Milner). We have also shown that GEOCH is Jock, so then

MACGEACHY = JACKSON. Nine Englishmen out of ten would say

McOUAT as a form of McWAT: son of Walter, WATTY = WATSON, but that would be McQUAT. McOUAT is formed on

McHowit, and Howit is = Tulloch : a little hill, probably *con.* the Biblical Tell : a hill, as Tell-abib : hill of corn = Cornhill. Tel-el-Kebir : strong hill = Montfort. "Then I came to them of the captivity at *Tell-Abib,* that dwelt by the river Chebar."

Howe (John), from which McOuat is formed : a hill = Fell, whence Felton, when not from field =

Hilton = Craig : man living on a crag. Howe also = Knowe, whence

Knolls, Knollys, Knowles, Knox, and Knee. From the man Howe we have the patronymical diminutive Howie, like Dix, Dixie. "I wish I was in Dixie" = Dixon, Dickson,—

> " Gae bring my gude auld harp ance mair,
> Gae bring it free and fast ;
> For I maun sing anither sang,
> Ere a' my glee be past,
> And trow ye as I sing, my lads.
> The burden o't shall be,
> Auld Scotland's *howes*, and Scotland's *knowes*,
> And Scotland's hills for me !
> I'll drink a cup to Scotland yet,
> Wi' a' the honours three."

Adam takes the *dim.* Ennan (Adam eoghan) : little Adam, giving

(Mc)Lennan (L phonetic), *cor.* to (Mc)Lennand, which becomes Cleland (Burns).

(Mc)Grory is formed on (Mc)Rory, from Roderic. In like manner

(Mc)Farland (N.Y. fame) is a form of McFarlane of Parlan, of Paul.

Zetland is by some given as a form of Shetland, by others from Yet for Gate, and so land enclosed and entered only by a gate, and yet others demand its being *con.* Zee for Sea, as Zealand : sea land = Attica, Pontus, Pomerania : foreshore countries.

Torquil, Tormaid (famous Scottish names) are formations on our esteemed friend Thor. Tormaid is the Gaelic equivalent for

Norman : north man, whence Norval, Normandy, Norway : way to the north.

Torquil gives the Highland (Mc)Corckle, whence (Mc)Corkindale. We have seen that the Gaels compared with the Germans have few trade names of those.

(Mc)Creach : a ploughman = Plews.

An account of the awful results forth-flowing from Highlanders doffing their kilts comes from the United States, to which one McLean had emigrated. By some unpatriotic freak he dropped his lawful Mac, and put in his appearance on the pages of the "Boston Directory" as bare Lean. His punishment soon overtook him. A bookwright giving an account of proper names exhibited him as LEAN, the opposite of fat.

THE SPANISH AND PORTUGUESE PATRONYMIC

is formed by *az* or *ez* affixed. The two are variations of the tail of Filius : a son, as

ALVAREZ : son of ALVA : pale, from ALBIS : white, answering to VANE for BAIN.

DIAZ (Bartholomew) : of DIEGO, for JAGO, from James, and so = FITZJAMES.

PEREZ (as in Perez de la Rua, who gave name to Peru) : Peter = PEARSON.

ENRIQUEZ : of Henry = HENDRICKS, from HENDRY, for Henry.

GOMEZ (Carlist general) : of JOAM, for John = GAMGEE, GANGE, *con.* GAMBETTA, JANTJEE, which consult.

JUAREZ (Mexican) : JUAN, for John = our JOHNSON.

LOPEZ (Paraguayan dictator) : LOBOS = WOLF, so that LOPEZ = LUPSON. The commonest of all names amongst the Spanish speaking race are LOPEZ and DIAZ, like our SMITH and JONES.

MENDEZ : Clement, which through Spanish love of the sonorous *o* becomes MENDOZA,—

> "And how he had storm'd, and treated her ill,
> Because she refused to go down to a mill,
> She didn't know where, but remember'd still,
> That the miller's name was *Mendoza*."

MELENDEZ, however, means of the Æmilian *gens.*, Roman descent.

LAINEZ (Jesuit general) : of LANE : last born.

BARTHEZ ("History of Savans") : Bartholomew = MACFARLANE.

NARVAEZ (premier) : of NERVIUS, which is also a *pat.* meaning *son of Nerva.* Italian and Spanish families affect derivation from Romans.

VASQUEZ : Gascon, Basque, whence Gasconade : a boast.

· VELASQUEZ (painter) : Velasco. DOMINIQUEZ : Dominic, "Desperdicios, or *Dominiguez*, the famous torreador, lies dying, having been frightfully wounded by a bull in the ring of Puerto de Santa Maria, in the presence of ten thousand spectators."

DESPERDICIOS : desperate (fellow) : a Madrid nickname, of which PERDITA may be termed a *fem.*

VALDEZ : son of Valens, who gave name to Valentia. The *d* formative.

RUIZ : of Ru, from Roderigo for Roderick.

COBEZ : Jacob = our JACOBS, when *s* is patronymical = BEN YACOUB. In South America names in *az* or *ez* change to *iz*. Though many names ending in *az, ez,* or *iz* are *pats.*, yet some so ending are the mere outcome of Spanish fondness for *z*, whereby words ending in *s* or *x* blend into *z* or *ez* without patronymical force. Thus

JUEZ : for Judex : a judge = DEMPSTER, DAY : and the lady name

INEZ for Agnes ; as also Luz for Lux : light. So CORTEZ (discovered California) for Cortes, our

COURT : a courtier, well bred = CURTIS : courteous, TOWNLY : town like.

HOFFMAN : court man. Hoff is identical with Haff, Have, Haven = Hithe, Hyde : where ships hide from storm. Havre de Grace : harbour of grace. Frischhaff : fresh water haven. Hoff: a temple, court, farm, harbour : these all have one underlying sense, protection. Hoff gives

HOVEY : a farmer, HOFRICHTER : court judge, a judicial title. The Spanish patronymical sign was got by the Spaniards from the Goths, previously to whose arrival they used HIJO, from Filius : a son, a name to be numbered by thousands, and may be formulated as = HOPPS, INGO. Hence we derive the grand title and well known name

HIDALGO (filius de al Goth) : son of the Goth. Filius gave *hijo* and *ez* to the Peninsula, *fitz* to Normandy, *vitch* to Russia, *fi* to Hungary, *figli* and *li* to Italy, but nothing of that nature to England. LOPEZ being like our Smith, Jones, Robinson, one of that name termed himself.

LE LUBEZ : the LOPEZ, as the Irish have The O'Donaghue.

SUARIUS : a swine herd, gives SUAREZ (Jesuit author).

THE ITALIAN PATRONYMIC

was sometimes formed by placing the name of a son before that of a his father, as

GALILEO GALILEI : Galileo, the son of Galilei : a crusading name.

GALILEO, *con.* Galilee, one distinguishing himself there = our well known

CROSSKEY : who in the crusades carried the Papal standard, Peter's two keys.

SPERON SPERONI : Speron, the son of Speroni. SPERON : hopeful, *con.* Nil desperandum.

MASATONIO : Thomas, the son of Antony.

GIANCARLO : John, son of Charles. This mode of expressing filial relationship was adopted from the Greeks, who have a class of names similarly formed, as

DION CASSIUS : Dion, son of Cassius. It is used in Muscovy, as
PAULINA PETROWNA : Pauline, daughter of Peter. And also
PAUL-PETROWICH : Paul, son of Peter. This is a more exact
expression, sonship, than ours, and so may be termed the
definite patronymic. Contrast it with

WILSON : son of Will, which ? If we said TAM WILL :
Thomas, son of William, we should be more exact. Now, this
is done in the Yorkshire dales.

GIANFIGLIAZZI : John, the son of AZI. Then AZI : strong,
con. Ases. The French also form patronymics after this
pattern.

BASSOMPIERRE (marshal) : Bassom, the son of Peter. And
the original

BASSOM : short, *con.* Base : the foundation, BASSI (Ugo), and
our

BISSET : a dwarf = CURCI : curt = BASS (ale), SHORT, PETTET,
KLEIN. Consult

BASVECCHI, capable of meaning little old man = SEACHLAN.

VECCHI : old = AULD, is in common use all through Italy.
But our

VEITCH is from De Vesci (vetus civitas) : of the old town =
OLDHAM.

ROBESPIERRE : Robert, son of Peter. Italians often use *di*
for *de*, as

ANDREUCCIO DI PIETRO : Andreuccio, the son of Peter.
Andreuccio : little Andrew. Occasionally *filius, figli* ter-
minates a name, as

MACCHIAVELLI : Michael's son = MACMICKING. Napoleon
said, " Macchiavel is the only author really worth reading."

BENEDETTO IL FERONDI : Benedict (il for filius) son of
Ferondi.

FERONDI (*con. fero*cious) : stern = SEVERUS, SUWARROW.
Filius forms *fi* in certain Spanish names, as

FIGUEROLA (senor) : son of GUEROLA : great warrior, Guerre:
war. Italy is given over to a passion for the sonorous *o*, as
Serb : a native of Servia, is formed into SERVONI. So her
genius is illustrated in the last of these names:—ECOLAMPADIUS
(Greek) : house lamp, HAUSSCHEIN (German) : house shine,
HOUSEGO (English) : house joy, HUMBERT (king), UMBERTO
(Italian) : house brightness : birth names. COCCAPIELLA (*con.*
our cock : of a gun and Pello : I drive) is the Italian name
answering to ARCUBALLISTER : arrow thrower, ALABASTER
(ballo).

Here it becomes me to acknowledge my indebtedness to
Padre Gavazzi, who, in 1858, gave me valuable information on
the patronymics of his charming Italian language.

THE RUSSIAN PATRONYMIC

is *itch* for a son, *of*, *ef*, or *if* for a grandson or descendant. The latter is called a *papponymic*, similar to the Celtic O. This *of*, *ef*, *if* forms *owna*, *ova*, or *ina* for wife or daughter, as the Celtic O forms *ua:* a daughter.

ROMANOVITCH JOURIFF: son of Romain, grandson of Joury. JOURY, JURY: George. The name IFF: a grandson, one of good descent = ATHELING. Names in *ski* are generally local, that meaning city, as

KOPINSKI: the town of St. James, *con.* Jacob, Coppock.

Tobolsk: ski on the Tobol river. Okotsk: ski on the Okota.

Peteropaulski: city of Peter and Paul, saints or czars. Muscovites are as fond of *ski* as Spaniards of *ez*, and so use it as verbal padding. Thus two Russian nobles took the names

NEWSKY and SUDANOWSKY, the former for Swedes on the Neva, the latter for Turks on the *south* bank of the *Dan*au, Danube, *con.* ONDERDONK.

CZARINA: wife of the Czar. KLAWINA: daughter of Nicholas.

ALEXANDRINA (our own): daughter of Alexander. KATH-AROWNA: of Catherine, one of the rare instances of a daughter named from her mother.

IVANOWNA: daughter of John. NICHOLALJEWITCH = NICHOLSON.

PHILIPPOVA (Nihilist leader): daughter of Philip, nearly = our PHILIPPA (queen).

PASKIEVITCH (prince of Poland): born at passover time.

LANGIEWITZ (patriotic Pole): son of LANGE, the German form of Long.

STOJANOVITS = STEVENSON. BASILOWITZ, VASSILOVITCH: son of a king =

RAJAHPUTRA, FITZROY, CREE, RENE. CZAROWITZ: Czar's son = the old Greek CRESSIDAS.

CZAR is not from Cæsar, but from the ancient SAR: a military prince, *con.* SARAI: princess.

FEODOROVITCH: of Theodorus = DOROKOFF. " General *Dorokoff* captured a whole regiment of Westphalians."

ROMANOFF (dynasty): descended from ROMAIN: son of Rome.

IVANOFF = JOHNSON. KORNILOFF (admiral): of Cornelius.

MOURAVIEFF (prince): of Moravian ancestry.

MENSCHIKOFF (Alma): of little, less (*con.* Minus), given by empress Katharine.

YOUSSUPOFF (diplomatist): of Joseph. ORLOFF (count): of Orlow. IGNATIEFF (diplomatist): of Ignatius.

ORLOW: an eagle = AQUILA, NINUS, from whom Nineveh.

TREPOFF (shot by Nihilist): son of the *steppe*, a foundling.

SCOBELOFF (Plevna): Jacob's son = FITZJAMES. POPOFF (admiral): of a priest = MACPHERSON.

MELIKOFF (governor of St. Petersburg): son of Meles, an Armenian river, near which the original MELIKOFF dwelt.

MELIKOFF (Loris) answers closely, and yet by chance coincidence, to

MELESIGINES: son of Meles, a river near Smyrna, which gave Homer one of his poetic bye names, suggesting

NILOGENES: son of the Nile, Moses. The name of the father of epic poetry,

HOMER: a hostage = BORROWS, BORROWMAN: one borrowed from the foe to be given back.

ARSNIEW: descended from a lion, *con.* ALP ARSLAN: the lion. The Russians took it from the Turks, having the same right to their names as to their lands,—

"Though led by *Arsniew*, that great son of slaughter."

Off becomes *ew*, and when needed *jew*.

GREGORJEW: descended from Gregory. Apart from the difficulty of deciphering Sclavonic words, we have to contend with a difficulty hardly less when trying to identify familiar names in a Muscovite uniform. Who but a Russian could see Simson in

SENTSCH, or Elizabeth in ELZE, Abraham in OBRYS, or the classical Euphrosyne in PHROUZKA? It is is said that Russian children do not speak Sclavonic till months later than those born at the same time in sunny Hesperia can freely speak Italian. That says something for the taste of babies seeing light under the shadow of the Bear,—

"How shall I spell the name of each Cossaque
Who were immortal, could one tell their story?
Alas! what to their memory can lack?
Achilles' self was not more grim and gory
Than thousands of this new and polished nation,
Whose names want nothing—but pronunciation.

．　　．　　．　　．　　．　　．

And Tschitsshakoff, and Roguennoff, Chokenoff,
And others of twelve consonants apiece
Ending with 'ischskin,' 'ousckin,' 'iffshcchy,' 'ouski,'
Of whom we can insert but Rousamouski."

DEMIDOFF (prince): descended from Demetrius.

DIERKOFF: descendant of Theodoric. LADISLAUS, WLADIS-LAW: glorious chief or ruler = CLEARCHUS (retreating myriad).

JAROSLAV (Crimean prince): glorious George. RADOSLAV (king of the Bosnians): glorious Conrad.

PETROSLAV : glorious Peter. BOLESLAUS, BOGOSLAV : the glory of God. Certain of the above are obviously not patronymical, yet connection justifies this grouping. Howbeit, we will part company with our newly acquired friends by giving a genuine *pat.* in *ow* for *off*, viz. :

SUWARROW (crossed Alps) : son of Severus, a severe man.

THE MODERN GREEK PATRONYMIC

assumes the forms *pulos, oula,* as in the names

NICOLOPULOS : son of Nicholas = COLLINGS. STASOULA : of Anastasius.

KARAGEORGEOPULOS : son of Black George : PAPPADOPULOS : of a priest = POPOFF : of a father.

THEOPHILOPOULA : of Theophilus. And, strange to add, CHRISTOPULOS (Otho's premier) : son of Christ = CHRISTIE.

CHRISTOS : our Christ, is common in the Athens of 1883, and is often given to brigands and other pests of civilisation.

THE GERMAN, DUTCH, SWEDISH, AND LAPLAND PATRONYMICS.

are SOHN, *zen, sen, son, zoon* and *dotter*, as

MENDELSSOHN (musical composer) : son of Mendel, for Clement = MENDEZ, whence MENDOZA.

HEINZEN : of John = VAN HAHN, ANSON, JOHNSON, *con.* HEYNE.

HARPERTZOON : of Harper. CLAUSSEN, KOLSEN : of Nicholas = COULSON. TONSEN : of Antony.

HUESSEN : of Hugh. DEITRICHESSEN (almanack) : of Theodoric.

THORWALDSEN : of THORWALD : *wielder* of Thor's hammer, powerful.

LARSDOTTER : son of Lars, and LARS, a form of Lawrence. "Christina Catharina *Larsdotter*, the Lapland giantess, stands seven feet two inches, was born at Brennas. Her parents are of diminutive stature, not exceeding four feet in height." No terror should be exhibited at a girl being called

LARSDOTTER · son of Lars, as no Laplander would be terrified at hearing of Mary *Wilson*. Dotter means offspring, *con.* DODDS, without respect of sex, then it is limited to a son, although philologically identical with

THUGATER (giving Thyatira, so called in honour of a royal daughter being born), and DAUGHTER.

HANSDOTTER is the Laplandic for JOHNSON, Dotter gives TOT, the pet name for a little girl. HERTZEN (Alexander) = MACARTHUR.

DIRK WILLEMZOON : Theodoric Williamson. "Amongst the

persecuted people was a poor protestant named *Dirk Willem-zoon*, who was condemned to death by the Blood Council."

Zoon, by itself, is common among the northern nations = our

Kyd, Young (which does not mean juvenile but first born son) =

Hiji, Hopps, Ingo, Juvenal, Idas, Maggot, etc.

Brodersen : brother's son, like his uncle = Nepos (Cornelius).

The Lithuanian Patronymic.

Those ancient people, the Lithuanians, though rapidly losing their characteristics in the absorbing militarian action of Russia, had a language and literature all their own. Their patronymic, still used, the monument of a lost nationality, is *aitis, ait*, or *at*, used as an affix thus :—

Adomaitis: son of Adam = Badams.   Jokubaitis: Jacob = Cobbet.

Tammasait: Thomas = MacOmish.   Jurgaitis: of George = Jorgez and Jouresen.

Obrigakat : Abraham = Tabraham.   These suffice to illustrate the truth that names looking horridly strange are only foreign modification of household words, as Negroes, Chinese, and Lapps, are but variations of Adam : man.

The Hindostanee Patronymic

is *putra* added as an affix, as

Brahmaputra (river god): son of Bram, Brahma = Tiberius: son of Tiber, *con.* Tobermory.

Rajaputra : king's son = Tyrannion : of Tyrannus : a king.

Vishnaputra (very common): of Vishnu, of the Hindoo Tri-mutri.

Indraputra: of Indra, mythically applied to Delhi.   Indra, the god of heaven, the Indian Jove.   The Maharatta's use *jee*, as

Shahjee : king's son = Machree, Regan, Price, Fitzroy.

Sivajee (founder of⋆Maharatta confederation): of the god Siva.

Siva : destroyer = Apollyon, Agag, Beor.   Add to these

Jamsetjee (well known Bombay merchant): son of a man named Jamset as Gamgee (professor) = Jantjee.

The Chinese Patronymic

is *tse* or *se* used as an affix, as in the name of the Chinese Socrates,

Kung-fut-se : Kung, the son of Fo, for Buddha, whence Confucius.

BUDDHA: wise, giving Botan for Buddha Stan: country of Fo.
TAO-TSE: son of the sickle, applied to a farmer, answers
surprisingly to CURRAN.
HOANG-TSE: son of Augustus, Hoang being the Chinese for it.
Yang-tse-Kiang: river, son of the ocean, very large river.
The majority of Chinese personal names are drawn from a
sacred poem written by the emperor Tao, which does not contain more than 408 choice names, but by permutation they
suffice the vast population of Sinim. The popular Christian
names in Britain are not more than 20, while those for women
are even fewer, but these would allow of every human being
bearing a' different appellation. We have seen how unrecognisable the Cossacks made well known names, but the pigtail
man exceeds the worst Muscovite in such baseness. Who
would identify Jeremiah in Pekin where he is called JALE-
MEIOHANG? This is no translation, merely a pure (?) transfer.
Sinalogues (learned in Chinese) surely suffer occasional puzzle-
ment! Our commonest name is Smith, of those in the flowery
Empire, CHANG = RIVERS, STROMIER, RIBAS, in the sense of
living in or near a stream. On that great river, the river St.
Lawrence, notable for its rapids, the most noteworthy is La
Chine: the Chinese. The early navigators thought that was
the way to China, as Columbus thought India could be reached
by sailing west. When passing along the streets of Montreal,
in 1880, I saw a laundry, the sign of which was Sing Long.
My name being Long, I entered and parleyed with a Mongolian
featured man, having eyes like button holes cut upside down,
and a skin coloured like cod liver oil. He was washing a shirt
in a basin a few sizes larger than what we use for sugar. I
was anxious to learn something of my name in Chinese. Alas!
the man seemed a negative quantity, knowing, apparently, a
trifle less than nothing. I walked away in disgust, and the
impression made by the circumstances gradually began to fade.
Three months after I was strolling down a street in New York
when I saw on a sign board "Sing Long, Chinese Laundry."
Of course, the impression made at Montreal was deepened, and
I was doubly puzzled. Howbeit, that was little to this:—The
next day, while passing through a street in Brooklyn another
Chinese laundry thrust itself upon my notice, this time kept
by one Sam Long. Now, as my late father was named
Samuel Long, and fifty years before I had heard familiar
friends call him Sam Long, my surprise was inexpressible.
Flesh and blood could endure no more. Learning that not far
from Dr. Talmage's Tabernacle was the Brooklyn Young Men's
Christian Association, whereat was held a Chinese Sunday
school, I made therefor. One part of the instruction was in
Cantonese, the other in English. When hearing the grotesque

20

sons of the Flowery Land sing our hymns, and seeing them
chalk on the black board portions of our holy faith, I was
forcibly reminded of Isa. xlix. 12, " Behold these shall come
from far : and, look, these from the land of Sinim :" the Sinoe,
which gives Sindon : fine linen, the product of Chinese looms,
as Calico from Calcutta, the work of the Indian weaver. Rev.
xviii. 12. I seemed to hear One saying, "This day is this
scripture fulfilled in your ears." At the close of the address I
spoke to the sinalogue and learned, " What you took for names
were mere signs posted there partly as horse-shoes are nailed
over doors to keep away witches." As the Greeks and
Romans concealed city names, in fact, gave them two names,
one true and secret, the other sham and popular, lest enemies
should get hold of its designation, and by incantations bring
calamities upon the city, so these Chinese hide their names.
When Balak desired Balaam to curse God's people, he gave
their precise name, or else the sorcerer would have had nothing
to work upon : " Come, curse me *Jacob*, and come, defy *Israel.*"
Though he had that material he goes to work with this
result : " Surely no enchantment against Jacob, neither any
divination against Israel." In China, LONG : fortunate,
successful, lucky. SING LONG : much luck, elliptical for " I
hope I shall have much luck." SAM LONG : great success (I
hope to have). So Rev. ii. 17, " I will give him a new name
written, which *no man knoweth* saving he that receiveth it,"
i.e., No one shall hurt him, and he shall prosper. I then saw
that Sing Long of Montreal had deceived H. A. Long of
Glasgow. He was no negative quantity. I was. Nevertheless, as I had learned something of the Chinese customs in
spite of China men, in gratitude I sent my linen to a Chinese
laundryman, who passed it through his bason, sending it home
like a snow drift, accompanied by semi-invisible paper covered
with tea-chest oddities, by which two dollars fifty cents. was
laid to my charge. As we have seen, Charm is the root of
Harm, whence HARMER : a wizard, a drew, a magus.

THE LATIN PATRONYMIC

is *ilius*, originally *idius*, from the Greek *idas*. Thus
HOSTILIUS : son of Hostis, originally written Hostidius.
HOSTIS : a stranger, ger, alien = XENO, AGUR, LESTRANGE,
GALL, Balaam, L'HOSTE.
HOSTILIUS : son of a stranger, exactly = GALLYON, GALLACHER.
POMPILIUS (for Pompidius) : of Pompey. POPILIUS : of the
people, becomes
PUBLIUS. ICILIUS (Icidius) : equal son (to his father in
fame) =

PATROBAS. "*Icilius* her lover boldly opposed the decrees, and obliged Claudius," etc.

MANLIUS (Manilius, Manidius): son of the morning, morning born, suggesting

PHOSPHORUS : LUCIFER : light bringer. SPURIUS : of Spura. SPURA : a sower, *con.* spores. AQUILIUS : of an eagle, swift footed. In later times, *enus, inus, anus, ianus, onius* prevailed, probably finding an origin in the Greek patronymical sign *uion, uios, on.* Thus we have Labienus, Rufinus, Tebanus, Hadrianus, Vipsianus, Sidonius, etc.

LABIENUS (Titus): son of Labeo. LABEO : thick lipped, slow speaker = CHILO, *con.* ACHILLES.

HADRIANUS : of ADRIAN, from Ater : black (soil) = SWART-ZERD. Hence Adriatic : sea of Adria (n) and Adrianople : Hadrian's city. Of the above patronymical signs, *ianus* pertains to adoption, as

EMILIANUS : the adopted son of Æmilian ; SEJANUS : Sejii.

SEJI : sower = SPURA, early agricultural names. When *ianus* applied to daughters it became *iana,* as

PUDENTIANA (St.): adopted daughter of Pudens. And

PUDENS : shame faced, modest. But the usual patronymic form for daughter was *eja,* as

CICEREJA: Cicero's daughter. Parallel with Celtic *ni, nic,* as

CAITRIN NIC SEAIN : Catherine, daughter of John, and the well known

MAIBLE NI NEILL : Mable, daughter of Neil. Of course the Highland form is the more definite, but both forms are obsolete.

MABLE: merry, joyous, Mab like = LETITIA, whence LETTICE. We owe the word name to the Latins, it being a form of nomen, for notamen, from Noto : I mark, de*note,* from Nosco : I know, recog*nise.* The Romans said,—" Nomen et omen : " a name is a sign, *omin*ous. With Roman names were not only to be won, but, in later years, told of *gens* (clan), or *familiæ,* a subdivision of gens. Familiar means of the same family. Defective names argued ignoble descent. GENTLEMAN : man of gens, noble origin. Cicero complained that he was only known through himself, *i.e.,* his name was not famous until he made it so. When children were named, a feast was observed called nominalia, kept on the eighth day after birth, if a female, but the ninth day when a male. After single names fell into disuse a second name was added, which, ceasing to satisfy, a third was appropriated, and, in some cases, a fourth, termed Agnomen : to the name. Those of later periods are divided under three heads.

Prænomen : fore name, answering to our Christian name.

Nomen : *the* name, indicating descent, or place of birth.

Cognomen: with the name, added through a family being distinguished. Thus

Marcus Junius Brutus. MARCUS is the prænomen, like our MARK, and means polished, urbane,

JUNIUS, the nomen, describes his age, *juniority.*

BRUTUS, the cognomen, intimates he was of the gens Brutii.

BRUTUS: a fugitive slave = PHYG-ELLUS (*con.* Fugio: I flee), was descriptive of the original applying to Marcus Junius genealogically. His name, stripped of appendages, was Junius. No person can have more than one name save by a figure. Our Prince of Wales is named Edward Albert Guelph. If crowned, he would be Edward VII. His name is one, GUELPH : Wolf. The possession of three names was the sole privilege of free Romans. Thus: " Habet tria nomina : " he has three names, came to signify he is a free citizen. Such names were to dwellers on the Tiber what long names were to dwellers on the Ilissus in the age of Pericles, and what two names were on the banks of the Thames in the reign of King Richard. No slave dare have a prænomen, so that its absence was fatal to a man's admission into *good society.* Hence the force of the line—

" Gaudent prænomine mollis auriculæ : "

delicate ears love the prænomen. Much of this ceased after A.D. 212, when Caracalla enfranchised most of the Roman provinces, upon which myriads of the *one named* at once availed themselves of the ability to take as many names as fancy dictated, to the confusion of society of the time being.

THE GREEK PATRONYMICS

is *idas,* modified to *ida, ides, id, i, od.* Also, but not so widely spread through classic Greek, we have *ion, on, one,* and *an* (like the Celtic *an,* from eoghan) from UIOS : a son. Likewise *genes* and *goni,* formations on Geno : I beget. To *idas* we owe *ite,* so familiar in such words as

Ammonite: a descendant of Ammon. A Celt would say O'Ammon or MacAmmon; the Russians would have Ammonoff; Hebrews would say Ammoni, like Gibeoni: a Gibeonite. The following is a selection of best known examples of its use.

ARISTIDES : son of Ariston = BETSON : son of Best.

ARISTOS : most like Ares, Mars. BEST for beatest, who beats all, *con.* ARISTOGITON : best neighbour = NEIGHBOUR.

SIRACHIDES (Jesus): son of Sirach.

ASCELPIADES (Bythinian physician): of Esculapius, figurative for a clever medical man.

BASILIDES (father of Herodotus) = TYRANION (Cæsar's

friend): son of a king, of royal descent = AHIMELECH, MACHREE.

CRŒSUS (king): a governor, CRESSIDAS: son of a king, CRESSIDA: royal daughter = RENE.

PYLADES (and Orestes): of Pyleus, *Pyleus:* son of Pyle, and PYLE: a gate, having charge of city gate = our SOUTHGATE, *con.* Pylorus: gate keeper, Hecatompylæ: hundred gates, Thebes, Thermopylæ: gate of hot springs.

PELOPIDAS: of Pelops. PELOPS: dark face = DUFF, SWARTZ.

EPAMINONDAS ("who at Leuctra bled"): of Epamnon.

EPAMNON: a defender = HECTOR, WEIR, WARE, BAILEY.

LEONIDAS: of Leon. LEON: a lion. The royal beast was common in Greece up to the time of the Persian invasion.

LYCIDAS: son of Luke. HEROD (the Idumean) for Heroidas, Herodias: son of a hero.

HERODIAS for Herodiah, like Elias for Elijah, is its *fem.* form.

TOLMIDES: descendants of Ptolemy, here dynastic as HERACLIDE: of Hercules. EPIGONI: sons of the seven (epta) who came from the siege of Troy.

THEOGONIS: begotten of a god. POLYGONUS: one of many children.

TELEGONUS: last born = LANE, IMOGEN, *con.* Telephone.

ERIGONE (the constellation of Virgo): Eris (strife) born, born at the time of battle, *op.* of SHALLUM, IRENE: time of peace.

EUMENIDES: daughters of Eumenes and EUMENES: of a good mind, genial—a propitiatory name applied to the Furies through fear of them. Some say daughters of memory, remorse.

SIMONIDES (poet): of Simon. SIMON, from Semi: half, half nosed, simice like.

HESPERIDES: daughters of the west = ATLANTIADES, *con.*

NEREIDES: daughters of Nereus. NEREUS: sparkling sea, phosphorescent waves.

HYPERIDES: of Hyperion. HYPERION (uper, super): of above, the sun.

SARRONIDE: of Sarron (a Celtic king, the Solomon of his age), applied to a philosopher. But SARONIDAS: son of an oak, robust = BENHAIL, DARROCH, ECHIUS.

SARONY: an oak = ECK, or EYCK. Oak from Eke: to grow. Eke out: to prolong.

MEONIDES (Homer): son or Meonia, Asia Minor, whence Meander: Meonian river. One of the few cases where a country gives name to a river as Indus from India.

MELESIGINES (Homer): of Meles, a river near Smyrna = MELIKOFF.

HYADES (stars so called): daughters of rain, bring wet weather, *con.* Hudor: water, whence Sudor: sweat, *i.e.,* wet.

TRIONES: three daughters. ARCTURUS: son of the bear,—

"Hic canit errantem Lunam, Solisque labores;
Unde hominum genus, et pecudes; unde imber, et ignes:
Arcturum, pluviasque *Hyades*, geminosque TRIONES."

THEOSEBIUS: of Theosebes. THEOSEBES: worshipper of God in opposition to polytheism = GOTOBED, GOTOBEDDE.

EUSEBIUS (historian): good worshipper, devotee = GODFREY.

ACTEON (and dogs): of sea shore, dweller on, *con.* Attica: coast line = COSTA (Rica: rich): coast. COSTIGAN: young Costa.

EURIPIDES (tragedy): of Euripus, born near it. Aristotle is said to have drowned himself therein because he could not discover reason for its ebb and flow. Now called Negropont: black bridge, from one connecting island with mainland.

MARCION (heresiarch): of Mark = MARCELLUS.

CÆSARION (child of Cleopatra by): of CÆSAR. MILTO: beautiful, gives

MILTIADES (Cimon's son): of Milto. MARSYAS (flayed): son of Mars = ARIUS (Arianism) of Ares.

PALLADIUS: of Pallas. EUCLID (of Megara): of Eucleos.

EUCLEOS: good glory, famous = MARR, BRIGHT, SHEM.

APOLLOS ("may plant"): of Apollo, eloquent. APOLLYON: of Apollo, destroyer, slaying like sunstroke.

HORMISDAS (pope): of the god Ormuzd, the antagonist of Arimanes.

DIOGENES (tub): god begotten, of divine ancestry = THEO-GONIS. ÆOLAS: variegated, tatooed, a warrior, *con.* ÆOLUS (king of winds): variable, as the winds are.

AIOLID: soldier bred = HERRING, HEROD, WICKLIFFE.

ASTERION: of a star. ALEXIUS: of Alexis. ALEXIS: a helper, *con.* elixir.

ASCANIUS (puer): of the old stock, of Æsc: the ash, the Asir Adam. SU: bear hunter, for SUAGROS, *con.* Ursa: grunter, gives

SUIDAS (grammatist): son of Su, or son of the bearhunter.

LAPIDE (Cornelius a): of James = our JAMIESON.

RASSELAS (Johnson): of an apostle, walker in the true faith = DE FOE and DE SANTOS.

When the *pat.* is *fem.* it softens from *uios* to *eis*, *on* becomes *one*, while *genes* become *genia*, and *idas* forms *ida*.

CHRYSEIS: daughter of CHRYSES, while CHRYSES: golden haired = FLAVIUS.

BRYSEIS: daughter of Bryses, and BRYSES: strong, athletic.

PYROIS (one of the mares of the sun): daughter of fire, swift as lightning.

DIONE (mother of Venus): divine daughter = BETHULIA.

HERMIONE (wife of Cadmus): daughter of Mercury = HERMOGENES.

THEMISTO (T formative): daughter of Themis, and THEMIS: right, justice.

THEMISTOCLES: glory of Themis. OUIDA: no one's daughter, orphanee. *On* passes into the gentile *pat. ian*, as Arab*ian*, Wallach*ian;* also into *ine*, as Philist*ine*.

ENDYMION (enthymion, from Thumis: animus, mens): son of mind, intellectual—originally applied to an observer of heavenly bodies, like son of harmony for a musician. This *pat.* form *uios, os, an* enables us to analyse names which else might seem uncompounded. Thus

TYRANN-OS is from Turra, Turris: a tower, from Terra: earth, an earth-work, giving

TURANN: son of a tower, its governor; now he who governed it was called its king, in keeping with what children say, " I'm king of the castle," hence we have

TYRANNOS: royal, kingly bred, castle born, ultimately giving Tyrant. So

DUNCAN: head of the fort = TIERNY (in which *t*, *r*, *n* are identical with consonants in Turann): castle king, earth work lord = *Kenealy, con.*, HEALY: a rampart or rath.

TIGHEARNA: son of a king or lord. Thus from Domus: a house, we derive

DOMINUS: a house lord. So Kir: a wall, a walled city, giving Carthage, gives

KURIOS: son of the city, its governor = ASTYANAX: king of the city, *con.* Senex.

CYRUS: city king, is a form of Kurios. So the name of the Cilician

OPPIAN: not son of Ops, nor yet earth born, *i.e.*, autochthonal, but son of earth work builder, tower maker = TYRANNOS TIGHEARNA, DOMINUS (domus inos), KURIOS, CYRUS, and OPPIAN may all be viewed as *pats.*, similar to

O'BRIAN: son of the great house, castle, palace: all being like

PORPHYROGENETUS: palace born. There can be no doubt the Latin

TERENCE and the Irish TERENCE are identical, and not by chance, but identity of origin, each signifying a tower lord, the raiser of an earth work, and =

CAREY, when not from Carus: dear. Castles were the foci of civilization from Greece to Ireland.

Purgos: a tower, *con.* Pergamos, whence *parchment* is from Ge: earth. Burglar was one who dug through a dried mud wall. The *g* in Purgos, Geometry, and Burglar, is the same.

ONION (Alexandrian temple): son of ON: the sun, divinely born = DIOGENES and DIOSCORIDES.

The Hebrew Patronymic

proper is *ben* from Eben : a stone, from Banah : to build.
Sons build families as stones do houses. When John said,
" God is able of these stones to raise up sons unto Abraham,"
probably he meant such act was as easy to God as it was for a
scribe to make *eben,* by omitting the tittle, into *ben.* The
Jews adopted Bar : a son, from the Babylonians. The Chaldees
used Bar in the sense of lofty, elevated, superior, which was
primarily applied to an eminence, and is identical with our
Barr, as

Barskimming : the hill at the bend of the river. Hence
Skimming, whence M'Skimming. Barrhead = Hillhead. It
was first said of eminent places and then of eminent persons,
in contrast with captives, slaves, and servants : " Kiss the
Bar lest He be angry," *i.e.,* obey Him who is the Lofty One,
the Uplifted.

Naib : a prophet, a seer, gives Nebo : the god whose oracles
told futurity. The god was worshipped on Mount Nebo.

Barnaib : son of a prophet, whence Barnabas : of consolation, as a good son is a great consolation =

Scipio : a staff (to his father), *con.* Sceptre : leant upon,
patriarchal staff. Thence our Barnaby (Rudge) and Barnardo
(cardinal), and Bernardo (orphans), if not from Bernard.

Rudge : a hill, *con.* rig, ridge = Barr : one dwelling on a
hill = Hills. But Longridge : big farm.

Barzillai : of Zillai, and Zillai : blacksmith. Zillai : iron,
the sounding metal. This is the first use of iron in the Bible,
" Which took a wife of *Barzillai* the Gileadite."

Barkos (nethinim) : son after his father = Barabbas : of his
father = Icilius, Patrobas, Papias. " Now Barabbas was a
robber." Assumes form of Barkas.

Bar Jesus : of Joshua (Jehovah Hosea). Berosus (historian) :
of Hosea, and Hosea : saviour = Soter, Hafiz, as

Hafiz-Allah = Joshua : saviour of Jehovah. Calmet says,
Dict. p. 152,

Bar-Jona, should be Bar Johanna : son of John = Van
Hahn and Gamgee, usually given

Bar-Jona : of Jonah. As Jonah : a dove, and Livy : a
dove = Tortola (tur, tur), Tovey (from dove), we cannot be
far wrong by saying that literally Barjona = Livius.

Bartholomew : of Tolmai, gives Bartlemy : born Aug.
24th, at St. Bartholomew's mass, Bartlemy Fair. Bartlett,
Batt, Bates (when not boatman), Batty (equestrian), Barth
(African explorer), Bartle (Sir), Barletta, Badcock, according to some authors it corrupts in Spain to Balthazar (wiseman). Barthez : son of Bartholomew.

TOLMAI : a furrow, tall as = LONGFELLOW, AULAY.

BARTIMEUS : of Timeus. TIMEUS : honourable = TIMON (of Athens), TITUS, which some make into TATE, whence

TATIUS = TATLOCK : little Tate, or son of Titus, which differ little from BARTIMEUS. But the Spanish

TATO : the tacit, silent = TACITUS, MUDO, MUDIE, MOODIE, STILL. About the time Israel was waiting her Messiah, an impostor arose, calling himself

BARCHOCAB : son of a star = ASTERION. " There shall come a star out of Jacob." Facts falsifying his promises, he was called

BARCOSBA : son of a lie, *con.* COSBI (slain by dart) : ensnarer, deceiver, not greatly differing from the better known

REBECCA : a snare, a fascinating woman = SPOONER, PACK, THUG, and DOLON.

BARSABAS (Joseph) : seventh son, as BATHSHEBA : seventh daughter. The use of the Chaldee *pat. bar* is but a parenthesis in Hebrew onamatology. Their *ben* was used long before it, and is now in use after *bar* has become obsolete. That *ben* was used early is plain from

BEN-AMMI : son of my people = AMMON : my people, as also

REUBEN : see! a son. BENJAMIN : son of my right hand. BENONI : son of my sorrow. That it is still in use is manifest from the following modern names.

BOLIVAR (gave name to Bolivia), for Ben Oliver = OLIVAREZ.

BADAMS is Ben Adam = MACADAM, whence Macadamise : to pave after his recipe. ODAMS is a form of Adams forming ODY : little Adams. The Jews call those of their blood born in Egypt

Beni Masr : sons of Mizraim. Beni for benim. Hence *i*, a gentile *pat.*, as

Beni Shem : children of Syria, Beni Franza : sons of France, applied by Turkish Jews to all western foreigners. Let us get back to our Bible, where we have

BENHAIL : son of strength, strong born, about = MEIKLE-WEAN : big baby, as

MEIKLEHEAD : much head = TESTA, MEIKLEREID : great man of the Reid's. " In the third year of Jehosaphat's reign, he sent to his princes, even to *Benhail*."

BENHANAN : son of compassion, pitiful, *con.* ANANUS, whom John calls, xviii. 13, ANNAS : gracious, merciful.

ZOHETH : (who is) taken away, born when parents changed residence.

BEN-ZOHETH : son of removal, who emigrates against parental advice. " The sons of ISHI were *Zoheth* and Ben-zoheth."

ISHI (from Ish: a man) for Ishim : men = to many men = PERIANDER, MANNUS.

BENE-BARAK : sons of lightning, whose spears and swords flash and glitter. They were Danites. Dagger is from Dag: day, because it flashes like day light. BARAK (and Deborah) : lightning = LLEWELLYN.

BOANERGES : thunder bolts (James and John). We meet with

BEN-GEBER: son of the strong, exactly = the Saxon WHITING. Certain Hebrew names intimate relationship to God as *father, son, daughter, brother.* Those of the first are professions of faith and claims to sonship that surprise us the more they are studied. Nowhere in the Old Testament are men invited so to do, nor is permission to do so even intimated. The others seem to intimate holiness, godliness, as

AHIMELECH : king's brother, *i.e.*, kingly, magnificent = REGULUS, ROYLE, RYLE, CORTEREAL (*con.* cort, curt, roy), fine fellows all.

ELIAH : God my father = ABIEL. " Kish the son of *Abiel.*"

JOAB : Jehovah father = ABIJAH. " *Joab,* son of Zeruiah."

BARIAH : son of Jehovah = BENAHIAH. " *Benahiah,* son of Jehoidah.

BETHUEL : daughter of God, a pure person = BITHIAH : of Jehovah. "These are the sons of *Bithiah,* the daughter of Pharaoh." She being of Egypt, her husband, Mered, is supposed to have dropt her Coptic designation and called her thus, signifying she was to be a pure worshipper of Jehovah.

AHIAH : brother of Jehovah, his servant = JOAH. " *Joah,* the son of Asaph, the recorder." Bold strange names, any of which I should be unwilling to bear.

ABITAL (David's wife) : (whose) father (is as) dew ; he gave one who refreshed, consoled.

BEN - JOSEPH corresponds to the latinised Greek form JOSEPHUS (uios) : son of Joseph.

.*. Some only of the above are patronymical, but all are given as illustrations of our main subject.

SUPERADDENDA.

WINDTHORST (opposition): winding wood, allied by original position to the following queer folk, viz.: QUESTION, QUIDDY, QUILT, QUITTACUS; wood dwellers all, *con.* With, Wid, Quid: a wood. TARTUFFE: a truffle eater, living luxuriously, and yet pulling a long visage. TITHONUS: narrow chested like a locust, the *op.* of PETION and = AGABUS. MARTYR (Justin): one who *witnessed* for the truth by blood. MARBLE: worker in. MARVEL (Andrew). TANZ is a form of ATHANASIUS (creed): deathless = AMBROISE, formed on AMBROSE: not mortal. POULIN (current French Canadian): a foal, *con.* palfrey and = COLT (revolver): wild a wee. PANGBORN (pen burn): brook head = PENGELLY, KINGLASS. ARIEL: aery, fairy like. GOSSIP (chess): God sib: related through God by baptism, a godfather. As people focussing the baby babble somewhat, GOSSIP became a verb, *gossip:* to chatter inanities about neighbours. Amongst the few biblical trade names is HERESH: a carpenter ("Heresh and Galal"). ULLATHORNE: a settler among elm trees and thorn bushes = BRACKENBURY.

GAU (Nubia), Hebrew for a stranger. XENOS, Greek, whence Euxine: good (safe) for strangers, Hostis, L'HOSTE = GAU, HOSPITALIS: stranger receiver = PRENDERGAST and LIEBGAST, answers to the Scoto English FRAME: frae far, *con., from* a distance. PUNCH: tunbodied = PUNSHON, PANSA, WAMBA, MICKLEWAIM, HOGARTH, which consult. Bohn ('s library): bean planter = CYAMITAS, giving the grotesque BONES, BONE. ZUKERTORT (lit., *sugar tart*): a pastry baker = MAZARIN. TANHAUSER: pine wood dweller = TANGUYE. STROMBI (Guiseppe): trumpet-voiced = TRUMPF, TRUMP (*uncon.*, trump at cards) = BELCHER. Stromboli: mountain making a rumbling noise like a trumpet. OSTERWALD (commentator) answers to our EASTWOOD. Probably twenty per cent. of all known names are corrupted thrice, twice or once, generally through the ignorance of the corrupter as to the form or meaning of the name subjected to violence. It is usually done on the principle of the Irish preacher's, "Putting what sinse he could into this text." Thus SNAEFELL: snow hill, where snow remained the year round was tortured into SNOWBALL, and the Spanish

HIJO, from Filius: son, was disguised into IGO, which few would think meant a son, but turns up unexpectedly in Jo. "John Anderson, my jo," loved like a son.

INGO: a son, MAR: glorious, INGOMAR: glorious son, *cor.* to INKHAMMER.

BODKIN (bodykin): a dwarf = CURTIN: short. CROOKS (in some cases), CROCKETT: crooked = BOSSUE: humped. The German is rich in birth names, amongst the most beautiful of which is MORGANSTERN: morning star, born at the appearance of = GAD, VERGILIUS. When MORGAN is not Cambrian, in which it signifies a mariner, it is German, and means *morning born* = MANIUS. Amongst Boston names I find ZOUCH: the stock of a notable tree = BUMM, ATTREE. A writer of that learned city gives in his voluminous work on names, FEVRE, as a case of personal names derived from diseases! Of course, a form of LE FEVRE. COYLE: a wood, gives KELLY. ALBUQUERQUE: white oak. AHAZIAH: held (of) Jehovah, Heb. ii. 16. ANDROMEDUS: commander of men, great general, *con.* ALCANDER: strong man. ARDMILLAN: bald mountain = MONTCALM. LEWIS shades off into (Mc) LEISH.

MURRAY is formed on Moray (shire), said to obtain its name from Moravian settlers.

BEER is formed on BAUER: a boor. CADI, KADI: a judge, *fem.,* CADIJALI. KADIJAH (Mahomet's wife) = HYPATIA, CONSUELIA. BRIGHAM (Young) = Bridgeton, PONT, which see. EPISCOPUS (*con.* microscope): overseer = BISHOP, gives EPISCOPIUS (*lit.*): son of a bishop. CONCEIT is a form of CONCETTA. BLACKMONSTER (minister): living in a Dominican house. PUFFENDORF = PRESTON: priest's town. BUDGE (Montreal, Y.M.C.A.) for Bodger: Cooper gives *dim.* BUDGETT. SEDIGITUS: born with six fingers. VOSS, VOCIUS, FOSS, *con.* FOX: crafty and cruel. AURELIUS: golden-haired, giving AURELIA = FULVIA. PAMPHILON (*con.* DUPANLOUP, FOULIS) = our PENCOIT, WOODHEAD. SABBADINI (Irridentist): learned = SAGE, and *con. sapio, savoir.* SABELLIUS (Sabellian): one of the Sabelli: aborigines of Italy, and who, with the Sabines, are supposed to have been named in connection with star worship, *con.* Sab: an army, sabaism, Sabaoth.

THE END.

INDEX

OF NAMES, TITLES, OR DESIGNATIONS.

21

22

23

24

25

26

27